De-Westernizing Film Studies

De-Westernizing Film Studies considers what form a challenge to the enduring vision of film as a medium – and film studies as a discipline – modelled on "Western" ideologies, theoretical and historical frameworks, critical perspectives and institutional and artistic practices, might take today. The book combines a range of scholarly writing with critical reflection from filmmakers, artists, and industry professionals, comprising experience and knowledge from a wide range of geographical areas, film cultures, and (trans-)national perspectives. In their own ways, the contributors problematize a binary mode of thinking that continues to promote an idea of "the West and the rest" in relation to questions of production, distribution, reception, and representation within an artistic medium (cinema) that, as part of contemporary moving image culture, is more globalized and diversified than at any time in its history. In so doing, *De-Westernizing Film Studies* complicates and/or rethinks how local, national and regional film cultures "connect" globally, seeking polycentric, multi-directional, non-essentialized alternatives to Eurocentric theoretical and historical perspectives found in film as both an artistic medium and an academic field of study.

Saër Maty Bâ has taught film studies at the universities of Bangor, East London, Portsmouth and St Andrews. His research blurs boundaries between diaspora, film, media, and cultural studies. His articles and reviews have appeared in journals such as *Studies in Documentary Film, Film International* and *Cultural Studies Review*. He is co-editor with Will Higbee of a special edition of the *Journal of Media Practice: Re-presenting Diaspora in Cinema and New (Digital) Media* (2010). Bâ is an associate editor of the *Encyclopedia of Global Human Migration* (2013) and an editorial board member of the journal *Working USA*.

Will Higbee is a senior lecturer in film studies at the University of Exeter. He is the author of *Mathieu Kassovitz* (2007) and the co-editor with Sarah Leahy of *Studies in French Cinema: UK Perspectives, 1985–2010* (2010) and with Saër Maty Bâ of a special edition of the *Journal of Media Practice: Re-presenting Diaspora in Cinema and New (Digital) Media*. He is a member of the editorial board of the journal *Studies in French Cinema* and has published various articles on contemporary French cinema, cinemas of the North African diaspora in France, and questions of transnational cinemas in journals such as *Transnational Cinemas, French Cultural Studies,* and *Africultures*.

De-Westernizing Film Studies

Edited by
Saër Maty Bâ and Will Higbee

Routledge
Taylor & Francis Group

LONDON AND NEW YORK

First published 2012
by Routledge
2 Park Square, Milton Park, Abingdon OX14 4RN

Simultaneously published in the USA and Canada
by Routledge
711 Third Avenue, New York, NY 10017

Routledge is an imprint of the Taylor & Francis Group, an informa business

British Library Cataloguing in Publication Data
A catalogue record for this book is available from the British Library

Library of Congress Cataloging in Publication Data
De-westernizing film studies / edited by Saër Maty Bâ and Will Higbee.
p. cm.
Includes bibliographical references and index.
1. Motion pictures – Philosophy. 2. Film criticism – Developing countries.
I. Bâ, Saër Maty. II. Higbee, Will.
PN1995.D49 2012
791.4301 – dc23
2011051418

ISBN: 978-0-415-68783-6 (hbk)
ISBN: 978-0-415-68784-3 (pbk)
ISBN: 978-0-203-14424-4 (ebk)

Typeset in Baskerville
by Taylor and Francis Books

Printed and bound by CPI Group (UK) Ltd, Croydon, CR0 4YY

Contents

Illustrations

Contributors

Nathan Abrams is a senior lecturer in film studies at Bangor University. His most recent book is *The New Jew in Film: Exploring Jewishness and Judaism in Contemporary Cinema* (2010).

John Akomfrah, originally from Ghana, is one of Britain's leading filmmakers, a governor of the British Film Institute and founder member of the London-based Black Audio Film Collective with whom he directed a range of highly acclaimed films, including *Handsworth Songs* (1986) and *Seven Songs for Malcolm X* (1993). In 1998, with producers Lina Gopaul and David Lawson, he founded Smoking Dogs Films and has directed a series of digital films, artworks, and television documentaries for the BBC and Channel 4, including *Urban Soul: The Making of Modern R&B* (2004). One of his latest projects includes a cine-essay focused on the theme of migration, *Mnemosyne* (2010). A critic as well as filmmaker, Akomfrah has written widely about cinema.

Saër Maty Bâ has taught film studies at the universities of Bangor, East London, Portsmouth and St Andrews. His research blurs boundaries between diaspora, film, media, and cultural studies. His articles and reviews have appeared in journals such as *Studies in Documentary Film*, *Film International* and *Cultural Studies Review*. He is co-editor with Will Higbee of a special edition of the *Journal of Media Practice: Re-presenting Diaspora in Cinema and New (Digital) Media* (2010). Bâ is an associate editor of the *Encyclopedia of Global Human Migration* (2013) and an editorial board member of the journal *Working USA*.

Mohammed Bakrim is a film critic, screenwriter, and President of L'Association Marocaine pour les Études Cinématographiques (the Moroccan Association for Cinema Studies).

Olivier Barlet is a member of the Syndicat Français de la Critique de Cinéma and the African Federation of Film Critics. He is Film Correspondent (and former Chief Editor) for the African cultural journal *Africultures*. His award-winning book, *Les Cinémas d'Afrique noire: le regard en question* (1996) has been translated into English and Italian.

Farida Benlyazid is a Moroccan filmmaker. Her first documentary, *Identité de femme/Womanlight* (1979), was made for the French TV channel FR3. Since then she has directed a number of very successful TV dramas, including *Nia taghleb* (2000), *El Boukma* (2001), and *Secret de famille/Family Secret* (2009). She has also directed feature-length films that focus on the experiences of women, including *Ruses de femmes* (1999), *Casablanca, Casablanca* (2002), and *Juanita de Tanger/La Vida Perra de Juanita Narboni* (2005). Her scriptwriter's credits include *Poupées de roseaux* (1980) and *Badis de* (1986).

Yifen T. Beus holds a Ph.D. in comparative literature from Indiana University and is currently Associate Professor and Chair of International Cultural Studies at Brigham Young University, Hawaii. Her recent publications include: "Postcolonial Beaux' Stratagem: Dancing and Singing Back with Carmen" in *Storytelling in World Cinemas* (forthcoming), "Authorship and Criticism in Self-Reflexive African Cinema" in *African Films and Criticism* (2010), and "Colonialism, Democracy, and the Politics of Representation in Alain Corneau's *Le Prince du Pacifique*" in *New Zealand, France and the Pacific Anthology* (forthcoming).

Kuljit Bhamra is a musician, composer, and producer. He has worked, both independently and collaboratively, on film scores including *Bhaji on the Beach* (1993), *The Winter of Love* (2011), and *Bend It Like Beckham* (2002). He has also made musical appearances on *A Little Princess* (1995), *The Guru* (2002), *Alexander* (2004), *Brick Lane* (2007), *The Four Feathers* (2002), and *Charlie and the Chocolate Factory* (2005).

William Brown is a senior lecturer in film studies at Roehampton University. He is the co-author (with Dina Iordanova and Leshu Torchin) of *Moving People, Moving Images: Cinema and Trafficking in the New Europe* (2010) as well of various articles and book chapters that analyze (digital) cinema in a range of national and transnational contexts.

Campbell X is the filmmaker (director, sound and camera person) behind the film production outlet BlackmanVision, which makes films that are experimental and/or address issues of memory, forgetting and untold stories. She started out in making films for UK television. She also collaborates with other filmmakers.

Jonnie Clementi-Smith is a British independent filmmaker and video artist of Sri-Lankan descent as well as a film/media lecturer. He recently moved to Hong Kong where he now works as a founder member of the Hong Kong Film Collective. The collective's first film, *The Surroundings* (2011), was commissioned by the Freshwave Film Festival (Hong Kong). His work includes a restaging of Maya Deren's *Divine Horsemen* (2005) and a documentary installation called *People Inbetween* (2007).

Shahab Esfandiary had a short career as a film critic and cultural journalist before he joined the Iranian television where he was involved in foreign program acquisition and feature production. His publications include a chapter on the Iranian war film director Ebrahim Hatami-Kia in *War in Iranian Cinema* (2010) and an article on the veteran Iranian director Daryush Mehrjui in the peer-reviewed journal *Iranian Studies*. His doctoral thesis "National Cinema and Globalization" (2009) has been commissioned for publication.

Flow Motion is a London-based duo comprising electronic musicians, artists, and filmmakers Edward George and Anna Piva. Flow Motion produce multi-media installations and sound art performances. Their work has been shown at the Barcelona Museum of Contemporary Art, the Pompidou Centre (Paris), the International Institute of Visual Art, the Science Museum's Dana Centre in London, the Steirischer Herbst Arts Festival in Austria, Star City's historic Cosmonaut's Club, and Sadler's Wells's Lilian Baylis Theatre. In 2007 Flow Motion completed *Invisible,* the second of a three-part multimedia sound art and science project. Flow Motion's most recent project *Promised Lands* (2008–2010) can be viewed via www.promisedlands.info. Flow Motion's written texts have been published in *Leonardo Journal* and *Journal of Media Practice* and in anthologies and exhibition publications such as *Changing States: Art and Ideas in an Era of Globalisation* (2004), and *Sonic Process: a New Geography of Sound* (2002).

Coco Fusco is a New York-based interdisciplinary artist, writer, and director of Intermedia Initiatives at Parsons New School for Design. She has performed, lectured, exhibited, and curated around the world since 1988. She is a recipient of a 2003 Herp Albert Award in the Arts. She is the author of *English is Broken Here: Notes on Cultural Fusion in the Americas* (1995), *The Bodies That Were Not Ours and Other Writings* (2001) and *A Field Guide for Female Interrogators* (2008). Some of her recent work deals with the role of female interrogators in the War on Terror, such as *A Room of One's Own* (2006) a monologue about female interrogators, a perfor-mance that explores the "Black Codes" that were established in the Americas after Slavery, and a research project on the experience of incarceration in the USA.

Patti Gaal-Holmes is an art historian and artist/filmmaker. Her doctoral thesis, "A History of 1970s British Experimental Filmmaking," was completed at the University of Portsmouth in 2011. Her research interests include discourses on exile, migration, colonialism/postcolonialism, and relationships between theory and practice. She is Reviews Editor for the journal *Transnational Cinemas*.

Will Higbee is a senior lecturer in film studies at the University of Exeter. He is the author of *Mathieu Kassovitz* (2007) and the co-editor with Sarah Leahy of *Studies in French Cinema: UK Perspectives, 1985–2010* (2010) and with Saër Maty Bâ of a special edition of the *Journal of Media Practice: Re-presenting Diaspora in Cinema and New (Digital) Media.* He is a member of the editorial board of the journal *Studies in French Cinema* and has published various articles on contemporary French cinema, cinemas of the North African diaspora in France, and questions of trans-national cinemas in journals such as *Transnational Cinemas, French Cultural Studies,* and *Africultures.* He is currently completing a monograph entitled *Post-Beur Cinema: Maghrebi-French and North African Émigré Filmmaking in France since 2000.*

Katharina Lindner's Ph.D. (University of Glasgow) was concerned with cinematic articulations of female athleticism, physicality, and bodily performance. Her research engages with debates around gender, sexuality and representation, cinema, and embodiment as well as with phenomenological approaches to film. Her work has been published in a range of academic journals, including *Feminist Media Studies*, *Journal of International Women's Studies*, and *New Review of Film and Television Studies*.

Daniel Lindvall is Editor-in-Chief of *Film International*. He is a cultural journalist and independent scholar. His interests include Marxism and cultural politics, the labour movement and class relations on screen and participatory culture as a means of democratic social change. He is a regular film critic for the Swedish Syndicalist weekly, *Arbetaren*.

Teddy E. Mattera is a South African film writer, director, and producer. He wrote the short documentary *Waiting for Valdez* (2003) and wrote and directed several films, including *Max and Mona* (2004). More recently, he has directed five episodes for the television series *One Way* (2006–2007) and the short film *Telegraph to the Sky* (2009) for the 2009 cultural festival in Algiers. A longer version of the latter film is currently screened on Mzansi, a cable channel in South Africa.

Sheila J. Petty is Dean of the Faculty of Fine Arts and Professor of Media Studies at the University of Regina, Canada. She is also an adjunct scientist (new media) at TRLabs, Regina. She is the author of *Contact Zones: Memory, Origin, and Discourses in Black Diasporic Cinema* (2008) and has written extensively on issues of cultural representation, identity, and nation in African and African diasporic cinema and new media. She has curated film, television, and new media exhibitions for galleries across Canada.

Deborah Shaw is Reader in Film Studies at the University of Portsmouth. She is founding co-editor of the journal *Transnational Cinemas*, and her books include *The Three Amigos: The Transnational Films of Guillermo del Toro, Alejandro González Iñárritu, and Alfonso Cuarón*, (forthcoming), *Contemporary Latin American Cinema: Ten Key Films* (2003), and *Contemporary Latin American Cinema: Breaking into the Global Market* (2007).

Rod Stoneman is Director of the Huston School of Film and Digital Media. Before moving to NUI Galway, he was Chief Executive of Bord Scannán na hÉireann/The Irish Film Board and previously a deputy commissioning editor in the independent film and video department at Channel 4 Television. He is the author of *Chávez: The Revolution Will Not Be Televised: A Case Study of Politics and the Media* (2008). His most recent films include *A Tourist Excursion to the Burren* (2006), *12,000 Years of Blindness* (2007), and *The Spindle: How Life Works* (2009).

Kate E. Taylor-Jones is a lecturer in visual culture at Bangor University. Her research specialism includes the visual culture of Japan and South Korean and gender and visual culture. She is the author of *Rising Sun Divided Land: Japanese and Korean Cinema* (forthcoming) and has published widely on a variety of topics including colonial Japanese and Korean cinema, domestic violence and the Internet, and prostitution and the sex trade in East Asia.

Acknowledgments

The Editors of *De-Westernizing Film Studies* would like to thank the following individuals for their assistance and support with this publication. To Natalie Foster, Senior Editor at Routledge, for originally commissioning the project as well as for her advice and support in bringing the book to completion. To the academics, friends, and colleagues who have supported this project at various stages since its inception, especially Professor Graeme Harper (Oakland University, USA), Dr Elisabetta Girelli (University of St Andrews), Dr Roshini Kempadoo (University of East London), and Dr Pedram Khosronejad (University of St Andrews). We are also grateful to the readers of the original book proposal for providing us with encouraging feedback and constructive criticism in equal measure.

Special thanks to the filmmakers, critics, composers, writers, and academics who generously gave of their time to be interviewed for this book as well as to the authors of individual chapters for enriching the book's intellectual content and scope. To John Akomfrah, Lina Gopaul, and David Lawson at Smoking Dogs Films for giving us permission to use the image from *The Call of Mist* (1998) for the book cover, and to Dr Coco Fusco for allowing us to use images from *A Room of One's Own: Women and Power in the New America* (2005) and *Two Undiscovered Amerindians Visit the West* (1992–1994) for inclusion inside the book. We are also grateful to Chris Mearing and Jon Primrose (Department of Drama, Exeter University) for technical assistance with recording the interviews for this book which were conducted online.

Finally, the editors would like to express a special thanks to their respective families for their patience, love, and support over the months that have been spent working on this project.

Foreword

If studying film originates somewhere is it therefore only from, and of, that place? According to such a definition, historically speaking some might imagine that film analysis lives in Paris, somewhere around the Grand Café on the Boulevard des Capucines, where in December 1895 the Lumière Brothers exhibited the film *Sortie des Usines Lumière à Lyon Workers Leaving the Lumière Factory*, among other short films. Thus emerged a mass, though arguably lay, inaugural audience of film critics! Or maybe film analysis lives on the outskirts of Lyon, at 25 rue St. Victor Montplaisir, where the Lumière factory was based at the time, and where *Workers Leaving the Lumière Factory* was shot. Or was that just the making of that one film, not the ongoing analyzing of many films?

As we quickly realize, all these suggestions make absolutely no sense. And yet, in analytical terms, they might as well make sense because the hegemony of critical discourse, one prominent over another, one embraced, another discouraged, one established, another trying to emerge, suggests that there is a centrality to the studying of film. But whose centrality is this, and why does it exist?

For an art involving so many human intersections and interactions, film has occasionally produced some intriguing narrowness of analysis. Not necessarily because of a lack of intellectual ability in a particular analyst. Not even because one film critic or another has consciously sought to promote a primary socio-economic, cultural or political viewpoint, or to elicit just a small range of these. Instead, simply because hegemony works this way: it insists on domination, superiority, and centrality. Regardless of whether we believe many films emerge around a central subjective core, it is impossible not to recognize that the film arts are not about narrowing human interactions. Rather, they are fundamentally about extending them. And this is the case whether we think in terms of the making of film – the principles of communication, collaboration, and exchange that are necessary for a film to be made, distributed, and consumed – or whether we think in terms of many individuals and the group, the relationship between singular creative visions and a wider cultural perspective, between makers, academic critics, and general film audiences.

With all this in mind, the idea that the academic discipline of film studies or, more specifically, the application of film theory, could be (or should only be) "Western" must surely collapse, even under the smallest amount of scrutiny. In many ways it has not – or, more accurately, it has not yet. Go further, and consider the notion that the analysis of film should rightly consider and embrace the perspectives of the world's filmmakers and film audiences that represent multiple cultural perspectives, personal as well as cultural and socioeconomic, local as well as national and global, and the concept of a hegemonic disciplinary focus for film studies becomes decidedly wrong.

We must always be wary of holding a blinkered academe-centric view of human phenomenon if we are to approach the possibility of producing genuine truths about the nature of our world. This wariness should not be viewed as a trend to be explored today in universities and colleges. Instead, it should surely *always* be a key element of us being responsible, engaged members and makers of universities. Similarly, we all recognize that film itself tells us it is not one thing but many, not one set of creative achievements but many; that it is not adequately approached by a singular critical perspective but only truly approachable, truly analyzable, through an understanding of many perspectives.

To suggest the need for *De-Westernizing Film Studies*, as this current book expertly does, is effectively to argue for the critical reintroduction of the human into the intensely human practice of filmmaking and film viewing. Unconscious as much of the removal of the human might have been, the fact that we have participated in it by compartmentalizing film critique into nations and periods, preferred theoretical schools of thought and Western ideological vantage points might well mean some of us have *Westernized* it by a lack of attention to alternative possibilities.

All this is not a condemnation of the progress made by a great many film scholars over the past century. But it is to say that though film originally emerged from somewhere it has more importantly traveled elsewhere, to very many places in fact; been embraced, reinvented, made, watched, analyzed, configured by a multiplicity of people for a multiplicity of purposes and with a multiplicity of results. A de-Westernized film studies, therefore, does not involve an art being returned to its origins. Nor does it involve the seeking of a progenitor for an academic discipline. As an art, film is global, globally made, and globally received. With this in mind, a de-Westernized film studies is a film studies recognizing the collaborative human brilliance of film and empowering individual and cultural difference in response to filmmaking. This book, *De-Westernizing Film Studies*, makes plain that to de-Westernize is to reinvigorate, is to empower, is to *create* a film studies that is both appropriate and significant here in our transnational twenty-first century.

Professor Graeme Harper
Director, The Honors College
Oakland University, Michigan, USA

Introduction

De-Westernizing film studies

Saër Maty Bâ and Will Higbee

Each age and society recreates its others.

(Said 1995: 332)

[T]here seems to me to be ways in which one could reconfigure a history of cinema without mentioning Méliès or Godard but still be just as legitimate, because the questions this new history would raise would be just as pertinent and just as real.

(Akomfrah 2010: 28)

What is at stake is not only the hegemony of Western cultures, but also their identities as unified cultures; in other words the realization that there is a Third World in every first and vice-versa.

(Minh-ha 1989: 3)

Preamble: definitions of a process

The principle aim of *De-Westernizing Film Studies* is to consider what forms a challenge to the enduring vision of film as a medium – and film studies as a discipline – modeled on "Western" ideologies, theoretical and historical frameworks, critical perspectives as well as institutional and artistic practices, might take today. The range of scholarly writing, interviews with filmmakers and industry professionals, and critical reflection contained within this volume – comprising experience and knowledge from a wide range of geographical areas, film cultures, and (trans-)national perspectives – seeks to problematize a binary mode of thinking that continues to promote an idea of "the West and the rest" in relation to questions of production, distribution, reception, and representation within an artistic medium (cinema) that, as part of contemporary moving image culture, is more globalized and diversified than at any time in its history. In so doing, *De-Westernizing Film Studies* complicates and/or rethinks how local, national, and regional film cultures "connect" globally, seeking polycentric, multi-directional, non-essentialized alternatives to Eurocentric theoretical and historical perspectives found in film as both an artistic medium and an academic field of study.

For our purposes in *De-Westernizing Film Studies*, the "West" is not considered primarily as a fixed geographical location, nor bound to a specific historical period. Rather it is an ideologically inflected mode of being in and seeing, perceiving or representing the world, or, what Žižek describes as: "a contemplative attitude that misrecognizes its dependence on social reality" (Žižek 1994: 3). Moreover, the "West" as a category is always (necessarily) shifting, in motion, and therefore unstable: one's geographical "West" is always another's "East." The "West" therefore becomes a geo-cultural or geo-political framework that one can subject to a range of theoretical analyses across disciplines that contemporary film studies encompasses or interconnects with: screen studies, (new) media studies, cultural studies, language studies, research methods, education, history, philosophy, and so on.

Following this line of thinking, a process of "de-Westernizing" essentially avoids perceiving the West/Western solely as, or through, geographical frameworks. Locating the West is also a question of perspective. As the Moroccan filmmaker Farida Benlyazid notes in her interview for this volume, while Morocco may be seen by Europe and North America as part of the Orient/East, in the Arab world it forms part of Al-Maghrib, meaning, literally, the "West" or "Occident" (the term denotes the Western most territories that fell to the Islamic conquests of the seventh century). Furthermore, just as Morocco is clearly identified for linguistic, cultural, and religious reasons as part of the Arab world, similar arguments can also be made for it belonging to a "Mediterranean" group of nations, simultaneously confirming and blurring the supposed certainties of the East/West, Orient/Occident binary. This instability of a supposedly fixed Occident/Orient binary is further complicated by the legacy of European (French) colonial rule that has shaped and transformed cultural contact and exchange between France and Morocco – both in the territory of the former protectorate but also in the former *métropole* itself through the presence of the Moroccan diaspora in France consisting of Moroccan immigrants and their French-born descendants.

The idea of West and East, Occident and Orient as representing fixed geographical coordinates or unified cultural entities is thus repeatedly problematized by various authors and interviewees across this volume and repeatedly exposed as uncertain. In a similar way, the notion of de-Westernizing as it is debated throughout this volume resists a straightforward inversion of Eurocentric binaries, diachronic histories or centers, or an oversimplified equation that simplistically reads de-Westernizing as "anti-Western" or, indeed, "anti-Hollywood." As the term "de-*Western*izing" itself suggests, the influence of the "West" and its film cultures remain a very clear presence as well as a very real part of the debate. Moreover, as a number of contributors to this volume argue (see for example chapters by Abrams on a *midrashic* reading of Kubrick's *The Shining* (1980), Bâ's exploration of "black" diasporic cinema as symptom, Lindner's analysis of queer aesthetics in contemporary American cinema, and Brown's discussion of continuity editing as a "common" cinematic language), the process of de-Westernizing is one that can (and indeed must) take place simultaneously outside of and *within* Western ideological, intellectual, academic, institutional, industrial, and cinematic territories themselves. As Daniel Lindvall suggests in his interview for this book, a refusal of the West/non-West binary is vital, for to accept such as to a position is to present "a false choice of allegiance between 'Western' and 'non-Western' that obscures the complex history of human development as well as real conflicts of interest within nations/regions (notably class conflicts) as well as real common interests between groups (such as classes) across the 'Western'-'non-Western' divide."

Therefore we do not understand "de-Westernizing" as a fixed, fully formed or unmediated theoretical position (though, to be sure, the question of film theory is foregrounded in much of the discussion of de-Westernizing contained within this book). Rather, we view "de-Westernizing" as an ongoing *process* that enables debate and negotiation between academics (theorists, historians), critics, and filmmakers whose position is defined more in terms of a shared attitude toward the need for a more diverse approach to film theory, film history, and film practice than a given geographical location, political/artistic affiliation; otherwise we would be legitimizing ideology, "a systematically distorted communication" (Žižek 1994: 10) that functions by defending "the existing system against any serious critique, legitimizing it as a direct expression of human nature" (Žižek 2009: 27). In this context, the aim of de-Westernizing also becomes the act (through theory and practice) of exposing, challenging, and thus repositioning the West's dominance (real and imagined) as a conceptual "force," representational norm, epistemological center, and ontological "fact," in cinema, as well as questioning the hierarchies that are produced in film studies as a result of studying "cinema" under these conditions.

Tracing de-Westernizing gestures in film theory and practice

Identifying a "Western" bias and the pursuit of an alternative, non-Eurocentric perspective is not, in and of itself, a new approach in film studies and filmmaking. Even though the global reach of European colonial and imperial rule ensured that for many non-European peoples (especially those in Africa and the Arab world) it would be more than fifty years into cinema's first century before they were able to access the means of production of the twentieth century's most important art form, indigenous filmmaking nonetheless established itself as an industrial and artistic presence in countries such as China, India, Egypt, and Japan well before the 1950s. With decolonization in the 1950s and 1960s many newly liberated postcolonial nations – distinctively in Algeria, to take one example – sought to nationalize the film industry and use cinema as a form of propaganda as well as an educational tool. Elsewhere in Latin America, the camera became a radical weapon of resistance against oppressive state control and dictatorships. In terms of theorizing and scholarship, at least as early as the late 1970s and into the 1980s Western critics and academics were considering alternative or under-represented modes of non-European film practice most obviously in relation to Japanese cinema (Burch 1979), Indian cinema (Willemen and Gandhy 1982), West-African cinema (Pfaff 1984) but also the cinemas of central and southern America and the Caribbean (Johnson and Stam 1982; Chanan 1985; Fusco 1987) as well as more wide-ranging attempts to, on the one hand, define "Third World" filmmaking *in relation to* the West (Armes 1987) and, on the other, propose Third

(World) cinema as presenting a direct challenge (political and aesthetic) to First World (Western) filmmaking (Gabriel 1982). Much of this critical engagement with these non-Western cinemas and modes of filmmaking came in response to the films, theorizing and activism of Third (World) cinema that emerged first from Latin America in the late 1960s with the Grupo Ciné Liberacion's *La Hora de los hornos/Hour of the Furnaces* (1968), which was followed a year later by a manifesto based on the experiences of making the film, entitled *Hacia un tercer cine/Towards a Third Cinema: Notes and Experiences on the Development of a Cinema of Liberation*, written by two of the group, Fernando Solanas and Octavio Getino (Chanan 1997: 373). This key intervention by these militant politicized Argentine filmmakers was the inspiration for the emergence of a broader conception of "Third Cinema" – formulated in the work of Teshome H. Gabriel (1982) as an anti-imperialist cinema that through both its content and aesthetics was opposed to all forms of imperialism and class oppression and was defined as much by its politics as by the location of production. The question of Third Cinema's relevance for film and video practitioners two decades after Solanas and Getino's original intervention, as well as more specifically the relation of Third Cinema to diasporic filmmakers living and working in the metropolitan centers of the West was further addressed in Pines and Willemen's seminal collection *Questions of Third Cinema* (1989). Following on from this, Anthony R. Guneratne and Wimal Dissanayake's edited collection *Re-Thinking Third Cinema* (2003) offered an incisive, informed and wide-ranging re-evaluation of the continued relevance of "the only branch of film theory that did not originate within a specifically Euro-American context" (Guneratne 2003: 7) whose relative neglect amongst film theorists Guneratne perceives as symptomatic of the discipline's more general tendency to overlook the cinemas from outside of the industrialized Global North (Guneratne 2003: 1).

The growing importance of diasporic cinemas, in particular cinemas of the African diaspora since the 1980s, and the subsequent attention given to these films and filmmakers by a substantial body of academic publications – e.g., Mercer 1994 – was evidenced by the publication of Michael T. Martin's groundbreaking anthology *Cinemas of the Black Diaspora: Diversity, Dependence and Oppositionality* in 1995. This work has been complemented in the early 2000s by that of Hamid Naficy's *An Accented Cinema* (2001) and Laura U. Marks *The Skin of Film* (2000), which have showed the impact postcolonial and diasporic filmmakers from the Global South was having (albeit from the peripheries of the industry) in national cinemas of the Global North – as well as, in the case of Marks's work, illustrating how the wider theoretical agenda (in relation to a "haptic" cinema of sensation and affect) could be driven by the filmmakers and artists, whose work was traditionally located beyond the sightlines of the Euro-American bastion of grand theory. Finally, in the arena of diasporic cinema, Sheila Petty's *Contact Zones* (2008) provides a cogent and forceful analysis of how more recent Western preoccupations surrounding questions of origins, migration, the blurring of national identities, and the "pressures and fissures created by globalization" have been alive and ongoing issues for members of the African diaspora and how the films that emerge from the black diaspora "have much to offer in the current debate surrounding globalizing cultural spaces" (Petty 2008: 1–2). As in the academy, such changes and transformations were also being noted by Western and non-Western film critics and historians working outside of the university system during the 1980s, 1990s, and 2000s (e.g., Olivier Barlet, interviewed in this volume, and Férid Boughedir). Their work explored the ways that both the anti-imperial politics and aesthetics of film could be applied to a critique of Western political and economic hegemony in a global film industry that appeared intent on maintaining the modes of domination and exclusion that had held sway over most of the globe throughout the nineteenth and first part of the twentieth century in the form of European colonialism.

In addition to the theoretical, intellectual, and practical de-Westernizing approaches outlined above, questions surrounding the relationship between Western and non-Western cultures, political economies, forms of representation, and systems of knowledge contained within these studies of national, regional, and ethnic film cultures, were further informed by a broader set of academic discourses aligned to postmodern and poststructuralist theory; namely postcolonial theory. The work of scholars originating from indigenous, settler, and diasporic contexts (intellectually and culturally) aligned with postcolonial theory (Hall, Bhabha, Minh-ha, Spivak, Said, Ashcroft et al.) brought to the fore the question of representation of the marginal or subaltern and the recognition of empowering forms of hybridity and difference in the face of hegemonic (Western, capitalist, neo-colonial) discourse. Of all these theorists, it is arguably Edward Said's seminal study *Orientalism,* with its emphasis on the West's construction of an ontological and epistemological binary between Orient and Occident (Said 1995), that can be most obviously aligned with concerns of the various contributors to *De-Westernizing Film Studies.* However, they also find resonance in Trinh T. Minh-ha's refusal of "Master Territories" and her insistence on the blurring of boundaries between insider/ outsider, colonized/colonizer, Western/non-Western (Minh-ha 1989: 133–149), or even in Ashcroft's more recent concept of "post-colonial transformation," whereby the (former) colonized's challenge to Western (imperial) control has frequently been characterized by "a remarkable facility to use the modes of the dominant [colonial] discourse against itself and transform it in ways that have been both profound and lasting" (Ashcroft 2001: 13).

The limitations and dangers of postcolonial theory's globalizing "gesture" in downplaying multiplicities of location (historical, cultural, temporal) have already been widely recognized (Shohat and Stam 1994: 37–40). However, the refusal of post-colonial theory to commit to a fixed binary, what Hall terms its "double inscription" is precisely where its value lies, since it permits "a decentred, diasporic or global re-writing of earlier, nation centred imperial grand narratives" (Hall 1996: 247). Moreover, this breaking down of the "grand narratives" of (Western) imperialism takes place not only within the boundaries of formerly colonized nations and cultures but also within the multicultural postcolonial spaces of contemporary Western society, where, as Žižek puts it in another context, "one has to learn fully to accept that there is no big Other" (2009: 149).

For the purposes of this volume, James D. Le Sueur's (2003) definition of colonialism and decolonization as "dialogical" is helpful for moving beyond the perceived theoretical restriction of postcolonial theory in relation to the idea of de-Westernizing; more specifically for the way that it perceives decolonization as an awkwardness to be embraced rather than decried since "when researchers study issues posed by decolonization they inevitably enter into a field of inquiry whose very subject is that of contest and change" (Le Sueur 2003: 2).

One final scholarly intervention that must be included in this overview of theoretical approaches to "de-Westernizing" is that of *Unthinking Eurocentrism: Multiculturalism and the Media* (Shohat and Stam 1994), a text that did so much to influence thinking on the hegemonic hold of the Western media on the global cultural imaginary and in particular, Shohat and Stam's notion of "polycentric multiculturalism." Polycentric multiculturalism is thus defined as a radical approach that globalizes and discusses issues of multiculturalism, colonialism, and race within a "web of relationality" from multiple vantage points and "in relation to social power" – whereby sympathy is clearly and consistently expressed with the marginalized and oppressed. It contends that "no single community or part of the world, whatever its economic or political power, should be epistemologically privileged." Finally, it rejects fixed or essentialized concept of identities (be they individual or communal) preferring to view them as polymorphous, dialogic, and in a process of becoming: "within an ongoing struggle of hegemony and resistance, each act of cultural interlocution leaves both interlocutors changed" (Shohat and Stam 1994: 46–49). This understanding of multiple perspectives and dialogic negotiations between individuals and communities operating at both a local/national and global/transnational level has been highly influential in film studies' recent engagement with the conceptual terms of transnational and world cinema (Ezra and Rowden 2005; Dennison and Lim 2006; Ďurovičová and Newman 2009). Most recently, Shohat and Stam's concept has been adapted by Nagib, Perriam, and Dudrah in *Theorizing World Cinema* (2012) to a "polycentric approach to Film Studies" which refuses to define world cinema negatively as "non-Hollywood cinema," preferring to see it instead as: "a polycentric phenomenon with peaks of creation in different places and periods. Once notions of single centre, primacies, and dichronicities are discarded, everything can be put on the world cinema map on an equal footing, even Hollywood, which instead of a threat becomes a cinema among others" (Nagib et al. 2012: xxii–xxiii).

De-Westenizing Film Studies shares the widely accepted idea expressed in *Theorizing World Cinema* that escaping binarisms opens up a space for original theorizing to take place and emerge from both within and across a variety of national and regional film cultures. However, the explicit attention paid to imbalances of power (economic, political, industrial, social) in Shohat and Stam's original conceptualization of polycentrism means that we must advance with extreme caution when considering Hollywood (or Bollywood and Nollywood for that matter) as merely one cinema among others. "All cinemas are equal, but some are more equal than others," we might say. In this book, questions of national and transnational cinema are thus dealt with through a de-Westernizing optique that is equally attentive to escaping binary notions of national/transnational (and indeed the very notion of the national as primarily a Western construct) as they are of the often uneven balances of history, power, and displacement involved in the construction of national or transnational film cultures. (In this context, see the chapters in Part II by Higbee on reimagining community in Tunisian national cinema, Beus's comparative analysis of storytelling traditions as theoretical framework in Pacific Island and African cinemas, and Esfandiary's exploration of "banal transnationalism" in the recent films of Iranian exilic auteur Mohsen Makhmalbaf.)

De-Westernizing and the moves of alterity

It would seem then that the resultant point for us is one of setting de-Westernizing up as a non-given, as unclearly defined. The point of the book is indeed to extrapolate a series of thoughts, ideas, and writings as to what de-Westernizing might actually mean, for example a chaotic mix of moves of alterity. This is precisely why we find Akomfrah's concept of a "double move of alterity" insightful (see his interview in this book) because, irrespective of the fact that the double mover's gesture depends on location and is therefore cultural, aesthetic, political or economic, the double move itself is always already implicit within that same gesture, adopting more or less the following shape or pattern: "always characterized by [. . .] that 'double move,' which is a move for elevating a space – and it's very much a space of difference – informed by an understanding. Otherwise it's not [a de-Westernizing gesture]."

In addition, the question of where that space of difference leads reasoning on de-Westernizing seems to us to be just as important. These zones of the "double move" are "contact zones" (Clifford 1994; Petty 2008) at the same time as they produce third spaces (i.e. beyond the double move(r)'s first and second spaces) of meaning, or clusters of such spaces, within the same zones.[1] Put differently, the double move becomes a quadruple move in a motion that turns exponential; the de-Westernizing gesture (or process or body) is penetrated, invaded even, by an exponentiality in "more or less the way a virus is implanted in a cell," to invoke Jameson's post-modern against-the-grain concept of hybridity (2010: 316). From this line of thinking, depending on the subject's/de-Westernizer's location(s), that gesture would increase or decrease but never cease to be in motion and unpredictable. As a case in point, our own editors' gesture produces meaning by mobilizing the "I" and the "You" of a statement (e.g., West/Western on the one hand, and non-Western on the other), two places of communication, which are then activated "in the passage of a Third Space," decolonized and decolonizing, where relation between "the general condition of language and the specific implication of [our] utterance" result in ambivalence (Bhabha 2004: 53). Again, de-Westernizing as a non-given which, akin to "[t]he intervention of the Third Space of enunciation," is a deliberately ambivalent process that shatters "this mirror of representation in which cultural knowledge is customarily revealed as an integrated, open, expanding code" (Bhabha 2004: 54). Our proposed perception of the de-Westernizing gesture and process does not therefore aim to homogenize, unify or authenticate: it disrupts, displaces, de-homogenizes,

muddies both "West"/"Western" on the one hand, and the de-Westernizing ges-
ture-processes at work in/on/through West or Western on the other hand. Such
a perception is ours and *De-Westernizing Film Studies'* "pact of interpretation"
(Bhabha 2004: 53).

Thus, our version of de-Westernizing is about an increasing connectivity within
zones of contact always already threatening to overspill its contents (disruptions,
displacements, de-homogenizations, muddy waters, and so on) into spaces
beyond itself in an unpredictable fashion. This is because de-Westernizing does not
buy into, nor is it a flawed and idealistic notion of, political internationalization or
a metaphorical idea of the global-local. Instead, it is (and embraces) the reality of
how, economically and culturally, films, filmmakers, and our analyses, function
across national and/or cultural borders and boundaries in the current phase of
globalization. This functioning takes place in a way that (paradoxically) challenges
the hegemony of the West at the same time as it appears to reinforce it. The
apparent reinforcement, it must be clear, befalls only those who fail to see that
the (p)act of interpretation is never merely a binary "act of communication
between the I and the You designated in the statement" (Bhabha 2004: 53). For if
it were so, it would not have been possible to perceive "Western" in the terms
Lindvall insightfully does in his interview for this book as "an ideological
framework of ideas shared by Triad (European Union, North America, Japan)
ruling classes." While this Triad advances its own goals and serves the interests of
ruling classes globally, one which is already being challenged by the rise of other
emerging industrial/economic superpowers (e.g., Brazil, India, China), the ostensibly Western construct of "nation," as shown in this book, remains relevant to
de-Westernizing thought processes and acts.

At the same time, migration and diaspora beyond the nation (both as recent
engagement with host nations and a more sedentary presence) impact on our idea
of de-Westernizing. Reference is being made here to ways in which de-Westernizing
has to account for "the discordant movements of modernity, the massive migrations"
marking out the twentieth and twenty-first centuries (Baziel and Mannur 2003: 3).
De-Westernizing's exponential quadruple move adds a further treble movement
to its dynamics – i.e. embodiment, scattering, and regrouping "into new points of
becoming" (Baziel and Mannur 2003: 3) – that is "not always westerly" (Naficy
2010: 13).[2] Filmmakers' (or other artists') migrations are not in "one vertical
direction from [. . .] home to exile" (Naficy 2010: 13). Instead, as evidenced in
Esfandiary's chapter on Mohsen Makhmalbaf, and Gaal-Holmes's, Bhamra's, and
Campbell's respective interviews for this book, these bodies may move back
home, may remain there, but their frequent movements are also horizontal since
they lead to "other transitional locations, third countries or to a series of temporary homes in diaspora" (Naficy 2010: 13). In other words, de-Westernization
is understood here as able to not preclude the non-crossing of national borderlines – an in-situ de-Westernization caused/accented by forms of globalization
like "economic privatisation, media restructuring, digitization and the Internet"
(Naficy 2010: 13) – but also to acknowledge and embody border crossings,
migrations, and diasporas as constitutive elements of a de-Westernizing ontology.

From this line of thinking, our idea of de-Westernizing stays away from recent attempts to make an incision-distinction between what constitutes a "migrant" and a "diasporic" filmmaker respectively.[3] Such a distinction is tenuous and cannot account for the seven moves of the de-Westernizing gesture-process or the complexities of migration and diaspora.

From the above discussion, it should be clear then that de-Westernizing is not synonymous with de-centering. Rather, it is an attempt to emphasize ways in which non-Western influences, experiences and modes of thinking, theorizing and *making* film (which may well emanate from within a Euro-American orbit) can take their place alongside those from within the West. To this end, while the West may remain dominant in economic terms, there are also in the creative industries multiple centers of production and multiple mainstreams for, among other achievements, "together, globalisation and the digital shift carry out an inevitable adjustment of international balances [and] intensify the circulation of information" (Martel 2010: 445). The mainstream multiplies and diversifies creatively to an extent that "we have less and less 'cultural products' and more and more 'services' and fluxes" (Martel 2010: 444). De-Westernizing must therefore reckon with differing ways of mainstreaming, particularly those emanating from contemporary "young leaders of creative industries from emerging countries" eager "to disseminate their services all over the world" (Martel 2010: 444).[4] These leaders can operate from within, across, and/or outside the West. And of course, the current age of digital dissemination is bringing into closer proximity a variety of mainstream and avant-garde cinemas, as Akomfrah's comments, in his interview for this volume, about leaving the Rio cinema in London having seen *The Tree of Life* (dir. Terrence Malik, 2011) and being able to purchase Nollywood DVDs just across the road, make clear. De-Westernizing processes must thus be ready to grapple with such complex creative and reception trajectories as they disfigure, beyond recognition, the-West-and-the-rest-type debates while at the same time having a lasting and substantial bearing on film studies.

In line with this logic, de-Westernizing cannot be about making hegemonies disappear; hegemonies, just like mainstreaming, scatter, and that is precisely our argument so far – i.e. from double move to multiply-diverse mainstreams. Indeed, one must not miss how de-Westernizing (still) speaks to ideas of center/periphery and global/local. De-Westernizing is acutely aware that "location is still an important category that influences the specific manifestations of transnational formations" (Grewal and Kaplan 1994: 16). Moreover, de-Westernizing is mindful of how discrete diasporas differ in terms of agenda and politics. Put differently, as Petty's chapter on African film studies, Bâ's on questioning discourses of diaspora, and Taylor-Jones's on East Asian co-productions amply demonstrate, one must first learn to recognize diasporas, and then attempt to isolate them for analysis. Once this plane, or rather pact of interpretation, is reached, three types of evidence become clear: de-Westernizing de-colonizes (like transnational feminist practices);[5] the articulation of de-Westernizing comes through its relation to scattered hegemonies; and de-Westernizing, though enabling scholars and practitioners (scattered, in transit, or regrouped), is not a new term.[6] The third type of evidence points to the fact that de-Westernizing is a new perception of existing phenomena that are in motion toward futures or beyonds that in turn are always already uncertain.

The issue of newly perceived existing phenomena (i.e. space, place, race, gender, practice, imaginary, discourse, ideology, politics, and so on) needs further unpacking. *De-Westernizing Film Studies* is positioned at the borderlines between the "representational" and the "non-representational." The vortex of motions and flexible dynamics at play in the book taken as a whole, in terms of space – place, race, gender, practice, imaginary, discourse, ideology, politics, and so on – show that some matters do not resist representation: they are non-representational. If dismissing representation altogether would be reckless, allowing it to become a tyranny would be equally uncalled for. Re-presentation, a process of repetition different from representation, seems more suited to perceiving existing phenomena anew. As cases in point, see chapters by Bâ and Taylor-Jones, Lindner, Flow Motion, and Abrams, as well as Barlet's interview in this book.

Furthermore, for de-Westernizing to be as complex, elusive, and unpredictable as it should be, the contact zone of its expressivity must not only re-present but also bring its representational and non-representational aspects in conversation. This is how, in our view, de-Westernizing processes emulate three key elements from non-representational theory as proposed by Nigel Thrift (2008). First, to give equal weight to "the vast spillage of *things*" (cf. with the zone of contact threatening over-spillage invoked above) because "things answer back" (Thrift 2008: 9). Second, de-Westernizing is unapologetically "experimental," something which connotes unpredictability, surprise and a trans-disciplinary impulse, or in Thrift's words, "[seeing] what happens [and] let the event sing you" (Thrift 2008: 12), as our decision to begin the collection and its section of "academic" chapters with a piece by Flow Motion (soundscape artists and electronic musicians) displays. Third, de-Westernizing aims "to get in touch with the full range of registers of thought by stressing affect and sensation" while not "dropping the human subject entirely" (Thrift 2008: 12, 13). De-Westernizing, in other words, is neither anti-humanist nor degenerative. Instead it seeks and embraces "a generalized ethics of out-of-jointness" (Thrift 2008: 12) (cf. with Le Sueur's awkward decolonization idea mentioned above) or of originality and innovation, and ethics which embodies "a form of answerability" that is in itself an opportunity to construct novel, albeit strange forms – of life, for example (Thrift 2008: 12).

From this line of thinking, we would argue that the amount of material treated in the volume that originates in the USA or Europe (the "West"?) is a mark of distinction useful in destabilizing the East/West binary, as already invoked through the Triad and other examples; in fact, we would claim this mark fully as part of our contribution. This is because it is a political and cultural statement against a tyranny-hegemony that has claimed many an edited volume cognate to *De-Westernizing Film Studies*: to place a premium on geography or on geographical location of both contributors and material covered.

To return to the issue of location, the amount of material treated in the book and located in the "West" (?) signifies a lack of trust in the same West's capacity to imagine itself as de-Westernized: what the West tends to do is reimagine its own hegemony, not least because of the tyranny just mentioned. Thus, Hall's (1996: 247) exposure of nation-centered imperial grand narratives (see above) went further and asked when the postcolonial actually *was*. Similarly, Young's *White Mythologies* (1990) argued that, in Europe, anti-colonialism was as old as colonialism itself; what was new in the years since World War II when Europe lost most of its empires through decolonization was the complementary efforts "to decolonize European thought" and the shapes of its history (Young 1990: 119). Consequently, Young went on to argue, these years marked "[a] fundamental shift" (1990: 119). We would argue that in issues of film studies and the West that type scale of shift is yet to happen – so-called centrifugal film studies books (from Europe/center to periphery/other), are in fact deeply centripetal, talking at readers and/or doing nothing for the so-called "Other" (who has not asked for anything in the first place). Similarly, if film studies books that are genuinely centripetal manage to avoid the above pitfall, they tend to fall into another one: an attempt to theorize a capacious, super-cinema cinema – as demonstrated so well by the otherwise extremely useful *European Cinema in Motion* (2010).[7] In short then, we would argue that if this book's overwhelming amount of material and locations within the West are a form of change, they are a more profound change than found in current books cognate to *De-Westernizing Film Studies*.

De-Westernizing film studies as emergent method

If, as the earlier overview of de-Westernizing approaches in theory and practice would suggest, considerable attention has already been paid by certain film studies scholars to the question of de-Westernizing in a variety of theoretical guises, the question must become: "What is the need for this current book and what is it doing differently?" A succinct reply can be offered as follows. First, despite the pioneering work listed above, in relation to the global output in film studies this remains, as Guneratne suggested (2000: 1, 4), a relatively neglected and, in theoretical terms at least, an underdeveloped and under-represented (some might even say under-*respected*) area of film studies, where studies of individual *auteurs* and national cinemas privilege a thematic or historical approach rather than a theoretical one. Moreover, a decade on from Guneratne's assessment of the field and we could argue that the "de-Westernizing" theoretical concerns of a politicized and aesthetic analysis such as "Third Cinema" has given way to a polycentric approach to transnational or world cinemas that is often more concerned with a comparative investigation of global and local conditions of production, distribution and exhibition rather than theorizing the political and representational consequences of a continued imbalance of power between the Global North and South in terms of both production and representation. It should also be stressed at this juncture that, whilst many of the essays in *De-Westernizing Film Studies* are clearly concerned with exploring the implications of de-Westernizing on film theory, they also understand the importance of historical and empirical and institutional studies (such as that offered by Flow Motion or Kate Taylor-Jones in this book) as well as the need to understand the industry – hence the reason for the extended dialogue with practitioners, artists, and industry professionals found in the final interview section of this book. Thus, while much has already been done by a range of scholars over previous decades to lay the groundwork for *De-Westernizing Film Studies*, much remains to be achieved – not least in relation to a more extended range of theoretical and comparative analysis of a far wider range of film cultures, industries, and national cinemas with a specific eye on the attendant debates signaled by the notion of de-Westernizing. More specifically, in the area of film theory there is also a need to break away from the Euro-American dominance of theoretical models, to explore new theoretical positions that can emerge from sources outside of the traditional Western spheres of influence as well as understanding how case studies drawn from a range of global film cultures can inform contemporary debates in film theory – e.g., the analysis found in chapters by Bâ and Taylor-Jones (affective passions) and Lindner (queering the body) – in which the recent affective turn is analyzed, or in William Brown's consideration of continuity editing as a "common" film language. Finally *De-Westernizing Film Studies* intends to consider how current conditions and developments within cinema (the ongoing transformation of the audiovisual landscape caused by the rapid development and access of digital filmmaking technologies) are also forcing us to reassess what is at stake for non-Western filmmakers and film cultures working both within and outside of the Western film industry. These are precisely the issue explored in the interview with Coco Fusco contained within the book.

De-Westernizing film studies therefore evokes and acknowledges its shared aims with earlier theoretical discourses and movements but responds to the changing conditions in which the terms of these debates are taking place. Unlike the postcolonial, de-Westernizing is not bound exclusively to a colonial/postcolonial binary that leads, on the one hand, to a very specific set of historical "moments" and, on the other, to a conflation of histories, cultures, locations, and struggles of resistance into the hybrid "postcolonial subject." In a similar fashion, while the intervention of Third Cinema in the 1960s is a key reference point for earlier thinking and theorizing around the question of non-Western film cultures, *De-Westernizing Film Studies* must (necessarily) move beyond the historical and ideological coordinates that appear to locate the discourse of Third Cinema in a set of given certainties relating to the struggles against imperialism and oppression that, as Coco Fusco notes in her interview for this book, are no longer so fixed and secure. Moreover, it is that such debates and practices have been transformed by a shifting geo-political map at the same time as they have been rewritten due to advances in access to production and distribution networks, both mainstream and alternative, that opened up in the digital age. In this respect, "de-Westernizing" is also an attempt to reconsider how film studies and cinema/new media/moving image culture negotiates its position within a changing economic, cultural, and political order that has transformed previous and supposed "certainties" of East/West, capitalism/communism, as well as race, gender, and nation but within which these binary and Eurocentric modes still hold immense power (including in the film industry itself).

What the above analysis leads us to is a position in which the call being made in this book for a "de-Westernizing gesture" (as John Akomfrah puts it in his interview for this book) as a means of rethinking analyses of cinemas across the globe is at once familiar and unknown; a tried and tested path and new territory; a return to well-trodden academic paths and a new methodological departure. The intention of this book, then, is to unpick a series of ideas and approaches to the concept of "de-Westernizing" in order to better understand what it means or how, it might be applied to an analysis of cinemas from across the globe. In *The Handbook for Emergent Methods* Hesse-Biber and Leavy describe innovative approaches for gathering the necessary data in order to answer research questions that "illuminate something about social life" as "contact methodological zones," which stress "the interconnectedness between *epistemology*, who can know and what can be known; *methodology*, theoretical perspectives and research procedures that emanate from a given epistemology and *method*, the specific techniques utilized to study a given research problem" (Hesse-Biber and Leavy 2010: 2).

Hence, in the context of this book, exploring what "de-Westernizing" film studies might mean becomes a method of rethinking a binary or Eurocentric approach to film studies in particular in relation to the west and the rest in cinema (as the term "world cinema" has tended to suggest) in order to propose new methodologies that will lead to an alternative "un-centered" version of knowledge that gives credit to multiple viewpoints in order to arrive at original and innovative ways of studying film history, theory and practice in a globalized context. Above all, this notion of emergent methods requires, on the one hand, a flexibility to methodological approach at the same time as inviting "multiple meanings and contradictions due to the fact that different paradigms offer different and often opposing interpretations" (Hesse-Biber and Leavy 2010: 4). Thus, as already stated, our understanding of "de-Westernizing" film studies offers no guarantees, givens or certainties. Instead, the aim of this book is, in part, to problematize the notion of de-Westernizing itself at the same time as bringing into question the fixed binaries of Western and non-Western, simply by placing the concept in the wider academic and cinematic domain for further debate and discussion. In this respect, rather than staking a claim for yet another theoretical position or simply adding to the existing lexicography of accented, postcolonial, Third, trans- or intercultural cinema, *De-Westernizing Film Studies* presents itself as an emergent method for studying the balance of power in cinema as a global and local cultural force.

A variety of (non-academic) writing styles and forms of expression have been incorporated into *De-Westernizing Film Studies*, and we would claim this itself as a form of de-Westernizing. Interviews in the latter section of the book switch between informal and conversational to formal and highly theoretical, whilst always rigorously engaging with the issue of de-Westernizing. Rod Stoneman's (academic, film producer), Akomfrah's (writer, producer, director) and Kuljit Bhamra's (musician, film music composer) are potent cases in point. Similarly, *De-Westernizing Film Studies* requires from readers, especially academics, regular dis-placements and re-positionings, sometimes within one single contribution, but not always in terms of style of writing. In other words, thought processes, perceptions of West/Western and/or de-Westernizing included in this volume (should) cause positive vertigos of displacement in the reader: "[o]pacities must be preserved; an appetite for opportune obscurity in translation must be created; and falsely convenient vehicular sabirs must be relentlessly refuted" (Glissant 1997: 120).

Notes

1 Please note that we are not yet referring to Bhabha's (1994) "Third Space" (see below), but to the ordinal number "third" connected the to (plural) "spaces" because the latter, in a third move that opens up to a fourth move and then turns exponential, will scatter like shrapnel.
2 Naficy is describing his past writing on "the movement of people and cultural capital," including filmmakers who physically cross national borders to produce bodies of work he calls "acccented cinema, or accented for television" (2010: 13).
3 Berghahn and Sternberg argue for such a distinction in *European Cinema in Motion: Migrant and Diasporic Film in Contemporary Europe* (2010).
4 These include but are not limited to Brasil, Indonesia, India, Lebanon, Hong Kong, Saudi Arabia, Mexico, and South Korea.
5 Grewel and Kaplan argue that "[m]any women who participate in decolonizing efforts [. . .] have rejected the term 'feminism' in favour of 'womanist' or have defined their feminism through class or race or other ethnic, religious, or regional struggles" (1994: 17).
6 Routledge published the edited collection *De-Westernizing Media Studies* (2000).
7 One of its proposed six "distinctive features" states that "[i]t is a cinema of identity politics that probes difference along the multiple coordinates of race, colour, ethnicity, nationality, regionality, language, religion, generation, class, gender and sexuality" (Berghahn and Sternberg 2010: 41).

References

Akomfrah, J. (2010) "Digitopia and the Specters of Diaspora," *Journal of Media Practice,* 11 (1): 21–30.
Armes, R. (1987) *Third World Filmmaking and the West,* Berkeley, Calif.: University of California Press.
Ashcroft, B. (2001) *Postcolonial Transformation,* London and New York: Routledge.
Baziel, J. A. and Mannur, A. (2003) (eds.) *Theorizing Diaspora: A Reader,* Malden, Mass.: Blackwell.
Berghahn, D. and Sternberg, G. (2010) *European Cinema in Motion: Migrant and Diasporic Film in Contemporary Europe,* Basingstoke: Palgrave Macmillan.
Bhabha, H. K. (2004) *The Location of Culture,* London and New York: Routledge.
Burch, N. (1979) *To the Distant Observer: Form and Meaning in Japanese Cinema,* Berkeley, Calif.: University of California Press.
Chanan, M. (1985) *The Cuban Image,* London: BFI Publishing.
——(1997) "The Changing Geography of Third Cinema," *Screen,* 38 (4): 372–388.
Clifford, J. (1994) "Diasporas," *Cultural Anthropology,* 9 (3): 302–338.
Dennison, S. and Lim, S. H. (eds.) (2006) *Remapping World Cinema: Identity, Culture and Politics in Film,* London and New York: Wallflower Press.
Ďurovičová, N. and Newman, K. E. (eds.) (2009), *World Cinemas, Transnational Perspectives,* London and New York: Routledge.
Ezra, E. and Rowden, T. (eds.) (2005) *Transnational Cinema: The Film Reader,* London and New York: Routledge.

Fusco, C. (ed.) (1987) *Reviewing Histories: Selections from New Latin American Cinema*, New York: Hallwells.

Gabriel, T. H. (1982) *Third Cinema in the Third World*, Ann Arbor, Mich.: UMI Press.

Glissant, É. (1997) *Poetics of Relation*, trans. by B. Wyng, Ann Arbor, Mich.: University of Michigan Press.

Grewal, I. and Kaplan, C. (1994) *Scattered Hegemonies: Postmodernity and Transnational Feminist Practices*, Minneapolis, Minn.: University of Minnesota Press.

Guneratne, A. R. (2003) "Introduction: Rethinking Third Cinema," in A. R. Guneratne and R. W. Dissanayake (eds.), *Re-thinking Third Cinema*, London and New York: Routledge, pp. 1–28.

Hall, S. (1996) "When Was the Post-Colonial? Thinking at the Limit," in I. Chambers and L. Curti (eds.), *The Post-Colonial Question: Common Skies, Divided Horizons*, London and New York: Routledge, pp. 242–260.

Hesse-Biber, S. N. and Leavy, N. (eds.) (2010) *Emerging Methods in Social Research*, New York: The Guilford Press.

Jameson, F. (2010) "Globalization and Hybridization," in N. Ďurovičová and K. Newman (eds.), *World Cinemas, Transnational Perspectives*, London and New York: Routledge, pp. 315– 319.

Johnson, R. and Stam, R. (eds.) (1982) *Brazilian Cinema*, East Brunswick, NJ: Associated University Presses.

Le Sueur, J. D. (ed.) (2003) *The Decolonization Reader*, London and New York: Routledge.

Marks, L. U. (2000) *The Skin of the Film: Intercultural Cinema, Embodiment, and the Senses*, Durham, NC: Duke University Press.

Martel, F. (2010) *Mainstream: enquête sur cette culture qui plaît à tout monde*, Paris: Flammarion.

Martin, M. T. (ed.) (1995) *Cinemas of the Black Diaspora: Diversity, Dependence and Oppositionality*, Detroit, Mich.: Wayne State University Press.

Mercer, K. (1994) *Welcome to the Jungle: New Positions in Black Cultural Studies*, London and New York: Routledge.

Minh-ha, T. (1989) "Outside In, Inside Out," in J. Pines and P. Willemen (eds.), *Questions of Third Cinema*, London: BFI Publishing, pp. 133–149.

Naficy, H. (2001) *An Accented Cinema: Exilic and Diasporic Filmmaking*, Princeton, NJ: Princeton University Press.

——(2010) "Multiplicity and Multiplexing in Today's Cinema," *Journal of Media Practice*, 11 (1): 11–20.

Nagib, L., Perriam, C., and Dudrah, R. (eds.) (2012) *Theorizing World Cinema*, London and New York: I. B. Tauris.

Petty, S. J. (2008) *Contact Zones: Memory, Origin, and Discourses in Black Diasporic Cinema*, Detroit, Mich.: Wayne State University Press.

Pfaff, F. (1984) *The Cinema of Ousmane Sembène: A Pioneer of African Film*, Westport, Conn.: Greenwood Press.

Said, E. W. (1995) *Orientalism: Western Concepts of the Orient*, 2nd edn, London: Penguin Books.

Shohat, E. and Stam, R. (1994) *Unthinking Eurocentrism: Multiculturalism and the Media*, London and New York: Routledge.

Thrift, N. (2008) *Non-Representational Theory: Space, Politics, Affect*, London and New York: Routledge.

Willemen, P. and Gandhy, B. (eds.) (1982) *Indian Cinema*, London: BFI Publishing.

Young, R. (1990) *White Mythologies: Writing History and the West*, London and New York: Routledge.

Žižek, S. (ed.) (1994) *Mapping Ideology*, London and New York: Verso.

——(2009) *First as Tragedy, then as Farce*, London and New York: Verso.

Part I

(Dis-)Continuities of the cinematic imaginary

(Non-)representation, discourse, and theory

1 Imag(in)ing the universe

Cosmos, otherness, and cinema

Edward George and Anna Piva (Flow Motion)

The closing of the frontier and the beginnings of American cinema

In 1790 the population of the United States of America was just over 3 million, mostly concentrated along the Atlantic seaboard. Indigenes of the First Nation dominated the landscape as they had done for thousands of years. White settlements extended no more than a few hundred miles (Porter et al. 1890: xix). Within a hundred years settlers had run out of spaces to claim. The American frontier, the line of movement that marked their growing presence – 3,200 miles long in 1790 (Turner 1921: xix) – had reached its limit.

The Bureau of the Census's *Report on Population of the United States at the Eleventh Census: 1890* announced that the idea of a frontier had reached the end of the line; that the frontier line had in fact been broken and didn't really mean anything anymore, because American settlers were, more or less, all over the continent.

The dissolution and transformation of the (frontier) line – from a (border) line of movement into regions of gradually cohering, opaque sentient clusters of whiteness, an opacity of settler presences whose linearity is prescribed by its national borders – is itself bordered by inventions that transformed moving pictures into mass entertainment: significantly, the Edison Company's Kinetograph motor-powered motion picture camera of 1881 and its Kinetoscope film projector in 1891, patented in 1897. America's first film production studio, Edison's Kinetographic Theatre, opens in February 1893; the country's first commercial movie theatre, the Kinetoscope Parlour, opens on Broadway two months later.

The fading of the frontier line coincides with the appearance of the Western landscape, in the cinematic frame, in the urban landscape. Early cinema provides a technology of nostalgia. Contained within its evocation of the frontier, distinctions between fiction, non-fiction, and meta-fiction are casualties of its preoccupation with performance and re-enactment: vanquished by settlement, the indigene returns. A fabrication of (cinematic) light, an anomaly of whiteness (a trick of forgetting), he is now the Indian, other than himself in name alone, condemned by light to return, and return again: as ethnographic display (*Esquimaux Village* [Edison, 1901]), as sexual threat, as figure of recurrent fantasies of recent conquest (*Sioux Ghost Dance* [Edison, 1894]).

The indigene returns as a figure of mimesis, a cinematic extension of minstrel theatre's tradition of masking[1] (of something terrible that has happened, will happen, here, if not there, to you the Negro, you the Indian, and, perhaps, even you . . .) and make believe (because something awful has not happened; not to you, the Indian, the Negro. . .).

Beneath and above the clouds: new frontiers

The emergence, the invention, of the Indian as the Other of American cinema, coincident with the last great act of land divestment (the Dawes Severalty Act of 1887, by which around 90 million acres of Native American land became the property of white Americans) marks the return of the indigene as a trick of the darkness (a nightmare figure of the frontier imagination, haunting the darkness of the plains, invading the dreams of the settler, forever threatening to halt the movement and destroy the line of settlement), and marks also the emergence of the frontier as a textual space of remembrance and forgetting.

The frontier as mnemonic trope finds its first comprehensive expression in Frederick Jackson Turner's *The Frontier in American History* (1921), an anthology of texts written by Turner between 1893 and 1918. For Turner, the frontier is a mobile space in which the conditions of a distinctly white male European American identity are created, a physical space whose closure signaled the end of what Catherine Gouge calls "a frontier 'of mind' – a fear of loss of an imaginative space that could rhetorically and conceptually structure American nationalism" (Gouge 2007: 1).

The frontier as a spatial metaphor is kept alive through political discourse. Nineteen thirty-two presidential nominee Franklin D. Roosevelt evokes the frontier as a negation – a barely existent space, no longer a viable alternative for the victims of the Depression (Roosevelt 1932: 6). For President Roosevelt's Vice President, Henry A. Wallace, a "new frontier" line borders a space wholly different to the Western lands, to be conquered by "men whose hearts are aflame with the extraordinary beauty of the scientific, artistic and spiritual wealth now before us" (Wallace 1934: 277).

In *Science, The Endless Frontier: A Report to the President (July 1945)*, a document shaped by correspondence between Roosevelt and Vannevar Bush, Director of the Office of Scientific Research and Development, the lands beyond Wallace's new frontier would be secured by the corporate and academic receipt of state funding for an agency for "civilian initiated and civilian controlled military research," to "conduct long-range scientific research on the Services' research on the improvement of existing weapons" (Bush 1945: 25).

In 1944, in a letter to Bush, Roosevelt wrote: "New frontiers of the mind are before us" (Bush 1945: 4). Fast forward to 1961 and John F. Kennedy's *Special Message to the Congress on Urgent National Needs:* space is the new frontier. . .

Cosmos, space of colonial fantasy

American cinema begins with the figure of the Indian. The film with which Edison premiered his new invention, the Kinetoscope, at the Chicago Columbian World Exposition of 1893, is none other than *Hopi Snake Dance* (Edison, 1893).

The movie with which Hollywood announces itself to the world is *The Squaw Man* (DeMille, 1914).

The repressed memory of the barbarism of settlement returns in American cinema as something similar to and other than itself. The body of American cinema's first Other, the Indian (first figure of American cinema's unconscious), returns as a spatial matrix (an arrangement of light, history, memory, darkness, silence, technology).

Even in the absence of the Indian, this matrix demarcates the space of subsequent figurations of Otherness, providing the figure of the pioneer with his ontological counterpoint. The body and the land of the Indian serve as the pioneer's projection screen of forgetting: something terrible did not happen here.

Greg Grewell argues that "Underlying most science fiction plots is the colonial narrative, whether or not readers and viewers of science fiction readily recognize it" (2001: 4). American cinema's narrative of spatial colonization begins with the figure (of flesh and fantasy) and the lands (as phantasmatic space, geophysical space) of the Native American. Its narrative of extra terrestrial space colonization could be said to begin with the transposition of the space of the frontier from the Western lands into the spaces of science fiction. Mascot Pictures' series *Phantom Empire* (Brower and Eason, 1935) was the first to merge the western with science fiction: Universal Studios' *Flash Gordon* series (Stephani, 1936) inaugurates America's projection of its pioneering adventurer, the frontiersman of the nineteenth century, into the cosmos in the figure of Alex Raymond's Euro-American hero, the comic book descendant of American science fiction's first colonizing hero, Edgar Rice Burroughs' *John Carter of Mars* (1912).

Clifford Vaughan's Wagnerian score for *Flash Gordon* (1936) set the emotional and historical tone for the eponymous hero's adventures (and for the future use of orchestral music in science-fiction cinema). *Flash Gordon* begins with a martial planet ruled by a despotic Asian, on collision with Earth; the fantasy of the colonizer under threat of destruction from an aggressive, colonizing force could be said to have one of its cinematic beginnings here.

The figure of American cinema's first Other returns, recurrently, in the image of another, then another, Other. We could trace the figure of Ming the Merciless up and down a metonymic chain of inhuman non-whiteness: backward, to Sax Rohmer's *Fu Manchu* in 1913, forward, to the Red Mongols of the first *Buck Rogers* comic strip in 1929 ("Half breeds!" yells Buck's girlfriend, blasting a Mongol from the sky), and further forward, to Ridley Scott and H. R. Geiger's, nameless, unwhite, inhuman non-human, alien (*Alien* [Scott, 1979]).

Always different, always the same, the Other announces the settler's re-visioning, his/her return, to the space of the founding drama (the founding trauma) of the violent Othering of the body and space of the indigene, foretold by the first delineation of the frontier line.

Perhaps the trauma is mutual: like the European colonizer, the Euro-American settler is condemned to configure as space of fantasy (always different, always the same) the space of trauma prefigured by the absent Indian, by the all but invisible indigene. The Euro-American imagines himself/herself as the about to be (but never) colonized.

The frontier, "the meeting point between savagery and civilization" (Turner 1893: 5), the founding space of the formation of Euro-American identity, is never final, never closed.

The nature of the frontier changes over time: the disappearance of the land frontier is superseded by the appearance of "spiritual and mental frontiers yet to be conquered" (Wallace 1934: 271–273). The original trauma, reanimated as metonym for that which cannot be contained by the retelling of the frontier narrative, presents not so much new openings as endless revisitations of that which cinema (still) cannot (fully) yet speak.

The endless cosmos, never an end in itself, presents an opening, in the darkness of space, onto the interior of an ongoing national-racial project; "In place of old frontiers of wilderness, there are new frontiers of unwon fields of science, fruitful for the needs of the race" (Turner 1914: 301).

Here, high above the clouds, there is always savagery, always civilization, always a wilderness, a new world, in which something of the past – an obliterative accretion of incidents and events of settler violence, a silencing, beneath the silence of silent cinema, beneath the noise of sound cinema, of that which must remain out of the frame. The massacre of the Ghost Dance movement at Wounded Knee in the winter of 1890 will not begin to haunt the cinematic frame until long after all concerned in the making of *Sioux Ghost Dance* (Edison, 1894) are themselves ghosts.

In 1924 Native Americans were granted citizenship of the USA. In 1931, the year of Edison's death, they were still barred from voting. American cinema grants the indigene a return as a matrix of conquest and forgetting, as some thing, some time, some place – a kingdom beneath the ground in *Phantom Empire*, a city in the sky in *Flash Gordon* – as some event, here, in living memory in 1894, or there, a "long time ago, in a galaxy far, far away" (*Star Wars* [Lucas, 1977]).

It does this on the condition that the indigene, as matrix of remembrance, announces themselves as other than themselves, if at all. And yet, in his/her absence, the indigene, as matrix of trauma, haunts, even now, this metaphor of settlement and identity formation, this grapheme, this line of movement (settler movement, camera movement; line of migration, line of thought, arc of narrative) that is the frontier.

Dream space, passive space, empty space. . .

With its first forays into outer space, American cinema reduces the size of the universe as it inaugurates its Othering – the universe, in diegetic space, is a tiny space in which "the race" renews its founding settler tropes without fear of disappearing into the vast darkness between the stars. No more (or less) alien than the wilderness beneath the earth's atmosphere, the universe, in diegetic space, is a domestic space, a space-in-waiting for Euro-American (self-)discovery, a clearing for an exceptionalism-to-come.

American cinema arrives in outer space after the French and the Soviets; *A Trip to the Moon* (Méliès, 1902) and *Aelita, Queen of Mars* (Protazanov, 1924) are among the earliest examples from those two countries.

There is a shared perception in these examples of early, silent cinema, an evocation of the universe as something with few properties of its own.

The universe is a space in a dream: the Mars of Protazanov's dream-spaces form a counterpoint to the material realities of building Communism. It is a space of fantasy: in *A Trip to the Moon,* a magician-director's moon finds its colonial correlative in the moon's spear wielding indigenes, the Selenites, a shoe-in as much for the Others of Jules Verne's and Orson Welles's worlds as the spear wielding sub-humans of the colonial imagination. The contents of the universe are as anthropomorphemes; the sun, the moon, and the stars, beyond their functions as luminous markers of the expanded scale on which the most familiar of dramas could be performed, eternally, throughout infinity, are as passive and inert as the darkness between them.

In a later silent movie, Fritz Lang's *Woman in the Moon* (1929), the emptiness of space is a space of convergence of astronomical and literary-cinematic speculation: "The day will come when a manned rocket will fly to the moon," reads the intertitle proclamation of the film's scientist, Professor Manfeldt. And in 1929, or 1924, or 1902, the moon would never have been closer or brighter than in a movie theatre, in whose darkness planet Earth would be viewed in its entirety for the first time, before disappearing into the darkness of diegetic space, viewed from the window of a rocket ship, from the frame of the screen.

The universe as it is imaged by astronomical cinematography is prefigured by the universe(s) of the cinematic imagination. The cosmos, imag(in)ed for the imagination by cinema, begins as an image of movement, as spectacular, onto-dramaturgic space. Cinema first illuminated the moon as a fiction in which the impossible scenario of lunar colonialism is suggestive of France's colonial expansion and the impossible scenario of its failure (Méliès).

Cinema first illuminated the emptiness of outer space as a space between (space of interference; dream as interference between) making material the meaning of being-Communist (Protazanov), as well as a space of the discovery of the meaning of being-Euro-American, through the body, in the body, through combat: a space of (self)knowledge through the triumph over the body of another (Stephani's *Flash Gordon*).

The cosmos in early cinema is the onto-political frontier, the meeting point, of historical memory and historical fiction. These films initiate cosmos-themed science-fiction cinema's engagement with pre-Heideggerian questions of philosophy; the idea of the universe as the space of engagement with questions of the meaning of Being has yet to come:[2] it will be signaled in *2001: A Space Odyssey* (Kubrick, 1968).

"Space is open to us now"

Astronomical cinematography begins in White Sands, New Mexico, in 1946, at the US Army Ordnance Proving Grounds, with the launch of V2 Rocket number 12. A DeVry Automatic 35mm motion picture camera is attached to the former Nazi rocket weapon, now owned by the US military, and produces the first moving images of Earth from outer space. The launch and the flight footage are shown in American movie theatres – in one of the many *Universal Newsreels* news documentaries made by Universal Studios. From *White Sands NM V-2 rocket, 1946/11/21:* "Rivaling the fantastic imagination of Jules Verne, the camera brought back the record of a flight into the heavens."

There was also coverage of the launch in the February 1947 edition of *Science Illustrated.* The photo caption beneath the news item, *"Armoured Camera Survives V-2 Flight, Photographs Earth at 65-Mile Height,"* begins with the line "How we'd look to passengers aboard a rocket. . ."

The newsreel and popular science magazine evoke the literary predecessor of outer space cine science fiction – Verne's science fantasy *From the Earth to the Moon* (1865) – as a point of departure for astronomical thinking. The newsreel's evocation of the literary imagination confers on the rocket launch a literary memory, gives astronomical aspiration a beginning in popular culture, even as it announces the limit of speculative (literary, cinematic) thinking. The camera, in the service of science, travels where literature and cinema cannot.

The *Science Illustrated* report of the launch marks the moment in which the eye of the camera in the service of astronomy is first used to generate narratives that, in time, will shape the meaning(s) of outer space in science fiction. The report does this even as it positions, in the place of the point of view of the camera, the point of view of a possibly alien, potentially hostile, protagonist from a science-fiction scenario. Through science fiction, the report returns the reader to the space of the movie theatre, where Earth was first observed, a vanishing point in the diegetic darkness of Lang, Méliès, Protazanov, and others. . .

In Cold War America, science-fiction cinema prefigures the political rationale for the arrival of the first human on the moon as it echoes national fears of Soviet encroachment. In *Destination Moon* (Pichel, 1950) the fear of Soviet domination of America, and even of a Communist invasion of America, frames the event. These fears provide the journey with its impetus, and inform, by way of (cultural, cinematic) echo, the 1961 address by President Kennedy that will inaugurate Apollo 11's moon landing in 1969 as a symbol of American technological and ideological supremacy – a project in which American political ambition, launched into space, becomes a synonym for human development, personified in the figure of the "free man" (Kennedy, 1961) whose Other is Soviet Communism, a project whose object is to determine the meaning and the material potential of space: "This is not merely a race. Space is open to us now; and our eagerness to share its meaning is not governed by the efforts of others. We go into space because whatever mankind must undertake, free men must fully share" (Kennedy 1961: 1).

A nationalist project, which defines space as national space: Kennedy tells Congress that if it supports his idea, "it will not be one man going to the moon [. . .] it will be an entire nation." (Kennedy 1961: 2). Science-fiction cinema (as a feature of present possibility, and of a future-in-waiting) effectively prepared television for the image of an American on the moon. Cinematography, in the service of Kennedy's goal, presents the cosmos as a metaphysical space whose origin is grounded in textual space: over the grainy footage of a lunar sunrise, we hear (but do not see) the crew of the Apollo 8 read the first chapters from the book of

Genesis in a broadcast from Lunar orbit on Christmas Eve, 1968 (*The Apollo 8 Christmas Eve Broadcast*, NASA, 1968).

The broadcast of the Apollo 11 moon landing in 1969 synchronizes the astronaut's body and voice in a triumph of body over voice, noise over message. What had been first witnessed as the apogee of the cinematic imagination, was now supplemented, confirmed and made redundant, by the detritus of communication, the static and crackle of the air to ground communication through which the voices of the astronauts of Apollo 11 emerged.

Avant-garde music and the universe as space of transcendence

Electronic sound enters the diegetic universe of science-fiction cinema as composition: Louise and Bebe Barron's electronic score for *Forbidden Planet* (Wilcox, 1950) introduces avant-garde music to science-fiction cinema.

In the film, United Planets Cruiser C57-D is sent sixteen light years across the universe to find out what became of the crew of an expedition sent twenty years previously to colonize planet Altair IV. The Barrons' score functions as a feature of the world of the film, to sonify the alien nature of planet Altair IV (the darkness of unclaimed colonial space). The score also functions as a characteristic of the world in the film, as the music of the planet's ancient civilization. Through this second function, the score evokes a (non-avant-garde) Euro-American sound world (and its corresponding world of thought and feeling) as an absent, interplanetary norm.

Science-fiction cinema, in its first encounter with avant-garde music, casts the music into the remote distance sixteen light years out of earshot. Avant-garde music enters science-fiction cinema as a sonic Other. Its function is to (pre)serve the relation of orchestral soundtracks in science fiction to time as prescribed in Vaughan's score for *Flash Gordon*.

Against the futurity of the visual components of *Forbidden Planet* – or indeed *Flash Gordon* – the relation of sound to time serves to signify the cosmos as the nineteenth-century location for the post-twentieth-century adventures of distinctly nineteenth-century kinds of hero (romantic, epic, messianic).[3] This relation also establishes a continuity of the science-fiction "space opera" (Turner, 1941) and the *Gesamtkunstwerk* – or "total art work" – (Trahndorff, 1827).

Nonetheless, it is through avant-garde music, particularly the music of György Ligeti, that the transcendental is invoked in space-themed science-fiction cinema. In *2001: A Space Odyssey* (Kubrick, 1968), the universe is figured as a space of becoming and transcendence through avant-garde music – and as the space of the play of tensions between screenwriter Arthur C. Clarke's secular humanism (Anders 2011: 3) and Kubrick's speculative creationism (Nordern 1968: 49, 50). György Ligeti's *Atmospheres* (1961) gives this tension its gravitas and drive.

Ligeti's *Requiem* (1963–1965) underscores the presence of *2001*'s enigmatic monoliths: a montage comprising *Atmospheres* (1961), *Aventures* (1962), and *Lux Eterna* (1966) propels the film's final act, *Jupiter and Beyond the Infinite*, and orchestrates the film's impossible, counter-rational moments – of movement through space-time, beyond the speed of light, of the expansion of space, of the evolution of human biology and the movement of the agency of intelligence.

The film's closing sequences occupy Ligeti's micro-polyphonic sound world, and from within this space orchestrate the possibility of an end of the idea of the Other as other than the figure of the pioneer. The dissonant space of Ligeti's sound world comprises the space of the distant galaxy in which Bowman, the film's astronaut protagonist, discovers he is the Other of himself, one of many, experienced by an older, other version of himself, as a ghostly, fleeting presence. Here (in micro-polyphonic space) there is no Other: there is the rhythm of renewal and movement of consciousness through space-time, of the movement of consciousness as the pre-condition of the body.

Distance, difference, and the hologram's impossible death

Ligeti's compositions signify *2001*'s conceptual distance from the film's generic predecessors. They announce the space-themed sci-fi genre's coming of age and the development of an awareness of itself as a form with a past: the *Star Wars* franchise (Lucas, 1977–1985) revises the serial science-fiction format and acoustic orchestral tropes of *Flash Gordon* – and *Buck Rogers*. *Star Wars'* use of *musique concrète*, pioneered by Pierre Schaffer and introduced in science-fiction cinema by Walter Murch in *THX 1138* (Lucas, 1971), ensures the universe of the film will sound distantly familiar.[4] The invention of surround sound cinema technology for screenings of the film guarantees that the sound of the universe leaves no space empty.

The universe of diegetic space as the location of science fiction's self-reflexivity begins with a cannibalizing gesture, with the inclusion, at the beginning of *THX 1138*, of the trailer for *Buck Rogers: Tragedy on Saturn* (Beebe, Goodkind, 1939) – a stitching in time of two future worlds (both films are set in the same but different twenty-fifth century), a weaving of a lineage of heroism between Rogers and Lucas's protagonist, THX, which finds its limit (the end of the line) in the figure of the film's African-American hologram who, lacking the technological knowledge pertinent to the most basic act of heroic escape (driving a vehicle), perishes by his own ineptitude.

"I'm not real," the hologram says, and the African American enters (and exits) the future as a trick of the light made flesh, his death (impossible: in what sense is a former hologram, turned almost human, alive?) signals the reanimation of the structuring role of the first Other of American cinematic space, in science fiction's performance of being as non being, as the sign of non-being, to signal the repetition of the death of the Other.

The hologram discloses a wish: "I always wanted to be part of the real world." The future, his exit suggests, is no place for the Other, other than the place of his recurring death, his many deaths. No place other than as space-time-in-waiting for the impossible demand of the expanding frontier, that the Other recognizes the imposition of this new, sub-human identity as the truth of his/its being. A space-time-in-waiting for the projection, across the body, across the land of the

Native American, of that (terrible event) which the pioneer's heroic self perception refuses to imag(in)e, other than as the drama – always different, always the same, of the movement, in and across diegetic space – of the Other's becoming inhuman, non-human, post-human, augmented human.

The diminished humanity of the settler (above the clouds, beneath the clouds) shapes and haunts the settler's creation, speaks through the silence of the chain of being-Indian, being-virtual, being alien, in the act of clearing a space for settlement, in which the "real world" (the Real of psychoanalysis) would be given form and force.

On turning away and the value (and limits) of noise

The universe first enters diegetic space through the technology of television. It does so as noise – as crackle, hiss, and static, buried in the interference interrupting television's flow of sound and image, present between channels and in the empty space left after a station has ceased transmission.

In 1965 radio astronomers Arno Penzias and Robert Wilson identified this noise. It is the Cosmic Microwave Background Radiation, the ubiquitous afterglow of the Big Bang. The universe enters domestic space as sonic detritus, prefiguring and interrupting the triumphal event of the 1969 moon landing.

Radio astronomy begins with noise, with Karl Jansky's discovery, in 1931, of the sound of radio waves, galactic signals emanating from the center of the Milky Way. Prefiguring the emergence of *musique concrète* in 1948, radio astronomy offers the universe to *musique concrète* as a gift in waiting, an extra-terrestrial space of expansion of *musique concrète's* terrestrial sound world "of the voice, the sounds of nature, of sound producing instruments" (Schaeffer, interviewed by Hodgkinson 1987: 3).

Jansky's discovery is the first sign of a new scientific understanding of the universe. Far from the empty, silent space of *2001*'s universe, the spaces between visible cosmic phenomena are alive with intergalactic events and invisible phenomena, which contain the possibility for transformation into sound. Far from being a passive locale given symbolic meaning through cinematic narrative, the phenomena of the universe comprise a non-human drama of forces material and immaterial, visible and invisible.

Contained in the activity of these forces is the possibility for a non-figurative, non-narrative, cinematic engagement with the cosmos – a turning away from space-themed science-fiction cinema's Westernizing impulses and lineal tropes, which could not be achieved within the confines of the genre, but was nonetheless suggested by the presence in the cinematic frame of the sonic avant-garde, itself the creation of another kind of turning away from another Westernizing impulse.

With *musique concrète*, Schaeffer attempted a turning away from Arnold Schoenberg's twelve-tone, dodecaphonic compositional method (Hodgkinson 1987: 2), through which Schoenberg proposed, in 1921, the global pre-eminence of a particularly German Western art music tradition whose greatest exponent in the nineteenth century had been Wagner, and whose greatest exponent, in the twentieth century, would be Schoenberg himself. The twelve-tone system would, Schoenberg believed, last "for the next hundred years" (Schoenberg 2006: 314). Like Schaeffer, Ligeti's oeuvre also represents a turning away from Schoenberg (Tusa 1999).

Having managed a radical turning away from a musical Westernizing impulse, these avant-gardes were then used in the service of giving continuity to a cinematic, Westernizing impulse. Ben Burtt's use of *musique concrète* for "special dialogue and sound effects" in *Star Wars: Episode IV – A New Hope* (Lucas, 1977), framed by John Williams's original music, brought a sonic newness to George Lucas's rejuvenatory conservation of the space opera and its sub-textual frontier mythos. Murch's use of *musique concrète* in his sound design for *THX 1388* signals the film's formal and sonic difference from its predecessors. Framed by Lalo Schiffrin's score, Murch's sound design also foregrounds the film's intimate proximity to the genre's narrative tropes and traditions.

A hybrid cinema of the invisible universe

Freed from its diegetic moorings, experimental music offers cinematic practice a series of openings. A new opening onto the cosmos, and an opening for experimental cinema that also allows for a critical engagement with experimental music – and its racial Others – an opening for a collaborative dialogue and practice across the disciplines of digital art, cinema, and science. A series of openings, in which *musique concrète's* founding ideas – that environmental sounds can be materials for musical objects, and that sound recording technologies can function as mediating technologies in music making – are extended and transformed in *Astro Black Morphologies/Astro Dub Morphologies* (Flow Motion, 2004).

In *Astro Black Morphologies/Astro Dub Morphologies*, diegetic space is created through the transformation not of environmental sound, but of numbers – digital data, in a process in which a cinematographic recording technology, NASA's three camera All Sky Monitor component of the Rossi X-ray Timing Explorer satellite, functions as a mediating technology for film and music making.

In 2002 a press release from the Royal Astronomical Society announced that the satellite's documentation of the patterns of variations in the X-ray emissions of a black hole, Cygnus X1, were similar to music:

> For the past six years, Dr Phil Uttley and Prof. Ian McHardy at the University of Southampton, together with other colleagues, have used NASA's Rossi X-ray Timing Explorer (RXTE) satellite to monitor the X-ray variations of several active galaxies. Their aim is to compare the slow variations in the X-ray output of active galaxies with the much more rapid variations (on time-scales of milliseconds to seconds) of black hole X-ray binary systems (BHXRBs): black holes that are a million times smaller than the monsters in galaxy centers and feed off gas from normal, "companion" stars.
>
> Dr Uttley explains: "The X-ray variations of active galaxies and BHXRBs can be likened to music, showing small variations – single notes – on short time-scales, and larger variations – whole key changes – on longer time-scales. What we are finding with our RXTE monitoring is that the time-scales for these note

and key changes to take place are about a million or more times longer in active galaxies than in BHXRBs. In other words, take the tune played out in X-rays by a black hole X-ray binary and slow down the tape by a factor of a million or so and you get the kind of variations we are seeing in active galaxies.

(Bond and Mitton, quoted in Flow Motion 2010: 52)

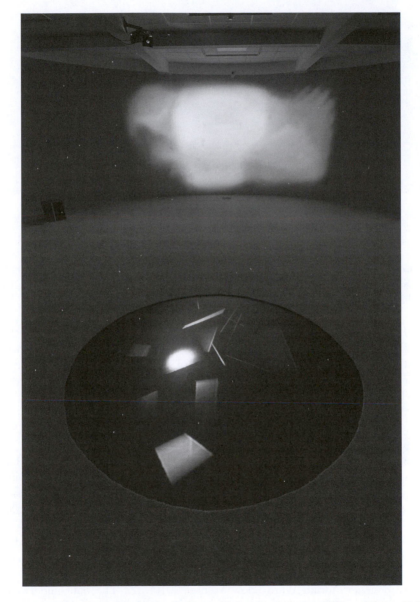

Figure 1.1 Astro Black Morphologies/Astro Dub Morphologies (©Flow Motion/Adrian Ward, 2005) Photo: Steve Shrimpton, courtesy of John Hansard Gallery.

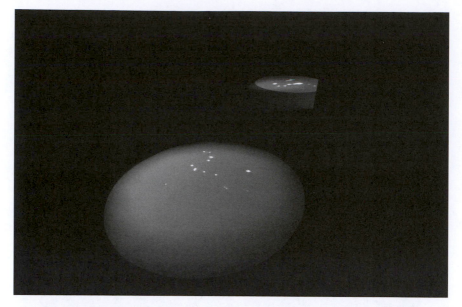

Figure 1.2 Astro Black Morphologies/Astro Dub Morphologies (©Flow Motion/Adrian Ward, 2005) Photo: Steve Shrimpton, courtesy of John Hansard Gallery.

Part of the task of documenting the emissions of Cygnus X1 was achieved by the All Sky Monitor, described by NASA as three cameras mounted on the RXTE satellite:

> Inside each camera is a proportional camera sensitive to energies in the 2–10 keV range. Each camera is able to look at a different region of the sky; two of the cameras have an overlapping field of view. The entire boom that the cameras are mounted on rotates by 6 degrees once every 90 seconds. Through this sequence of rotating and then staying fixed for 90 seconds, etc., the ASM covers 80% of the sky in 90 minutes.
>
> (Lochner et al. 2001)

When Uttley announced the findings of the RXTE, there was no "music of black holes," and no cinematographic image. The satellite documented the invisible X-ray output as numbers representing fluctuations in the black hole's emissions. These numbers, as well as their subsequent graphic reassemblage, Cygnus X1's light curve, were made available by Uttley to Flow Motion.

The artists collaborated with Dr Tim O'Brien, astrophysicist at Jodrell Bank Observatory, on devising a methodology for the sonification of the light curve (Flow Motion 2006: 26). They then converted the data into images with generative designer Adrian Ward (Flow Motion 2010: 52). The data underwent a succession of transformations, through a bricolage (Hodgkinson 1987: 2) not of sounds, but of processes – of sound transformation ideas and approaches drawn from astrophysics, European experimental music, Caribbean sonic experimentation, and cine-sound history – framed and informed by their reading of the term dub as a trope of sonic and cinematic process (Flow Motion 2010: 48).

Astro Black Morphologies/Astro Dub Morphologies presents a rethinking of the presence of the cosmos in the space of the movie theatre, where the universe first entered the public imagination. The work comprises the installation's curvilinear, doubled spaces of darkness and light. Walls and floors function as both multi-projection surfaces and sound projection locations.

The work's cinematic and sonic components reflect the conditional nature of physical experience of the universe's non-material forces. Its multiple movies and sound sources (re)present these forces as the product of multiple mediations from which emerge cine-sonic objects for aesthetic engagement in the absence of the (impossible) experience of the enigmas of the invisible universe.

Astro Black Morphologies/Astro Dub Morphologies thus constitutes a hybridic cinematic (sound art performance-installation) space, in which cinematographic technology is a distant component (above the clouds) in a chain of mediations and transformations for a cinema of light (curves), and yet which foregrounds the (re)presentation of the universe's invisible components as sensorial phenomena possessed of their own dynamic forces. Here the creation of diegetic space is achieved in the absence of a founding cinematographic image, heightening the distinction between the movie camera's function for non-narrative cinema, and its function for astronomy.

Cinematographic astronomy in the service of space-themed, non-narrative cinema makes possible a cinema of the cosmos in which the dynamic of the Self-Other is dissolved through an evocation of the cosmos as an object of aesthetic experience.

Here, there is a turning away from the idea of the universe as the dramaturgical space of the territorializing imagination and the frontier trope's spatial metaphors of linearity. There is the evocation of the cosmos through the language of experimental music processes: the grain of sound (via granular synthesis), the trace of sound (via dub process), the cloud of sound (via micro-polyphonic composition).

And there is the body, already comprised of the stuff of stars, understood here, through the work of physicist H. Eugene Stanley's research group, as the bearer, at its cellular level, of patterns of variation and predictability, theorized by mathematician Benoit Mandelbrot as Flicker noise, discovered by Clarke and Voss (1975: 317, 318) to be ubiquitous in nature, and later discovered, by Uttley and his colleagues, to be a feature of the universe, present in Cygnus X1's X-ray output (Flow Motion 2006: 25–26). Here, in the body, is the universe; here, in diegetic space, in hybrid cinematic space, is the universe to which we have always belonged, and which has always resided in us.

Notes

1 Dancer William Henry Lane is cited by Nick Tosches (2002) and Jacqui Malone (1996) as the first documented American to perform in blackface; Lane, inventor of tap dance, appears, unnamed, in Charles Dickens's *American Notes for Circulation* (London: Chapman & Hall, 1842).

2 The central question of philosopher Martin Heidegger's oeuvre is that of the meaning of being, addressed initially in his major early work, *Being and Time* (1929) and summarized on the book's first page: "Do we in our time have an answer to the question of what we really mean by the word 'being'? Not at all. So it is fitting that we should raise anew the question of the meaning of Being. But are we nowadays even perplexed at our inability to understand the expression 'Being'? Not at all. So first of all we must reawaken an understanding for the meaning of this question."

3 Brad Eden (2005) credits Simon Williams with identifying these kinds of heroism in the operas of Richard Wagner.

4 Tim Hodgkinson (1987) defines *musique concrète* as follows: "[It is] music made of raw sounds: thunderstorms, steam-engines, waterfalls, steel foundries [. . .] The sounds are not produced by traditional acoustic musical instruments. They are captured on tape (originally, before tape, on disk) and manipulated to form soundstructures. The work method is therefore empirical. It starts from the concrete sounds and moves toward a structure. In contrast, traditional classical music starts from an abstract musical schema. This is then notated and only expressed in concrete sound as a last stage, when it is performed. *Musique concrète* emerged in Paris in 1948 at the RTF (Radio Télévision Française). Its originator, leading researcher and articulate spokesman was Pierre Schaeffer – at that time working as an electro-acoustic engineer with the RTF."

References

Anders, L. (2011) *A Star Has Gone Out: Tribute to Arthur C. Clarke.* Available online at www.secularhumanism.org/index.php?section=library&page=anders_28_4 (accessed September 20, 2011).

Anon. (1947) "Armored Camera Survives V-2 Flight, Photographs Earth at 65-Mile Height," *Science Illustrated*, February, 47.

Bond, P. and Mitton, J. (2002) *Music of Black Holes: They All Play the Same Tune*, Royal Astronomical Society, April. Available online at www.ras.org.uk/news-and-press/72-news2002/434-pn02-09-nam3 (accessed July 2, 2011).

Bush, V. (1945) *Science: The Endless Frontier – A Report to the President by Director of the Office of Scientific Research and Development, July 1945.* United States Government Printing Office, Washington. Available online at www.nsf.gov/od/lpa/nsf50/vbush1945.htm (accessed September 1, 2011).

Calkins, R. (1929) "Buck Rogers 2429: The Sleeper," *Worcester Evening Gazette*, February 4. Available online at http://rolandanderson.se/comics/buckrogers/buckstrips.php (accessed July 18, 2011).

Case, D. S. and Voluck, D. A. (2002) *Alaska Natives and American Laws*, Fairbanks, Ala.: University of Alaska Press.

Clarke, J. and Voss, R. F. (1975) "1/f Noise in Music and Speech," *Nature*, 258 (November): 317–318.

Dirks, T. (2011) "The History of Film: The Pre-1920s, Early Cinematic Origins, and the Infancy of Film, Part 1." Available online at www.filmsite.org/pre20sintro.html (accessed July 20, 2011).

Eden, B. (2005) "Williams: Wagner and the Romantic Hero," *Opera Today*. Available online at www.operatoday.com/content/000720print.html (accessed July 4, 2011).

Flow Motion (2006) "Astro Black Morphologies: Music and Science Lovers," *Leonardo Journal*, 39 (1): 23–27.

——(2010) "Astro Dub Morphologies," *Journal of Media Practice*, 11 (1): 47–58.

Gouge, C. (2007) "The American Frontier: History, Rhetoric, Concept," *Americana: The Journal of American Popular Culture (1900–present)*, 6 (1). Available online at www.americanpopularculture.com/journal/articles/spring_2007/gouge.htm (accessed July 20, 2011).

Grewell, G. (2001) "Colonizing the Universe: Science Fictions Then, Now, and in the (Imagined) Future," *Rocky Mountain Review of Language and Literature,* 55 (2): 25–47.

Hodgkinson, T. (1987) "An Interview with Pierre Schaeffer: Pioneer of Musique Concrète," *ReR Quarterly,* 2 (1).

Kennedy, J. F. (1961) *Special Message to the Congress on Urgent National Needs, May 25.* Available online at www.nasa.gov/pdf/59595main_jfk.speech.pdf (accessed October 4, 2011).

Lochner, J. et al. (2001) *About RXTE,* The Rossi X-ray Timing Explorer Learning Centre, National Aeronautics and Space Administration. Available online at http://heasarc.nasa. gov/docs/xte/learning_center/what_is_RXTE.html (accessed July 2, 2011).

Malone, J. (1996) *'Steppin' on the Blues: The Visible Rhythms of African American Dance,* Urbana, Ill.: University of Illinois Press.

National Aeronautics and Space Administration (1968) *The Apollo 8 Christmas Eve Broadcast,* NASA, December 24. Available online at http://nssdc.gsfc.nasa.gov/planetary/lunar/ apollo8_xmas.html (accessed September 4, 2011).

Nordern, E. (1968) "Playboy Interview: Stanley Kubrick," *Playboy,* September.

Porter, R., Gannett, H., and Hunt, W. (1890) "Progress of the Nation, 1790 to 1890," in *Report on Population of the United States at the Eleventh Census: 1890, Part 1,* US Census Bureau.

Roosevelt, F. D. (1932) *Commonwealth Club Address,* September 23, 1932, San Francisco, California. Available online at www.americanrhetoric.com/speeches/fdrcommonwealth. htm (accessed September 1, 2011).

Schoenberg, A. (eds.) (2006) *The Musical Idea and the Logic, Technique and Art of its Presentation,* ed. by P. Carpenter and S. Neff, Bloomington, Ind.: Indiana University Press.

Tosches, N. (2002) *Where Dead Voices Gather,* London: Jonathan Cape.

Turner, F. J. (1893) "The Significance of the Frontier in American History," in *The Frontier in American History,* New York: Holt & Company, pp. 1–38.

——(1914) "The West and American Ideals," in *The Frontier in American History,* New York: Holt & Co., pp. 290–310.

——(1920a) "The First Official Frontier of the Massachusetts Bay," in *The Frontier in American History,* New York: Holt & Co., pp. 39–66.

——(1920b) "Preface," in *The Frontier in American History,* New York: Holt & Co., pp. v–vi.

Tusa, J. (1999) "The John Tusa Interviews: Gyorgy Ligeti," *BBC Radio 3.* Available online at www.bbc.co.uk/radio3/johntusainterview/ligeti_transcript.shtml (accessed September 14, 2011).

Wallace, H. A. (1934) "Beyond the Frontier," in *New Frontiers,* New York: Reynal & Hitchcock, pp. 269–291.

Wrobel, D. M. (1996) *The End of American Exceptionalism: Frontier Anxiety from the Old West to the New Deal,* Lawrence, Kans.: University Press of Kansas.

2 Questioning discourses of *diaspora*

"Black" cinema as symptom

Saër Maty Bâ

> The history of the black Atlantic since [Columbus] [. . .] provides a means to re-examine the problems of nationality, location, identity, and historical memory. [. . .] The specificity of [. . .] the black Atlantic can be defined, on one level, through this desire to transcend both the structures of the nation state and the constraints of ethnicity and national particularity.
>
> (Gilroy 1994: 16, 19)

> I want to advance a theory of contemporary black cinema that accords with the fact that biological criteria are neither necessary nor sufficient for the application of the concept of black cinema. I refer to this theory as a no-theory theory, because I want to avoid any commitment to an essentialized notion by not giving a definition of black cinema.
>
> (Lott 1995: 42)

This chapter reflects on "black" as a term, category and trace informed, shaped, and marked by "race" (a language and relation, not fixed, and fleeting). It attempts to rethink and reposition "black" while relating a predicate of being called "black," as a de-Westernizing tool, to the West/Western. "Black" becomes a category of thought and process that shifts grammatically between adjective and noun.

With "black" in mind, the chapter respectfully enters into dialogue, at the same time as it shows the limitations of, and transcends, problematic theoretical frameworks of diaspora, specifically Paul Gilroy's notion of the Black Atlantic. It also analyzes films/moving images for three main purposes. First, to unpack the terms "discourse," "thought," "cinema," and their interconnections, considered within the context and discussion of what ascriptions "black" may embody within "black diasporic cinema."[1] Second, to examine discourses of diaspora studies, particularly the ocean-framed "Black Atlantic." Third, to suggest that the act and process of generating dialogue between "black" diasporic discourses has implications beyond "black" diasporas themselves.

Thus, the chapter suggests meanings and proposes interconnections within studies of "black" peoples, their cultures, and their diasporas while referencing the historical, cultural, and/or political circumstances of films discussed. Additionally, it implicitly embodies three questions: What does "black" say about the "West"?[2] What is "Western"? And, finally, does the West/Western not always reside wherever or emerge whenever perceptions of de-Westernization are possible and/ or unfolding through and across difference but with no obsession with origins?[3] Following this line of thinking, the chapter aims to expose not the content allegedly concealed by the form (which is to say "black" concealed by the West/Western) but the secret of the form itself. This secret-form is an ideological universal, unity or falsity, broken and laid open by "black" symptoms, the latter being understood as "the exception which disturbs the surface of the false appearance" (Žižek 2008a: x; see also Žižek 2008b: 161 and Žižek 1994: 296, 306). Thus, the creation, workings, mutations, and/or reproduction of the form must be seen, known, and understood, but not before the manifestation called "discourse" and its connections to ideology are unpacked.

Enfolding "black" symptoms

Discourse is a process. All discursive processes are inscribed in ideological connections and "internally moulded by their pressure" while ideology itself signifies "a set of complex effects internal to discourse" (Eagleton 1991: 194–195, 198). Every discourse emerges from "some tendentious 'subject position'" and aims to produce specific effects in its addressees (Eagleton 1991: 201). Therefore, connections between "the political, cultural, economic and the rest" depend on discourse just as ideology, signifying "the point where power impacts upon certain utterances and inscribes itself tacitly within them," is "a matter of 'discourse'" (Eagleton 1991: 204, 223). In short: there is no "post-ideological world" and we need to "[detect] the faults in an ideological edifice" (Žižek 2008a: ix), something which "black" Caribbean poet and activist Aimé Césaire's book *Discourse on Colonialism* (1950) epitomizes as it reveals how "the circulation of [the racially and culturally hierarchical] colonial ideology" was as fundamental to colonial control as "police and corvée labor [while] drawing a direct link between the logic of colonialism and the rise of fascism" (Kelley 2002: 175). Discourse is indeed both its author's discourse on a given topic and her/his critique of that topic's own discourse. Following Robin Kelley's analysis of Césaire's book, this chapter posits the term "discourse" (relating to sociocultural practice, process, and to ideology) as a poetry of revolt, a "revolutionary graffiti painted in bold strokes across the great texts of Western civilization; [and] a call for us to plumb the depths of the imagination for a different way forward" (Kelley 2002: 180–181).

The 1960s–1980s were symptomatic of attempts to craft such ways of revolt and reimaginings, something that entailed multiple ruptures of rigid imaginaries such as the triangular slave trade, geographic and oceanic frameworks of thinking diaspora.[4] These decades were contact zones – for Africa, antiwar, and counter-cultural movements – where, Powell (2005: 9) argues, "alterable and interchangeable black identities" encountered satire and fantasy, raised "the specters of inauthenticity and mutability in identity-centred discourses," exchanged gazes, and clashed with "assertive *Blacks*" resisting cultural and racial ambiguity/ obscurity.[5] The point was and remains that whether looking back toward beginnings in saltwater slave trading or forwards to Afro-futures unknown, on a diasporic scale "blackness" in 1960s–1980s was introducing into visual culture the following issues: an aesthetic split and "psychological tumult"; cracks and mayhem that were uncontainable by "racial oratory, political dictates, or the demand for 'positive images'"; and a mushrooming identity and "disfigured racial psyche" (Powell 2005: 10, 13).[6] Those ruptures, combined with contemporary historiography,[7] recentered traditional African cultural and belief systems within the lost-and-rediscovered school of "non-western erudition & folklore" that blacks actively embraced just as that school was being fissured by film and photography (Powell 2005: 24). Examples would include *Black Orpheus* (Camus, 1958), which mixes archival footage with staged performances and features "black" Brazilian actors, actresses, and performers; *Space Is the Place* (Coney, 1976), starring composer, band-leader and so-called Afro-futurist Sun Ra; or photographer Jean-Paul Goude and Jamaican model and singer Grace Jones's *Nigger Arabesque* (1978), featuring Jones's jet-black, supple, scantily clad, and luminous body.

Adapted from Vinicius de Moraes's play *Orfeu de Conceiçao* (itself influenced by French culture), *Black Orpheus* Westernizes "black" experience in Rio via a Helle-nic myth (Orpheus) dipped in Brazilian *samba* and presenting a romanticized "French touristic view of carnival" (Stam 1995: 282). It also offers challenges and ruptures that problematize blackness beyond/despite geo-oceanic frameworks, even though Camus himself seems ignorant about "black" Brazil. Indeed, carni-val's cultural connections with Africa had been "reassembled" on Brazilian soil just like "Candomblé, musical rhythms, Capoeira, and palm-oil based cuisine" (Pinho 2010: 33). Simultaneously, *Black Orpheus* challenges viewers who must not confuse pageantry with "black" social values; who see carnival as a militant critique against injustice and distinguish it from "black" archetypes; and who consider how blackness, Brazilianness, and carnival collectively expose "the metaphysical trans-cendence against a postcard backdrop" (Stam 1995: 282). Similarly, while *Space Is the Place* puzzles with its mix of film genres (US blaxploitation, science fiction, art, comedy) and music concert, *Nigger Arabesque,* though riddled with stereotypes, was symptomatic of a noticeable shift from and contrapuntal "mindset" to more than twenty years of struggles asserting positive "black" visibility in visual culture, a visibility which was currently enfolding "into a world of sanctioned diversity & fashionable defiance" (Powell 2005: 26).

In summary, it is provisionally suggested that, within studies of blacks and their diasporas, "discourse" connects "thought" and "cinema" while all three terms, in association, become interchangeable because they refuse to either be post-ideological or ignore the unconscious illusion that structures "our real, effective relation to reality [. . .] what may be called *the ideological fantasy*" (emphasis in original; Žižek 1994: 316). Moreover, discourse ruptures and disfigures its enunciator(s) and its effects; at once, it fractures the non-Western and obscures and complicates posi-tive gains regarding "black" cultural visibility in the so-called New World. Indeed, the symptom "black" is varied, defiant, and perpetually in motion within and between liminal spaces; it is within such spaces that the "black" in/and "black diasporic cinema" can be investigated.

As Andrew (2010: xiv) recently suggested, "Traditional film studies is indeed on the defensive, for the 'idea of cinema' is changing underneath us." Moreover, the recurrent question "What is black in black diasporic cinema?" always already transforms Andrew's statement into a metaphor for "black" presence or absence in Western visual cultures and is a challenge to Western discourse, thought, and cinema.[8] This is because "black" is always inspirational and proactive in changing ideations of cinema within different contexts, times, and places, a fact expounded by Lott's "no-theory theory" (Lott 1995). Focusing on "black" filmmaking practices and political objectives within US blaxploitation cinema and Third Cinema, no-theory theory prioritizes complex contemporary meanings associated with such aspirations and is "designed to be discarded" when these meanings stop being "applicable" (Lott 1995: 41, 42). To discuss "black" or "black diasporic cinema" is therefore to identify a no-theory theory for, beyond the shared characteristics outlined thus far, "black"/"black diasporic cinema" and Lott's theory are always already ruins from which new knowledge must emerge.[9]

Following this line of thinking, the idea of an indelibly raced "black representational space," "cultural territory" or "conceptual terrain" seems limited.[10] Contemporary perceptions of "black" seem to preclude discussion of a raced space because, if "black" is raced, its "condition of raciality" must be evoked and perhaps "profitably understood as the question of the unthought, as a dimension of potentiality."[11] Arguably, potentiality is always empirically located, notwithstanding the "black" trace's circulation within and/or between pedagogical imperatives, cultures, continents, film genres, film festivals, television channels, and art galleries. These spaces are elusive, impermanent, time-determined, and only imbued with afterlives by a "black" that is theorized as a no-theory, i.e. fragmented and mutating. This type of "black" is echoed in "ciné-geography" because it functions as "a material index of social relations, capable at unexpected moments and in tangential ways, of reanimating intense moments of upheaval."[12] This "black" has also been shrapnelizing skin/colour politics – e.g., through Césaire, Ra, Jones, Lott, BAFC – beyond recognition and well before "the capitalist western world s[ought] to exclude" and demonize all "impoverished strangers" with "xeno-racism" (Sivanandan, cited in Fekete 2009: 19–20).

Thus, "black" is in and relates to the world through continuous social interactions with a twofold meaning: first, as a sign with value because it displays what Marks calls in another context the "ability to be taken up, to germinate, to communicate" (2007: 294); second, as transformation from unthought to thought. Furthermore, if meaning "is destined for the future," then "black" thought becomes valuable when connected to other thoughts; accordingly, its ultimate value would rest not on the community – i.e. "individual, passing human beings" – but on "black" as "the thought that outlasts the community" (Marks 2007: 300). It follows that, once dislocated from the triangular slave trade paradigm, albeit temporarily, "black" (thought, discourse, cinema, and so on) becomes a constant desire and self-interest to migrate (see Marx 1998; Bâ 2010a: 349).

Put differently, oceanic frameworks (such as formulated in Gilroy's *Black Atlantic*) may not be able to grasp this "black," which is a two-pronged problematic of cognitive psychology: it only challenges the higher brain/cortex while at the same time being perceptually inconstant (in size, shape, colour, and location); like an image projected on the retina, "black" changes each time one encounters it;[13] it is also a "rich and constant process of mediation, a continuum between impression, perception and thought" (Marks 2007: 286). Oceanic frameworks cannot grasp this "black" because they get confused – at least – whenever one cracks open liminal spaces separating "a postmodern turn from history" from "a nomadic turn" concerned with "the very parameters" of discrete historical moments (Baziel and Mannur 2003: 3). Likewise, one cannot grasp "black" as a problematic of cognitive psychology by using "diasporic traversals" to sufficiently question the inflexibilities of identity. Indeed, what if there is no turn (e.g., when "black" belongs to neither of the above two turns but still generates new meanings)? What is to be done if/when, in the postcolonial moment, arts, intellects, theories and practices are brought "face to face with a reconfigured subaltern articulation of a new cultural and political discourse" (Enwezor 2007: 116)?

It would seem that "black" thought and "black" cinema have managed to answer such questions whenever "black" and "thought" or "black" and "cinema" have been linked, irrespective of geography, geo-politics, geo-culture or temporality.[14] Thus, it is not a question of "resisting representation" (Enwezor 2007: 114). Rather, it is about transforming the moment of "black" contact(s) with thought, cinema, and so on from within the above-mentioned cracked-open space. That space might be justifiably named "postcolonial" in order to locate a discrete "black" potentiality, but the perceptually inconstant "black" complicates location in two more ways. First, "black" transnationalism (in image, intention, and act) always precedes the postcolonial moment, despite the "shared history and experience of colonisation" underlining notions like "transnational postcolonialism" associated with BAFC and similar groups (Enwezor 2007: 117). Second, film projects that may be described as "black," though conceived at precise moments within chronological time, become diegetic fragments of "cinematic image" made of shots "already filled with time" (Tarkovsky 1989: 114; Bâ 2010a: 349–351) and therefore able to throw into crisis any humanly graspable notion of time. "Black" effects transnational rhizomorphic time transformations for which the "postcolonial" is but one fleeting, minor, un(der)privileged moment.

As a result, the complications inherent in locating "black" call for frameworks of no-theory theory to expose chronology-contingent time while allowing a redis-covery of diegetic cinematic images that are imbued with multiple and unpredictable crossings of time within and between shots/worlds.[15] Moreover, the ability of diegetic time to traverse shots across films justifies comparing the non-Western, ancient "black" African art of storytelling with "modern-day" cinematic storytelling; they share methods like narrative structures imbued with heterogeneous "med-iating elements" like "continuity and discontinuity of time, and the relationship between image and sound" (Ukadike 1994: 24). Similarly, when diaspora and cinema are brought together, as Akomfrah (Ghanaian-British filmmaker and a BAFC founder member) argues, one may construct "a completely new sense of not simply what is cinema but how to define it," "to do something which Godard's *Histoire(s) du cinéma* is [. . .] a symptom of. As a series of essays, you could watch them without realizing that black people have been in the cinema. It is these profound ellipses and omissions and glosses that now seem to me to be part of an analogic stack in which histories are privileged on the basis of what is available."

(Akomfrah 2010: 28)

Akomfrah uses "black" to argue for a radical and justified reperception of cinema history that challenges Western discourse, thought and cinema via selective restoration and/or transcendence of its deep oversights. As Akomfrah shows us, it can be argued that "black cinema" is an "archipelized" cinema (a provisional, intermediate state)[16] an ideation of cinema mutating from underneath us, and a metaphor made of proto-cinema, intertextuality and accented engagements with archives (written, audio and/or visual).[17] "Black cinema" both chooses to be proto-cinematic and has this status imposed upon it from without,[18] but its constitutive proto-ness always opens up intertextual possibilities whereby text, sound, and image are reworked from archives whose meanings are destined for the future. These archives, which also function as traces-residues, or incubating "ghost machine[s]" (Enwezor 2007), embody potentials for de-Westernizing film from within any given framework (imperial, hegemonic, subaltern, and so on).

BAFC thus considered "the archive of empire" as a location for "rewriting the narratives of empire" (Enwezor 2007: 118), while Fusco (New York-based interdisciplinary artist, academic, and moving image director), working with Mexican artist Guillermo Gómez-Peña, could create and star in a live performance-turned-video that exposes racist and pseudo-scientific exclusion, *The Couple in the Cage: A Guatinaui Odyssey* (Heredia and Fusco, 1993; hereafter *Couple in the Cage*). Here, Fusco and Gómez-Peña display their bodies with doubly fake(d) referents attached: they were/are no "undiscovered" Amerindians while the Guatinaui people are inexistent. Yet *Couple in the Cage*'s rationale manages to hark back to a tangible historical past (seventeenth to early twentieth century) when "black" bodies were transported by "whites" for display, entertainment, and visual objectification. Simultaneously, the Fusco–Gómez-Peña project echoes Marks on meaning being destined for the future because *Couple in the Cage* looks toward a time-in-becoming where contemporary forms of exclusions might be displaced and rendered unviable. Thus, a combined, treble reinscription of referents operates in and through *Couple in the Cage* as follows: Fusco's body invokes Saartjee Bartman, a South African woman displayed in eighteenth-century western Europe, scantily clad or naked for "white" visual pleasure;[19] Gómez-Peña's evokes "the cannibal, [. . .] the warrior, this threatening masculine Other" causing fear to viewers (Johnson 1993); and their performance problematizes contemporary notions of spectacle, amusement, objectification, and exclusion. They "have touched on a colonial wound in this piece" (Johnson 1993, quoting Gómez-Peña).

It is worth emphasizing though that Fusco's work is never stuck in a post-colonial moment because it plays on "complex notions of colonial desire, entrapment, exile and display, and the historical exclusion of black subjectivities from

Figure 2.1 The Couple in the Cage: A Guatinaui Odyssey (Heredia and Fusco, 1993).

modernity" (Barson and Gorshlüter 2010: 21). Fusco locates potentialities within contexts able to draw past and future into the present. Her documentary *Operation Atropos* (2006) shows her experience of training with retired US army interrogators in order to create a touring one-woman show called *A Room of One's Own*, featuring Fusco as a US Army interrogator "who likes her job and [. . .] finds [. . .] nothing wrong with receiving orders to engage in actions that would be defined as torture [. . .] outside the United States" (Fusco 2010: 81). Both projects epitomize an urgent and constant need to rethink one's politics and the moving image, notably regarding "race," given that, as Fusco explained in 2007: "the [US] war machine is run by a black woman [Condoleezza Rice] and the entire legal structure of the legitimation of torture has been created by ethnic minorities" such as John Yu (Asian-American Law professor), Alberto Gonzales (Mexican-American attorney general) and his "Vietnamese assistant attorney general" (Fusco 2010: 91).

This type of sharp analysis exposes the term "post-black" as a discourse/recourse evading tough questions inevitably attached to mutations of blackness; faults must be detected in an ideological structure and the alterability and interchangeable aspects of identity addressed within a (non-"post") discursive-ideological world. If black people's "social position and self-definition," which "post-black" supposedly refers to (Barson and Gorshlüter 2010: 182), are always-already shifting, then "post-black" becomes a central paradox in "black" cinema/thought/discourse and, as shown below, in diaspora.[20] Claiming post-blackness leads one back to black representational space debates that no-theory theory – designed to be abandoned when meanings linked to its aspirations become inapplicable – debunks. Evasion is not interventionist, avoidance is unable to challenge racial categorizations, and post-race is a myth by which some choose to live (see Bâ 2011a).

"Black" diversity and fashionable defiance are not necessarily un-raced or de-raced, mainly when seen through "the fluid intertextual shiftiness of [film/moving image] genre" put in contact with the "black" diasporic (Bâ 2007: 49; see also Bâ 2008). Crucially, this coming together of genre, film/moving image, and diaspora also constitutes a bridge toward further problematizing oceanic frameworks by applying analytical tools that suggest the limitations of the oceanic's value, both in and beyond texts per se. Within cracked-open spaces of/created by the black diaspora, the oceanic framework, to extend the metaphor, becomes a conceptually dried-up or permanently drained concept. Freed from this unique focus on the oceanic, it is possible to play on the (term) "western" and its own linkages to blackness to argue, for example, that other frameworks must be used to connect disparate films and tropes that may belong to the "western" genre. This is how *Posse* (Mario Van Peebles, 1993) connects with tropes of the "western" at play in the Senegalese Diop-Mambéty's films and *Death in Timbuktu*, a spoof "western" inserted within *Bamako* (Sissako, 2006) and set in Mali.[21]

Beginning in 1898 Cuba, near the end of the Spanish-American War, *Posse* is about Jesse Lee (Van Peebles) and his men. Betrayed by their "white" military commander (Billie Zane), they escape with a reserve of gold to the USA. Lee obsessively tracks down the Ku Klux Klan (KKK) raiders who had lynched his father King David (Robert Hooks), creator of the "black" town of Freemanville. *Posse* signifies on a US/Hollywood-dominated genre by foregrounding outsiders therein: its heretofore untold story line is "black" and Native American; its *mise-en-scène* does target evils of "whiteness" (e.g., gun shooting practice on wooden KKK heads); and it features numerous "black" actors/stars.[22]

Posse's opening and closing sequences frame Lee's story as a long flashback within which his own memories lead to further flashbacks. The sequences raise issues of history, memory, and time and highlight the reasons why oceanic frameworks do not work for "black" diasporic cinema. *Posse* opens with an unnamed man's apparent monologue (Woody Strode) contextualizing Lee's story with the help of archival photographs, low-angle, and medium close-up shots:[23]

"They got us believe that Columbus discovered America [though] the Indians were already here. [. . .] There's one thing about time: no matter how much or how little passes, it changes things. [. . .] people forget that one out of every two cowboys were black. [. . .] over half of the original settlers of Los Angeles were black, but [. . .] we never hear their stories."

The closing sequence reveals that Strode is the orphan Lee rescues and adopts in *Posse*; that he is being recorded by two "black" journalists and his picture taken.[24] Therefore, at the contact zone of diegesis and real life the orphan/Strode hands "black" history and memory to journalists/real-life filmmakers for contemporary and future generations; stylistically, the sequence links diegetic time to the 1990s through written words, flame-colored on a black-and-white photograph of Van Peebles's Lee and his posse:

> "Today, approximately twelve per cent of Americans are African-Americans. However, that [percentage] owns less than one half of one per cent of America's wealth. Although ignored by Hollywood [. . .] the memory of the more than 8,000 Blacks that roamed the early West lives on."

These words condemn racism in the USA and (the) Hollywood ("western"); *Posse* bridges past, present, and future while disrupting "white" supremacist filmic accounts of history;[25] and literally and metaphorically *Posse* de-Westernizes film (in terms of filmmaking, history, aesthetics, and genre) from within a/the West. Aware of "black" presence in the Americas and the complex alliances between "Blacks" and Native Americans, *Posse* squarely locates its de-Westernizing fight within the Americas' boarders – Cuba, New Orleans, the Western Frontier, Freemanville, and Cutterstown – during a specific time frame. Moreover, this double location links *Posse* to Diop-Mambéty's tropes of the "western" and Sissako's spoof of the genre in *Bamako*, via analogy and transcendence of saltwater slave trading without proclaiming "black" social death.[26]

As early as eight years of age, Diop-Mambéty (1945–1998) regularly sneaked out of home at night to stand outside theatres and listen to films with friends; he told an interviewer, "the Westerns were my favourite films" (Givanni 1995: 30). After listening to "westerns," the friends would reconstruct them – or create new ones – in their homes' courtyards using a white sheet, candles, human figures, and horses cut from cardboard as well as their voices as diegetic sound (Givanni 1995: 30). In short, young Africans were signifying upon a genre that had emerged from within the West (in this instance, Hollywood, or Italy for "spaghetti westerns").

Figure 2.2 Posse (Mario Van Peebles, 1993).

These listening-recreating experiences of westerns bled into the adult Diop-Mambéty's ironic, playful, and parody-riddled fictional films such as *Badou Boy* (1966 and 1971), *Touki-Bouki* (1974), and *Hyenas* (1992), through tropes of the face-off or duel; good-bad-and-ugly narrative structures; greed and betrayal; and fantasizing about, going to, discovering, and/or returning from the "West" (Europe and the USA). *Touki-Bouki* features a scene where Mory (Magaye Niang) rounds up his bull-horn-decorated motorbike like a western cowboy to the sound of "black" music-hall star Josephine Baker's song "Paris." This complex web of references emerging from just one playful scene supports the thesis that the oceanic reference is insufficient. Yet Diop-Mambéty's tropes are barely discernible in Hollywood and spaghetti westerns because, as just shown, tropes of the Western western genre that pervade his films are always-already transformed. Diop-Mambéty's tropes connote a meeting of Senegal, the USA, "African" practices of listening,[27] the sonic apparatus of the cinema, class (young Diop-Mambéty could not afford cinema tickets), and his desire for creative freedom via imagined alternatives to contemporary sociopolitical conditions.

It follows that Diop-Mambéty de-Westernizes film by departing from caco-phonous western film-fragments (akin to Derridian ruins) in order to birth new films with no impediments, binaries, linearity, borders or rules attached. This is how he can make sense as a precursor to a movement such as Dogma 95.[28] Diop-Mambéty called for "a filiation untouched by revenge but bustling with recovery" or "a here-and-nowness for Africa" (Cousins 2007: 28) that was or displayed an openness to the world; eight years after his death Sissako responded creatively to this call with *Death in Timbuktu*.

Death in Timbuktu is undoubtedly a metaphor "for the narrow-mindedness of Westerners' views of Africa" but, akin to Diop-Mambéty's work or to *Bamako* (the film within which this film is located) it is not "a simple diatribe against the West" (Ukadike 2007: 39). Therefore, keeping Diop-Mambéty firmly in the picture, three points become relevant:[29] *Death in Timbuktu* pays homage to spaghetti westerns; it also "exposes Hollywood's predominance of African screens (small and big)" and inserts extra, playful space within *Bamako*'s condemnation of the IMF and the World Bank. Sissako also resignifies on the western genre by using font types typical of western film iconography, Malian desert landscapes that recall US/European westerns, and the costumes and presence of Danny Glover (African-American actor), Zéka Laplaine (DR Congolese actor-director), Sissako (starring as Dramane Bassaro), and Elia Suleiman (Israeli-Arab director and actor).

In summary, the complex linkages between *Posse*, Diop-Mambéty's films, and *Death in Timbuktu* cannot be made by applying the oceanic frameworks of diaspora. They are, moreover, indicative of the fact that nowadays diasporic constitutions and connections result more from flying over (conceptually arid) oceans than sailing/floating upon them;[30] that the (re)appropriation of cinema technology by those denied access to it for long periods is no longer a novel or nascent phenomenon; and, finally, that *Posse* is told in African storytelling mode, i.e. via an elderly figure telling legendary stories to younger generations. That the nar-rative structures in Diop-Mambéty's films, *Bamako* and *Posse* use digressions and circularities characteristic of "black" African oral storytelling traditions clarifies that these films can only be connected effectively if/when each is considered part of what is called, in relation to *Bamako* and Africa, "a pan-African cinematic tradition of telling the truth – a truth [. . .] against the West" (Ukadike 2007: 39).[31] Furthermore, this tradition is historical: it bridges time(s) and space(s) without recourse to oceanic frameworks, reiterating the earlier discussion in this chapter about discourse as revolutionary graffiti, multiple ruptures of rigid imaginaries, liminal cracked-open spaces, and no-theory theory of "black cinema."

As we shall see, the concept of diaspora asks questions that oceans can neither handle nor contain: "what happens when one cannot or does not want to look back for political or economic reasons? [. . .] when future generations do not know how to look back [. . .]?" (Baziel and Mannur 2003: 9)

"Black" questioning frameworks

> The use of the term *diaspora* [. . .] is not that it offers the comfort of abstraction, an easy recourse to origins, but that it forces us to consider discourses of cultural and political linkage only through and across difference.
>
> (Edwards 2001: 62)

Edwards's essay "The Uses of *Diaspora*" (2001) is conducive to perceiving diaspora "as a more dynamic and dialectical concept" (Bâ 2010b: 59); it also helps this chapter posit early elements of a non-oceanic framework of diasporic discourses as the latter lays the groundwork for exposing the conceptual aridity of oceanic frameworks.[32] Indeed, Edwards warns that Gilroy's *The Black Atlantic* "threatens continually (despite Gilroy's own qualifications) to conflate diaspora [. . .] with Gilroy's proposition of that field he calls the "black Atlantic'" in order to force a debate on "the *politics of nominalization*" (emphasis in original; 2001: 45, 46). More recently, Glissant called for a radical departure from the "Black Atlantic" field because "the Atlantic is a continent, not an archipelago. And we are inhabitants of an archipelago. When Africa was attacked by the colonizers, it was not a continent, but an archipelago. [. . .] [T]he arrival of the Africans within the phenomenon of slavery is not about the Atlantic, but the Caribbean" (Diawara 2010a: 60; see also Edwards 2001).[33]

Of course, because diaspora is open to "ideological appropriation," namely by nationalists and racial essentialists (Edwards 2001: 52), following historians Joseph Harris and Locksley Edmondson, its historiography must be resuscitated by advancing concepts of (Africans') "involuntary diaspora" (inside the African continent, and via Arab and European slave trades) and "mobilized diaspora" (a twentieth-century phenomenon) (Edwards 2001: 53; see also Diawara 2010a: 59). In doing so one can argue that "a discourse of diaspora becomes necessary in the same period that the 'mobilized diaspora' is taking shape" (Edwards 2001: 54), while at the same time allowing this argument's full complexity to emerge as follows: involuntary diaspora must be freed from its strict historical location and allowed to roam across time and space. For example, Akomfrah's 1960s migration to the

UK from Ghana (with his mother and siblings) was voluntary only in part, for it resulted from the death of his father following the collapse of President Kwame Nkrumah's regime.[34] Similarly, this chapter's questioning of diaspora theories takes place at the contact zone(s) of involuntary and mobilized diasporas, a cracked-open, third and multi-sited space where meanings are always moving.

Consequently, Edwards' *décalage*, "the kernel of precisely that which cannot be transferred or exchanged, the received biases that refuse to pass over when one crosses the water or [. . .] a different kind of interface" (2001: 63), is useful to this author's thinking, which, located at the limits of involuntary and mobilized diasporas, questions frameworks through a politics of diaspora "reject[ing] Western assumptions about a link between knowledge production and the nation" (Edwards 2001: 54)[35] and acknowledges "the West"/"Western" as an unstable and mutable category. Put differently, during the late nineteenth and twentieth centuries the "black" diasporas shaped by early transatlantic and slave trades transmuted into many "fractured diasporas" resulting in movements from South to North, "across the Western hemisphere – from Port au Prince to Montréal, from Kingston to New York – and from West to East across the Atlantic ocean again" (Baziel and Mannur 2003: 2). It follows that in the twenty-first century concepts of diaspora must speak "to diverse groups of displaced persons and communities moving across the globe" (Baziel and Mannur 2003: 2); hence the questions: Where is the West/the Western? What is Western? As shown so far the West/Western is (always) wherever or whenever a perception of de-Westernization is possible and/ or unfolding through and across difference, without obsession with origins.

Thus, at this juncture, the chapter echoes Glissant's statement on African diasporas of the post-transatlantic slave trade, i.e. that "every diaspora is the passage from unity to multiplicity" (Diawara 2010a: 59), and reinvokes Edwards and Glissant in order to discard geo-oceanic frameworks of diaspora. It is worth reiterating the chapter's motion beyond both a moment of transatlantic dispersal and Black Atlantic theory; its interest is in what emerges from what Glissant sees as the system that started "to contain and signify the existence of the Blacks" to the Caribbean (Diawara 2010a: 60). This is because, instead of the Gilroyan oceanic frameworks' attempt "to open the box and let the sea flows take the lead" (Naro et al. 2007: 4), the chapter concurs with Glissant that "the 'archipelisation' of the deportation of the Africans is a reality, a precious one" (Diawara 2010a: 60).

It is crucial to note that Glissant is not retracing "black" people's geo-oceanic source and origin but those of a system always-already removed from a moment of idealized pre-archipelization. Otherwise one may not comprehend "black" folk traditions, performance-based celebrations, and rituals such as Brazilian carnival, Ecuadorian *Semana Santa*, or *congadas* (festivals) celebrating *carnaval* in Portobello (Panama). The latter event and practice emanate from groups calling themselves Congos whose *congadas* derive predominantly from "sixteenth- and seventeenth-century practices which in turn may refer back to [. . .] central Africa" (Bettelheim 2004: 288). These groups, and "black" Panamanians, do not enter a "national dialogue" inside Panama regarding nationhood and modernity for they (c)are about "the particular status of the powerful and threatening free *cimarrón* (maroon) communities [. . .] that populated the entire Atlantic coast" (Bettelheim 2004: 290); Panama Congos' historical connection with Africa is outer-national and yet geo-oceanic frameworks and their discourses of diaspora cannot explain spaces that Congos occupy. Oceanic trajectories can no longer help because Congos have gone through manifold and successive, metaphorical and literal, archipelizations.

Legacy (dir. Inge Blackman 2006) provides an example of aesthetic resonances between the *congada* dance and the Jamaican *Kumina*.[36] The former features couples moving around one another in a circular configuration with almost-motionless upper bodies and non-syncopated shoulders. In contrast, their lower bodies move in a swing-shuffle pattern with arms "held low" and swinging/swaying in a similar side-to-side motion (Bettelheim 2004: 294). These features echo Jamaican *Kumina* where hip motion and feet shuffling follow a noticeably similar configuration, while additionally Jamaican *Kumina* shares with the *congada* dance a "Congo heritage [. . .] Congo-based vocabulary and belief system" and resonance with "a Central African Congo aesthetic" (Bettelheim 2004: 294).

Shot in Trinidad, *Legacy* is a "cross-fertilizing, teleology-interrupting meditation on black history and memory, using the 'body' as a site for an (oral) excavation of multiple discourses on gender and sexuality, matrilineal heritage and oppression, but also hope" (Bâ 2007: 49; see also Blackman/Campbell 2006: 17–25). *Legacy*'s Jamaican *Kumina* is performed by Campbell and her mother. On the beach at sundown, they move in a circular pattern and with shuffling footwork within a candlelit circle. This dance differs from the *congada* because, while arms are kept close or stuck to the body (from elbows up), forearms move up (to shoulder level) and down (to hip level) in parallel with the footwork. However, continuity – African, or between *congada* and *Kumina* – is established through memory and corporeal witnessing. This is because *Legacy*'s *Kumina* provides a linkage to Campbell's ancestors dancing the *Kumina* at night and away from "white" eyes.[37] Campbell's mother was only able to access Africa and corporeal witnessing through her own grandmother who had not received a colonial education.[38] Crucially, therefore, such a convoluted route is the only one through which Campbell's mother can create some form of continuity from/back to Africa via *Kumina*.

'Black" connections or discourses coming through *Kumina* can therefore only make sense if one grasps that, as with scientific and ideological discourses on Africa, "traditions (*traditio*) means discontinuities through a dynamic continuation and possible conversion of *tradita* (legacies). As such, it is part of a history in the making" (Mudimbe 1988: 189). The act of discontinuing if not rupturing – which can be historical, cultural, aesthetic, performative, and so on – does preclude linearity (time-based or not), while at the same time creating other forms of continuities via transformation or conversion. Therefore, *Kumina, congada*, cognate dances, and their discrete performances, become (part of) a never-ending process of making "black" history/discourse/thought/cinema/diasporas. The Congo and Africa have become ideations, traces, transformations, resignifications, or simply metaphors experiencing perpetual vertigos of displacement that geo-oceans can neither cope with nor grasp.[39] This justifies why Campbell, Trinidad-born, nurtured in Jamaican culture, and self-declared of Coromantee ancestry via her maternal grandmother's Maroon/*cimarrón* blood, can make diasporic sense when performing a Jamaican *Kumina* within (a film shot in) twenty-first-century Trinidad.[40] The same process of geo-ocean-free rupturing allows Campbell to claim *Kumina* as a project that triggers beginnings but "no end" while using performance to bring about archipelized "collective ancestral memories" (Blackman/Campbell 2006: 18). Certainly, like Brazilian carnival or Portobello *congadas*, *Legacy* reinvents "blackness" and Africa by giving "visual pleasure to the audience, while challenging 'us'" (Blackman/Campbell 2006: 18).

Ending beginning: (to the) beyond(s of) "black" diasporas

What then are the implications of putting "black" diasporic discourses in dialogue? What are the outcomes of dialogic "black" diasporic discourses that necessarily (involve) going beyond the black diasporas? The tropes, filmmakers, and films discussed above provide collective beginnings of answers through their: locations between involuntary, mobilized, and twenty-first-century diaspora concepts; embodiment of *décalage*, which exposes limitations of water crossings; and archipelized retracings/questionings of systems of "black" containment. What we are left with therefore are tropes, filmmakers, and films that resist "post-black," display a creative freedom defying geo-oceanic frameworks of diaspora – and still make sense.

Of course these stances are present in more films and filmmakers than space restrictions have allowed this author to explore. The BAFC's use of Soviet filmmaker Sergo Paradzhanov's film aesthetics in *Seven Songs for Malcolm X* (Akomfrah, 1993),[41] of Polish composer and conductor Krysztof Penderecki's trauma-echoing music in *Testament* (Akomfrah, 1988), and Edward George's writing for and presence in BAFC films, especially *Last Angel of History* (Akomfrah, 1996) would be potent places to pursue the questioning processes begun here.

Acknowledgments

The author is grateful to Will Higbee, Edward George, and Anna Piva for feedback on earlier versions of this chapter.

Notes

1 In this chapter, words and phrases in inverted commas are mostly followed by a reference. However, exceptions arise with constructs central to its thesis: here inverted commas denote acknowledgment of the latter's (positive) instability and fluidity in ways epitomized by how "black" is addressed in the text.

2 Here, no interest is expressed in the implicit/transparent presence of "white" as a category due to the latter's potential for binary positioning and self-privileging as center.

3 Of course, relation with beginnings and their locales may remain obsessive without relation itself becoming pathological, fixed or singular.

4 The triangular slave trade is a constant reaction to modernity, while English-language scholarship on the Atlantic world has "largely ignored or overlooked" the important "Portuguese relationship with the Atlantic" (Naro et al. 2007: 5, 7). Yet acknowledging

this relationship does not reach or affect the bases of what generated the triangular paradigm in the first place; it just perpetuates it through a different geometrical form.

5 Alterable and interchangeable black identities were visible in advertisements for mail-ordered, Taiwan-manufactured wigs in "popular African American" magazines; satire and fantasy were manifest in playwright George C. Wolfe's *Hairpiece* where two talking wig stands compete for "the loyalty and adornment of a black woman"; and assertive Blacks were those who took US Civil Rights movement gains beyond the "American melting pot" and into the core of a forceful yet far-sighted racial awareness (Powell 2005: 9).

6 "Saltwater" is borrowed from Smallwood's book *Saltwater Slavery* (2008).

7 The Senegalese Cheikh Anta Diop's work is a case point.

8 See Martin (1995), Stam (1995), Bâ (2007), and Malik (2010).

9 The term "ruin" as used here echoes philosopher Jacques Derrida's thought according to which everything is or is about to be in ruin, and every structure is ephemeral. For a recent discussion, see Richards (2008).

10 English (2007: 27–70) discusses such a space insightfully.

11 Quotes drawn from Eshun on the condition at play in the name "Black Audio Film Collective" (BAFC, 1982–1998) (2007: 75). BAFC's sixteen-year existence (1982–1998) within a Global North metropolis (London) is an example of potentiality.

12 Eshun and Gray (2011: 2) advance this concept in relation to the militant image or intention. However, we shall see that "black" challenges geography and is not always militant in terms of image or intention.

13 Racist reactions to "black," more animal than human, always emanate from the lower brain area. For "perceptual constancy" and other basic cognitive psychology notions, see introductory works such as Anderson (1995) and Malim (1994); on thought, the human mind, representation, and cognitive science see Crane (2003).

14 It is this author's contention that this figuring out of answers had begun well before the 1980s, which is where Okuwi Enwezor's analysis of BAFC locates it (2007). Compare this with the point made above about the 1960s to the 1980s as a period of multiple ruptures of rigid imaginaries.

15 This is why one can discuss "black" in past tenses or organize retrospectives. See, for example, Eshun and Sagar's touring exhibition "The Ghosts of Songs: A Retrospective of the Black Audio Film Collective, February 2–April 1, 2007." That any cinema can be described as such may be undeniable. However, to discuss "white" in this context means having to begin with addressing what Heidegger calls presencing or "the enduring of that which, having arrived in unconcealment, remains there" (1977: 161). "White" was/is never opaque, invisible and/or concealed: it has always been subject(ed) by "white" hegemony to what Snead calls "mythification" and "marking" (1989: 4, 5).

16 "Archipelized" is adapted from Glissant's "archipelisation," which he constructs via his argument that transatlantic slave trade Africans arrived "in Louisiana, the islands, Cuba, Jamaica, Martinique, and spread from there across the new continent" (Diawara 2010a: 60).

17 Enwezor (2007: 117–118) identifies these characteristics in BAFC's inaugural project *Expeditions One/Two: Signs of Empire/Images of Nationality* (1982–1984) and *Handsworth Songs* (1986) taken together.

18 For difficult access to means of audiovisual production, see Bowser (1999) on "Black Documentary Film."

19 See *Vénus noire* (Kechiche, 2010). Arguably, in *Nigger Arabesque* Jones's body fulfils functions similar to Fusco's.

20 The fact that perhaps in the USA, Europe, and significant sections of continental Africa social positions are not always-already shifting in socioeconomic terms further questions the soundness of "post-black" discourse/recourse.

21 A link could also be made to *Le Retour d'un aventurier/The Return of an Adventurer* (dir. Alassane, 1966) where, returning to his village in Niger after time in the USA, an African man brings gifts of cowboy outfits which his friends wear and then proceed to play at "Cowboys and Indians."

22 For how *Posse* relates to and departs from conventions of the American Western, see Gleiberman (1993). These actors/stars include Van Peebles' father Melvin, Pam Grier, and Isaac Hayes. Melvin directed the groundbreaking film *Sweet Sweetback's Baadasssss Song* (1971); Grier and Hayes are icons of 1970s US blaxploitation cinema; and Mario was already known for his urban-gangster film *New Jack City* (1991).

23 Strode (1914–1994) was a prolific actor who featured in over eighty-five films, including Hollywood and spaghetti westerns.

24 Filmmakers Reginald and Warrington Hudlin; Reginald directed *House Party* (1990) and *Boomerang* (1992).

25 Compare with Buscombe's statement on 1980s and 1990s westerns: "History is a rich source of material for those who would offer narratives other than those dominated by the macho white male. [. . .] However, Hollywood seems reluctant to take the plunge. While it no longer has confidence in the certainties of the traditional western, it lacks the ability to imagine what would take their place" (2007: 381). *Posse* was daringly able to imagine such a replacement.

26 Regarding analogy and black social death, this author is taking exception to Wilderson who argues that "[w]hereas Humans exist on some plane of being and thus can become existentially present through some struggle for, of, or through recognition, Blacks cannot reach that plane" (2010: 38) and dismisses analogy as a method. For further details see Wilderson (2010: 35–63) or Bâ (2011b).

27 A type of listening shaped by oral storytelling traditions that "African" children like Diop-Mambéty and this author have repeatedly experienced.

28 Here Wynchank (2003: 98) must be acknowledged but also critiqued; she makes an insightful link between Diop-Mambéty's *La Petite Vendeuse de soleil/The Little Girl who Sold "The Sun"* (1999) and Dogma, while overlooking two crucial issues: first, what they share (regarding technology, shooting style, camerawork, and story design) permeate the whole of Diop-Mambéty's work – not just one film – and second, Diop-Mambéty's "extreme simplicity" when using technology did not "echo" Von Trier, Vinterberg, and Dogma (Wynchank 2003: 98), it had simply forerun them.

29 Points drawn from this author's forthcoming essay "Abderrahmane Sissako: Cineaste of the Horizon."

30 This "aeriality" trope informed Flow Motion's multimedia interactive project *Promised Lands* (2009–). *Promised Lands* supports this chapter's contention, especially regarding limits of oceanic frameworks in forging diasporic connections and bridging diverse temporal zones and spaces. See www.iniva.net/pl/main-page (accessed September 25, 2011).

31 On "black" African storytelling see Ukadike (1994: 21–24).

32 Unless otherwise indicated, all references to diaspora and/or Edwards come from this 2001 essay. Therefore, only the year and page numbers are given in the text.

33 On Gilroy's Black Atlantic (theory and book) and his theories of "race" in cinema, visual culture, and/or cultural studies, see Palumbo-Liu (2004), Oboe and Scacchi (2008), Bâ (2010a and 2011b), Barson and Gorshlüter (2010), and Glissant in Diawara (2010a).

34 Email correspondence between Akomfrah and author, July 29, 2011.

35 Edwards suggests that 1960s–1970s US black studies used the same strategy.

36 Blackman has since changed her full name to "Campbell X" and is interviewed in this volume.

37 "My grandmother was well educated in those days, i.e. up to high school level – it was the colonial system which brainwashed people in British ways; so she was very much leaning toward Britishness. She did know some traditions and had to stand up to my grandfather's Eurocentrism [. . .] even though [. . .] he also practised African traditions. So it is the attitude to the traditions practised that is more significant than whether or not they did practice them. To some varying degree everyone does in the Caribbean, but most look down on these traditions with shame" (Campbell, email correspondence with the author, July 29, 2011).

38 "My great grandmother was not educated at all because education was not considered
    necessary for women like her – poor and working class. So, her knowledge was what
    had been passed down orally and through her mother and beyond. Ironically then, she
    retained the Africanness and traditions and oral culture and was not ashamed of it, but
    knew she had to keep it quiet" (Campbell, email correspondence with the author, July
    29, 2011). Campbell's grandmother, married to a "Caucasian"/"white" man, chose not
    to teach Campbell's mother the *Kumina* because, according to the latter in the film, "it
    was too African" and Campbell's grandmother "preferred things British," having been
    formally educated out of African traditions.
39 Concerning the geographically situated African Congos, one may also ask which one/s
    is/are (to be) pin-pointed or privileged today?
40 Coromantees or Coromantins are of *Akan* culture (Ghana) and were renowned for
    organizing and carrying out countless "slave" rebellions on slave ships and in the Car-
    ibbean. They have culturally influenced Jamaica and the Maroons (see Rediker 2005,
    Smallwood 2007, or Taylor 2006).
41 See Bâ (2006: 156–164), unpublished Ph.D. thesis, "Malcolm X and Documentary
    Film Representation" (Exeter). See also Bâ (2008: 137–148).

References

Akomfrah, J. (2010) "Digitopia and the Specters of Diaspora," *Journal of Media Practice*,
    11 (1): 21–30.
Anderson, J. R. (1995) *Cognitive Psychology and its Implications*, 4th edn, New York:
    W. H. Freeman & Co.
Andrew, D. (2010) *What Cinema Is! Bazin's Quest and its Charge*, Malden, Mass.: Wiley-Blackwell.
Bâ, S. M. (2007) "*Voix noires:* Black Documentary Theory," in D. A. Bailey (ed.), *The Black
    Moving Cube: Black Figuration and the Moving Image*, Berlin: The Green Box, pp. 31–54.
——(2008) "Visualising Rhythm, Transforming Relationship: Jazz and *Seven Songs for Mal-
    colm X* (1993)," *Studies in Documentary Film*, 2 (2): 137–148.
——(2010a) "Diegetic Masculinities: Reading the Black Body in Epic Cinema," in
    R. Burgoyne (ed.), *The Epic Film in World Culture*, London and New York: Routledge,
    pp. 346–374.
——(2010b) "Affective Power/Formal Knowledge: Diaspora, African Cinema and Film
    Festivals outside Africa," *Film International*, 8 (5): 54–69.
——(2011a) "'Planetary Humanism' Calling: New Sightings of "Black" Bodies in Epic Films,"
    Film International. Available online at http://filmint.nu/?p=911 (accessed June 25, 2011).
——(2011b) "The US De-Centred: From Black Social Death to Cultural Transformation,"
    Cultural Studies Review, 17 (2). Available online at www.csreview.unimelb.edu.au (accessed
    October 31, 2011).
——(forthcoming) "Abderrahmane Sissako: Cineaste of the Horizon," in B. Stephenson
    and S. J. Petty (eds.), *The Directory of World Cinema: Africa*, Bristol, UK: Intellect Publishing.
Barson, T. and Gorshlüter, P. (eds.) (2010) *Afro Modern: Journeys through the Black Atlantic*,
    Liverpool: Tate Liverpool.
Baziel, J. A. and Mannur, A. (eds.) (2003) *Theorizing Diaspora: A Reader*, Malden, Mass., and
    Oxford: Blackwell.
Bettelheim, J. (2004) "Carnaval of Los Congos in Portobelo, Panama: Feathered Men and
    Queens," in G. Fabre and K. Benesch (eds), *African Diasporas in the New and Old Worlds:
    Consciousness and Imagination*, Amsterdam and New York: Rodopi, pp. 287–312.
Blackman, I. (2006) "Legacy," in D. A. Bailey (ed.), *The Black Moving Cube: Black Figuration
    and the Moving Image*, Berlin: The Green Box, pp. 17–25.

Bowser, P. (1999) "Pioneers of Black Documentary Film," in P. R. Klotman and J. K. Cutler (eds.), *Struggles for Representation: African American Documentary Film and Video*, Bloomington, Ind.: Indiana University Press, pp. 1–33.

Buscombe, E. (2007) "Westerns in the 1980s and 1990s," in P. Cook (ed.), *The Cinema Book*, 3rd edn, London: BFI Publishing, p. 381.

Césaire, A. (2000) *Discourse on Colonialism*, New York: Monthly Review Press.

Cousins, M. (2007) "African Cinema: Invisible Classics," *Sight and Sound*, 17 (1): 26–30.

Crane, T. (2003) *The Mechanical Mind*, 2nd edn, London and New York: Routledge.

Diawara, M. (2010a) "A Conversation with Édouard Glissant aboard the Queen Mary II," in T. Barson and P. Gorshlüter (eds.), *Afro Modern: Journeys through the Black Atlantic*, Liverpool: Tate Liverpool, pp. 58–63.

——(2010b) *African Film: New Forms of Aesthetics and Politics*, Munich: Prestel.

Eagleton, T. (1991) *Ideology*, London: Verso.

Edwards, B. H. (2001) "The Uses of *Diaspora*," *Social Text*, 19 (1): 45–71.

English, D. (2007) *How to See a Work of Art in Total Darkness*, Cambridge, Mass.: MIT Press.

Enwezor, O. (2007) 'Coalition Building: Black Audio Film Collective and Transnational Post-Colonialism', in K. Eshun and A. Sagar (eds), *The Ghosts of Songs: The Film Art of the Black Audio Film Collective*, Liverpool: Liverpool University Press, pp. 106–129.

Eshun, K. (2004) "Untimely Meditations: Reflections on the Black Audio Film Collective," *NKA Journal of Contemporary African Art*, 19 (summer): 38–45.

——(2007), "Drawing the Forms of Things Unknown," in K. Eshun and A. Sagar (eds.), *The Ghosts of Songs: The Film Art of the Black Audio Film Collective*, Liverpool: Liverpool University Press, pp. 74–105.

Fekete, L. (2009) *A Suitable Enemy: Racism, Migration and Islamophobia in Europe*, New York: Pluto Press.

Flow Motion (2009–) *promised lands*. Available online at www.iniva.org/press/2009/promised_lands (accessed August 31, 2011).

Fusco, C. (2010) "Operation Atropos," *Journal of Media Practice*, 11 (1): 81–94.

Gilroy, P. (1994) *The Black Atlantic: Modernity and Double Consciousness*, London: Verso.

——(2000) *Between Camps: Nations, Cultures and the Allures of Race*, London: Penguin.

Givanni, J. (1995) "African conversations," *Sight & Sound*, 5 (9): 30.

Glieberman, O. (1993) *"Posse"* (Review). *Entertainment Weekly*, May 21. Available online at www.ew.com/ew/article/0,306613,00.html (accessed June 23, 2011).

Johnson, A. (1993) "Coco Fusco and Guillermo Gómez-Peña," *Bomb*, 42 (winter). Available online at http://bombsite.com/issues/42/articles/1599 (accessed June 23, 2011).

Heidegger, M. (1977) *The Question Concerning Technology and other Essays*, trans. W. Lovitt, London: Harper Perennial.

Kelley, R. (2002) *Freedom Dreams: The Black Radical Imagination*, Boston, Mass.: Beacon Press.

Lott, T. (1995) "A No-Theory Theory of Contemporary Black Cinema," in M. T. Martin (ed.), *Cinemas of the Black Diaspora: Diversity, Dependence and Oppositionality*, Detroit, Mich.: Wayne State University Press, pp. 40–55.

Malik, S. (2010) "The Dark Side of Hybridity: Contemporary Black and Asian British Cinema," in D. Berghahn and C. Sternberg (eds.), *European Cinema in Motion: Migrant and Diasporic Film in Contemporary Europe*, Basingstoke: Palgrave Macmillan, pp. 132–151.

Malim, T. (1994) *Cognitive Processes*, Basingstoke: Macmillan.

Martin, M. T. (1995) "Framing the "Black" in Black Diasporic Cinemas," in M. T. Martin (ed.), *Cinemas of the Black Diaspora: Diversity, Dependence and Oppositionality*, Detroit, Mich.: Wayne State University Press, pp. 1–24.

Marks, L. U. (2007), "Immigrant Semiosis," in J. Marchessault and S. Lord (eds.), *Fluid Screens, Expanded Cinema*, Toronto: University of Toronto Press, pp. 284–303.

Marx, A. W. (1998) *Making Race and Nation: A Comparison of the United States, South Africa and Brazil*, Cambridge: Cambridge University Press.

Maslin, J. (1993) "A Western in the Hands of a Revisionist," *New York Times*, May 14. Available online at http://movies.nytimes.com/movie/review?res=9F0CE4D81430F937 A25756C0A965958260 (accessed June 24, 2011).

Mudimbe, V. Y. (1988) *The Invention of Africa: Gnosis, Philosophy and the Order of Knowledge*, London: James Currey.

Naro, N. P., Sansi-Roca, R., and Treece, D. H. (eds.) (2007) *Cultures of the Lusophone Black Atlantic*, Basinstoke: Palgrave Macmillan.

Oboe, A. and Scacchi, A. (2008) *Recharting the Black Atlantic: Modern Cultures, Local Communities, Global Connections*, London and New York: Routledge.

Palumbo-Liu, D. (2004) "*Against Race:* Yes, But At What Cost?," in G. Fabre and K. Benesch (eds.), *African Diasporas in the New World: Consciousness and Imagination*, Amsterdam: Rodopi, pp. 39–58.

Petty, S. J. (2008) *Contact Zones: Memory, Origin, and Discourses in Black Diasporic Cinema*, Detroit, Mich.: Wayne State University Press.

Pinho, P. (2010) *Mama Africa: Reinventing Blackness in Bahia*, Durham, NC: Duke University Press.

Powell, R. J. (2005) "Racial Imaginaries, from Charles White's Preacher to Jean-Paul Goude's and Grace Jones's Nigger Arabesque," in D. A. Bailey (ed.), *Back to Black: Art, Cinema and the Racial Imaginary*, London: The New Art Gallery Walsall, pp. 8–27.

Rediker, M. (2005) *The Slave Ship: A Human History*, London: John Murray.

Richards, K. M. (2008) *Derrida Reframed*, London: I. B. Tauris.

Smallwood, S. E. (2007) *Saltwater Slavery*, Cambridge, Mass.: Harvard University Press.

Snead, J. (1989) *White Screens/Black Images*, London and New York: Routledge.

Stam, R. (1995) "Samba, Candomblé, Quilombo: Black Performance in Brazilian Cinema," in M. T. Martin (ed.), *Cinemas of the Black Diaspora: Diversity, Dependence and Oppositionality*, Detroit, Mich.: Wayne State University Press, pp. 281–304.

Tarkovsky, A. (1989) *Sculpting in Time: Reflections on the Cinema*, trans. K. Hunter-Blair, London: Faber and Faber.

Taylor, E. R. (2006) *If We Must Die: Shipboard Insurrections in the Era of the Atlantic Slave Trade*, Baton Rouge, La.: Louisiana Sate University Press.

Ukadike, N. F. (1994), *Black African Cinema*, Berkeley, Calif.: University of California Press.

——(2007) "Calling to Account," *Sight and Sound*, 17 (1): 38–39.

Wilderson, F. B., III (2010) *Red, Black and White: Cinema and the Structure of US Antagonisms*, Durham, NC: Duke University Press.

Wynchank, A. (2003) "Djibrill Diop-Mambety, Fondateur d'us Cinéma nouveau" *Cinémaction/Cinémas africains, une oasis dans le desert?*, 106 (1er trimestre 2003): pp. 93–98.

Žižek, S. (1994) "How Did Marx Invent the Symptom?" in S. Žižek (ed.), *Mapping Ideology*, London and New York: Verso, pp. 296–331.

——(2008a) *Enjoy Your Symptom: Jacques Lacan in Hollywood and Out*, London and New York: Routledge.

——(2008b) *The Plague of Fantasies*, London and New York: Verso.

3 Affective passions

The dancing female body and colonial rupture in *Zouzou* (1934) and *Karmen Geï* (2001)

Saër Maty Bâ and Kate E. Taylor-Jones

This chapter will examine two films that are over sixty-seven years and a continent apart in creation. *Zouzou* (Allégret, 1934) was one of the earliest vehicles for the talents of one of the most popular stars of the French music hall, the African American Josephine Baker (Zouzou). *Karmen Geï* (Gaï Ramaka, 2001) is a Senegalese reworking of Bizet's opera *Carmen* and stars Djeïnaba Diop Gaï as the ill-fated seductive lead (Karmen). The chapter will explore how an affective reading of the dancing body can reveal new pathways for free interpretation and challenge the Western (and) patriarchal construction of the African-American/African "black" female body.[1] As we shall see, an affective study offers a method through which the (bodies of) protagonists, in this instance the female leads Karmen and Zouzou, can move outside the boundaries of transitional meaning in order to present an alternative fertile contact zone of meanings.

Constructing affective power

The recent "affective turn" in the visual and cultural arts is one that "invites a transdisciplinary approach to theory and method" (Clough 2007: 3). Consequently, this chapter will utilize the vision of affect presented by Brian Massumi that focuses on the "body without an image," an approach which sees the body as an "accumulation of relative perspectives and the passages between them" (Massumi 2002: 57) and one that also "refuses to cohere into a distinctive image" (Featherstone 2010: 195). The term "image," as related to visual artifacts such as film, is clearly problematic in the context of patriarchal (and) Western construction of the black female body. Colonial expansion, enslavement and "science" all contributed to the ways in which that body came to be regarded within visual and actual European Culture (Gilman 1989: 100). As Nelson states, "identity often comes down to the meanings that are attached to bodies when they are rendered as objects of vision. . . Vision and the visual are western tools of social ordering" (2007: 234). The image of the black female body within this structure is one that has historically and culturally been "probed and catalogued, watched and desired, named and misnamed" (Henderson 2010: 4). Subjectivity of the black female body has, therefore, often been denied and repressed. However, as Wilson et al. state in *Rerouting the Postcolonial,* affect signals the turning "from identity politics to subjectivity itself" (2010: 6). Affect is about placing the body at the center of discourse, since affect *proceeds* from the body and an *in-betweenness* of bodily interaction (Featherstone 2010). And yet, this is not about the dismissal of the body as a cultural and historical entity.[2] Instead, affect allows us to see the body as:

> no longer the obstacle that separates thought from itself. . . It is on the contrary that which it plunges into. . . in order to reach the unthought. . . the body. . . forces us to think what is concealed from thought, life. . . To think is to learn what a non-thinking body is capable of, its capacity, its postures.
>
> (Deleuze 1986: 189)

In this absolute rejection of the mind–body dualism, affect seems to hold what Massumi calls "the key to rethinking modern power" since "at the affective moment when the image first assaults us, we are temporarily outside meaning" (1996: 235). Affect is about engagement with "the creative and political possibility of the body" (Nayar 2009: 19); it is about the disruption of the status quo and the dominant social strata. This chapter is focused on "affect as potential: a body's capacity to affect and be affected" (Gregg and Seigworth 2011: 2). The above theoretical debates thus open up a methodological framework for this chapter to analyze the cultural and historical intricacies of the "black" female body on film whilst simultaneously seeing the body as the site of positive and affirming affective power relations.

The need to acknowledge the cultural and historical positioning of the bodies in question is important. As Hardt and Negri state in their examination of the intricacies and legacies of Empire, the "multitude must confront directly with an adequate consciousness the central repressed operations of Empire" (2000: 399). Such a confrontation must also be aware of Hardt and Negri's (2000) idea of a post-industrial world (synonymous with a prison). For and in that world, the body – raced and gendered – may nonetheless remain coherent, disputed, the ultimate refuge of civil society, and an imagined/real fertile contesting contact zone. For Bhabha (1986), three conditions underlie "the process of identification in the analytic of desire": first, one exists when "called into being in relation to an Otherness, its looks or locus" (1986: xv); second, identification, trapped "in the tension of demand and desire, is a space of splitting" (1986: xv); and third, identification is the constant "production of an "image" of identity and the transformation of the subject in assuming that image" (1986: xvi).[3] The thinking of both Hardt and Negri and Bhabha is echoed in Bignall's claim that:

> describing a movement towards genuinely postcolonial forms of society, post-colonialisation should introduce a discontinuity or a difference into colonial histories; this historical discontinuity is required if post-colonial societies are to "exit" from habitually [Western] imperial assumption and practices of relations.
>
> (Bignall 2010: 3)

Thinking through Bhabha's notion of postcolonial identification in the context of the more recent "affective turn" in critical theory, we can describe Zouzou and

Karmen as desired affective bodies in motion within spaces of splitting (whether resisted spaces or not) where they assume transforming/transformative images and articulate difference. To summarize the films, in *Zouzou*, ("black") Zouzou and ("white") Jean (Jean Gabin) are the adopted (or maybe, abducted) children of a circus ringmaster-barker called Papa Mélé (Pierre Larquey). As adults, Zouzou falls in love with Jean who loves another, "white" woman. *Zouzou* is tailored to Baker's body and performance ability, while accenting race mixture as "deformity and exoticism" (Jules-Rosette 2007: 84). In *Karmen Geï*, Karmen, having escaped from prison returns to her home and her criminal gang. The story is told via a heady mix of song and dance as we see Karmen engage in love and crime in equal measure. Her affair with high-ranking police officer Lamine (Magaye Niang) leads to her death when in a fit of jealous rage he murders her in the opera house where her story is being performed as she dies.

As metaphors for critical writing on the "postcolonial," these two bodies try to disrupt both "the Western discourses of modernity through [. . .] displacing, interrogative subaltern or postslavery narratives" and the perspectives the latter engender (Bhabha 1994: 241). Thus, interruption meets conscious displacing and interrogation within an articulation or representation of difference or an issue of "the not-one, the minus in the origin and repetition of cultural signs in a doubling that will not be sublated into a similitude" (Bhabha 1994: 245). Such a temporal break dictates that the positing of dancing bodies in direct confrontation to the colonial/repressed empire must emerge from the bodies' own perspectives as a composite continuing "negotiation" seeking to sanction the "cultural hybridities" surfacing "in moments of historical transformation" (Bhabha 1994: 2). It also demands that the positing be imagined in "a more transnational and translational sense" (Bhabha 1994: 5).

Of course, hybridity, "a difference within," a subject that inhabits the rim of an "in-between reality" (Bhabha 1994: 13) needs new problematizing in a de-Westernizing context, a process already begun through the idea of contesting contact zones raised in relation to Hardt and Negri above.[4] Affect will further this process by deciphering hybridity within and between discrete dancing bodies. This in turn enables this chapter to produce new ruptures of the past–present continuum, while remaining what Bhabha (1994: 7) would refer to as an "insurgent" cultural act. The past (here represented by the historical colonial narrative of Zouzou/*Zouzou*) is not just recalled, it is renewed and refigured so as to innovate, interrupt, displace, and/or interrogate the performance of "the present" offered by Karmen in *Karmen Geï*. Moreover, as we shall see, the dynamic of past and present invokes notions of being "unhomed" and the "unhomely" due to the distance (in both space and time) between Zouzou and Karmen's dancing bodies. The unhomely provides "a 'non-continuist' problematic that dramatizes – in the figure of woman–" paradoxical boundary drawings (Bhabha 1994: 10), since, as Bhabha reminds us, "To be unhomed is not to be homeless, nor can the 'unhomely' be easily accommodated in that familiar division of social life into private and public spheres." (Bhabha 1994: 9).[5] Zouzou and Karmen's dancing bodies thus problematize and transcend the public–private spatial binary by performing at its interstice, producing what might be best described as a "corporeal-performative-spatial positioning"; which opens up at the point where "we speak of humanity through its differentiations – gender, race, class – that mark an excessive marginality of modernity" (Bhabha 1994: 238). Therefore, when and where past and present "touch contingently, [with] their spatial boundaries metonymically overlapping, [. . .] their margins are (time-)lagged, sutured, by the indeterminate articulation of the "disjunctive" present. The dancing bodies of Karmen and Zouzou thus perform "in the time-lag *in-between* sign and symbol" (Bhabha 1994: 254; emphasis in original). In short, time-lag empowers dancing bodies to rest in a "*performative, deformative* structure that does not simply revalue the contents of a cultural tradition, or transpose values "cross-culturally" (Bhabha 1994: 241; emphasis in original).

Dance, power, and politics

It bears repeating that the key aim of this chapter is to focus on the powers of affect being exercised in two films, which have as central element the African-American/African "black" female dancing body. As Castaldi (2006) notes, the importance of dance in many African societies was used by European colonizers as evidence that Africans were more primitive. However, Neveu Kringelback observes that "dance may well be one of the human activities in which the inseparable nature of reason and emotion becomes evident" (2007: 253). Scholars such as Turner (1968) and Cohen (1993) interpret bodily performance as a potential site of either rebellion or the social control of dangerous emotions. Such work puts in bolder relief Thomas's (2003: 174) argument that dance does not convey "the authentic expressions of the body," which stresses the importance of attending to the functions of dance and dancing forms. Instead, dance overcomes "mind and body dualisms" because it is "a situated embodied practice" able to "highlight and reflect [their] presence in the cultural domain" while crafting a place for investigating the limits and exceptional "possibilities of the "physical body" (Thomas 2003: 93). The chapter shall now explore how an Africanist aesthetic of dance is crucial to Zouzou's and Karmen's dancing bodies, as well as to the chapter's process of "de-Westernizing" their bodies and performance.

The word "Africanist" "include[s] diasporan concepts, practices, attitudes, or forms that have roots or origins in Africa" (Gottschild 2001: 89); its basic non-linear aesthetic and logic challenge Eurocentric perspectives, subconsciously and cognitively, through "Irony, paradox and double entendre, rather than the classical European linear logic of cause, effect, and resolution" (Gottschild 2001: 91). Yet, rather than simply reduce Karmen's and Zouzou's performances to this model or dismiss European dance aesthetics altogether, this chapter proposes to open up a time-lag and craft a contested contact zone that doubles as an unhomed and unhomely space.

Thus, not only is the chapter's emergent/insurgent approach potentially de-Westernizing, it is also a "beyond-binaries" strike at an exhausted but still insidious colonial trope about dance and "black" bodies: the African(ist) presence as primitive. Building on Castaldi, the authors of this chapter argue that the "primitive" is a European psychological pathology that emerged from a purported Enlightenment period to posit "the black (dancing) body as the screen upon which Europeans projected" their irrational fears, dreams, and wishes: "the European concept of the Other" could not exist without this trope (Gottschild 2001: 92). These authors' perception of "primitive" highlights the latter's additional significations of threat, prohibition/illegitimacy, stylishness and seductiveness, not least because most of "modern dance is 'primitive to a degree' and some have totally borrowed the primitive mould" (Gottschild 2001: 92, paraphrasing Louis Horst). Put differently, the "primitive" re-turned into a dance political weapon.[6]

In "a rationalized and technocratic culture [. . .], the mind and the body" represent "culture" and "nature" respectively (Thomas 1995: 6). The body is supposedly "pre-linguistic," represents some inner emotional condition, exists hypothetically "outside language," and does not experience "the (cultural) conventions of discourse" (Thomas 1995: 6). Consequently, body motion is a "material reality" only able to reveal a speaker's real attitude, while speech constitutes the representation because it can "cover over that [same] 'real' attitude" (Thomas 1995: 6).

The chapter's point here is to emulate Thomas and locate the origin of her assertion within Western thought. Descartes's "Cogito, ergo sum" or "I am thinking, therefore I exist" (Cottingham 2000: 107), emphatically made thinking by its very nature separate from the material sphere and thus constitutive of the human subject, "capable of existing without any physical substrate whatsoever" (Cottingham 2000: 107). Western cultural thought grabbed Descartes's idea only to be "dominated by the privileging of the rational thinking subject and the relegation of the Other to a subservient position": i.e., reason over emotions, culture over nature, objectivity over subjectivity (Thomas 1995: 6).

In short, the much-debated mind/body split must be de-Westernized through Zouzou's and Karmen's dancing bodies, but without advancing some form of "proliferation of 'alternative histories of the excluded'" (Bhabha 1994: 6). Instead, within a de-Westernizing framework, this chapter affects/transforms the basis "for making international connections," the "currency of critical comparativism, or aesthetic judgement" (Bhabha 1994: 6). Accordingly, its de-Westernizing process and theory is unhomed or unhomely at the same time as it unhomes Zouzou's and Karmen's dancing bodies from Western canons of interpretation – feminist, or otherwise. Given that "[d]ifferences in culture and power are constituted through the social conditions of enunciation" (Bhabha 1994: 242), this chapter de-Westernizes Zouzou and Karmen/the "black" body and affect by introducing a transcendent time-lag, a split, but also by transforming sites of enunciation so as to expose "the fact that the hegemonic structures of power are maintained in a position of authority through a *shift* in vocabulary in the position of authority" (Bhabha 1994: 242). This introduction-transformation process can only succeed in full if combined with the Africanist dance aesthetic, which must now be broken down into interconnected characteristics. Gottschild (2001) suggests the following five: (1) the all-encompassing aesthetic of "the cool";[7] (2) embracing the conflict; (3) polycentrism/polyrhythm; (4) high-effect juxtaposition; and (5) ephebism.[8]

From Zouzou to Karmen: constructing the affective female body

Zouzou is a film that has the performativity of the lead actress – Josephine Baker – at the center of the narrative. As a key "black" female figure of tremendous cultural importance, any engagement with Baker needs to examine "challenges to the politics of the visible that her work and legacy pose" (Cheng 2011: 39). Previous academic focus on *Zouzou* is one that has clearly been placed in the context of time and space as it relates to France rather than the African/ist experience in Europe (see Sherzer 2006, Ezra 1996, Conway 2004). Although all different, these approaches all have one key element in common; they place their readings of *Zouzou* firmly in the historical and cultural context of "French cinema," with little or no interrogation of that terminology. Julian comments that Baker's films, seen from this angle, are no more "than vehicles for *French* exploration of racial identity and national belonging" (2009: 48; emphasis in original).

Baker starred in four "French" films.[9] Playing a Martinican in *Zouzou* (her first sound film), Baker is one of the most publicized figures representing "the racist and sexist history of objectification and of desire that makes up the phenomenon of European primitivism, or conversely, the idealization of black female agency" (Cheng 2011: 3). Located between these two poles, Baker's dancing body can be seen as an affective rendering of gendered agency whilst acknowledging the surrounding colonial and imperial discourses which cannot be unfound(ed)/divorced fully from the space, narrative and reception of the film text *Zouzou*.

Following this line of thinking, it is worth emphasizing that Baker was an uncontested star in 1920s and 1930s French cinema, which was going through a predominantly colonial-imperialist period routinely depicting "black" people's so-called inability to embrace French culture, as shown in all four films from this period that feature Baker. In all these films, she is corporeally ambiguous, her

Figure 3.1 Zouzou (Marc Allégret, 1934).

Afro-diasporic blackness is a construct-gaze pregnant with historical, theoretical, and critical bearings on French "National" cinema; Baker had to make up for being an untrained actress not fluent in French who, additionally, had to bring her culturally imbued stage skills (for example, music hall) to the movie screen. Her dancing body, e.g., as Zouzou, refused/refuses any form of imprisonment; it questions the essence of European civilization and thought and resignifies if not politicizes the notion of the primitive. In this context, Lepécki (2004: 136) rightly asks: "how can we discuss [Baker's] performances in terms of a practice of complexity with counteracts of resistance performed by less visible bodies of colonized Africans?" Lepécki's question raises, in turn, the issue of agency that this chapter looks at through Zouzou's dancing body and an acknowledgment of what Avery Gordon identified as "improperly buried bodies": abject bodies, even in death, denied place and peace by history's hegemonies (Lepécki 2004: 136; quoting Gordon). Zouzou transforms performance into a contested space where "performativity," i.e. that which is hidden or disguised, might be investigated. Indeed, Diamond reminds us that the "real" is always mediated, and presence always traceable and retraceable by what it appears to exclude (2000: 67). As this chapter aims to demonstrate, the affective embodiment of Zouzou is, in fact, the site of a colonial rupture and time-lag and unhomeliness that challenges the very foundations of the colonial narrative.

At a midpoint in *Zouzou*, the girls in the costume department dress (or rather, undress) Zouzou as a chorus girl. Thrilled, she runs to show her new glamorous look to Jean and begins to dance on the stage. Baker's dance on the stage is remarkable. Previously in the film, we see the highly structured, heavily choreographed dances of the chorus girls, but Zouzou's first stage presentation is pure dynamism. Rejecting all attempts at restraint, order or style she moves her body as she pleases. Engaging with her own shadow, Zouzou moves her fingers in an imitation of a child's shadow puppet display and proceeds to imitate a variety of popular dance movements such as the Charleston, the Shimmy and (the ironically named) Black Bottom. However, as Gottschild notes, although the "white" audience would be able to recognize, in Baker's dancing, styles they themselves practiced, Baker was actually engaging in "black dances" which included the "improvised torso and limb movements emblematic of the Africanist dancing body. . . that rhythmically articulated the breasts, belly and buttocks and were essentially the movements of 1920 American fad dances" (2003: 158). Whether or not the average 1930s dancer was aware of this, many of these popular dances had been based on African dance movements such as the Juba that saw dancers use their own bodies to create rhythms via the slapping of areas such as backs, buttocks, and cheeks. These complex polyrhythms moved from Africa, often via the slave plantations, and in turn directly influenced popular dance styles such as ragtime, jazz and even rock 'n' roll (Dehn 1989). Therefore, "the black dancing body (a fiction based on reality, a fact based on illusion)" had "infiltrated and informed the shapes and changes of the American dancing body" (Gottschild 2003: 14). In this way, Baker's dancing body acts as self-aware site of disruption and de-Westernization. In one section of the above dance she mimics soldiers shooting, she utilizes a vision of "white" supremacy and yet disrupts it via her laughing and parodic attitude. Her body itself is simultaneously the embodiment of the colonial tradition and the site of its disruption. As Francis notes, "objectified, she mobilized the power of objects in the mise-en-scène of her films and the staging of her live performances to represent her ideas about herself and the world" (2009: 249). In this way the affective body is one that engages with the structures in process of self-awareness and self-knowledge and engages the viewer in an act of disruption via the refusal to be a "known" body. In the process of affect, as previously stated, there can never be a universal pattern or construction of "knowing" the bodily space (Gregg and Seigworth 2011: 3). In her dance, Zouzou (Baker) points to, and then parodies, the tensions and social structure that would seek to contain her body. Her final song, trapped in a birdcage dressed in fine white feathers, singing about her long lost Haiti (which the film has already clearly stated she is not from), highlights the racial and national tensions that result in Zouzou being unable to claim Jean as her own. When Zouzou sings in that cage, her sense of loss is centered on her own subjectivity. If she is mourning "an end of an era," as Ezra (2000: 112–113) argues, then Zouzou's lament is a desire to escape from Martinique (domination/French colonial imperialism) to Haiti (a free country). Consequently, because she can aspire to Haiti – a symbol of freedom – she should be allowed an outer-national (historical) point of enunciation since she cannot be positioned as de-facto accomplice, agent of or apologist for French colonial imperialism. The birdcage song needs an outside-in reading (Haiti/San Domingo-France) doubling as an outer-national perspective. Crucial to this reading model is the collapse of the French colonial imperialist structure caused by the only victorious "black" slave revolt in the New World, i.e. the late-eighteenth-century San Domingo revolution led by Toussaint L'Ouverture (see James 1963; Scott 2004). Toussaint L'Ouverture and the San Domingo revolt can

Figure 3.2 Zouzou (Marc Allégret, 1934).

signify Zouzou's literal escape or jump from the birdcage, as well as giving Zouzou her symbol of freedom (Haiti) back. Conversely, Zouzou's escape or jump cannot be interpreted solely from the perspective of either the collapsed structure of European colonial imperialism (in San Domingo) or "the ruins of the [mid-1930s French] Third Republic" (Ezra 2000: 102).

Moving from *Zouzou* to *Karmen Geï* this chapter relocates its study from an Africanist woman in colonial France to an African woman in postcolonial Senegal. It is pursuing its exploration of how an affective reading of the dancing body reveals new pathways for free interpretation and challenge of the Western (and) patriarchal constructions of the "black" female body.

As Brennan states in her study on the transmission of affect, "when you walk in a room you can often *feel* the atmosphere" (2004: 2; emphasis added). The opening scene of *Karmen Geï* offers an ideal example of this. Situated in a female prison in the notorious Gorée Island, the camera opens to Karmen; tall, beautiful, and highly sensual she sits facing the camera, with her legs exposed from upper inner thigh down, opening and closing in time to the beat of the drums that surround her. She moves to standing and starts to dance. The crowd of surrounding women goes wild. Her body calls toward and is responded to by the beat of the drum as she searches for the face that she wishes to engage with; she locates and captures it in her stare and dances closer. The seated woman stares captivated at her. Her green police uniform and her seated position indicate a position of authority but the dancing woman controls the arena. Her dancing movements become smaller, her arms lower, her feet move along the ground and her hips and legs begin to offer more definite and more undulating thrusts until she reaches the site of her attention. She lifts her black loincloth (*sër*), seemingly held around her waist by a string of (white) beads known as *fer* (highly sensual/eroticized by both women and men) to expose the inner, red, short wrapping (*bèèco*), and she dances between the seated woman's legs and gradually pulls her up to dance with her. The crowd of moving, shouting, and cheering women heightens the mood, and as the drums become even more frenetic they surround the two dancing figures that are now engaged fully in their dance. As the heightened sense of lesbian

Figure 3.3 Karmen Geï (Joseph Gaï-Ramaka, 2001).

eroticism grows, the taller woman controls the green-clad woman's movements by controlling the rhythm via holding her shirt and moving her legs in a clearly sexual rhythm between her dance partner's legs. As the camera pulls back we see the walls of a prison and the cityscape of modern-day Dakar behind it.

Charting in words the movements of the body is a challenge that has faced dance studies since its conception and to convey an "atmosphere" or "force of affect", such as we experience in the opening sequence of *Karmen Geï*, is even more difficult. With reference to the affective body, two elements are key. The first is that all bodies, regardless of race, gender age or ethnicity, are never defined by themselves alone, they are not singular items but always engage in "the field or context of [their] force-relations" (Gregg and Seigworth 2011: 3). The second is the Spinozan notion of "not yet knowing" a body (Gregg and Seigworth 2011: 4). The body is in constant flux and there can never be a universal pattern or construction of "knowing" the bodily space and its vicarious "doings" and "undoings" (Gregg and Seigworth 2011: 3). Referring to the above dance sequence we can see demonstrations and articulations of these tensions. Returning to Gottschild's articulation of the cool, we see that despite the highly energetic movements of Karmen's limbs and the highly suggestive thrusts of her pelvis, her face remains engaged and smiling. She is calm (not frenzied like many of the women around her) and in control of her actions (cool), whilst simultaneously her body seems to flow and move on its own volition (hot). She personifies Gottschild's Africanist "high-affect juxtaposition" (2001: 96). Surrounding her we have the control of the prison walls and guards but she expresses a state of absolute freedom. The act of seduction is itself a disruptive act, as the exchange is between two women, and Karmen excludes any male/patriarchal gaze from her interactions with Angelique. She engages in a "nonlinear, non-narrative, movement experience" (Gottschild 2001: 13); she cannot be simply defined but instead becomes the site of multiple forces, doings and undoings. The interplay between her open and moving clothing is placed in contrast to Angelique's set and rigid police uniform. Thomas notes that societal desire to control and hide the body has resulted in the move toward the "control and privatisation of the body. . . (the body) to be classified as the dangerous 'other; to culture'" (Thomas 1995: 7). Clothing and adornments, as items which cover/uncover the body, are as "demonstration of identity. . . an inevitable political act" (Ross 2008: 12). In *sabar,* the dance style being performed by Karmen, Castaldi notes "the more skilled the dancer, the more she will undress and expose in the dancing circle" (2006: 82). Thus, it is not Karmen's casual display of her body that is in itself a challenge to Senegalese culture and society since, as Dovey notes, it is permissible in the *sabar* ritual and tradition (2009: 245); what Karmen demonstrates is her ability to disrupt the structures of power and control in her open embrace and control of the political body (Angelique), something that she will continue in her impact on Lamine (the high-ranking police officer who becomes her lover, and eventual killer). In parts of Africa, dance "serves as an index to the value system that enables the community to interpret and express the various events of life" (Nii-Yartey 2009: 17). With this in mind, Karmen is imbued with the historical, political, and social life of Senegal (or what we might refer to as the force-relations of life in Senegal). She is more than an embodiment of cultural politics; she is a moving, vibrant body who will engage with all aspects of herself and her physical presence as a living part of the system that surrounds her. As Wendy James notes, "What can be said in language does not fully match what is going on in life" (2003: 92). This relates directly with Clough's notion of affectivity "as a substrate of potential bodily response, often automatic responses in excess of consciousness" (Clough 2007: 2). As the above analysis of the opening sequence illustrates, therein Karmen is "temporarily outside meaning" (Massumi 1996: 235); she becomes temporarily "unhomed" from dominant dialogues of race and gender and in short, she is performing "in the time-lag *in-between* sign and symbol" (Bhabha 1994: 254; emphasis in original). In her affective moment she defies the aim to constrain her to the dialogue of Carmen (negative) and offers an African engagement with a new mode of female being. She is not a "black Carmen." Rather, as Castaldi notes the dance acts as "the privileged space between the material and the spiritual [. . .] the living memory of a dialogue between past and present, time and space, ancestral spirit and quotidian life" (2006: 3). In this way Karmen engages not only in the "here and now," but operates as a locus of the affective rendering of historical, social and cultural experiences and narratives. Like with Zouzou, misrecognition can take place in those who desire to utilize Karmen's body to support their own narratives. This misrecognition would allow for Zouzou to be reduced to no more than the black female "Other" in French cinema and Karmen to become an exotic rendering of a Western narrative. However, although she engages with past renderings of an archetypal female figure, Karmen is far from a universalized vision of womanhood (which removes the specificity of her black body), not a saint or a sinner (reduced to a purely sexual subject), and not a figure to aspire to or one to lament (female victim). She is not a singular entity; she is the locus of the force-relations that surround her within her temporary unhomedness or the time-lag between sign and symbol where she performs. She is "anchored in a time, place, a particular culture" (Dovey 2009: 248), and she is an embodied site of affective power. Dovey accurately criticizes Hutcheons' reading of Karmen as a simple indigenizing of the Carmen narrative to conclude "*Karmen Geï* renders the very idea of

Figure 3.4 Karmen Geï (Joseph Gaï-Ramaka, 2001).

indigenization irrelevant" (Dovey 2009: 251). Unlike Bizet's Carmen, she will not die a shamed woman, but one to be exulted and admired, an Africanist vision of affective passion. With reference to the purposes of the de-Westernization project, the reframing of *Karmen Geï* as an intricate part of a film aesthetics in an "African" cinema tradition seeking to articulate new modes of being is a highly important one.

Conclusion

This chapter began by stating that "the past" of Zouzou/*Zouzou* is not just recalled, it is renewed and refigured so as to innovate, interrupt, displace, and/or interrogate "the performance of the present" found in Karmen/*Karmen Geï*. Its affected reading of Karmen and Zouzou's discrete bodies has openly sought not to constrain, control or reduce the body to stereotypes. Rather, the chapter has juxtaposed these bodies in order to more clearly posit them as both sites of motion and sites in movement. The moving, but also desired, affective and transformative, bodies of Karmen and Zouzou articulate, through their very being, questions of difference and the gaps or schisms in time and place: they exist in a time-lag, as a contact zone between past and present and sign and symbol and, as such, allow an interrogation of these terms. They act also as a point of rupture in colonial/postcolonial narratives: Karmen does not die like Bizet's tragic heroine, she moves toward a new state of being (via the song and dance unfolding below the site of her "real" death); while Zouzou clearly does not dance only at the behest of colonial France. Instead, they are "unhomed" from Western canons of interpretation and toward a new mode of understanding.

Notes

1 This chapter is using the terms "black" and/or "African/ist" dependent on the topic being discussed. However, it needs to be acknowledged that these are problematic terms and this is not a conflation of non-white women into the over-arching category of "black." Rather, space dictates a choice of terms and these were felt most applicable to this work.
2 See Robinson and Tormey (2010) for issues related to this.
3 Therefore, these authors take exception to Hardt and Negri's (2000: 143–145) simplistic objection that the "postcolonial" is defined by writers like Homi Bhabha "as critical of, yet, caught up in an old model of power defined by binary opposition and sovereign domination."
4 Contact zones in this instance refers to areas/forms which allow the intermingling of two or more cultures (Pratt 1992).
5 Bhabha's context, different from these authors', is specifically about the ambivalent structure of "the civil State as it draws its rather paradoxical boundary between the private and the public spheres."
6 The complex work of Katherine Dunham (1909–2006), "black" American anthropologist, singer, famous choreographer and dancer, embodies potent illustrations of these issues. See Perpener (2001: 129–155).
7 It is an attitude wherein to be cool is to not be cold, snobbish or detached.
8 Ephebism means youth in ancient Greek. For further details on these five characteristics of the Africanist dance aesthetic, see Gottschild (2001: 96, 93, 94, and 95).
9 In addition to *Zouzou*, Baker starred in *The Siren of the Tropics* (1927), *Princesse Tam-Tam* (dir. Edmond T. Gréville, 1935) and *Fausse Alerte* (dir. Jacques de Baroncelli, 1940).

References

Bhabha, H. K. (1986) "Foreword: Remembering Fanon – Self, Psyche and the Colonial Condition," in F. Fanon, *Black Skin, White Masks,* London: Pluto Press, pp. vii–xxv.

——(1994) *The Location of Culture,* London and New York: Routledge.

Bignall, S. (2010) *Postcolonial Agency: Critique and Constructivism,* Edinburgh: Edinburgh University Press.

Brennan, T. (2004) *The Transmission of Affect,* Ithaca, NY: Cornell University Press.

Castaldi, F. (2006) *Choreographies of African Identities: Negritude, Dance, and the National Ballet of Senegal,* Urbana, Ill.: University of Illinois Press.

Cheng, A. A. (2011) *Second Skin: Josephine Baker and the Modern Surface,* Oxford: Oxford University Press.

Clough, P. T. (ed.) (2007) *The Affective Turn: Theorising the Social,* Durham, NC: Duke University Press.

Cohen, B. B. (1993) *Sensing, Feeling, and Action: The Experiential Anatomy of Body-Mind Centering,* North Hampton, Mass.: Contact Editions.

Conway, K. (2004) *Chanteuse in the City: The Realist Singer in French Film,* Berkeley, Calif.: University of California Press.

Cottingham, J. (2000) "Descartes," in R. Monk and F. Rapahael (eds.), *The Great Philosophers,* London: Phoenix Paperbacks, pp. 93–134.

Dehn, M. (1989) *The Spirit Moves: A History of Black Social Dance on Film, 1900–1986,* New York: Dance Time Publications.

Deleuze, G. (1986) *Cinema 1: The Movement Image,* Minneapolis, Minn.: University of Minnesota Press.

Diamond, E. (2000) "Performance and Cultural Politics," in L. Goodman and J. de Gay (eds.), *The Routledge Reader in Politics and Performance,* London and New York: Routledge, pp. 66–70.

Dovey, L. (2009) *African Film and Literature: Adapting Violence to the Screen,* New York: Columbia University Press.

Ezra, E. (1996) "Silents Are Golden: Staging Community in *Zouzou,*" *French Cultural Studies,* 7 (20): 149–161.

——(2000) *The Colonial Unconscious: Race and Culture in Interwar France,* Ithaca, NY: Cornell University Press.

Featherstone, M. (2010) "Body, Image and Affect in Consumer Culture," *Body and Society,* 16 (1): 193–221.

Francis, T. (2009) "The Audacious Josephine Baker: Stardom, Cinema and Paris," in D. C. Hine, T. D. Keaton, and S. Small (eds.), *Black Europe and the African Diaspora,* Urbana, Ill.: University of Illinois Press, pp. 238–259.

Gilman, S. (1989) *Sexuality: An Illustrated History,* London: Wiley.

Gottschild, B. D. (2001) "Stripping the Emperor: The Africanist Presence in American Concert Dance," in S. S. Walker (ed.), *African Roots/American Cultures: Africa in the Creation of the Americas,* Lanham, Md.: Rowman & Littlefield, pp. 89–103.

——(2003) *The Black Dancing Body: A Geography from Coon to Cool,* Basingstoke: Palgrave Macmillian.

Gregg, M. and Seigworth, G. (2011) *The Affect Theory Reader,* Durham, NC: Duke University Press.

Hardt, M. and Negri, A. (2000) *Empire,* Cambridge, Mass.: Harvard University Press.

Henderson, C. (2010) *Imagining the Black Female Body: Reconciling Image in Print and Visual Culture,* Basingstoke: Palgrave Macmillan.

James, C. L. R. (1963) *The Black Jacobins: Toussaint L'Ouverture and the San Domingo Revolution*, New York: Vintage. First published 1938.

James, W. (2003) *The Ceremonial Animal: A New Portrait of Anthropology*, Oxford: Oxford University Press.

Jules-Rosette, B. (2007) *Josephine Baker in Art and Life: The Icon and the Image*, Urbana, Ill.: University of Illinois Press.

Julian, E. (2009) "Now You See It Now You Don't: Josephine Baker's Films of the 1930s and the Problem of Color," in D. C. Hine, T. D. Keaton, and S. Small (eds.), *Black Europe and the African Diaspora*, Urbana, Ill.: University of Illinois Press, pp. 48–62.

Lepécki, A. (2004) "The Melancholic Influence of the Postcolonial Spectral: Vera Montero Summons Josephine Baker," in H. Raphael-Fernandez (ed.), *Blackening Europe: The African American Presence*, London and New York: Routledge, pp. 121–139.

Massumi, B. (1996) "The Autonomy of Affect," in P. Patton (ed.), *Deleuze: A Critical Reader*, Oxford: Blackwell.

——(2002) *Parables for the Virtual: Movement, Affect, Sensation (Post-Contemporary Interventions)*, Durham, NC: Duke University Press.

Nayar, P. K. (2009) "Postcolonial Affects: Victim Life Narratives and Human Rights in Contemporary India 1," *Postcolonial Text*, 5 (4): 1–22.

Neveu Kringelbach, H. (2007) "'Cool Play': Emotionality in Dance as Resource in Senegalese Urban Women's Associations," in H. Wulff (ed.), *The Emotions: A Cultural Reader*, Oxford and New York: Berg Press.

Nelson, S. (2007) *The Color of Stone: Sculpting the Black Female Subject in Nineteenth-Century America*, Minneapolis, Minn.: University of Minnesota Press.

Nii-Yartey, F. (2009) "Principles of African Choreography: Some Perspectives from Ghana," in J. Butterworth and L. Wildschut (eds.), *Contemporary Choreography: A Critical Reader*, London and New York: Routledge, pp. 254–258.

Perpener, J. O., III (2001) *African-American Concert Dance: The Harlem Renaissance and Beyond*, Urbana, Ill.: University of Illinois Press.

Pratt, M. L. (1992) *Imperial Eyes: Travel Writing and Transculturation*, London and New York: Routledge.

Robinson, A. and Tormey, S. (2010) "Living in Smooth Space: Deleuze, Post Colonialism and the Subaltern," in S. Bignall and P. Patton (eds.), *Deleuze and the Postcolonial*, London and New York: Routledge, pp. 41–61.

Ross, R. (2008) *Clothing: A Global History*, London and New York: Polity Press.

Shaviro, S. (2010) *Post Cinematic Affect*, Winchester: Zero Books.

Scott, D. (2004) *Conscripts of Modernity: The Tragedy of Colonial Enlightenment*, Durham, NC: Duke University Press.

Sherzer, D. (2006) "Nationalizing and Segregating Performance: Josephine Baker and Stardom in *Zouzou* (1934)," *Post-Script*, 26 (1): 13–19.

Turner, V. (1968) *The Drums of Affliction: a Study of Religious Processes Among the Ndembu of Zambia*, Oxford: Clarendon Press.

Thomas, H. (1995) *Dance, Modernity and Culture: Explorations in the Sociology of Dance*, London and New York: Routledge.

——(2003) *The Body, Dance, and Memory*, Basingstoke: Palgrave Macmillan.

Wilson, J., Sandru, C., and Welsh, S. L. (2010) 'General Introduction', in J. Wilson, C. Sandru, and S. Welsh (eds), *Rerouting the Postcolonial: New Directions for the New Millennium*, London and New York: Routledge, pp. 1–14.

4 African frameworks of analysis for African film studies

Sheila J. Petty

The primacy of Western thought in the disciplines of digital theory and art history has become a much debated subject of late, with globalization, knowledge economies, and the accompanying digital evolution often considered through Western criteria. Certainly, as Chika Okeke-Agulu notes, "this tendency to insinuate the importance of European cultural traditions" of art history disseminated through globalization processes, shuts down any possibility for exploring how alternative concepts of art might derive from other traditions (2007: 206). Furthermore, Okeke-Agulu argues that there are two ways to view this new form of colonization. The first involves the predominance of Westocentric criteria with indigenous cultures being forced to adopt these standards even though this will result in an extermination of "alternative or opposing discourses from the non-Western world" (Okeke-Agulu 2007: 206). The second view involves indigenous discourses forging a globalized art history by forming alternative configurations of art histories, creating transnational dialogue across cultures (Okeke-Agulu 2007: 207).

The second view offers the potential for resistance and more closely parallels the preoccupations of some African artists and filmmakers working in postcolonial contexts. This chapter will draw on Okeke-Agulu's assertions and apply them to African film theory. It will begin by questioning the very nature of "postcolonial frameworks" and notions of "the global" and their relevance to African film studies. It will go on to demonstrate that African and African diasporic theory not only has a critical role in the discussion of African and African diasporic film texts, but also a long-established history of contributing in a meaningful way to debates surrounding the nature of globalization and its effects on culture. Finally, the chapter will then turn to Édouard Glissant's notion of relational poetics because it visualizes culture and art production as an unfolding process, subject to both internal and external cultural contacts where the "synthesis/genesis" of identity and aesthetics is continually evolving (Glissant 1997: 174). Difference and commonality, then, can both be accommodated in this system as artistic expression (in this case, cinema) and becomes a process rather than a static concept. Ultimately, the chapter hopes to demonstrate that simply transposing Western theories and methods from "Western-based" film studies to African and African diasporic cinemas can be interventionist and does not always adequately uncover the deep meaning of the African texts, and hence, this chapter advocates the adoption of an African "world sense" to use Oyeronke Oyewumi's term.

One of the factors most overlooked in discussions of African and African diasporic theories is that they were among the first to engage the processes of colonialism, postcolonialism, and the transnational nature of contemporary cultural identities within the auspices of globalization. The twin poles from which early theory was derived, namely Middle Passage slavery and colonization, are counted among the first markers in the development of the industrial revolution. As Martha Donkor notes, "colonization was the accumulation of wealth through the exploitation of foreign resources, both human and natural" and it "siphoned wealth from colonized territories to shore up industries in their countries, while colonized sites remained marginal to the political economy that industrialization engendered" (Donkor 2005: 28). In this sense, without the global circulation of labor and goods from Africa and the diaspora, the prosperity of Europe, the Caribbean and North and South America would have been severely truncated. Yet, as Michael Hanchard argues, "people of African descent have often been depicted as the antithesis of Western modernism and modern subjectivity" (1999: 245). More to the point, what has been and continues to be overlooked is the fact that thinkers and theorists of African descent "have utilized ideas about racial selfhood and collective identity, capitalism and socialism, justice and democracy that emerged as the economic, political, normative, religious, and cultural consequences of the epoch in which they lived" (Hanchard 1999: 245). Like Foucault, Benjamin, Lacan, and other Western theorists, African and African diasporic writers and theorists such as W. E. B. Du Bois, Frantz Fanon, Édouard Glissant, Paul Gilroy, Achille Mbembe, V. Y. Mudimbe, Léopold Sédar Senghor, and Kwame Nkrumah, among many others, have sought to explicate their understanding of the world from their own unique positions in the flow of global histories. Perhaps most importantly, many African and African diasporic subjects possess specific knowledge of what it means to live African and African diasporic identity both historically and personally.

The goal of de-Westernizing theory when analyzing African and African diasporic works is not to restrict the application of Western theory but rather to broaden such analysis by bringing to the fore imperatives within such artworks that may be overlooked or minimized through the use of purely Western standards. The problem is a complex one because there is understanding to be gained by the application of outside theory in terms of freshening debate or providing new perspectives. Certainly African and African diasporic thinkers and theorists tap into Western or European theory in the course of their work. The problem arises when outside theoretical paradigms or imperatives become defining criteria without qualification. For example, to use Benjamin or Foucault's theories of culture to discuss African or African diasporic film without also acknowledging their Western limitations is to impose criteria on artworks that were not framed with those imperatives in mind. To further the argument, let us consider how Foucault's notion of Bentham's panopticon (1977: 165–168) might be used as a potential metaphor for the power mechanism of colonialism. In such a reading, the colonial authorities might become the occupants of the panopticon's tower, surveilling colonized subjects who are held passive by laws that denigrate their cultures and religions and often deprive them of their traditional lands. On the surface it is a promising metaphor: colonial authorities control language, education, economic, and political activities and have the right to determine where an individual might dwell. In other words, Foucault's notion of discipline and power can definitely account for how colonial authorities function as oppressors. Taken at face value, Foucault's position would seem to suggest that Africans were passive victims of colonialism, which deprives them of their long histories of resistance. The insistence on the passivity of those under the tower's control is a limitation of Foucault's original work and therefore does not allow for consideration of challenge, resistance, subversion, and rebellion experienced by ex-colonized subjects. The tower may control the gaze out, but the oppressed control the gaze back.

Hanchard makes a salient point when he writes that African and African diasporic peoples have often been treated by Western theory as having no history of their own (1999: 250–251). The thinkers and theorists generated by these cultures have responded by creating counter histories with the "project of historical recovery that at the same time presupposes a new or, at minimum, distinctive, collective consciousness for African and African-derived peoples in the face of a perceived erasure of history by the West" (Hanchard 1999: 252). The exact nature of this collective consciousness may be highly debated by African and African diasporic theory, but it is the interchange of ideas on what constitutes black history, identity and culture that makes these theories so rich in application (Petty 2008: 15).

W. E. B. Du Bois offers a case in point. His most well-known work, *The Souls of Black Folk*, was originally published in 1903 and is considered to be one of the most important early works on African-American identity and one that still generates debate today. Written at a time when the segregationist Jim Crow laws in the American South signaled the failure of governments to deliver on the equality promised to African Americans following the Civil War, *The Souls of Black Folk* takes stock of the social, economic, and political situation faced by African Americans in the south. Du Bois's re-evaluation of slavery and the ultimate failure of emancipation led him to develop the notion of "double-consciousness" as a means of explicating the disjunction felt by many of his African-American contemporaries. Du Bois describes double-consciousness as a state of irresolvable tension in which "one ever feels his two-ness, – an American, a Negro; two souls, two thoughts, two unreconciled strivings; two warring ideals in one dark body, whose dogged strength alone keeps it from being torn asunder" (1994: 2). From this perspective, the promise of emancipation (true equality and access to citizenship), cut down by the imposition of segregation (denial of equality and citizenship based on racial difference), placed African Americans in an untenable position: do they cleave to the validity of their own culture or do they accept the denigration of that culture on the faint hope of acceptance as an American citizen? Although the Jim Crow laws have been repealed for some decades, the continued racism in American society still renders Du Bois's concept timely and open for debate.

In the film *Daughters of the Dust* (1991), filmmaker Julie Dash, influenced by Du Bois's work, tells the semi-fictional story of the Peazant family who have gathered together in the Sea Islands off South Carolina in 1902 prior to a planned migration to the mainland (Foster 1997: 67). The film, structured in a series of vignettes, focuses primarily on the interplay of the Peazant women whose varying opinions on the reasons for and against migration provide the locus for debate, conflict, and reconciliation. At the center of the narrative is the character of Nana Peazant, the family's elderly matriarch. Nana Peazant comes to represent the preservation of the Gullah culture that the family shares and provides a living connection to the African slaves who founded the culture in the Sea Islands. Still practicing the African spirituality and magic of her African and slave ancestors, Nana Peazant's adherence to the past serves as a marker to measure African-American identity.

Dash illustrates double-consciousness through two of the Peazant women, Viola and Haagar. In Viola's case, she returns from the mainland to join her family for the gathering, bringing with her seemingly rigid Christian missionary beliefs. Haagar, on the other hand, has lived all her life in the Sea Islands but also possesses strong Christian beliefs. Haagar views migration to the mainland as a means of advancing her family economically. At first glance, this may resemble a situation where the colonizing effects of Christianity are responsible for both women valorizing the white cultural imperatives from the mainland. When viewed in the light of double-consciousness, however, the belief systems of both women become much more conflicted and racially charged.

Du Bois writes powerfully that double-consciousness generates a "longing to attain self-conscious manhood, to merge his double self into a better and truer self," without losing what is intrinsic to African American identity (1994: 3). In this light, Viola's religious zeal is based on more than a true faith: Christianity provides her with a cloak of protection against a racist world, a place of acceptance where she is socially powerful and able to mask the importance of race in her life. Over the course of the film, however, she finds her own beliefs challenged by the respect she has for Nana Peazant. Similarly, Haagar's desire to migrate is based on more than the simple desire to further her family's prospects. She sees the opportunity to acculturate to white standards as a means of shedding the legacy of slavery and all it entails. Her strident disregard for Nana Peazant's ways indicates an internalization of the long-term denigration of African American culture that began with slavery and never really abated. In this context, if Christianity is Viola's mask and a means to end the psychological tension of double-consciousness, outright repudiation of her African American heritage becomes Haagar's means of doing the same.

Significantly, Dash resists the urge to offer a tidy solution to the women's conflict. Near the end of the film, Nana Peazant offers the family a charm shaped like a hand and tied to a bible. This offering serves as an act of reconciliation and signals Nana Peazant's desire to bridge the gap opened in the family by religion and migration by tangibly suggesting that the past (her beliefs), the present (represented by the Bible) and the future (distance created by migration) can be overcome by recognizing each is irrevocably connected by the thread of a shared history. When Nana Peazant asks the family to "kiss this hand full of me," Viola is initially reluctant to comply because of the idolatry the charm represents. Haagar furiously prevents her family by force from participating in "this Hoodoo mess," and retreats from the family without possibility of reconciliation. On the surface, Haagar's repudiation of her heritage might be viewed as simple rigidness. Instead, as Du Bois suggests, such refusal is the result of a process of self-hatred engendered by systemic racism and typified by the "inevitable self-questioning, self-disparagement, and lowering of ideals which ever accompany repression and breed in an atmosphere of contempt and hate" (Du Bois 1994: 6). Viola, on the other hand, solves her conflict in a more constructive way. Motivated by respect for Nana Peazant, she first kisses the Bible and then the charm, suggesting that she has regained respect for the African-American culture that underpins her history. Viola thus finds a solution to the tension caused by double-consciousness by coming to embrace both her family's history and her Christianity as complementary identity forces.

African and African diasporic theorists sometimes incorporate Western theory into their work. In doing so, such theorists often reinterpret, reinvent or transform Western theory to account for African and African diasporic imperatives.[1] The works of Frantz Fanon offer a case in point. Born in Martinique in 1925, Fanon belonged to a well-to-do family who had the financial wherewithal to provide him with an excellent French-based education that included such luminaries as Aimé Césaire among his instructors (McCulloch 1983: 2). Choosing to fight for France during World War II, Fanon was confronted by extreme racism which later fuelled his writing and generated such important works as *Black Skin, White Masks* (1952) and *The Wretched of the Earth* (1961) (Alessandrini 1999: 2).

Black Skin, White Masks is of special note here, not just because this was Fanon's first book but also because the volume served as his thesis in psychiatry. The influence of Freudian psychology is clearly evident in the work, but what makes *Black Skin, White Masks* unique is the fact that Fanon appropriated Western psychoanalytical theories to explicate the effect of colonialism on the psychology of both the colonizer and colonized. Among his many innovations in *Black Skin, White Masks,* Fanon mapped out the psychology of othering based on the notion of the gaze. In Fanon's estimation, the gaze of the black man is interpreted by the white colonizer as a threat to his power as if the goal of the black man is to displace him from his social position (1982: 128). This look is then internalized by the black subject as an act of "self-objectification" that compels her/him to internalize the degradation of racism (Fanon 1982: 129). Thus, for Fanon, blackness is a social construct that exists only when it is compared to whiteness (Fanon 1982: 110).

Med Hondo's *Soleil O* (1970) offers an illustrative example. The film chronicles the experiences of an unnamed African immigrant as he arrives in France in search of work. Using avant-garde techniques such as mock interviews, narration, and interpretive recreation scenes, the film explores how racism in the ex-colonial metropolis perpetuates the oppressive legacy of colonialism. Most importantly, the black immigrant goes from bewilderment to resistance by the end of the film.

Fanon's notion of the gaze is especially useful in exploring the interaction between the black immigrant and the white individuals he encounters on his journey through French culture. Initially, the black immigrant arrives in France with great joy for, as Fanon dryly notes, "the country represents the Tabernacle," for those colonized individuals who have embraced French language, education and culture as the epitome of civilization (Fanon 1982: 23). Certainly, the black immigrant shares this position as his narration in the arrival scene reverently intones, "One day I began to study your graphics, read your thoughts, talk Shakespeare and Molière and spout Rousseau." The selection of prominent European writers and philosopher indicates that, for the black immigrant, his French education is a promise of equality with white French culture.

This position is quickly dispelled through a series of scenes in which the black immigrant seeks employment. In each encounter, the black immigrant is measured and rejected based on the color of his skin and through the authoring power of the "white" look. In the first scene, the black immigrant attempts to answer a job posting at a construction site, only to be first sized up and then turned away based on the premise that all Africans are thieves. In the second scene, a hostile garage owner refuses to consider the black immigrant for a job, once again forcing the black immigrant to endure an openly derisive gaze by the garage owner. In a third scene, the black immigrant is confronted in a courtyard by an angry concierge who first takes his visual measure and then opines, "We have enough niggers as it is." Finally, provoked to respond directly, the black immigrant asks in desperation, "Can you please tell me where I came from?" As the concierge retreats in fear, the black immigrant is left to internalize his own frustration.

This process of the look creates, as Fanon argues, "a definitive structuring of the self and of the world – definitive because it creates a real dialectic between my body and the world" (Fanon 1982: 111). Thus, instead of his perception of himself as French, the black immigrant is faced with the knowledge that in France he is African and nothing else. The black immigrant's cry, "Can you please tell me where I came from?" echoes Fanon's own words when he asks, "Where am I to be classified? Or, if you prefer, tucked away" (Fanon 1982: 113). On the surface, this seems to suggest that not only is racism inevitable but so are its deleterious effects on the black psyche. For Fanon, however, racism and its effects may be inevitable, but the black subject possesses a powerful tool to fight back: resistance. Faced with what he describes as "an amputation, an excision, a hemorrhage that splattered my whole body with black blood," Fanon rejects such "revision" of his black identity and instead rebels against the strictures of racism (1982: 112). As Fanon persuasively argues, "there remained only one solution: to make myself known" and by doing so reassert his own subjectivity in the face of racism (1982: 115).

Like Fanon, Hondo is also interested in a revolutionary black identity. Oppressed in every direction from government agencies to employers to local Parisians, the black immigrant is plunged into a psychic break with reality. The end of the film finds the black immigrant howling out his anguish in the woods. Collapsing in exhaustion near an uprooted tree, the black immigrant finds himself circled by photographic images of iconic black and revolutionary leaders, including Patrice Lumumba, Che Guevara, and Malcolm X. The images, each "gazing" at the black immigrant, signals a reformulation of his identity, as he comes to a new revolutionary state. The film's final tag line, "To be continued. . ." suggests that this revelation is only a first step in creating a positive self-identity, which must be linked with revolutionary action. Thus, as Fanon suggests, individuals of color have an obligation to challenge "the historical, instrumental hypothesis" that frames systemic racism in order to "initiate the cycle of my freedom" (Fanon 1982: 231). Thus, like Viola who finds a constructive way to deal with double-consciousness, the black immigrant also discovers strength within himself to resist systemic racism.

Not all African and African diasporic theory is directly preoccupied with the nature of systemic racism: in fact, such theory can be as wide-ranging as the social, political, and cultural challenges faced by these communities. A case in point is Achille Mbembe, a Cameroonian theorist and philosopher whose landmark works such as *On the Postcolony* (2001) have challenged and redefined what it means to be African in a global flow of history and politics. Always provocative, Mbembe's subject matter has ranged from redefining cosmopolitanism to calling for change in the underpinning of African theories of self and culture.

In his essay, "Necropolitics," Mbembe takes on the mechanics of death and violence and considers how both contribute to ethnic violence, a cultural phenomenon that continues to plague Africa as well as other hotspots in the world at large. For Mbembe, "sovereignty" is inextricably linked with the right to "exercise control over mortality and to define life as the deployment and manifestation of power" (2003: 12). By this definition, we express our power as a society by determining how "bodies are inscribed in the order of power," usually through the rule of law or the exercise of politics (Mbembe 2003: 12). As Mbembe points out, many constructs describing this process inherit from modernity the utopic assumption that this power is wielded through politics by subjects who are free and equal agents as "a project of autonomy and the achieving of agreement among a collectivity through communication and recognition" (2003: 13). Yet, autonomy is not the only project of sovereignty: at times, the necropolitics of life and death are also exploited by those whose main goal is *"the generalized instrumentalization of human existence and the material destruction of human bodies and populations"* (Mbembe 2003: 14; emphasis in original). In this case, sovereignty becomes focused on the notion of enemies of the state, and death in particular becomes separated from the notion of equal subjects under a rule of law to unequal subjects whose status is often defined by ethnic terms.

This subject is explored in Fanta Régina Nacro's film, *The Night of Truth* (2004). Set in an imaginary African country, *The Night of Truth* focuses on the struggle between the imaginary Nayak and Bonandé ethnic groups as they struggle for sovereignty of their nation.[2] At the commencement of the film, Colonel Theo, leader of the Bonandé rebels, has called for a summit with President Miossoune, leader of the Nayak, in an attempt to bring peace. Despite reservations on both sides, an agreement is reached for a meeting at the Bonandé compound.

Beneath the surface of the film lies a series of important questions: How can reconciliation occur between ethnic factions when war atrocities have been committed by both sides? Who has the right to determine who lives or dies under those circumstances? What happens to ordinary people when politics become necropolitics based on hatred and prejudice? Is it possible to turn away from the process of necropolitics once its hatred has been unleashed? It is in this context that Nacro's choice to locate the narrative in a fictional country allows her to focus clearly on the human consequences such struggles entail without the restrictions that accompany the depiction of a historical place or event. Thus, these questions are embedded in the film's main sub-plot, which focuses on Edna, the wife of President Miossoune, whose son Michel was killed and then genitally mutilated by an unknown Bonandé soldier. Devastated by grief and rage, Edna is determined to find the identity of the murderer and to administer her form of justice.

The film does not portray Edna as a monster but instead humanizes her by demonstrating the depths of her grief as a mother. In an early scene, Edna visits Michel's grave, accompanied by the President and a host of bodyguards. During the visit, Michel's spirit appears to her, running through the men that surround her. The apparition causes her immense pain and makes her swear to seek revenge for her child's death. Moreover, the horror of Michel's mutilation, which involves the removal of his genitals and stuffing them into his mouth, is also calculated to make Edna's subsequent actions if not acceptable then at least understandable.

Later in the film, Colonel Theo is revealed to be the perpetrator of the war crimes enacted against Michel. Again, the film acts with restraint, portraying Theo as a deeply remorseful man, whose loss of self-control in a moment of blood rage has haunted him since its occurrence. Throughout the film, several of his staff and his wife, Soumari, a leader in her own right, question his single-minded dedication to pursuing peace talks just when the military campaign is on the verge of complete victory. His war crime, however, has made Theo question the validity of sovereignty at the cost of wholesale murder of the Nayaks. Thus, his brutal actions on the field of battle are humanized first by his remorse and then by his desire to find peace with his enemy.

Figure 4.1 The Night of Truth (Fanta Régina Nacro, 2004).

Although *The Night of Truth* takes a generalized overview of the conflict between the Nayak and Bonandé ethnic groups, the structure of this conflict mirrors a common arrangement. The Nayak have a past history of oppressing Bonandé by denying their rights as citizens. The Bonandé are not free of prejudice: throughout the film there are ample examples of the Nayaks described as snakes and the relation of half-truths intended to denigrate the Nayak culture. Mbembe offers insight into the mechanics of such hatred by suggesting "new technologies of destruction are less concerned with inscribing bodies within disciplinary apparatuses as inscribing them, when the time comes, within the order of the maximal economy now represented by the "massacre'" (Mbembe 2003: 34). Under this designation, military conflict is no longer restricted to the combat between soldiers but instead also focuses on doing as much lethal damage to civilians as possible. Annihilation of the other thus becomes the benchmark of success, however this is achieved.

When confronted by Edna at the summit concerning the identity of her son's murderer, Colonel Theo's deep remorse causes him to confess to the crime. Edna sets a trap for him, and eventually kills Theo by roasting him alive over a cooking fire. At first glance, this act of brutality might be read as a reiteration of the Eurocentric stereotype that portrays Africans as savages. In Edna's depiction, however, her act of violence becomes a sort of equivalent justice for the brutality enacted on her child and a testimony to how war can undermine social values. When her crime is discovered, the Nayak and Bonandé militia are on the verge of entering into a blood bath at the peace talks. This is forestalled by two actions. First, President Miossoune shoots his wife dead for her transgression. Then Soumari, Theo's wife, accepts the President's sacrifice and successfully intervenes by convincing the Bonandé militia to set down their weapons. Peace is thus forged by leaders on both sides willing to set aside their personal pain and differences in order to advance their societies in tandem. Whether or not the ending of the film is realistic or pure melodrama, *The Night of Truth* shares with *Daughters of the Dust* and *Soleil O* a desire to resist the inevitabilities of the social

Figure 4.2 The Night of Truth (Fanta Régina Nacro, 2004).

conditions that frame them. Although, as Mbembe argues, "under conditions of necropower, the lines between resistance and suicide, sacrifice and redemption, martyrdom and freedom are blurred," the film chooses to present the hope that collective social will can be a significant power in ending such conflicts (Mbembe 2003: 40).

In an era of slippage between borders and hybridization of cultures, narratives and aesthetic constructs through film art, it seems inevitable that Eurocentric linear configurations of nation and history are being subsumed by newer paradigms of postcoloniality and globalization. For African and African diasporic theorists, however, whose cultures have been forged through slavery and colonization, this is familiar ground. In considering the works of Du Bois, Fanon, Mbembe, or the many other black theorists and thinkers, one is struck by the sense that their concepts of identity are often posited at the confluence of competing flows of history. Édouard Glissant is one such theorist whose works in poetry, literature, journalism as well as theoretical writings are notable for expanding how the interaction between multiple histories and identity formulation are perceived. In particular, Glissant's concept of "le tout-monde" conceives "of the whole world as a network of interacting communities whose contacts result in constantly changing cultural formations" (Britton 2011). In this sense, identity is not a static state but rather one that shifts and continues to evolve as the subject comes into contact with myriad histories.

Born in Martinique and educated in France, Glissant shares with Fanon an Afro-Caribbean culture and a sense that slavery and colonization have had a profound effect on the development of such identities. He differs from Fanon, however, in the sense that Fanon found Afro-Caribbean identities to be fixed within the white gaze, whereas Glissant envisions identity as a "Poetics of Relation," an open-ended process based on "the rhizome of a multiple relationship with the Other" through interaction with global flows of culture and history (Glissant 1997: 16). Such a concept would, in Glissant's view, create a very different poetics for approaching aesthetic content in works of art that would, by necessity, be "latent, open, multilingual in intention, directly in contact with everything possible" (Glissant 1997: 32). From this perspective, aesthetic content would be measured on how it interacts within the text as well as taking into account how it intersects with the outside influences of its age.

Raoul Peck's *Sometimes in April* (2005) uses a relational style in its narrative structure to explore the Rwandan massacre. In many ways, Peck epitomizes transnationality as a filmmaker: born in Haiti, and raised in the Democratic Republic of Congo (former Zaire), Peck was educated in France and Germany, eventually returning to Haiti to serve as Minister of Culture. His works, similarly, have spanned the globe. His feature film, *Man by the Shore* (1993), is set in Haiti and depicts the struggle of a family to survive the Duvalier regime. His documentary, *Lumumba, Death of a Prophet* (Congo, 1991), explores the complex life and legacy of Patrice Lumumba, who rose to power in the Congo after the country achieved independence from Belgium in 1960. *Sometimes in April* shares with these previous works a commitment to exploring African and African diasporic experiences within the contexts of competing global histories and the conflicted relational interplay between Western, African and/or African diasporic imperatives.

The film's narrative structure provides a case in point. The film begins with a medium wide shot of a colonial map of Africa. In its initial composition, Africa is shown in a globalized context as Europe, India, Asia, and South America are visible in the shot. As the camera slowly zooms into the image of Africa, text scrolls up from the bottom of the screen, delineating how colonial strategies of divide and conquer disrupted previously peaceful relations between the Hutu, Tutsi, and Twa cultures of Rwanda. The fact that the shot begins wide and eventually zooms in to Rwanda indicates that the genocide about to be depicted is not simply an African problem: rather, it is an African problem rooted in global flows of history.

The narrative is organized in three distinct thrusts. In the first, the film presents a frame story set in April of 2004 and primarily centered on the character of Augustin Muganza, a Hutu survivor. Near the beginning of the film Augustin receives a letter from his brother, Honoré, who was a popular radio personality at the time of the genocide and whose propaganda broadcasts were instrumental in inflaming the violence. Now on trial in Tanzania by a United Nations Tribunal for his role in the genocide, Honoré asks Augustin to visit him so he can finally reveal how Augustin's wife, Jeanne and their two children died. The letter thus creates narrative suspense by revealing the existence of a mystery surrounding the fate of Augustin's family. The second story strand, which begins in April 1994, depicts the events of the genocide. Although organized around the tragedy that befalls Augustin's family, the story strand also portrays the general disintegration of Rwandan culture by exploring the complex notion of responsibility. In the third, Peck combines newscasts with the fictional struggle of Prudence Bushnell, a member of the US State Department, to spur the US government to action raising questions concerning Western responsibility and racism. This layered structure, which "disrupts the fixed linearity of time," and "abolishes the very notion of a centre and periphery," creates a "poetics of Relation" where static positions are subverted (Glissant 1997: 29, 27). Thus, the viewer must actively participate in weighing the relational implications, or "approximate truth" advanced by each story strand (Glissant 1997: 27).

The climax of the film, centered on the meeting between Augustin and his brother Honoré, demonstrates this principle. The two men are representative of the blurred filial relations characteristic of the genocide: as a broadcaster and member of the ruling Hutu group, Honoré epitomizes both the pursuit of absolute political power and personal ambiguity due to divided loyalties. For example, despite participating in hate propaganda against the Tutsi and urging his brother to be "on the right side" of the political struggle, Honoré rises to the occasion and tries to assist Augustin's family and children to flee to safety despite the personal danger it involves. Faced with the UN Tribunal, Honoré chooses to plead guilty to the criminal charges against him, yet in the film's climax, still remains defiant by accusing Augustin of judging him and "parading your good conscience around as if it's a crown." The statement thus implies that Honoré still feels that his actions were justified, raising questions concerning the legitimacy of the remorse previously expressed through his guilty plea. Peck thus uses such character inconsistencies as a relational tactic for raising debate.

In a later sequence, Jeanne and the boys, depicted in a flashback, are dragged from the car at the roadblock. As Honoré struggles with the soldiers holding him back, he pleads vainly that, "They're ours," a statement alluding to the boys' half-Hutu and half-Tutsi heritage. As the soldiers drive Augustin's young sons along the opposite side of the vehicle, they are visible in a series of fragmented frames seen through the architecture of the vehicle. When the soldiers force the boys to the ground, they disappear from sight. Thus, although the soldiers are visible as they raise their rifles and shoot the boys, the violence itself is masked. The film turns instead to Honoré's reaction as he stares in disbelief at the off-screen violence. This choice serves to emphasize the psychological trauma experienced by Honoré, thereby suggesting that the real cost of this violence is borne by those who witnessed it. Furthermore, the duration of the reaction and the fact that the spectators must imagine the sight Honoré is viewing allows a rest in the narrative for spectators to weigh the ideological merits of the action.

As Glissant argues, "evolving cultures infer Relation" through "the imaginary of the past: a knowledge of becoming" (1997: 1). *Sometimes in April* reflects this process because the film, by couching the Rwandan genocide in the flows of global histories and the relational interplay created by the film's characters, seeks to raise debate across a wide range of spectators. Thus, the film goes beyond a mere fictional recreation of the Rwandan genocide to pose complex questions of responsibility, and in doing so connects Africa to the world.

De-Westernizing African film studies does not involve simply banishing Western theory from discussion. Rather, the goal is to widen debate by the inclusion of African and African diasporic thinkers and theorists who offer a different perspective on history, culture, economics, and politics. As films such as *Soleil O, Daughters of the Dust, The Night of Truth*, and *Sometimes in April* demonstrate, the application of African and African diasporic theory reveals a richness in the films' depictions of history and race that might otherwise be masked by the application of solely Western theoretical criteria. As Du Bois's work suggests, race has a far-reaching role in shaping cultures and their social imperatives and to overlook this importance is to fail to understand an important aspect of social history. Moreover, theorists such as Mbembe, Fanon, and Glissant, who frequently engage and transform Eurocentric theory to suit African diasporic criteria, demonstrate that such theories can have a role in engaging African and African diasporic works through the transformative process. By providing counter histories to Western contexts, such theorists are able to demonstrate how sites of resistance shape their cultures and their art.

Acknowledgments

Special thanks to D. L. McGregor for assistance with and creative discussion of this essay.

Notes

1 Use of Western theory by a person of color is often fraught with tension. For example, Homi K. Bhabha's "The Commitment to Theory" offers in part a response to critics who question his use of "Eurocentric theory" by Lacan and Fanon. For an extended discussion, see Homi K. Bhabha, "Commitment to Theory" in Bhabha (2004).
2 Although beyond the scope of this work, it is worthwhile noting that Hollywood, in particular, has used African ethnic struggles as fertile subject matter. Such films include *Blackhawk Down* (dir. Scott, 2001) and *Hotel Rwanda* (dir. George, 2004).

References

Alessandrini, A. C. (1999) "Introduction: Fanon Studies, Cultural Studies, Cultural Politics," in Anthony C. Alessandrini (ed.), *Frantz Fanon: Critical Perspectives*, London and New York: Routledge, pp. 1–17.

Bhabha, H. K. (2004) *The Location of Culture*, London and New York: Routledge.

Britton, C. (2011) "Edouard Glissant," *The Guardian*, February 13.

Donkor, M. (2005), "Marching to the Tune: Colonization, Globalization, Immigration, and the Ghanaian Diaspora," *Africa Today*, 52 (1): 27–44.

Du Bois, W. E. B. (1994) *The Souls of Black Folk*, New York: Dover Publications Inc.

Fanon, Frantz (1982) *Black Skin, White Masks*, trans. by Charles Lam Markmann, New York: Grove Press.

Foster, G. A. (1997) *Women Filmmakers of the African and Asian Diaspora: Decolonizing the Gaze, Locating Subjectivity*, Carbondale, Ill.: Southern Illinois University Press.

Foucault, M. (1977) *Discipline and Punish: The Birth of a Prison*, New York: Pantheon Books.

Glissant, É. (1997) *Poetics of Relation*, trans. by B. Wing, Ann Arbor, Mich.: University of Michigan Press.

Hanchard, M. (1999) "Afro-Modernity: Temporality, Politics, and the African Diaspora," *Public Culture*, 11 (1): 245–268.

Hiddleston, J. (2009) *Understanding Postcolonialism*, Stocksfield: Acumen Publishing Limited.

Mbembe, A. (2001) *On the Postcolony*, Berkeley, Calif.: University of California Press.

——(2003) "Necropolitics," trans. by L. Meintjes, *Public Culture*, 15 (1): 11–40.

McCulloch, J. (1983) *Black Soul White Artifact: Fanon's Clinical Psychology and Social Theory*, Cambridge: Cambridge University Press.

Okeke-Agulu, C. (2007) "Art History and Globalization," in J. Elkins (ed.), *Is Art History Global?*, London and New York: Routledge, pp. 202–207.

Oyewumi, O. (1997) *The Invention of Women: Making an African Sense of Western Gender Discourses*, Minneapolis, Minn.: University of Minnesota Press.

Petty, S. (2008) *Contact Zones: Memory, Origin, and Discourses in Black Diasporic Cinema*, Detroit, Mich.: Wayne State University Press.

Part II

Narrating the (trans)nation, region, and community from non-Western perspectives

5 De-Westernizing national cinema

Reimagined communities in the films of Férid Boughedir

Will Higbee

The Maghreb must not form the outskirts of Europe or of the Orient. In my work, I say that we are a very important centre. It is here that there was Carthage, and works capable of arriving at a world level can emerge from Tunisian culture.

(Boughedir in Amarger 1994: 15)

[A]utonomous forms of imagination of the community were, and continue to be, overwhelmed and swamped by the history of the post-colonial state. Here lies the root of our post-colonial misery: not in our inability to think out new forms of modern community but in our surrender to the old forms of the modern state. If the nation is an imagined community and if nations must also take the theoretical language of states, then our theoretical language must allow us to talk about community and state at the same time.

(Chatterjee 1993: 11)

The term "transnational cinema" has, over the past decade, been employed in film studies with increasing frequency as a descriptive and conceptual marker as well as shorthand for an international or supranational mode of film production whose impact and reach extends well beyond that of the national sphere. So successful has the application of this conceptual approach been in the Anglo-American academy, that the "national" seems to have been largely displaced or negated, as if it ceases to exist or have any relevance. Yet the national continues to provoke strong opinions and prejudices in the context of cinema, as well as exerting the force of its presence within supposedly "transnational" filmmaking practices (Hjort and Petrie 2007: 12–13). This seems particularly true in the context of many Third or postcolonial cinemas, even if they are marked at the same time by transnational and diasporic cinematic configurations.[1] Filmmaking in the former French colonies of North Africa (Algeria, Morocco, and Tunisia) is a case in point: despite shared cultural, linguistic, and ethnic traits, a "common" history of colonial exploitation and migration to France, as well as regional initiatives such as "Maghreb Cinémas" (an organization founded at the Locarno film festival in 2005 by thirty North African directors with the aim of promoting and safeguarding the interests of "Maghrebi" cinema), the "national" impulse in these cinemas arguably remains stronger than at any time in their respective histories. What Hafez (2006: 226) describes as the "obsession" of Arab cinema with the question of the national reflects the fact that, even though the transnational realities of international or diasporic film production are clear in some, if not all, postcolonial film cultures, the formation or "aspiration" of the national in these cinemas (no matter how problematic it might be) arguably remains stronger than any transnational or "pan-national" impulse.[2]

Whilst not wishing to promote a discourse that simply privileges the national over the transnational – preferring to consider these terms as interdependent and interrelated, not mutually exclusive or in binary opposition – this chapter will, nonetheless, explore how we might "de-Westernize" the concept of the national in relation to non-Western (and more specifically postcolonial) film cultures by using national cinema as a means of thinking about new forms of community as they relate to nation.[3] To address the question of how national cinema might be rethought outside of Western frameworks of nationalism – and here it should be made clear that the concept of the West is seen as much in ideological terms as it is in relation to any geographical boundaries – this chapter draws on the interventions of the Indian political scientist Partha Chatterjee (1986, 1993). Chatterjee's theorizing of the national in (post-)colonial cultures offers fruitful ground for "de-Westernizing" national cinema as well as for analyzing how the concept has evolved following the "gradual eclipse of Third World nationalism" (Shohat 2003: 51) that informed the framing of debates around national cinema in the context of decolonization in the 1950s and 1960s, not to mention the theoretical and practical interventions of Third Cinema. While Chatterjee draws on examples from anticolonial nationalism in India, his arguments surrounding the construction of (post-)colonial nationalism – in particular his notion of the material and the spiritual realms of national cultural identity as a point of interchange between colonizer and colonized, West and East – are clearly presented to the reader in the context of a broader theory of de-imagining a European construct of nation that could be applied to other (post-)colonial nations and nationalisms. Moreover, when discussing the reimagining of (national) community in the films of Tunisian director Férid Boughedir – the other focus of this chapter – Chatterjee's approach allows us to consider the cultural specificity of Tunisian nationalism/national cinema in relation to Arab nationalism and the attendant concept of *watan*, without such specificity being over-determined by a pan-Arab nationalist world view from which Tunisia was often marginalized precisely because of its perceived "openness" or permeability to the West (Perkins 2004: 142).[4]

It is also worth at this juncture saying a few words about the choice of the semi-autobiographical feature films of Férid Boughedir *Halfawîn: Usfûr stah/ Halfaouine/Halfaouine: l'enfant des terrasses* (1990) (henceforth *Halfaouine*) and *Saîf halqu al-wâdiy/One Summer at La Goulette/Un été à la Goulette* (1997) (henceforth *Un été à la Goulette*) as case studies for this chapter. Despite an initial desire to direct narrative films (Boughedir in Aufderheide 1991: 30), Boughedir in fact established his reputation in the 1970s and 1980s as a documentary filmmaker, historian, and

critic of African and Arab cinema.[5] Indeed, it is possible to see his early documentaries as an extension of his film criticism and publications in this area.
Though released in the mid-1980s, *Caméra d'Afrique* (Boughedir, 1984) and *Caméra
arabe* (Boughedir, 1987) were actually projects that Boughedir had embarked on
in the mid-1970s, a time of sustained radicalism and optimism for the future of
African cinema. Boughedir was personally immersed in this milieu and its attendant debates due to his activities as a critic, historian, and academic. As such,
Caméra d'Afrique and *Caméra arabe* stand as important documents in relation to
African film history. The documentaries perform a role that is at once film history
(offering an "alternative" history of cinema, a non-Western history of African/
Arab cinema) archival (gathering excerpts from key Sub-Saharan African and
Arab films from the 1960s, 1970s, and early 1980s) and finally educational (using
the documentary format to extend issues and debates being conducted amongst
industry professionals and academics toward a broader audience).[6]

When interviewed, Boughedir has spoken candidly of the "duty" he felt in
making *Caméra d'Afrique* and *Caméra arabe,* whilst at the same time longing to make
the kind of films about everyday subjects that attracted him as a spectator:

> It took a long time – I was making *Caméra d'Afrique* between 1974 and 1983
> and during all this time I was applauding the courage of committed films.
> And that was necessary, and they were necessary. But at the same time
> I knew I wasn't going to make this kind of film. I was a little afraid of that
> feeling. I was worried – this was in the 1970s – that it was a reactionary way
> of thinking, just wanting to film daily life, the movement of women's hands
> when they are washing clothes for example. Then after finishing my two films
> I felt I had done my duty [. . .] now it's my turn to speak about the kind of
> cinema that I like. I made the kind of film [*Halfouine*] that is my kind of cinema.
> (Boughedir in Aufderheide 1991: 30)

On the surface, the above quote appears to endorse a simplistic reading of Boughedir's
career as divided into two distinct phases: an earlier, politically committed period of
documentary filmmaking and criticism that gives way to nostalgic representations
of the Tunisia of Boughedir's youth. The reality is, in fact, more complex. Boughedir
was born toward the end of the colonial period but was too young to fully comprehend or indeed influence the events leading to independence. However, he
belongs to a generation of Tunisian filmmakers who contribute to a "quest" to
"preserve an accurate memory, replete with both positive and negative features,
of the culture from which they had sprung" (Perkins 2004: 201).

Thus, while both *Halfaouine* and *Un été à la Goulette* are invested with nostalgia,
they cannot simply be dismissed as a depoliticized, individualistic retreat into the
locations, communities, and formative events of the director's youth. Rather, they
function to represent a discourse on the past, present, and potential future of the
Tunisian nation, through a reimagining of community that offers a clear alternative to a Western imagining of nation and (by extension) national cinema.
Unlike his earlier documentaries that focus on the politics of a (pan-)African or

Arab cinema, Boughedir's feature films from the 1990s attempt to re-present the relationship between community and nation. The everyday acts of "ordinary" Tunisians on screen function not as nostalgic indulgence but, rather, as a de-Westernizing gesture. Before we arrive at an analysis of these films, however, let us turn our attention to this idea of de-Westernizing the national through the theories of Chatterjee.

De-Westernizing the national/De-Westernizing concepts of national cinema

Broadly speaking, the origins of nation are perceived in Western thought to be "coeval with the birth of universal history" (a linear, collective past) and the development of post-Enlightenment discourses of progress, modernity, liberty, and humanism that coincide in the nineteenth century with the rise of industrialism and democracy (Chatterjee 1986: 2; Smith 1999). That this ideology also provided the justification for racism and violent oppression in the colonies is conveniently occluded in the grand (Western) historical narrative of the rise of European nationalism. In Western terms, the nation is, moreover, a sociopolitical entity that shares not only a common past but also an inevitable cultural homogeneity resulting as an essential concomitant of industrial society (Gellner 1983: 39). Finally, in Western modes of thought, the nation is, as Anderson (1983) has argued, an "imagined political community" that supersedes previous cultural systems of religious community, monarchy, and feudal states, and whose existence is the result of "a half fortuitous, but explosive interaction between a system of production and productive relations (capitalism), a technology of communications (print) and the fatality of human linguistic diversity" (Chatterjee 1986: 19).

In *Nationalist Thought and the Colonial World*, Chatterjee (1986) mounts a sustained analysis of how the development of nationalist discourses in postcolonial Africa and Asia – shaped, directed, and implemented almost exclusively by a Western-educated elite intellectual and political class – led to a paradoxical situation whereby, in setting out to assert its independence from European dominance by the former colonizer, nationalism in Africa and Asia remains a prisoner to the post-Enlightenment, modernist discourses of progress, universality, and liberty that have shaped Western ideologies of nationalism. Similarly, though film studies may have attempted in its engagement with the national to consider alternatives to Western or "First World" models of national cinema (see Armes 1994; Crofts 1993; Willemen 1989; MacKenzie 2000), the theoretical framework for analyzing national cinema has traditionally been modelled on Western discourses of nationalism such as those offered by Gellner, Anderson, Kedourie or Smith.[7] Though the emergence of this Eurocentric bias may, in part, be explained by the fact that the earliest theorizing on national cinemas emerged mainly from individual studies of European national cinemas and above all histories of the industry as a "metonym for the industrialisation of culture and a metaphor for modernity itself" (Vitali and Willemen 2006: 2–4), its continued prominence in studies of national cinema points to the need to reimagine or de-Westernize the national.

In the context of postcolonial "national" cinema, the hold of the Western imaginary over the formulation of nationalist discourse and cultural identity for newly liberated postcolonial nations in Africa and Asia in the 1950s and 1960s was compounded by the fact that, "the West invented nationalism. . . creating at one and the same time the hegemonic sense of national culture and the problem of national identity for the colonised territories" (Willemen 1989: 18). Thus, for the oppressed, indigenous colonial population (or at least for the urban, educated intellectual and political elite who spoke on their behalf) "the struggle for independence became inseparable from national identity" (Hafez 2006: 227). However, as Fanon's writing "On National Culture" (Fanon 1968) suggests, thinking and (institutionally speaking) organizing postcolonial culture within a national framework runs the risk of Third World nationalism simply mimicking the structures of the West. A version of European nationalism thus emerged in postcolonial states of the 1950s and 1960s that often mirrored the practices of imperialism, maintaining the same binary power relations and hierarchies (a neo-colonial elite ruling over the indigenous masses) while presenting "previously existing relations of domination and subordination as the natural state of things" (Willemen 1989: 19). Such criticism must, of course, be considered alongside the international realpolitik that required formerly colonized peoples to "adopt a practice and a discourse of the nation-state precisely in order to end colonialism" (Shohat and Stam 1994: 287). However, the problematic construction (or even possibility) of neo-colonial hierarchies replicating themselves led some theorists of Third Cinema to avoid the question of a specifically national cinema in favour of a committed internationalism (Gabriel 1982: 2). And yet the question of the national will simply not go away. Even if, for the postcolonial filmmaker, aligning with a broadly shared internationalist political ideology of anti-imperialism is logical, the individual cultural, political, and historical specificities inscribed in the space and time of the postcolonial nation cannot be ignored. Nor can we deny the fact that the creation of these postcolonial nations has often involved a problematic process of unification and partition of various ethnic groups and regions in a way that demanded newly formed postcolonial states to negotiate historical divisions often based on difference (be it religious, ethnic or cultural) that Western nationalism actively sought to deny with its myth of a culturally or historical homogeneous community.

A Eurocentric model of nationalism is, quite simply, inadequate for negotiating the differences that exist within virtually every nation-state. This is, precisely, one of the reasons that Western nationalism retreats into a discourse of homogeneity, a shared past and universalizing values, on the one hand, and the emphasis on the imagined community of a modern, industrialized democracy, on the other. However, this is not to say that the influence and continued legacy of what broadly speaking might be labelled "the West" can simply be evacuated from any attempt to conceptualize postcolonial nationalism or indeed the question of the national in non-Western film cultures that this chapter is specifically concerned with. As with Trinh T. Minh-ha's claim that there is a "Third World in every First World and vice versa" (Minh-ha in Crofts 1993: 64), a "pure" conceptualization of the nation in Third-Word or postcolonial nationalism cannot exist. Instead, a more complex understanding of nation (and by extension national cinema) emerges, one that attempts to construct a sense of shared national identity and "the right to speak in one's own cultural idioms" (Willemen 1989: 18) while simultaneously contending with issues such as relations of subordination and exclusion perpetuated by a neo-colonial elite, single dominant religious or ethnic group within the nation-state or the nostalgic and uncritical recourse into an idealized pre-colonial past. This reimagining of the nation/de-Westernizing of national cinema must therefore avoid fetishizing the postcolonial "moment" by acknowledging that the legacy of colonialism is not the only force at play in shaping the postcolonial nation-state. The impact of external forces on the local/nation-state – and the way that a continued influence of the West cannot simply be configured in "neo-colonial" terms but must be recognized in relation to multiple political, economic, and social structures of globalization – must also be addressed.

National cinema and its fragments: an alternative to a Eurocentric model of national cinema

In *The Nation and Its Fragments: Colonial and Postcolonial Histories* (1993), Chatterjee elaborates the problematic set out previously in *Nationalist Thought and the Colonial World* in order to offer an imagining of nation that is not bound by an exclusively Western frame of reference. He does this by identifying two spheres of interest for the development of a nationalist ideology or national cultural identity within the nascent postcolonial nation: the "material" and the "spiritual." The material is understood as the "outside" space, the realm of economy, statecraft, and technology; the domain where "Western superiority had to be acknowledged and its accomplishments carefully studied and replicated" (Chatterjee 1993: 6). In contrast, the "spiritual" or inner domain refers to aspects of culture such as language and religion, the domestic, personal or family life formed within the "sovereign territory of the nation" (Chatterjee 1993: 237). This dichotomy becomes key when it is understood that the spiritual was:

> of course premised upon a difference between the cultures of the colonizer and the colonized. The more nationalism engaged in its contest with the colonial power in the outer domain of politics, the more it insisted on displaying the marks of "essential" cultural difference so as to keep out the colonizer from that inner domain of national life and to proclaim its sovereignty over it.
>
> (Chatterjee 1993: 27)

There are two further elements that are key to Chatterjee's thinking here: first, that the distinction between the material (as the outer space dominated by imperial power) and the spiritual, as the private sphere from which cultural identity and thus colonial resistance emerges, allows us to understand how anti-colonial nationalism often creates its own domain of sovereignty long before the political struggle with colonial/imperial power has begun (Chatterjee 1993: 6). Second is that the association of this inner/spiritual sphere with notions of "community," and the observation that this community, which can be as localized as the family unit and as expansive as the imagined community of nation, challenges "capital" as the basis of modernized, industrialized nationalism of the West/Europe (Chatterjee 1993: 236–238). (As the subsequent analysis of *Un été à la Goulette* will show, Chatterjee's notion of "capital" can be extended beyond the European bourgeois liberalism to the conservative, Muslim property-owning class of Tunisia).

Though Chatterjee's broader formulation of the development of postcolonial nationalism has been criticized in some quarters for its perceived rigid dialectic approach to the complexity of the national question (Liu 1994: 39), the arguments put forward in *The Nation and Its Fragments* nonetheless offer a productive framework in which to rethink the question of national cinema from a "de-Westernizing" perspective. First, building on an understanding of cinema as both "an industry and a cluster of cultural strategies" (Vitali and Willemen 2006: 2), it provides an alternative to Western, colonial or Eurocentric modes of thinking and theorizing from which to examine the development of postcolonial or Third World nationalism/ national cinema while simultaneously acknowledging the continued presence and influence of the West at an ideological and material level. This becomes crucial if we begin to rethink the question of national cinema in an Arab nation such as Tunisia, where we are forced to acknowledge that cinema as a technological medium is a Western import (Shafik 1998: 4) and one that has for many years battled against the domination and exploitation of Western control of distribution and exhibition. Elsewhere in the Maghreb, the notable success of Tunisian auteur cinema in the 1980s and early 1990s and the spectacular commercial success of Moroccan cinema since the mid-1990s – to a point where Moroccan films are now successfully competing with American and Egyptian films at the box office – came about because of a system of funding and support modeled on that found in France, which allows the idiomatic expression of Moroccan culture to appear on the screen.[8] This example seems therefore to confirm Chatterjee's notion of the material as a space "where Western superiority had to be acknowledged and its accomplishments carefully studied and replicated" in order for the nation's "inner" national cultural identity to emerge on screen – in this instance in the form of popular Moroccan cinema. In the context of de-Westernizing or reimagining national cinema, Chatterjee's distinction between the spiritual and the material is also significant due to the complex relationship of a small national cinema such as that found in Tunisia between state (censorship) and national funding mechanisms, the ideological weight of a national filmic discourse within a postcolonial society as well as "the global context of cinema production and distribution" (Martin 2007: 213), which includes the need for international co-production[9] and the complicated relationship with France, as former colonizer and continuing partner in the co-production of Tunisian "national" cinema through funding mechanisms such as Fonds Sud.[10] Crucially, then, Chatterjee's "spiritual" domain as the site of personal expression, becomes the creative space from which a national discourse or cultural identity can be articulated by the postcolonial filmmaker, acting as a point of resistance to the continued control of the "material" domain by the state and other external forces.

Following on from this point, there is Chatterjee's link to the importance of community, which, rather than promoting a drive to an ethnic or religiously charged essentialist nationalism, promotes the possibility of multiple, culturally specific narratives to emerge and coexist within a larger political social unit – such as that of the nation-state. The aforementioned emphasis on the spiritual domain, thus points to difference as a key focus for structuring and articulating national cultural identity. The nation (and for our purposes national cinema) is not therefore constructed from one homogenous perspective or dominant historical, political or cultural discourse. Rather, it emerges from a collection of individual perspectives that incorporate the potential for questions of ethnicity, religious, and gender difference (amongst others) to be considered within the reimagining or de-Westernizing of the postcolonial nation.[11] However, the possibility of such difference emerging is also dependent on the industrial and institutional forces that determine the direction of any given national cinema. In relation to Arab cinema, it is, in fact, government censorship and state control of production and distribution that has – more, it can be argued, than any Western influence – prevented a truly open and heterogeneous national cinema from emerging. Thus, in postcolonial Tunisia, the need to elaborate a national narrative away from both the French and from the pre-colonial *bey* dynasties meant that cinema production, first under Habib Bourguiba and then Zine al-Abidine ben Ali, was a national(-ist) enterprise. Indeed, until the fall of ben Ali's regime on January 14, 2011, all images were effectively controlled by the government.[12] However, as we shall see in the final part of this chapter, Boughedir, like other Tunisian *auteurs* in the 1980s and 1990s such as Nouri Bouzid and Moufida Tlatli, found ways to circumvent such political and economic censure through elliptical representations of everyday cultural and political realities that Tunisian audiences could relate to.

Halfaouine: popular cinema and the nation "space"

Halfaouine, Boughedir's first solo-authored feature film, was made when the director was already forty-five years old. The film's affectionate, amusing, and sensuous depiction of life in the eponymous district of Tunis, seen through the eyes of a young boy on the cusp of adolescence, became the most popular film in the history of Tunisian cinema, attracting around 500,000 spectators (Armes 2005: 65–66). The film centers on daily life in Halfaouine, moving primarily between the family home and the local *hammam* (public baths) that Noura visits with his mother. The film's coming-of-age narrative depicts Noura as caught between the hypocritical patriarchal authority of his overbearing father, who beats his son for pestering young women in the street and then attempts to seduce the women who come into his shop, and the nurturing company of the women in the family home, who still see him as a child and so allow the teenager to accompany them on trips to the local baths. Noura's growing awareness of his own sexuality leads him to be ejected from the baths, bringing shame on the family, as he is caught voyeuristically gazing upon one of women bathers. As well as generating unprecedented success at the domestic box office, *Halfaouine* was enthusiastically received on the international festival circuit and "world" cinema distribution network. However, some have read the film's success with Western audiences and critics as due to the fact that *Halfaouine* "uses the awakening sexual curiosity of his adolescent protagonist to introduce the observer into the 'mysterious' world of Arab women" with the images of the Turkish bath in particular evoking "the harem subjects of nineteenth century orientalist painting in Europe" (Shafik 1998: 41).

Against these charges of neo-Orientalist and patriarchal representations of the exotic Arab woman, Armes offers a robust defense of the film, suggesting that, in order to understand the significance of the representation of Tunisian society being offered by Boughedir, we need to:

> [l]ose our Hollywood-fostered attitude that film is simply the art of manipulating time (in which the underlying principle is the combination of logic and surprise and a key element is the creation of suspense). We must turn our attention as well to questions of spatial division, spatial organisation and social conflict
>
> (Armes 2005: 143)

Armes could be said here to overstate the binary of Hollywood as a cinema that manipulates time and African/Arab cinema primarily as a cinema of spatial dynamics, since, through its reliance, broadly speaking, on continuity editing, *Halfaouine*'s construction of cinematic space and time is not radically different from that of Western cinema. Nevertheless, his assertion that we need to resist reading the construction of space and the relation of gender and power played out on screen in a "Western" context holds true. The film is, precisely, predicated on a representation of gendered space that is culturally specific to the traditions of the Arab world: clear distinctions between male and female space in the home; excessive and rigidly observed divisions between male and female in the public sphere. Without this understanding of gendered space in Arab society, the impact of the moments of female resistance in the public sphere that do appear in the film – such as when the young veiled women walking in the market reject and openly berate the advance made by Noura's two friends – are lost.

If we now apply Chatterjee's notion of the "spiritual" as a crucial point of resistance to a Westernizing interpretation of national identity to the above debate, we can see that the relationship between space and the personal in *Halfaouine* further refines our understanding of how the film functions as a national cinema text in a de-Westernizing framework. *Halfaouine* not only constructs diegetic space in relation to gender divisions in Arab/Tunisian society; it also refuses to play out this representation in relation to the theme of (Arabo-Muslim) tradition versus (Western) modernity. Rather than shifting between the neo-colonial part of the city and the medina, *Halfaouine* is set exclusively in one of the city's oldest neighborhoods and one that, as the film's credit sequence clearly shows, is within the medina and thus identifiably pre-colonial in terms of its architecture. Characters in the film do not struggle with a conflict between tradition and modernity; the film in fact shows a healthy disregard for obsessing over the continuing neo-colonial influence of France on the postcolonial Tunisian nation. And yet *Halfaouine* does not represent an unproblematic or naive retreat into a nostalgic view of a pre-colonial past. Instead, the film evidences Boughedir's own lack of a complex in terms of the perceived "inferiority" of the former colonized: the European/neo-colonial areas of the city are not shown quite simply because there is no need for them to appear. The film thus represents the public and private spaces of one of the popular (Arab) districts of Tunis, offering a vision of an "inner" or "spiritual" sphere – to borrow Chatterjee's terminology – that refuses the (former) colonizer's influence and remains as the privileged site of (cultural) resistance and the space in which national cultural identity is forged. Whilst acknowledging Stollery's claim (2001: 57) that *Halfaouine* depends on a location (the *hammam*) which is "no longer prevalent in present-day Muslim societies" – more the refuge of Western tourists than local residents – the fact remains that the representation of Tunis and Tunisian society offered in *Halfaouine* was enthusiastically endorsed by Tunisians themselves, who flocked to see the film in cinemas upon its release like no Tunisian film before or since. If we follow this interpretation of the construction of space in the film, the representations of women bathing in the *hammam* found in *Halfaouine* cannot be read categorically as neo-Orientalist images designed specifically to appeal to a Western audience or Western backer of the film. Instead, they offer a "local,"[13] "authentic" (or perhaps more accurately) "every-day" portrayal of social interaction in Arab/Tunisian culture that forms part of a national cultural identity. Indeed, we could say that such images in *Halfaouine* only risk becoming neo-Orientalist when disseminated, consumed, and "de-coded"[14] as such by Western audiences on Western screens. For it is, precisely, these everyday images of people/community/nation – not just women bathing in the *hammam* but also the sights and sounds of the market, men discussing politics in the local barbershop, women exchanging gossip as they sift grain on a rooftop terrace – that, as Boughedir suggested in his earlier quote, attracted him to the cinema; and which form a core "reality" of a reimagining of the national "community" and national cinema through Chatterjee's notion of the spiritual domain of anticolonial nationalism.

Figure 5.1 Halfaouine (Férid Boughedir, 1990).

Un été à la Goulette: community, memory, and the "time" of the national

If a non-Western reading of space in *Halfaouine* is crucial to unlocking the film's intended meaning, an understanding of *Un été à la Goulette* in relation to Chatterjee's concept of "community" as a key construct within postcolonial nationalist discourse reveals a film that is much more than simple nostalgia for an idealized moment in Tunisia's recent past. Instead, the film becomes an urgent plea for tolerance and recognition of the different communities that, historically, have shaped Tunisian society, and which Boughedir sees as essential for reimagining the nation's future. Thus the act of returning to the past to find an alternative "future" for Tunisia allows Boughedir to construct a non-Western mode of "narrating the nation" on screen via the difference found in the multicultural community of Goulette. The film tells the story of three families – one Jewish, one Arab, and one Catholic (Italian immigrant), but all ostensibly "Tunisian" – and the series of events that connect their lives during the summer of 1967 in Goulette, a seaside town only a few kilometers by train from Tunis and another local but iconic location selected by the director because of his personal connection to it.[15]

Whereas *Halfaouine* foregrounds father–son relationships, in *Un été à la Goulette* it is father–daughter relationships that are central to the narrative and become the means for Boughedir to expose the stifling and oppressive tactics of patriarchy on the young Tunisian women's lives. The film's narrative is driven by the friendship between three fathers (Youssef, Jojo, and Giuseppe) and their daughters (Meriem, Tina, and Gigi) and the vexed question of maintaining the young women's "honor" as they move toward sexual awakening.[16] This very personal family drama (located in a narrative space akin to that of Chatterjee's spiritual domain) is nonetheless placed within a broader national, transnational (pan-Arab) context by virtue of the narrative being set in the days leading up to the Arab–Israeli Six-Day War. Ultimately it is the combined effects of these two events – the personal "crisis" revolving around the fathers' need to preserve their daughters' honor set against the wider national and regional political crisis of the impending Arab–Israeli conflict – that threaten the peaceable coexistence of the multicultural community of La Goulette.

Hence, rather than looking to the present of a Tunisian society dominated in the 1990s by the autocratic rule of ben Ali's Western-educated elite, on the one hand, and the majority of ordinary Tunisians concerned with "preserving Tunisia's traditional Arabo-Muslim heritage from an onslaught of [Western] imported values and practices" on the other (Perkins 2004: 7), *Un été à la Goulette* effectively looks to a model of multicultural community from the nation's past. The decision to locate the narrative in the days leading up to the Six-Day War of 1967 is, of course, highly symbolic. The humiliating defeat suffered by the Arab states, led by Egyptian leader Gamal 'Abd al-Nasir, at the hands of the Israeli army effectively sounded the death-knell for Arab nationalism (and the aim of political unity for the Arab people), to be replaced by "other forces and ideologies such as state *wataniya* and radical Islam" (Dawisha 2003: 312). In the case of Tunisia, this defeat would lead to the eventual departure of virtually all Tunisian Jews and

Italian Catholics from the country. The events that effected a cultural and religious reconfiguring of the Tunisian nation are foreshadowed in the final moments of *Un été à la Goulette*, whereby a caption informing the spectator of the outcome for Tunisians of the Six-Day War is superimposed over a freeze-frame of Youssef, Jojo, and Giuseppe arm in arm. This Janus-faced image looks back to a "lost" moment of unity prior to the departure of Jews and Catholics from Tunisia at the same time as it offers a vision of an alternative future for the nation.

We could view this attempt to reimagine community in *Un été à la Goulette* as a de-Westernizing gesture, in the sense that it rejects the idea of a fixed, collective past as well as the belief in progress, both elements that are central to the discourse of European nationalism. Similarly, the film intersects with Chatterjee's notion of community that rejects the bourgeois consciousness upon which European nationalism emerged in the nineteenth century – whereby individuals come together on the basis of "shared preferences" – in favor of a "peasant consciousness" in which "collective action does not flow from a contract amongst individuals; rather individual identities themselves are derived from membership in a community" (Chatterjee 1993: 163). The colonial strategy of highlighting ethnic and religious difference amongst the indigenous population in order to divide the colonized majority and weaken collective opposition to colonial rule is thus challenged through anticolonial nationalism by a system in which people "living in different contextually defined, communities, can coexist peacefully, productively and creatively within large political units" (Chatterjee 1993: 238).

One of the more straightforward analogies for this peaceful coexistence described above is to be found in *Un été à la Goulette*'s use of food as a symbolic point of contact and exchange: at mealtimes the families literally share their respective cuisines, as the children carry plates of *gnaouia* (okra tajine), *bkaila* (spinach and haricot bean stew), and pasta from the dinner table of one apartment to the next. However, the most explicit plea from Boughedir for the type of "community" promoted by Chatterjee's proposed model of anticolonial nationalism comes in a scene roughly twenty minutes into the film, where, in Jojo's absence, Youssef and the local (Arab) bar owner defend the place of Jews in Tunisia. Challenging the open hostility of one of his Arab customers, who suggests that "traitorous" Tunisian Jews should leave the country "now they have their Israel," the bar owner responds:

> So you're Tunisian and Jojo isn't? Isn't your last name Tripolitan? Why don't you go back to where you came from? But which Tripoli is yours? The one in Lebanon, or the one in Libya? [. . .] And where were your Arab brothers during all this freedom fighting [for Tunisian independence from France]? There were plenty of traitors. . . There's good and bad everywhere. . . I bet you don't know about all the Tunisian Jews who went to prison fighting for us [Arabs]. . . Politics is about patriotism, not religion.

In the above example, the café is transformed from a place of idle talk or playful banter into a site of contestation and heated political debate about what is at stake in defining the Tunisian nation. Thus, while La Goulette offers the *potential* for peaceful coexistence and tolerance, it is not simply presented to the audience as a paradise from a bygone era. In addition to the confrontation in the café, the young women in particular confide in their mothers of their frustrations of living in the neighborhood and conforming to the oppressive demands of a traditional Mediterranean patriarchal society. Boughedir locates his narrative in the past to form a contact zone with the present as well as an imagined future for the Tunisian nation. The questioning of pan-Arab solidarity articulated by the bar owner's defense of Jojo ("Where were your Arab brothers during all this freedom fighting?") is indicative of Boughedir's refusal in *Un été à la Goulette* to define Tunisian cultural identity solely in terms of Arabo-Muslim heritage. A different vision of *watan* is therefore proposed by the film. The placing of three families, one Arab, one Jewish, and one (Italian) Catholic, at the center of the narrative is emblematic of Tunisia as a nation whose history and identity has been shaped by a variety of religions (Islam, Catholicism, Judaism), ethnicities, languages, and cultures. It is, moreover, a symbolic union informed by the country's geographical location on the north coast of Africa, in the Mediterranean, and at the heart of Carthaginian civilization, which had for centuries made it a natural point of connection and exchange for African, European, and Arab cultures.[17] The film thus refuses a definition of nation or community based on binary divisions of East/West, Arab/European or Muslim/Christian.

Interestingly, the character who most clearly represents conservative Arabo-Muslim culture (as well as a solidarity to the broader Arab community), the pious landlord El Hadj, is portrayed as a hypocritical and unsympathetic figure who lusts after Meriem (Youssef's daughter), finally offering to marry her on the pretence of preserving the family's honor. El Hadj is, furthermore, mocked by Youssef and his family as "Oriental" for affecting an accent modeled on the Arabic vernacular spoken in the Middle East – a comment that also highlights Tunisia's geographical location toward the periphery of the Arab world, Maghreb meaning "land where the sun sets" or "West" in Arabic. Most significantly, however, it is El Hadj, the conservative Arab patriarch and landowner, who displaces the Western bourgeois as the locus of capital in *Un été à la Goulette*. Witness, for example, the way that El Hadj sees the impending conflict between Egypt and Israel as a business opportunity (serving the individual and not the community) to purchase property cheaply from Tunisian Jews who may flee La Goulette as a result of the war. In the end, however, El Hadj's plans are thwarted: he literally drops dead from a heart attack at the feet of Meriem after she visits his home in secret and offers herself to him in an attempt to dissuade him from evicting the Jewish, Italian, and Arab families from one of his properties. Returning to Chatterjee's terminology, then, community becomes the site of resistance against capital (a fundamental element of European nationalism) and the contract of shared interests emanating from the (Western) bourgeoisie, that is embodied in this instance by the opposition of local residents from Goulette to El Hadj.

Conclusion

The intention of this chapter has not been to privilege the national as the exclusive framework within which North African, Arab or postcolonial filmmaking can be understood. Clearly, the national works as one positioning within a matrix of local and global (diasporic, transnational) reference points in which cinema functions and creates meaning – a point which Boughedir has himself acknowledged when writing about the significant contribution of exiled and diasporic filmmakers to New Arab cinema of the 1970s and 1980s (Boughedir 1987b: 10). Instead, the aim has been to revisit the question of the national in postcolonial North African or Arab cinema and in so doing to consider whether there is indeed a need to "de-Westernize" the frameworks within which the national/national cinema is understood. In this respect, Chatterjee's theory of postcolonial nationalism as based on spheres of the material and the spiritual permits a reimaging of national cinema in a North African or Arab context that accepts Western influences on the construction and development of a national cinema but also offers the possibility for a non-Western idiom of national cultural identity to emerge. In the more specific context of Tunisian cinema, part of the challenge offered in Boughedir's work is to displace or de-Westernize cinema as both cultural text and material object (a commodity for distribution and consumption) by constructing a national narrative that is clearly not predicated either on the binary of colonialism/European nationalist thought (colonizer/colonized, civilized/barbarity, modernity/tradition, the West and the rest) or in relation to a simple inversion of the colonial binary in the postcolonial moment. In other words, there are other centers – as well as multiple spaces and alternative times of the nation (past, present, and future) – just as there are other stories to be told outside a Western mode of nationalist discourse.

Acknowledgments

The author is grateful to Saër Maty Bâ and Florence Martin for feedback on previous drafts of this chapter.

Notes

1 Third Cinema, through both its content and aesthetics is opposed to all forms of imperialism and class oppression. It is defined as much by its politics as by the location of production (cf. Pines and Willemen [1989] and Chanan [1997]). Postcolonial cinema is a term that emerges after (and some might say as a consequence of) Third Cinema. While some postcolonial cinema may be incorporated into Third Cinema, its cultural, political, and temporal location is, necessarily, determined by the link to European colonialism. As such it is linked to former colonies, diasporas, and the *métropole* of the former colonizer.
2 Recent studies of North African cinema such as Armes (2005) and Brahimi (2009) – with sections focusing specifically on Algerian, Moroccan, and Tunisia cinema – show how Maghrebi cinemas continue to be framed in a national rather than regional (or transnational) framework.

3 For a more detailed discussion of this position, see Higbee and Lim (2010). For further discussion of the concept of transnational cinema, see Higson (2000), Ezra and Rowden (2006) and Ďurovičová and Newman (2009).

4 According to Choueiri, the concept of *watan* (homeland or "fatherland") emerged in the nineteenth century, identifying each particular Arab country as an "integral territory and reference point" within the wider Arab world. This resulted in the emergence of national historical writings centered on individual nations, whereby "national identity grew out of the long history of a particular fatherland sharing a common fund of Arab cultural values" (Choueiri 2000: 71).

5 Boughedir was awarded a Ph.D. for his thesis "Cinéma Africain et Décolonisation" from the Sorbonne in 1976 and has published numerous articles on African and Arab film history and criticism since the 1970s in Arabic, English, French, and Italian. Probably his best known work is *Le Cinéma Africain de A à Z* (1987).

6 It was in this context that *Caméra d'Afrique* was screened on British television (Channel 4) in the late 1980s. See Rod Stoneman's interview in this book for more details.

7 For example, though containing a section with individual contributions on Indonesian, Turkish, Indian cinema, and Third or "minor" cinema, Hjort and MacKenzie's excellent edited collection *Cinema and Nation* (2000) is, nonetheless, dominated, in sections entitled "The Sociology of Nationalism" and "The Concept of National Cinema," by political and socioeconomic models of nationalism that draw largely on Anderson and Gellner. MacKenzie's chapter (2000) on "mimetic nationhood" in relation to West African and Latin American cinema is atypical in the sense that it attempts to engage with the national outside of this Western paradigm. Elsewhere, Shaka's analysis of the national in African cinema (2004: 73–76) relies heavily on Crofts and Higson to make its argument. More recently, Vitali and Willemen's *Theorising National Cinema* (2006) brings together an impressive range of analysis of both Western and non-Western cinemas, offering alternatives to a Eurocentric national cinema model. However, none of these excellent essays explicitly or directly address a need to "de-Westernize" national cinema as a conceptual term.

8 Since the success of Tunisian filmmakers such as Boughedir, Tlatli, and Bouzid in the 1980s and 1990s, Tunisian cinema has experienced less success than Morocco and a more difficult climate for funding, distribution, and exhibition: cf. Armes (2005) and Martin (2007).

9 Both *Halfaouine* and *Un été à la Goulette* were funded through a combination of national/ international sources: the Tunisian Ministry of Culture, the French CNC, and European television companies such as ZDF, Canal+, and Channel 4.

10 Fonds Sud was created in 1984 to assist in the part-funding (up to €150,000) of production, post-production, and rewriting of films from all countries in Africa, Latin America and selected countries from the Near and Middle East and Asia and Central Europe. Funding is provided by the French Ministry of Culture and Communication (via the CNC) and the French Ministry of Foreign Affairs. While Michel Reilhac, a former president of the Fonds Sud, claimed at a round table at the Cannes Festival in 2004 that the fund's ethos was to "privilege those who made films in their country about their country" (quoted in Barlet 2004), Barlet has elsewhere questioned the extent to which the fund is actually geared to benefit France as much as the Southern Hemisphere filmmakers, since grants must be spent in France on post-production operations (Barlet 2000: 262). There is also a broader debate over how the reliance on Western funding for production can lead to pressure to pander to Western audiences' expectation of "African" cinema (Barlet 2000: 263).

11 In *The Nation and its Fragments*, the cultural resistance of middle-class Indian women to colonial domination is offered as an example of how gender difference can be articulated within the spiritual domain of the national (Chatterjee 1993: 135–158).

12 State censorship of all forms of media (internet, films, books, magazines) in Tunisia came to a dramatic end on January 14, 2011, with the fall of ben Ali's regime. While

there is undoubtedly now greater freedom of expression for Tunisian journalists and artists, the transition government secretly passed new censorship laws in May 2011 according to Tunisian news website Webdo. See http://www.webdo.tn/2011/05/07/la-censure-revient-en-tunisie-sur-ordre-du-tribunal-militaire (accessed October 11, 2011).

13 Serceau (2004: 196) describes Boughedir as "the most local of all Maghrebi film-makers" because of the close observation of social, cultural, and human interaction of Halfaouine and La Goulette found in his films.

14 This term is applied in the sense of Stuart Hall's de-coding (Hall 1980) which suggests an audience or viewer/listener that *actively* reconstructs meaning within a given text in relation to his or her ideological, sociocultural, and historical context, helping to explain how audiences can create multiple as well as often (ideologically) conflicting interpretations of the same text.

15 As with the Halfaouine neighbourhood in Tunis where he was born and raised, Boughedir spent the formative summers of his adolescence in the family home at La Goulette.

16 On this point the film's gender politics are somewhat ambiguous. Boughedir clearly displays sympathy for the young women – particularly in the dark and menacing sequence where they face the wrath of their fathers, having been discovered "messing around" with young men at a wedding reception. The film also opens up genuine spaces in the narrative for the young women to articulate their opinions and feelings. Elsewhere, however, Boughedir risks falling into objectifying clichés for comic effect – such as when the young boys from the neigbourhood spy on Gigi and Tina as they shower semi-naked on the roof of their apartment building. The scene has no apparent function in the narrative other than to establish the young women as sexually desirable to the young men of La Goulette.

17 This link to the Mediterranean has meant that, in the early years of the French protectorate in Tunisia (1880–1910), Italian settlers in fact outnumbered the French by five to one (Perkins 2004: 44).

References

Amarger, M. (1994) "La Parole aux cinéastes africains: Férid Boughedir," *Ecrans d'Afrique*, 9 (10): 15.

Anderson, B. (1983) *Imagined Communities: Reflections on the Origins and Spread of Nationalism*, London: Verso.

Armes, R. (1994) "Culture and National Identity," in M. T. Martin (ed.), *Cinemas of the Black Diaspora: Diversity, Dependence, and Oppositionality*, Detroit, Mich.: Wayne State University Press, pp. 25–39.

——(2005) *Post-Colonial Images: Studies in North African Film*, Bloomington, Ind.: Indiana University Press.

Aufderheide, P. (1991) "From the Terraces: Férid Boughedir," *Black Film Review*, 6 (4): 4–5, 29–31.

Barlet, O. (2000) *African Cinemas: Decolonizing the Gaze*, trans. C. Turner, London: Zed Books.

——(2004) "Les Vingt Ans du fonds sud," *Africultures*. Available online at www.africultures.com/php/index.php?nav=article&no=3422 (accessed October 9, 2011).

Boughedir, F. (1987a) *Le Cinéma Africain de A à Z*, Brussels: COIC.

——(1987b) "Malédictions des cinémas arabes," *CinémAction*, 43: 10–17.

——(1987c) "Panorama des cinémas maghrébins," *CinémAction*, 43: 59–71.

Brahimi, D. (2009) *50 ans de cinéma maghrébin*, Paris: Minerve.

Chanan, M. (1997) "The Changing Geography of Third Cinema," *Screen*, 38 (4): 372–388.

Chatterjee, P. (1986) *Nationalist Thought and the Colonial World: A Derivative Discourse*, London: Zed Books.

——(1993) *The Nation and Its Fragments: Colonial and Post-Colonial Histories*, Princeton, NJ: Princeton University Press.

Choueiri, Y. M. (2000) *Arab Nationalism: A History*, Oxford and Malden, Mass.: Blackwell.

Crofts, S. (1993) "Reconceptualising National Cinema/s," *Quarterly Review of Film and Video*, 14 (3): 49–67.

Dawisha, A. (2003) *Arab Nationalism in the Twentieth Century: From Triumph to Despair*, Princeton, NJ: Princeton University Press.

Ďurovičová, N. and Newman, K. E. (eds.) (2009) *World Cinemas, Transnational Perspectives*, London and New York: Routledge.

Ezra, E. and Rowden, T. (eds.) (2006) *Transnational Cinema: The Film Reader*, London and New York: Routledge.

Fanon, F. (1968) *The Wretched of the Earth*, trans. C. Farrington, London: MacGibbon & Kee. First published 1965.

Gabriel, T. H. (1982) *Third Cinema in the Third World*, Ann Arbor, Mich.: UMI Press.

Gellner, E. (1983) *Nations and Nationalism*, Oxford: Blackwell.

Hafez, S. (2006) "The Quest for/Obsession with National in Arabic Cinema," in V. Vitali and P. Willemen (eds.), *Theorising National Cinema*, London: BFI Publishing, pp. 226–255.

Hall, S. (1980) "Encoding/Decoding," in Centre for Contemporary Cultural Studies (ed.), *Culture, Media, Language: Working Papers in Cultural Studies, 1972–79*, London: Hutchinson, pp. 128–138.

Higbee, W. and Lim, S.-H. (2010) "Concepts of Transnational Cinema: Towards a Critical Transnationalism in Film Studies," *Transnational Cinemas*, 1 (1): 7–21.

Higson, A. (2000) "The Limiting Imagination of National Cinema," in M. Hjort and S. MacKenzie (eds.), *Cinema and Nation*, London and New York: Routledge, pp. 57–67.

Hjort, M. and MacKenzie, S. (eds.) (2000) *Cinema and Nation*, London and New York: Routledge.

Hjort, M. and Petrie, D. (2007) "Introduction," in M. Hjort and D. Petrie (eds.), *The Cinema of Small Nations*, Edinburgh: Edinburgh University Press, pp. 1–22.

Liu, L. (1994) "The Female Body and Nationalist Discourse: *The Field of Life and Death* Revisited," in I. Grewal and C. Kaplan (eds.), *Scattered Hegemonies: Postmodernity and Transnational Feminist Practices*, Minneapolis, Minn.: University of Minnesota Press, pp. 37–62.

MacKenzie, S. (2000) "Mimetic Nationhood: Ethnography and the National," in M. Hjort and S. MacKenzie (eds.), *Cinema and Nation*, London and New York: Routledge.

Martin, F. (2007) "Tunisia," in M. Hjort and D. Petrie (eds.), *The Cinema of Small Nations*, Bloomington, Ind.: Indiana University Press, pp. 213–228.

Ouerchefani, R. (2011) "La Censure de l'Internet revient en Tunisie sur ordre du Tribunal Militaire!" Available online at www.webdo.tn/2011/05/07/la-censure-revient-en-tunisie-sur-ordre-du-tribunal-militaire (accessed October 11, 2011).

Perkins, K. J. (2004) *A History of Modern Tunisia*, Cambridge: Cambridge University Press.

Pines, J. and Willemen (eds.) (1989) *Questions of Third Cinema*, London: BFI Publishing.

Serceau, M. (2004) "Halfaouine: le plus pénétrant et le plus utile des films maghrébins," *CinémAction*, 111: 196–201.

Shafik, V. (1998) *Arab Cinema: History and Cultural Identity*, Cairo: The American University in Cairo Press.

Shaka, F. O. (2004) *Modernity and the African Cinema: A Study in Colonialist Discourse, Post-Coloniality and Modern African Identities*, Trenton, NJ and Asmara, Eritrea: Africa World Press.

Shohat, E. (2003) "Post-Third Wordlist Culture, Gender, Nation and the Cinema," in A. R. Guneratne and W. Dissanayake (eds.), *Re-thinking Third Cinema*, London and New York: Routledge, pp. 51–78.

Shohat, E. and Stam, R. (1994) *Unthinking Eurocentrism: Multiculturalism and the Media*, London and New York: Routledge.

Smith, A. D. (1999) "History and Modernity: Reflections on the Theory of Nationalism," in D. Boswell and J. Evans (eds.), *Representing Nation: A Reader*, London and New York: Routledge, pp. 45–60.

Stollery, M. (2001) "Masculinities, Generations, and Cultural Transformations in Contemporary Tunisian Cinema," *Screen*, 42: 49–63.

Vitali, V. and Willemen, P. (2006) "Introduction," in V. Vitali and P. Willemen (eds.), *Theorising National Cinema*, London: BFI Publishing, pp. 1–16.

Willemen, P. (1989) "The Third Cinema Question: Notes and Reflections," in J. Pines and P. Willemen (eds.), *Questions of Third Cinema*, London: BFI Publishing, pp. 1–29.

6 Banal transnationalism

On Mohsen Makhmalbaf's "borderless" filmmaking

Shahab Esfandiary

In his book titled *Makhmalbaf at Large: The Making of a Rebel Filmmaker*, Hamid Dabashi rejects Jean Baudrillard's generalization that the postmodern world has created a transaesthetic realm of indifference in the field of arts (Dabashi 2008: 199). Dabashi accuses Baudrillard of Eurocentrism and refers to Mohsen Makhmalbaf's cinema as an example of emancipatory and liberating art in the age of the post-modern. Reflecting on Makhmalbaf's transnational filmmaking practices financed by European companies, Dabashi suggests that Makhmalbaf has applied "a guerrilla tactic of planting a Trojan Horse in the belly of globalising capital" (Dabashi 2008: 199).

Through analyses of Makhmalbaf's most recent film, as well as some of his interviews, this chapter presents a challenge to Dabashi's assessment. The argument here is also in contrast with the usual praise for, and celebratory readings of Makhmalbaf by American and European academics and critics such as Fredric Jameson (King 2003), Jonathan Rosenbaum (1999), Cynthia Weber (2005), and Eric Egan (2005). As shall be demonstrated below, it seems that in Makhmalbaf's case a limited, or to use Mette Hjort's categories, "weak" and "opportunistic" form of transnationalism (Hjort 2010), has resulted in certain outcomes which are far from the qualities and virtues attributed to "counterhegemonic" transnational cinema (Ezra and Rowden 2006). This case study, it is hoped, will contribute to recent critical elaborations on the meaning and value of the "transnational" within film studies, particularly those seeking to move beyond Eurocentric or Euro-American tendencies in reading such films.[1]

Transnational cinema: theorization and critique

In their contribution to the first issue of the journal *Transnational Cinemas*, Will Higbee and Song Hwee Lim shed light on some problems and limitations of the widely used concept of "transnational cinema." While acknowledging its potential-ities, they warn that taking this conceptual term for granted involves the danger of assuming that "the national simply becomes displaced or negated [. . .] as if it ceases to exist, when in fact the national continues to exert the force of its presence even within transnational filmmaking practices" (Higbee and Lim 2010: 10). Higbee and Lim also remind us of the risks of "celebrating the supranational flow or transnational exchange of peoples, images and cultures at the expense of the specific cultural, historical or ideological context in which these exchanges take place" (Higbee and Lim 2010: 11–12).

Similar concerns have also been raised by Hjort who proposes "a typology of cinematic transnationalisms," emphasizing that "[t]here is nothing inherently virtuous about transnationalism and there may even be reason to object to some forms of transnationalism" (Hjort 2010: 15). Regardless of the reservations one may have on Hjort's categories and their application beyond the, at times quite unique, examples used to describe them, it is notable that she values some forms of cinematic transnationalism "because they promote certain social, political, artistic, or aesthetic phenomena that *we* value" (Hjort 2010: 26, emphasis added). Hjort does not clarify who exactly this "we" is, nor does she reflect on the issue of diverse readings and/or values among audiences or critics from different geo-political and geo-cultural contexts. This reminds of some theorizations on the emergence of an "integrated, interconnected, transnational artworld" (Carroll 2007: 132) which, apart from a celebratory tone, have a rather elitist Euro-American orientation.

Noël Carroll, for instance, has suggested that, unlike the past, today artists and critics from different parts of the world "share a number of conceptual frameworks and hermeneutical strategies that facilitate understanding transnationally" (2007: 140). In his view, international art exhibitions and film festivals play a major role in this respect as they pave the way for "foreign language" and independent artists and filmmakers to exhibit their work. Such festivals, he writes "bring *sophisticated work* from everywhere to *serious audiences* in search of something different" (Carroll 2007: 133; emphasis added). Different variations of "progressive politics" and "a generic anti-establishmentarianism" are, in Carroll's view, the recurring themes in transnational art. The reappearance of similar themes in transnational art is merely seen as an indication of the fact that artists witness similar problems arising from capitalism and modernization in urban contexts. Again it is assumed that capitalism and modernization, as developed and experienced in Europe, are singular and universal phenomena, producing unified consequences across diverse national and cultural contexts.

In terms of form, Carroll considers pastiche, radical juxtaposition, de-familiarization, and de-contextualization as being widely common in transnational art. He suggests that these themes and forms together create "a worldwide discursive framework" or a "toolkit" for accessing and interpreting "a very great deal of ambitious art from all over" (Carroll 2007: 142). What we witness today, he concludes, is a "unified" transnational institution of art: "a culturescape with its own language games and networks of communication, distribution, and reception" (Carroll 2007: 142). This observation resembles the viewpoint of a critic/theorist located at the metropolitan "center" of the world who is clearly enthusiastic about having access to artworks from "the peripheries" and to "foreign language" films from other national cinemas. Rather than signaling a space of transnational dialogue and intercultural exchange though, this vision seems to imply the compliance of artists from around the world with the norms and values of a dominant intellectual discourse and aesthetic tradition originating from particular, yet powerful, geo-political and geo-cultural formations.

As Paul Willemen (2006) has noted, national boundaries have a "significant structuring impact" on sociocultural formations and thus should be accounted for in the way Western critics and academics approach and deal with cultural practices from elsewhere. Otherwise, he writes: "reading a Japanese film from within a British film studies framework may in fact be more like a cultural cross-border raid, or worse an attempt to annex another culture in a subordinate position by requiring it to conform to the raider's cultural practice" (Willemen 2006: 34). While Willemen, following Bakhtin, does acknowledge some potential advantages of an outsider's reading of texts from other sociocultural formations, he maintains that such dialogues with the other should also be used to "re-perceive and rethink one's own cultural constellation" (2006: 38). The critical study of other national cinemas, he thus suggests, should also be aimed at modifying "our Euro-American notions of cinema" (Willemen 2006: 38). Elsewhere Willemen has called for a "comparative film studies" (Willemen 2005) and also suggested a "transnational, critical collaboration," not only to elaborate "a *better* theory of cinema as a cultural form," but also "towards the never-to-be-reached goal of a comprehensive understanding of the way culture [. . .] works" (Willemen 2010: 253). Such an understanding, it seems, would not be possible if one is to rely on a self-made "toolkit" of themes and forms.

It would be insufficient for any study of "transnational cinema" to neglect the aforementioned concerns and to focus merely on the supposed ideal of the emergence of transnationalism in film. It is neither enough to suggest that that the "transnational" is a "more humble" substitute for globalization, due to the latter's negative connotations, overarching implications or prodigious use (Hannerz 1996: 6, cited in Bergfelder 2005: 321), nor to merely welcome the "transnational" for being an "intermediate" and "open" term between the "global" and the "international" (Ďurovičová 2010). What is needed, as Higbee and Lim have emphasized, is a "critical transnationalism" that recognizes "the interface between global and local, national and transnational," and moves away from Eurocentric tendencies in reading such films.

Filmmakers with(out) frontiers

During the 1980s Mohsen Makhmalbaf was a prolific and groundbreaking filmmaker in Iran who played a significant role in the foundation of the new Iranian cinema after the 1979 revolution (Dabashi 2001, 2002, 2007, 2008; Egan 2005; Donmez-Colin 2006). As a "disenchanted" Islamist, ex-revolutionary, and political prisoner of the Shah, Makhmalbaf became a major source of attraction to international festivals and Western critics in the 1990s. Yet since 1996 when he made his last film in Iran he has been experiencing a different kind of professional filmmaking which is apparently not confined to any particular territory. His reputation in the international festival circuit enabled him to secure funding for his films from sources outside of his homeland. He established a film company called Makhmalbaf Film House and, along with his wife and children, became involved in film productions that were financed, produced, and screened outside Iran. The most significant among these films was *Kandahar* (2001), the production of which has been described as follows:

> A prominent Iranian filmmaker makes a film about the status of women in Afghanistan, finances it by a French producer and distributor, premieres it in Cannes Film Festival in France, and from there it starts circulating the world, [. . .] before the events of September the Eleventh [. . .] make it a global sensation. The phenomenon is a text book case of globalization, with the corresponding ideas of cinematic nation, national cinema, and ultimately nation itself completely collapsing and superseded.
>
> (Dabashi 2008: 207, emphasis in original)

Makhmalbaf initially described his artistic disposition as "voluntary vagrancy": a strategy to escape censorship in Iran, and also to address wider "human issues" outside the country. He proposed the idea of "filmmakers without frontiers," defining them as filmmakers who "have fled their countries because of censorship [so that they] can create their work under more adequate conditions and their films will gradually reach their fellow citizens, but if they remain in their countries they will not be able to create any work" (Makhmalbaf 2005).

In 1998 Makhmalbaf was awarded one of France's most prestigious "national" awards, namely the Chevalier de la Légion d'honneur medal. In 2004, he officially became a French citizen and had until recently lived in Paris.[2] At the time of writing, *Sex and Philosophy* (2005) and *Scream of the Ants* (2006) are the most recent products of Makhmalbaf's transnational filmmaking career.[3] Both films are financed and distributed by the French company Wild Bunch. Like his earlier film *Silence* (1997), *Sex and Philosophy* was shot in Tajikistan with a Tajik cast. Although the film's diegetic world is in Tajikistan, there is little emphasis on local and national spaces in the film. *Scream of the Ants*, on the other hand, was entirely shot in India with a clear intention on the director's part to highlight certain aspects of local culture and rituals.

Scream of the Ants

A middle-class couple, originally from Iran but apparently resident abroad, travel to India on their honeymoon. The woman (Mahnoor Shadzi) believes in God and is in search of the *Ensan-e Kamel* (literally the perfect human). The man (Mahmood Shokrollahi) is an atheist and former communist.[4] The two squabble throughout the film over the existence of God, the causes of poverty, the meaning of beauty, and the importance of sex. The man has a peculiar character: in one scene we see him admiring his spouse with romantic words; in another he shouts at her and ridicules her religious views. He leaves his wife during their honeymoon after a quarrel, and spends the night enjoying sexual fantasies with an Indian prostitute. This includes asking her to pose as a table, on which he rests his goblet of wine.

While drunk, the man continues to discuss theology and philosophy with the statue of a bull: the "God of power." He loathes God for the sufferings of human beings yet admires him for creating women and wine. We also see the man applying soft clay over the naked woman's body, as if imitating God in creation. After these scenes which began with the couple's quarrel, we see the two in a taxi heading toward the residence of "the perfect human". They are hugging each other and laughing, as if nothing had ever happened.

Scream of the Ants depicts the traditional rituals and religious beliefs of Hindus and others from a rather scornful and even humiliating point of view. In one particularly disturbing scene we see graphically explicit images of naked old men and naked children jumping in the "sacred" river Ganges. Images of Indian beggars and poor people in the streets are edited in parallel with images of stray animals. The only "civilized" Indian we see in the film, apart from the prostitute, is a journalist who, like the tourist couple, carries a camera to document the exotic and primitive aspects of his own people. The statements of the atheist man are dominant throughout the film and interestingly find themselves echoed and amplified by a German adventurer. As the two men gaze scornfully at the Hindu rituals of burning the dead, the atheist man says "this universe is full of shit," to which the German replies:[5]

No [. . .] it is not only shit there [. . .] the shit is constantly raining on you. It is a process, shit is happening, continuously [. . .]. And then in the different cultures, they have found different answers to that [. . .] these are only worn out solutions by some who try to console the people, who try to help the people survive all that constant shit business.

(Makhmalbaf 2006)

When the couple ventures on their pilgrimage to meet "the perfect human," the man unravels the title of the film by emphasizing the number of ants they kill with every step that they take. The message appears to be: all quests for spirituality and metaphysics inevitably involve some kind of criminal activity at the material level. The scene where the couple meets "the perfect human" is also presented in a rather humorous manner, to the extent that it gives us every reason to suspect the wise man is either a fool or a fraud. There is however, a paradoxical twist at the end of the film when the poetic piece of advice that "the perfect man" has given to the woman is read out:

I crossed the seven seas, I climbed up the seven hills, I walked down all the valleys, I went into the deepness. Through all the seasons, I traveled around the world. And when I came back, I was humbled to see that the entire world was there, in a tiny drop of dew, on the leaf of the plant, in my home garden.

(Makhmalbaf 2006)

Here we find out that "the perfect human" did in fact possess some sort of wisdom. Moreover, we understand that the most recent film of a self-proclaimed "borderless" filmmaker who, over many years, has championed transnationalism and cosmopolitanism, ends with a rather "localist" conclusion: there is no need to travel and search all around the world. All is to be found in the local spaces where we are already situated.

Makhmalbaf's attitude toward India and its inhabitants in this film resembles the view of an eighteenth-century European anthropologist who is baffled by the (apparent) ignorance, barbarism, and superstitious beliefs of the people of the Orient, while also shedding tears for their extreme poverty. In fact, by exploiting the cultural and economic resources of India – such as exotic landscapes, Hindi rituals, colourful traditional clothing, naked bodies of local inhabitants, cheap cast and crew, cheap production and post-production costs – for a film produced by a European company, the whole project is also reminiscent of the project of colonialism. Rather than deconstructing colonialist and Orientalist discourses, as expected by a "rebel filmmaker," Makhmalbaf's film seems to be reproducing it.

In his 250-plus-page book, *Makhmalbaf at Large*, Dabashi only dedicates four pages to *Sex and Philosophy* and *Scream of the Ants* put together. This may not come as a surprise as the two films are not very helpful in supporting the subtitle of the book (*The Making of a Rebel Filmmaker*). Since Dabashi is a personal friend of Makhmalbaf and his voice is perhaps the most sympathetic we may find, the way he describes *Scream of the Ants* is quite revealing:

> two hopeless, graceless, boring and banal people, stranger to themselves than they are to us, doing as Makhhmalbaf's renewed fixation with absolutist terms of belief, conviction, truth, and reality tells them to do. They all fail – Makhmalbaf, his actors, his story [. . .]. Judged by this film, here in Paris, there in Afghanistan, or else in India, Makhmalbaf did not seem to be at home in his own craft any more [. . .] his creative courage seemed to have shied away from his worldly whereabouts.
>
> (Dabashi 2008: 216)

This strongly worded critique of Makhmalbaf's latest "borderless" film is clearly in sharp contrast with the image of the "rebel filmmaker" and transnational artist who had supposedly applied "a guerrilla tactic of planting a Trojan Horse in the belly of globalising capital" (Dabashi 2008: 199).

Transnational or "Westernized"?

It has been argued that one advantage of transnational and hybrid cultures is that they transcend local and national boundaries and are positioned "in-between" established cultural formations (Garcia Canclini 1995; Naficy 2001; Ezra and Rowden 2006). They can maintain, therefore, a critical distance from, and reflect on the two or more cultures that constitute them. In other words, they allow for a wider perspective which can acknowledge both the vices and virtues of the self and the other, of the local and the global, of the national and the transnational. Rather than acquiring the position of an intellectual who, in Edward Said's view, always maintains a degree of skepticism toward all received wisdoms (1996), Makhmalbaf's vision seems to have merely shifted from one dichotomist local perspective – in which "the Islamic" was glorified and "the West" was demonized – to another equally limited view in which "the West" is purified while "the Islamic" and even "the national" – in this case the Iranian nation – is reduced to its worst traits.

In a 2002 interview conducted in Paris after Makhmalbaf had left Iran, he uses a wide range of scornful generalizations to describe "the Iranians":

> In comparison to other nations, I feel the reason for our historical misery and depression lies in: first, absolutism; second violence and the sanctification of violence as revolutionary action; third indolence; fourth jealousy; and fifth lying, insincerity and hypocrisy. In my view Iranians are an arrogant, lazy and jealous nation.
>
> (Razi 2002)

Makhmalbaf's description of the "Iranians" stands in sharp contrast with the apparent passion that he expresses for three "other lands" in the same interview. These are: India, Afghanistan, and France. A closer examination of how he describes the first two, or the way he illustrates them in his films, however, leaves us with some indication of where his "true love" lies.

Makhmalbaf praises India "for Ghandi and his non-violence; for Satyajit Ray and his non-sentimentalism; for a nation with a thousand religions and traditions that live together in a high degree of tolerance and peace" (Razi 2002). Apart from the fact that he simply reduces a nation of almost a billion people to two individuals, Makhmalbaf's description of tolerance and peace in India fails to mention the violent sectarian bombings and terrorist attacks which have frequently taken place in India over the past decades. The Indian government's repression of Muslims in Kashmir is also totally neglected in Makhmalbaf's romanticized description. His apparent passion for India also seems incongruent with the gloomy – if not humiliating – image of this nation we see in *Scream of the Ants*.

Makhmalbaf's admiration for Afghanistan, however, is much more dubious since he in effect praises the country for its "primitiveness." He describes a journey on foot to Afghanistan as "a trip to humanity's primitive stages; to the first experiences of human beings in creating a basic, intimate and peculiar civilization" (Razi 2002). Such a view of Afghanistan arguably informs Makhmalbaf's feature film *Kandahar* (2001). As Slavoj Žižek has mentioned in an interview by Parviz Jahed, an Iranian critic, this film is "made for the west. Made to cater for western tastes" (Jahed 2009). The film tells the story of a white, blue-eyed, "liberated" female Canadian journalist of Afghan origin, who secretly travels to the Taliban-ruled Afghanistan to rescue her sister. While the film exploits Afghan women's colourful *burkas* to create some visually stunning images, the repression of Afghan women is reduced to the *burka* itself. The "liberation" of the Afghan people is therefore equated with "unveiling" their women. It is quite revealing that only days before the US military campaign on Afghanistan, in a speech after receiving the UNICEF Federico Fellini

Award for making *Kandahar*, Makhmalbaf publicly states, "I wish this award were bread that could be distributed among the hungry Afghanis. I wish that this award were rain that would pour over the arid land of Afghanistan. I wish this award were the breeze of freedom casting away the Afghan women's burka" (Dabashi 2008: 188).

In his next film, *Afghan Alphabet* (2001), Makhmalbaf goes even further than "wishing" for the *burka* to be "cast away," and practically gets involved in persuading a schoolgirl to lift her veil. This short film was commissioned by UNICEF to advertise the schooling projects for Afghan children in refugee camps inside Iran. For Makhmalbaf "not going to school" and "wearing a burka" are again conflated in this film as one single problem.[6] In a note on the film he explains, without irony, that the problem is that the girl does not know that she is imprisoned by "male chauvinism" (Makhmalbaf 2001). The double standard was not missed by UNICEF who had commissioned the film. According to Dabashi they ultimately rejected the film and refused to distribute it (Dabashi 2008: 191)

Only a few weeks after the USA began bombing Afghanistan, the White House made "an urgent request" for a private screening of *Kandahar* (Edemariam 2001). As Cynthia Weber notes in her in-depth analysis of the film (2005), the Bush administration used *Kandahar* to shift its justification of the war, from indiscriminate targeting of "the terrorists and those who harbour them," to the more popular narrative of "liberating the Afghan people." Although Weber, quite courteously, clears Makhmalbaf of any blame and suggests that the Bush administration appropriated the film against the intentions of its director, even in her reading of *Kandahar* we find elements that resemble the tone of Bush's "War on Terror":

> Kandahar codes humanity according to a simple dualism of light vs. dark. What is light is good; what is dark is evil. What is light and good is humanity; what is dark and evil are social, cultural, political, and religious forces within and beyond Afghanistan like the Taliban, civil wars, and proxy wars.
>
> (Weber 2005: 4)

We might also note that Makhmalbaf never objected to the "appropriation" of his film by the US administration. In fact according to Dabashi he was the first to break the news to the world on his official website that "President Bush has asked to see *Kandahar*," before it was officially confirmed (Dabashi 2008: 194). Makhmalbaf later went on to demonstrate that he has no problem even forming political alliances with Bush's "fellows." In the aftermath of the 2009 Iranian presidential elections, he issued a series of statements co-signed by Mohsen Sazgara: an ex-revolutionary guard, businessman, and political activist based in the USA who has close relations with the neo-conservatives and is a "research fellow" at the George W. Bush Presidential Centre. In these statements the two projected themselves as leaders of the Green Movement and from their residences in Europe or the USA, provided detailed guidance, tactical directions, and even slogans for the protestors inside Iran.[7] Given Makhmalbaf's earlier advocacy of "borderless" filmmaking and his previous engagement in humanitarian projects in Afghanistan, it is striking to see that one of the slogans he recommends to Iranian protestors in defiance of the Iranian government is *Na Ghazzeh, Na Lobnan. Janam fadaye Iran:* Neither for Gaza, Nor for Lebanon: I will sacrifice my life only for Iran (Makhmalbaf 2009).

Bearing in mind Makhmalbaf's comments about "the Iranians," and his attitude toward India and Afghanistan, his admiration of France in the same interview is quite sensational:

> For me France is the cultural capital of the world [. . .] particularly Paris with its cafés and their little round tables on the pavement where one can order just one cup of tea or coffee or a glass of wine and sit and read a 500 page novel through the whole day without being interrupted. It's a city where in every single day you have the option to choose and watch from among a thousand films that are being screened in cinemas, ranging from those of the early days of cinema to those of present times that may be made by an unknown young Vietnamese, Kazakhstani, Polish or Iranian filmmaker [. . .] and this is not just about cinema. During the past two centuries, the French have always accommodated unacknowledged artists from other nations. The history of painting after the Renaissance is the history of unknown painters and artists from other nations being admitted by the French.
>
> (Razi 2002)

Again we can find here a view that turns a blind eye to the global configuration of power and in particular those power relations within the history of colonialism. Makhmalbaf does not at all consider why artists "from other nations" should be "admitted," "accommodated" and "recognized" by the French or any other nation, in order to find a place in the world of art. Moreover, he neglects the poor record of "the French" in accommodating non-elite immigrants and fails to notice the widely discussed marginalization and subordination of large minorities, particularly of African and Arab origin, in French society, which has lead to various riots and violent clashes with the police (Cesari 2002; Freedman 2004; Hargreaves 2007). While enjoying Paris's cinemas and attending various film festivals in France, Makhmalbaf appears to have missed French films like *La Haine/Hate* (Kassovitz, 1995), *Caché/Hidden* (Haneke, 2005) and *Vivre au paradis/Living in Paradise* (Guerdjou, 1998) that deal with the inequalities, repression, and even brutal killing of minorities and immigrants by the French police (Higbee 2006; Crowly 2010; Hargreaves and Kealhofer 2011).

Rather than widening the filmmaker's perspective to allow for a more informed critical appraisal of local, national, and transnational cultures, and the power relations within or between them, it appears that Makhmalbaf's banal transnationalism (as evidenced in *Scream of the Ants* and *Kandahar*) has resulted in a much more parochial and dichotomist attitude. The latter simply denigrates the local and the national in favour of an alleged transnational that in fact turns out to have a local western European orientation. More troubling is the fact that this process also has the potential pitfall of reproducing the mentality of the (European) colonialists in the mind of a victim of (neo-)colonial and imperial projects. It can result in the work of a former political prisoner and "rebel filmmaker" serving the objectives of the neo-conservative onslaughts of the global age.

Kathleen Newman has stressed that "[w]e must ask whether the scale of the transnational evidenced in a cinematic text may operate differently from all other scales," and that whether in this particular scale "the connections established between the here and now of relatively distant locales overcome all the uneven relations of power of other scales such as the national, regional, continental, or international scales" (Newman 2010: 10). Taking account of Mohsen Makhmalbaf's transnational cinema, we may be in the position to say: not necessarily.

Notes

1 This chapter is a revised and updated version of a much longer chapter on Makhmalbaf published elsewhere (Esfandiary 2012). Due to the limits of space, here the analysis of Makhmalbaf's "borderless" filmmaking is be mainly focused on *Scream of the Ants*, with some references to *Kandahar*. I wish to thank the participants in the workshop *Where Are the Intellectuals? Culture, Identity and Community in the Modern Middle East* (University of Edinburgh, May 2010) for their comments on a paper based on the earlier version of this chapter. I am also very grateful to the editors of the present collection for their valuable feedback on the first draft of this chapter.

2 A recent CNN report on Makhmalbaf indicates that he has recently moved from France to the UK and currently resides in London: "Exiled Iranian Film Director's Flight to Freedom," September 22, 2011. Available online at http://edition.cnn.com/2011/09/22/world/meast/iran-film-director/index.html?hpt=imi_t4 (accessed September 27, 2011).

3 Despite leaving Iran in order to make films more freely, Makhmalbaf has not made any films over the past five years. There is currently no news of any film in development or production on the Makhmalbaf Film House website, www.makhmalbaf.com (accessed April 16, 2012).

4 Shadzi and Shokrollahi were appearing for their first time in a feature film and arguably have a very poor performance in the film. The former is an Iranian American, well known by many Iranians for her career as a young presenter in the Voice of America Persian satellite channel (affiliated to the US Department of State). The latter, also of Iranian origin, lives in France and has directed and produced a number of short films and documentaries. Taking into account Makhmalbaf's undisputable skills in selecting and working with non-professional actors, it is not entirely clear why he chose to work with these two individuals. It might be noted, however, that the news of the VOA female presenter appearing naked in a Makhmalbaf film spread quite rapidly inside Iran.

5 A very poor English transcription of the full dialogues of *Scream of the Ants* is available on the Makhmalbaf Film House website (Makhmalbaf 2006). By way of matching this script with the dialogues in the film some grammatical and spelling mistakes have been corrected by the author.

6 This is rather ironic given the fact that Makhmalbaf himself prevented his own children from attending schools in Iran because he believed it was a waste of their time. Instead he decided to teach them personally at home with lessons of his choice.

7 On November 27, 2009, Makhmalbaf appeared on David Frost's show on Al Jazeerah English, where he was introduced as the green movement's "official" and "key" spokesman. Available online at www.youtube.com/watch?v=OlKDd5JnJ5Y (accessed June 28, 2010). Mirhosein Musavi, the leader of the green movement, however, later denied having any spokesmen outside Iran (Musavi 2009).

References

Bergfelder, T. (2005) "National, Transnational or Supranational Cinema? Rethinking European Film Studies," *Media, Culture and Society*, 27 (3): 315–331.

Carroll, N. (2007) "Art and Globalisation: Then and Now," *Journal of Aesthetics and Art Criticism*, 1: 131–143.

Cesari, J. (2002) "Islam in France: The Shaping of a Religious Minority," in Y. Haddad-Yazbek (ed.), *Muslims in the West, from Sojourners to Citizens*, Oxford: Oxford University Press, pp.36–51.

Crowly, P. (2010) "When Forgetting Is Remembering: Haneke's *Caché* and the Events of October 17, 1961," in B. Price and J. D. Rhodes (eds.), *On Michael Haneke*, Detroit, Mich.: Wayne State University Press, pp. 267–280.

Dabashi, H. (2001) *Close Up: Iranian Cinema, Past, Present and Future*, London: Verso.

——(2002) "Dead Certainties: The Early Makhmalbaf," in R. Tapper (ed.), *The New Iranian Cinema: Politics, Representation and Identity*, London and New York: I. B. Tauris, pp. 117–153.

——(2007) *Masters and Masterpieces of Iranian Cinema*, Washington, DC: Mage.

——(2008) *Makhmalbaf at Large: The Making of a Rebel Filmmaker*, London: I. B. Tauris.

Danesh, M. (2007) "Darbareye Mohsene Makhmalbaf; parvaz ra bekhater bespar. . . (On Mohsen Makhmalbaf; Remember to fly. . .)," *Shahrvand-e Emruz*, 17, October 30. Available online at http://shahrvandemroz.blogfa.com/post-273.aspx (accessed December 27, 2007).

Donmez-Colin, G. (2006) *Cinemas of the Other*, Bristol: Intellect.

Ďurovičová, N. (2010) "Preface," in N. Ďurovičová and K. Newman (eds.), *World Cinemas, Transnational Perspectives*, London and New York: Routledge, pp. ix–xv.

Edemariam, A. (2001) "The Film Bush Asked to See," *The Guardian*, October 26. Available online at www.guardian.co.uk/film/2001/oct/26/artsfeatures (accessed December 27, 2007).

Egan, E. (2005) *The Films of Makhmalbaf: Cinema, Politics and Culture in Iran*, Washington DC: Mage Publishers.

Esfandiary, S. (2012) *Iranian Cinema and Globalisation: National, Transnational and Islamic Dimensions*, Bristol and Chicago: Intellect.

Ezra, E. and Rowden T. (2006) "General Introduction: What is Transnational Cinema?," in E. Ezra and T. Rowden (eds.), *Transnational Cinema: the Film Reader*, London and New York: Routledge, pp. 1–12.

Freedman, J. (2004) *Immigration and Insecurity in France*, London: Ashgate.

Garcia Canclini, N. (1995) *Hybrid Cultures: Strategies for Entering and Leaving Modernity*, Minneapolis, Minn.: University of Minnesota.

Hargreaves, A. G. (2007) *Multi-Ethnic France: Immigration, Politics, Culture and Society*, 2nd edn, London and New York: Routledge.

Hargreaves, A. G. and Kealhofer, L. (2011) "Back to the Future? Language Use in Films by Second Generation North Africans in France," in V. Berger and M. Komori (eds.), *Polyglot Cinema: Migration and Transcultural Narration in France, Italy, Portugal and Spain*, Vienna: Lit Verlag, pp. 75–88.

Higbee, W. (2006) *Mathieu Kassovitz*, Manchester: Manchester University Press.

Higbee, W. and Lim, S. H. (2010) "Concepts of Transnational Cinema: Towards a Critical Transnationalism in Film Studies," *Transnational Cinemas*, 1 (1): 7–21.

Hjort, M. (2010) "On the Plurality of Cinematic Transnationalism," in N. Ďurovičová and K. Newman (eds.), *World Cinemas, Transnational Perspectives*, London and New York: Routledge, pp. 12–33.

Jahed, P. (2009) "Žižek: Bayad no'ee sokoote tahdid konande bashid" (Žižek: You Should Have a Threatening Silence)," *Zamaneh*, July 10. Available online at http://zamaaneh. com/jahed/2009/07/post_367.html (accessed June 15, 2011).

King, N. (2003) "Going to Movies in the Morning: Fredric Jameson on Film," *Critical Quarterly*, 45 (1–2): 185–202.

Makhmalbaf, M. (2001) *"Afghan Alphabet*, Director's Note." Available online at www. makhmalbaf.com/movies.php?m=32 (accessed August 16, 2007).

——(2005) "Frequently asked Questions and Answers," Available online at www.makh-malbaf.com/news.php?lang=1& n = 31 (accessed August 16, 2007).

——(2006) *"Scream of the Ants* Dialogue List." Available online at www.makhmalbaf.com/ doc/070717060853ScreamoftheAnts.doc (accessed December 15, 2008).

——(2009) "Hoshdar be khabarnegarane khareji va hamintor khabar resanane jonbeshe sabz" (A Word of Caution to Foreign Correspondents and the Green Movement's Reporters). Available online at www.makhmalbaf.com/news.php?lang=2&n=65 (accessed June 14, 2011).

Musavi, M. (2009) "Goftogooye Kalameh ba Mirhosein Musavi piramun masaele mohemme keshvar" (Interview with Mirhosein Mousavi on the Important Issues of the Country), *Kalameh*. Available online at www.kaleme.com/1388/11/13/klm-10327 (accessed June 14, 2011).

Naficy, H. (2001) *An Accented Cinema: Exilic and Diasporic Filmmaking*, Princeton, NJ: Princeton University.

Newman, K. (2010) "Notes on Transnational Film Theory: Decentered Subjectivity, Decentered Capitalism," in N. Ďurovičová and K. Newman (eds.), *World Cinemas, Transnational Perspectives*, London and New York: Routledge, pp. 3–11.

Razi, A. (2002) "Besyar safar bayad ta pokhte shavad khami" (One Should Travel Much to Become Mature). Available online at www.makhmalbaf.com/articles.php?a=386 (accessed November 15, 2007).

Rosenbaum, J. (1999) "Makhmalbaf and Dostoevsky: A Limited Comparison," Available online at www.jonathanrosenbaum.com/?p=23026 (accessed June 15, 2010).

Weber, C. (2005) "Not Without My Sister(s): Imagining a Moral America in *Kandahar."* Available online at www.opendemocracy.net/content/articles/PDF/3006.pdf (accessed June 15, 2011).

Willemen, P. (2005) "For a Comparative Film Studies," *Inter-Asia Cultural Studies*, 6 (1): 98–112.

——(2006) "The National Revisited," in V. Vitali and P. Willemen (eds.), *Theorising National Cinema*, London: BFI, pp. 29–43.

——(2010) "Fantasy in Action," in N. Ďurovičová and K. Newman (eds.), *World Cinemas, Transnational Perspectives*, London and New York: Routledge, pp. 247–286.

7 Griots and talanoa speak

Storytelling as theoretical frames in African and Pacific Island cinemas

Yifen T. Beus

In discussing a decolonizing, rewriting process for postcolonial cinemas, Ousmane Sembène's film politics of refusing to mimic the West not only as an ideological stance but also as an ideal in film practice and analysis pioneered the debate and has been influential since the 1970s (Barlet 2000), followed by Teshome Gabriel's (1982) and Férid Boughedir's (1983) defining wave of thinking and practice. Filmmakers and critics have kept in mind this historical reality: cinema is a Western invention introduced to much of the non-Western world through colonization, and film aesthetics, philosophies, and even theories and methodologies have been dominated by Western, namely Euro-American, discourses and conventions (Getino and Solanas 1997; Armes 1987; Shohat and Stam 1994; Wayne 2001). As Western cinemas generally model after Hollywood's commercial films in the invisible style at the service of telling a goal-oriented, three-part story or follow the aesthetics of European art film (Wayne 2001), Sembène's likening of the filmmaker to a modern griot and an active cultural body engaged in both artistic expression and sociopolitical reform is particularly useful as a de-Westernizing framework in analyzing films from cultures with a strong oral tradition. Various critics have since discussed the relationship between the postcolonial African filmmaker and the traditional storyteller, the djeli or griot, not only as an "ambassador for tradition" but also as a modern-day bard (Barlet 2004).[1]

Dani Kouyaté's *Keïta! L'Héritage du griot* (1995) and Vilsoni Hereniko's *The Land Has Eyes* (2004) exemplify such de-Westernizing filmmaking by highlighting modernized indigenous storytelling strategies. Kouyaté, a griot by birth and caste, devoted his early professional life to advocating the work of the griot by touring from 1990 to 1996 in the USA and Europe with La Voix du Griot, a storytelling theatre founded by his father Sotigui Kouyaté, who played Djéliba (master griot) in the film. *Keïta!* aptly depicts Djéliba's journey into the city to initiate a schoolboy Mabo into his ancestral history by narrating to him the Mandé epic *Sundjata*. Hereniko, one of the first Pacific Islander filmmakers to win international acclaim, speaks of a similar urgency in an interview: "we [he and his wife as co-producers] really believed that storytelling is very important and, particularly in the medium of film, that Native people needed to see themselves reflected on screen" ("Vilsoni Hereniko Interview," 2004).[2] *The Land Has Eyes*, the result of Heriniko's desire to tell the native people's own stories, tells of a Rotuman girl Viki's experience of witnessing a neighbor's false accusation of stealing coconuts against her father, who cannot speak English to defend himself but insists on the indigenous way of justice: "Pear ta ma 'on maf ka ma 'on 'al ma inea jema ne sei te nojo" (The land has eyes and teeth and knows the truth), the Rotuman proverb that gives the film its title. Like Kouyaté, Heriniko was heavily influenced by his culture's oral tradition and intentionally structured this film not only around an important folk legend but also according to the framework of such storytelling. As the title of this chapter suggests, this author equates *talanoa*, a common word in Oceanian lexicon meaning "talk" or "discussion" and widely used in Oceania studies to connote cultural narrative or talk story, to the act and art of the African griot.[3]

Informed by previous discussions about the role of the filmmaker as contemporary griot in African cinema studies, this author hopes to first sketch out a theoretical framework to analyze Pacific Island films by directors who clearly have in mind a goal similar to that of Sembène in (re)telling their own stories and second to connect the two areas that are rarely discussed side by side through a common theme in what is commonly referred to as world cinema studies. Using Hereniko's pioneering work and Kouyaté's reflexive film on the heritage of the traditional storyteller as a point of reference also helps establish a foundation for future discussion on Pacific Island cinemas as *talanoa* or talk story and set a pattern for comparative studies. The repositioning of traditional storytelling as a key trope in de-Westernizing cinemas remains central to my analysis, which locates cinema as a transformed and modernized means of *talanoa* that engages African and Islander audiences with similar affect and a sense of (re)presence to that of traditional storytelling in a glocalized context.

The 1970s is a decade when many parts of the Pacific saw a wave of cultural renaissance, during which Pacific Islander literature flourished (Wendt 1973, Samoa; Grace 1975, New Zealand) under a unified banner of "New Oceania" and has emerged as a major subfield in Oceania studies.[4] As with African literary and cinema studies at its earlier stage, the textualization of oral narratives occupies an important part of the discipline (Williams 1986; Honko 2000; Winduo 2000; Ramsay 2010). While hybridized aesthetics and the issue of "twice-told tales" through textualization remain major concerns in Pacific and non-Western literary studies today, scholarship on visual popular culture in Oceania has been concerned mostly with images of the Pacific in Western art and cinema due to the scarcity of cinematic output by indigenous Islanders.[5] In particular, exotic native female images by Paul Gauguin have set the stage for many subsequent stereotypical depictions of this region (Taouma 2004: 35–46). Studies of the production history of images of the Pacific (O'Brien 2006), Hawai'i (Desmond 1999), and other South Pacific states (Wilson 2000) find such colonial types and practices a commonplace. Yet little has been written specifically on the representations of Oceania in European cinema, and the images of Oceania in popular Western cinema continue to perpetuate the same stereotypes since the colonial era (Beus 2011).[6]

Not surprisingly, although the writing about "true African cinema" or "African cinema by and for Africans" (Rouch 1962: 14–15) began as early as the 1960s, problematic perspectives still permeated decades of African cinema scholarship:

There was not a dynamic aesthetic proper to Africa due to the lack of African critics who know African traditions as well as the critical practice of the West, where the ethnocentrism of European and American film critics has limited them to evaluating African cinema through the prism of Western film language.

(Diawara 1988: 6)

Tomaselli, Shepperson, and Eke argue that Africa simply did not have the same modern and postmodern conditions and periodizations that warrant the same sets of theoretical assumptions employed by most film scholars (Tomaselli et al. 1995: 18–19) and that ontologies shaped by orality, a major cultural divergence in Africa, assume that the world consists of interacting forces of cosmological scale and significance rather than of discrete secularized concrete objects – a theory taken largely from Walter Ong (Tomaselli et al. 1995: 18, 32).[7] Thus, it is an imperative that we look at African cinema "straight in the eyes" (Diawara 1988: 6) and situate it in the appropriate historical and cultural context specific to Africa. In the past two decades, many African studies scholars have just done so to investigate the storytelling strategies that escape the norms of Europe's poststructuralist film theories as mentioned in the opening paragraph.

As with early scholarship on African cinema, Oceania studies is now facing similar challenges of lacking not only indigenous film scholars but also filmmakers. Unlike the Fédération Panafricaine des Cinéates (FEPACI), which gave African filmmakers a sense of unified charge in their efforts of decolonizing Western narratives about Africa through cinema, or the "New Oceania" concept that unifies post-colonial Pacific writers, the Pacific region does not have a similar organization or coalition of filmmakers to lead a Pan-Oceanian campaign in countering (neo) colonial and imperialist images of the Pacific Islanders. In fact, post-independence cinemas in the Pacific Islands have thus far come mostly from New Zealand and Australia, both settler nations. Moreover, it is only recently that we can speak of a visible presence or publicity of Pacific Island feature films. The first international film festival outside of New Zealand, Australia, and Hawai'i was the 2004 FIFO (Festival International du Film Documentaire Océanien/Pacific International Documentary Film Festival) in Papeete, French Polynesia, a festival sponsored by the French Polynesia Culture Ministry and French TV channel Canal Plus and considered "the place where the voice and the image of the Pacific people are acknowledged" (FIFO Website). But it is still dominated by New Zealander and Australian filmmakers in terms of the percentage of entries for competition.[8] This current state of scarce cinematic production in these regions within Oceania may be explained by Hereniko's statement in an interview about the Pacific Islanders' dissociation of themselves from cinema – a medium invented by and belonging to the West: "because for them filmmaking is for white people, for people in Hollywood, for movie stars" ("Vilsoni Hereniko Interview" 2004).

Despite the aforementioned scholarly attempt to set things straight and validate oral tradition's role in relation to literary work and other artistic expressions in contemporary Africa and Oceania, the author's main concern here is less with the textualization or adaptation of the actual oral stories. Instead, to echo Barlet's call to "subplant the archaic conception" [of the storyteller] and to "stop this figure from being distorted by rigid, reactionary discourse" (Barlet 2004), the author is concerned with storytelling as performance – the act and modes of storytelling that are still very much alive in the regions today. Thus Cham's taking issue with a thrice-told story in fact addresses a different set of concerns (Cham 2005: 298). Sembène's known equation of the filmmaker's role to that of the traditional griot refers exactly to such a relational "adaptation" of the director's art to a modified means of storytelling in the African or Oceanian context. The point is not about the (inter)textualization of the narratives but the material conditions under which narratives are (re)produced and told, the mode of speaking and acting as a narrative performance. It is a concern with the contextual relationship of the medium and the artist to its/his audience. Connecting contemporary art forms with orality is a process of such recontextualization (McArthur 2004: 64). McArthur observes that often key traditional narratives and talk stories can be converted and "adapted" into various modes of oral performance, such as a casual conversation, popular songs, or a political speech, to retain authoritative power in controlling the direction and content of the dialogue and negotiation or the form of expression (McArthur 2004: 62–68). Although in the case of filmmaking the medium of transmission is the camera/projector instead of the mouth, the performativity of the filmmaker remains as the source of power, which dictates how the discourse proceeds and how the listener/spectator receives and responds. Due to colonization and now through a decolonizing process, the modes of storytelling and other oral genres have inevitably evolved or been recast into new performance spaces (Barber 2009: 3). Thus, "multiforms" emerged (Honko 2000: 19–21), as did cinema as a form of communication and artistic expression, and the kind of "return to the source" cinemas can no longer address the contemporary complexities of a global screen culture (Bolgar-Smith 2010: 27).[9]

Although historically African griots and Oceanian storytellers served specific purposes in their own rights, their modern descendants now transcend their traditional functions and play a similar role in relation to their audiences in cinema. The term "strategic hybridity," instead of insisting on binaries of colonial/postcolonial, authenticity/essentialist difference, thus better describes and analyzes such a historical process across disciplines (Sharrad 2007). By resituating the performance of storytelling in a modern, contemporary space and "traveling" with the subjects in the process, the postcolonial performer/filmmaker reappropriates the power of the ancestor (the original storyteller) and the subjectivity of the colonizer (who introduced filmmaking to the colonies) while remaining reflexive of his/her own paradoxical positionings as product of a syncretic education from both the Western and non-Western traditions, a kind of "Afropolitanism" (Mbembe 2006) or "Oceanpolitanism" in a contemporary context.[10] For example, Kouyaté's cross-over from his caste and profession as a griot to a modern theatre and cinematic performer represents such flexible, hybridized "role play" and exhibition on the very topic of traditional storytelling afforded by a sort of postcolonial cosmopolitanism. Djéliba's last words to Mabo before he departs implies Kouyaté's optimism of a hybridized future symbolized by Mabo's character and reflected in his desire to continue his Western education as well as the traditional story:

> Do you know why the hunter always beats the lions in stories? It's because it's the hunter who tells the stories. If the lion told the stories, he would occasionally win. It's valuable for you. Think of it and be confident in the future. Always remember that it's an old world and that the future emerges from the past.

Likewise, Hereniko's own success and skills as a playwright, filmmaker, and an academic owe largely to his Western education, in addition to growing up listening to traditional stories, which has fostered in him a deep sense of who he is:

> In making the film Vilsoni [Hereniko] was in an ambiguous role – part insider, part outsider. As an insider, he drew on his own experiences growing up on the island; as an outsider he came to the task with years of academic conditioning. He had written about Rotuma before, but was unable to engage in a dialogue with the people he was writing about because, with very few exceptions, they had not read what he had written.
>
> (Howard 2006: 92)[11]

Despite the anxiety or liminal positions of these artists, their in-between-ness in fact allows them, as S. Hall (1994) and H. Bhabha (1994) have argued, flexibility and potentials to charter new grounds and innovate means of (re)telling stories through a synthesized identity and positioning. Especially, the preconditioning of

Figure 7.1 Kёita! The Heritage of the Griot (Dani Kouyaté, 1996).

the oral tradition provides a conceptual consistence with many African and Pacific cultures' general social structures, which still rely significantly on a kinship relationship and daily activities of oral nature, such as chants/songs in ceremonies and rituals, mediation of disputes and conflicts, moral value instruction through proverbs and myths, and very often casual gatherings with talk stories.

By highlighting the performance of storytelling in a modernized context, the author does not intend to replace a Euro-universalizing paradigm with another "universal" framework or with "brown mythologies" based solely on orality.[12] Despite the fact that the current anthropological approach to screen studies cannot represent oral traditions in "purely epistemological terms" (Tomaselli et al. 1995: 22) and that many Euro-American film theories can still apply in various productive ways, situating the cinemas as productions from cultures that have a similar thread connecting their worldviews, the communities, and people in such a context provides a useful, decentering schema in treating such cinemas as more than a text in the Western sense of representation and interpretation:

> Most specifically, griots serve to recover and preserve for exhibition in film, that which has been alienated from the present generation because of the disruption consequent to imposition of modernisation policies. In this sense, these filmmakers are also travellers between generations, and as griots they are the intergenerational counterparts of the medieval European troubadours who travelled in a more literally geographical sense.
>
> (Tomaselli et al. 1995: 24)

To recover the discursive space of the traditional griot and the connection between generations, Kouyaté toys with the notion of time in the main narrative as well as in the Sundjata story within the film *Keïta!*. The film's narrative maps out the lineage of the Keïta clan mediated through Djéliba's orature, which is in turn interjected with cinematic flashbacks to simulate the interaction between the storyteller and the audience in a live performance. It also displays the griots' complex relationships and proper roles with those they serve(d) – the court and the villagers in the past, Mabo and his family in the present, and the audience in each screening of the film. In so doing, the film's narrative structure subverts the temporal continuity typical of mainstream Western cinema by allowing the hunter, the ultimate storyteller, to travel between different storylines and generations. That is, while the two parallel narratives, past and present, do not end with a closure (Djéliba never finishes his story, and the audience never sees how Mabo negotiates between his education and his true calling as a griot after Djéliba leaves), they are intersected yet connected by the ostensibly same mysterious hunter. Moreover, key dramatic questions deal primarily with the timing of events: When will the hunter's prophecy be fulfilled? When will Sundjata begin to walk? When is Djéliba going to finish the story? The linearity is frequently interrupted by Mabo's questions, often edited in as sound bridges while the images of the past story are still in view, as well as by other daily activities. The narrative is thus punctuated by Mabo's persistent enquiries, which become the extradiegetic voice over the images of Djéliba's story – why certain things were the way they were, to which Djéliba always responds with the same answer "It is so. . . Be patient, you'll know everything." These dialogues, along with other interruptions, form a dynamic rhythm in the flow of the paralleled narratives, switching between the past and the present. Owing to these "intervals," the timing of breaks and exchanges will "make sense" only when resituated in a context of storytelling performance. However, the temporal boundaries of the individual oral performance are transcended by the continuation of the storytelling outside the filmic narrative: the heritage of the griot continues with the preservation/recording of the narratives as well as the performance on filmstrips or digitally and can be projected repeatedly in the future.

Similarly, in Oceania's oral tradition, the temporal and spatial connection within a community with its surroundings and the ancestors as well as contemporaries transcend the logical, linear boundaries and premises typically upheld in Euro-American film theories. Although the Island nations are divided by the ocean, in their cosmology, they are in fact extended and connected by none other than the ocean. The Pacific Ocean is part of their land and livelihood, and their ancient legends as well as contemporary talk stories reflect this worldview. Thus the functional similarity between African and Oceanian orality is significant in an attempt to indigenize theories that parallel with both regions' cosmologies and their folk traditions. The role and versatile functions of the storyteller, situated and engaged in a specific *vā* (space), reveal exactly the possible modes of reading and watching films.[13] For example, after Hereniko took *The Land Has Eyes* back to Fiji and Rotuma for the first time, he described an interesting experience:

> It was a very interactive experience where people kind of talked back and forth to what was going on on-screen, because they really know life on the island, and what they are watching on-screen is alive on the island at certain period in time. . . they saw themselves appear on-screen as a source of amusement. . . during several screenings, the audiences were ordered to shut up so the sound could be heard.
>
> ("Vilsoni Hereniko Interview" 2004; Hereniko 2010)

This weaving of past and present locations and moments made possible through cinematography, editing, and film projection functions similarly to a narratology that blurs the boundaries of real and fictional stories for the Rotumans. In their oral tradition, the present voice in a *talanoa* recounts the past events with a distinct tone, voice, and variation suitable to the specific moment in time and occasion. The audience then immediately makes a temporal link between the ancestors' circumstances and their own while maintaining the currency of the meaning and significance of the content. It is never a re-presentation of the stories as there is no set version, but rather a consistent sketch or outline of the same stories that are told in different parts of the islands or regions. Nor is it a representation in the political sense Spivak speaks of for the *talanoa* to serve as a proxy of the ancestors

Figure 7.2 The Land Has Eyes (Vilsoni Hereniko, 2004).

(Spivak 1988: 275–279). It is re-placing, instead of replacing, the storyteller's link with those that are "before" in the temporal and spatial sense through a master narrative that might have some details altered or modified in each act of telling/ performance.

Despite the intentional break of linearity of the intertwined narratives, the continuity both in the historical time and space as well as recontextualization of them can be maintained in a number of ways as exemplified in both films: reflexive storytelling motifs, rituals/ceremonies, and the use of proverbs. The narrative's progression in *Keïta!* relies on the telling of the Sundjata story (by Djéliba to Mabo or by Mabo to his friends) mixed with wise proverbs and is motivated by reconnecting Mabo and his generation back to their ancestors and passing unto Mabo the heritage of the griot – an act of linking and making whole fragmented past and present, whether it is under Djéliba's hammock or in the great Kapok tree. Not a mere coincident to foreground the oral tradition, *The Land Has Eyes* also opens with the protagonist's father telling her the legend of the warrior woman of the island. Although slightly different from the version told to the filmmaker when he was young, Marsh describes the filmmaker's reflexive gesture as universal:

> Whatever medium Hereniko uses, his tireless love for storytelling permeates his work and saves it from being reduced in filmic circles to the purely eth-nographic. The opening sequence of the film reveals one of humanity's oldest

and universal scenes: stories being told over the fire, stories handed down from one generation to the next.

(Marsh 2007: 308)

It is essential for both filmmakers to set up a "frame," to separate the master narrative, to which they constantly refer back to throughout the course of the films, from the body of the films' narrative. The *vā* of *talanoa* is thus established during the opening sequences: the father as the storyteller and the heroine as the receiver and carrier of the *mana* of the warrior woman in *The Land Has Eyes* and Mabo as an heir of the great Mandé Empire in *Keïta!*[14]

The storyteller's at times jester-like craft and at times chiefly authority, a type of transformation of oral performance McArthur refers to, can also resituate the master narrative in a transversal context. Like a trickster, he/she moves freely between gender and sociopolitical boundaries. In *Keïta!*, the Buffalo Woman, Do-Kamissa embodies the traits of both human and animal, male and female, and most importantly a storyteller (within the story) of what is to become. As buffalo, "he" (referred to by both Djéliba and the hunters as male) possesses the destructive power of a beast and terrorizes the land of Do, but as human, "she" displays the nurturing quality of a mother and poses as a progenitor of Sundjata (whose mother, Sogolon, is Do-Kamissa's adopted daughter). As storyteller, she in her human form reveals to the two hunter brothers the secret of her identity and ways to kill her as "I know everything. . . Everything has its end. My time has come," she claims. And like a wise griot/counsellor, she knows the timing of events, past and future. By reversing the roles (it is the hunter who tells the story according to Djéliba, not the Lion/beast), she foretells what is to happen in the future – the birth of Sundjata, a past event that is to be brought to the present through Djéliba's oral performance in the film's narrative.

The female trickster figure in *The Land Has Eyes* also traverses the discursive and social spaces. In the wedding scene, another storyteller, disguised as a female wedding clown, improvised a comic performance without a specific plot. Yet through her transgression of gender boundaries by commanding male chiefs and other male wedding guests at will, she is in fact reaffirming the gender-specific origin of the island by referring to the legendary warrior woman, who was the progenitor of all Rotumans. At the same time, she also repositions the chiefs and other males in their proper *vā* in relation to the storyteller/clown as well as other wedding guests to submit to her as her descendants by reminding them of the origin of the island and their proper responsibilities. Only in the setting of a playful performance can she re-present the authority of the island's mother in restoring the proper social order in a seemingly chaotic situation (Hereniko 1995: 65–102). This "ritual clowning" is in fact twice removed from the original story through a fictional performance within the film. However, to the actors in this wedding scene, "there was not clear separation between acting and being at the wedding" (Howard 2006: 82); it was both drama and reality at the same time as performance itself is a ritualistic act. As a result these actors demanded that a real wedding feast be served for it to be authentic in the film because "at a wedding you are fed, and fed well" (Howard 2006: 82). The wedding events, though within a fictional setting, not only had to look real, but they also had to be real to the actors who are simultaneously audiences, who witness the telling and retelling of the same story events captured on film. Thus there is no surprise during the screening that the audience, knowing that the actors all had a real, different life and profession outside the film, still marbled and giggled at the presence of these real life acquaintances in a fictional setting, which to them, serves not as a proxy, but as recontextualization, repositioning of what was, is, and to be, literally and symbolically (Howard 2006: 84–87).

When Fanon writes in "On National Culture" about the revived role of story-tellers in oral traditions in their decolonizing/de-Westernizing efforts, the tendency to "bring conflicts up to date" speaks powerful truth to contemporary writers and filmmakers in their creative work to establish their post-independence national culture through ever-changing means of storytelling:

> On another level, the oral tradition – stories, epics, and songs of the people – which formerly were filed away as set pieces are now beginning to change. The storytellers who used to relate inert episodes now bring them alive and introduce into them modifications which are increasingly fundamental. There is a tendency to bring conflicts up to date and to modernize the kinds of struggle which the stories evoke, together with the names of heroes and types of weapons.
>
> (Fanon 2005: 120)

N. Silva's definition of native pen-wielding as a "war of discourse" is a continuation of the tendency Fanon advocated (quoted in Brown 2005). Through a renewed consciousness, Kouyaté's and Hereniko's wielding of their cameras extends this "warfare" in a globalized digital era to a different tool of shooting back. Although written in 1961, Fanon's words remain current as both African and Oceanian filmmakers and scholars still face the urgent task of righting the wrong images and demystifying stories now created through an even wider variety of new popular media. W. E. B. Du Bois's notion of a "double consciousness" (Du Bois 1903: 3) – young person of color learns to recognize the practice of always looking at one's self through the eyes of others – also continues to serve as a compelling, self-reflexive reminder in theorizing:

> Perhaps we savages, plunged in darkness, do understand each other. What we share is the ability to see with the "third eye". . . the racially charged glance can induce one to see the very process which creates the internal splitting, to witness the conditions which give rise to the double consciousness. . .
>
> (Rony 1996: 4)

Only by investigating the positionings and roles of filmmakers influenced by traditional storytelling, who reposition themselves as the new storytellers to generate affect as well as effect that allow similar spatial and temporal relational interactions between the film/maker and the audience mediated through performance and camera lenses, can such a criticism and methodology look at African and Oceanian cinemas "straight in the eyes" and produce meaningful comparative studies in a glocal context.

Notes

1 As Bolgar-Smith explains, the term "griot" is a postcontact conflation of similar cultural figures in different parts of Africa, in particular the former Mandé Empire. Thus, one must understand that the griot has many roles (Bolgar-Smith 2010: 28–29). But it has become synonymous to the storyteller in African film scholarship largely due to Sembène's comments on this important cultural figure (Pfaff 1984). Other important works discussing the relationship between the filmmaker and the griot include Malkus and Armes (1991), Cham (1993), Diawara (1992), Ukadike (1995), and Tomaselli, Shepperson and Eke (1995).

2 Aotearoa, or New Zealand, is excluded here as it has a well established film industry, and much scholarly work has also been devoted to New Zealander cinema. As a settler nation, its history and issues concerning cultural identity are usually analyzed and treated differently from other Pacific Island nations by postcolonial scholars. For the same reason, I do not include cinemas from Australia although both are part of the Oceania area studies. Most Island nations' film industries, if any, have focused on producing documentaries or short narratives. Very few feature films from the Islands are known to the general public or have been anthologized.

3 *Talanoa* in other parts of Oceania than Fiji, Tonga, and Samoa also has its different names and various functions, such as gossip, mediation, negotiation, and casual talk. Like "griot," the term has acquired its currency as synonymous to storytelling in Oceanian scholarship.

4 Despite the fact that the Oceania covers such vast geographical areas and diverse cultures, the Pacific Islanders share a common Austronesian cultural origin and similar colonial histories. Albert Wendt's 1976 landmark work "Towards a New Oceania" addresses this unified postcolonial identity: "I belong to Oceania. . . This artistic renaissance is enriching our cultures further, reinforcing our identities/self-respect/and pride, and taking us through a genuine decolonisation; it is also acting as a unifying force in our region" (quoted in Hau'ofa 2008: 56).

5 Here the author is referring to Cham's (2004) terminology to summarize the process of textualizing oral stories. When discussing the complexity of filmic adaptation of traditional oral stories, Cham calls this "dubbing thrice-told tales." The stories went through textualization, transcription, and even translation when written down. They were then adapted into films, thus making it thrice removed from the original mode and context of storytelling.

6 See Y. Beus's introductory section. The most discussed European feature shot in the Pacific and about the Pacific people is F. W. Murnau's *Tabu* (1931).

7 Tomaselli and Eke's 1995 essay also addresses the relations between orality and literacy and specifically identifies problems of attempts to mesh visual codes with those of orality when dealing with a certain Third Cinema of Africa.

8 For example, 2011's competition included twenty-one, out of twenty-eight, entries from Australia and New Zealand. Except a handful of films from Vanuatu and New Caledonia, Micronesia and Melanesia had none. See the festival's catalog. Available online at http://fifo-tahiti.com/fifo_en/wp-content/uploads/2010/12/FIFOCATALOGUE2011.pdf (accessed June 30, 2011).

9 For related discussion, see also Bâ and Higbee's "Introduction" (2010).

10 See Harrow's preface (2007).

11 Alan Howard writes in this article a detailed account of the film's production and reception process and includes interviews with the filmmaker.

12 Reference is being made to R. Young's *White Mythologies* (2004) here.
13 See Tevita Ka'ili's (2005). Vā is a socio-spatial concept known in Tonga, Samoa, Rotuma, and Tahiti, where a nurturing relationship is developed. Ka'ili argues that this concept provides a key framework to the understanding of Tongan (and other Pacific) transnationality.
14 *Mana* in many Pacific languages refers to supernatural, divine power; it also connotes the impersonal, spiritual power or quality of an individual.

References

Armes, R. (1987) *Third World Film Making and the West,* Berkeley, Calif.: University of California Press.

Bâ, S. M. and Higbee, W. (2010) "Introduction: Re-presenting Diasporas in Cinema and New (Digital) Media," *Journal of Media Practice,* 11 (1): 3–10.

Barber, K. (2009) "Orality, the Media and New Popular Cultures in Africa," in K. Njogu and J. Middleton (eds.), *Media and Identity in Africa,* Bloomington, Ind.: Indiana University Press, pp. 3–18.

Barlet, O. (2000) *African Cinemas: Decolonizing the Gaze,* trans. C. Turner, London: Zed Books. First published 1996.

——(2004) "Modern-Day Griots," *Africultures* 61 (2004). Available online at www.africultures. com/php/index.php?nav=article&no=5727 (accessed January 25, 2011).

Beus, Y. (2011) "Colonialism, Democracy, and the Politics of Representation in Alain Corneau's *Le prince du Pacifique,*" in I. Conrich (ed.), *New Zealand, France and the Pacific,* London: Kakapo Books, pp. 91–108.

Bhabha, H. K. (1994) *The Location of Culture,* London and New York: Routledge.

Bolgar-Smith, K. (2010) "Questions of Source in African Cinema: The Heritage of the Griot in Dani Kouyaté's Films," *Journal of African Media Studies,* 2 (1): 25–38.

Brown, K. (2005) "Review of *The Land Has Eyes.*" Available online at www.kaiwakiloumoku. ksbe.edu/recipe& reviews/LandHasEyes.php (accessed May 29, 2011).

Cham, M. (1993) "Official History, Popular Memory: Reconfiguration of the African Past in the Films of Ousmane Sembène," in S. Gadjigo, R. Faulkingham, T. Cassirer, and R. Sander (eds.), *Ousmane Sembène: Dialogues with Critics and Writers,* Amherst, Mass.: Massachusetts University Press, pp. 22–28.

——(2005) "Oral Traditions, Literature, and Cinema in Africa," in R. Stam and A. Raengo (eds.), *Literature and Film: A Guide to the Theory and Practice of Film Adaptation,* Malden, Mass.: Wiley-Blackwell, pp. 295–312.

Desmond, J. (1999) *Staging Tourism: Bodies on Display from Waikiki to Sea World,* Chicago, Ill.: University of Chicago Press.

Diawara, M. (1988) "Popular Culture and Oral Traditions in African Film," *Film Quarterly,* 41 (3): 6–14.

——(1992) *African Cinema: Politics and Culture,* Bloomington, Ind.: Indiana University Press.

Du Bois, W. E. B. (1903) *The Souls of Black Folk,* Chicago, Ill.: A. C. McClurg & Co.

Fanon, F. (1961) "On National Culture," in B. Ashcroft, G. Griffiths, and H. Tiffin (eds.) (2005) *The Post-Colonial Studies Reader,* London: Routledge, pp. 119–122. First published 1961.

FIFO: Festival International du Film Documentaire Océanien. Available online at http://fifo-tahiti. com/ (accessed June 30, 2011).

Gabriel, T. (1982) *Third Cinema in the Third World: The Aesthetics of Liberation,* Ann Arbor, Mich.: UMI Research Press.

Getino, O. and Solanas, F. (1997) "Toward a Third Cinema," in M. T. Martin (ed.), *New Latin American Cinema* (2 vols.), vol. I: Theory, Practices and Transcontinental Articulations, Detroit, Mich.: Wayne State University Press, pp. 33–58. First published 1969.

Grace, P. (1975) *Waiariki*, Auckland: Longman Paul.

Hall, S. (1994) "Cultural Identity and Diaspora," in P. Williams and L. Chrisman (eds.), *Colonial Discourse and Post-colonial Theory: A Reader*, London: Harvester Wheatsheaf, pp. 392–401.

Harrow, K. (ed.) (1998) *African Cinema: Post-Colonial and Feminist Readings*, Trenton, NJ: Africa World Press, Inc.

——(2007) *Postcolonial African Cinema: From Political Engagement to Postmodernism*, Bloomington, Ind.: Indiana University Press.

Hau'ofa, E. (2008) *We Are the Ocean*, Honolulu, HI: University of Hawai'i Press.

Hereniko, V. (1995) *Woven Gods: Female Clowns and Power in Rotuma*, Honolulu, HI: University of Hawai'i Press.

——(2010) "Cultural Translation and Contemporary Filmmaking in Oceania," *Festschrift*, August 12–13, Rarotonga, Cook Islands. Available online at http://cookislandsresearch association.wordpress.com/2010/08/31/vilsoni-hereniko-at-festschrift (accessed January 23, 2011).

Honko, L. (2000) "Text as Process and Practice: The Textualization of Oral Epics," in L. Honko (ed.), *Textualization of Oral Epics*, Berlin: Mouton de Gruyter, pp. 3–54.

Howard, A. (2006) "The Making of the Film *The Land Has Eyes*," *Visual Anthropology Review*, 22 (1): 74–96.

Ka'ili, T. (2005) "Tauhi vā: Nurturing Tongan Sociospatial Ties in Maui and Beyond," *The Contemporary Pacific*, 17 (1): 83–114.

Keïta! L'héritage du griot (Keita! The Heritage of the Griot) (1995) Directed by Dani Kouyaté. AFIX, Lanterne, Sahélis, the Government of Burkina Faso, Burkina Faso/France.

The Land Has Eyes, or *Pear ta ma 'on maf* (2004) Directed by Vilsoni Hereniko. Te Maka Productions Inc., US/Fiji.

Malkus, L. and Armes, R. (1991) *Arab and African Film Making*, London and Burkina Faso: Zed Books.

Marsh, S. (2007) "*The Land Has Eyes: Pear ta ma 'on maf* (review)," *The Contemporary Pacific*, 19 (1): 308.

Mbembe, A. (2006) "Qu'est-ce que la pensée postcoloniale? (Entretien)," *Esprit*, December: 17–133.

McArthur, P. (2004) "Narrative, Cosmos, and Nation: Intertextuality and Power in the Marshall Islands," *Journal of American Folklore*, 117 (463): 55–80.

Nichols, B. (1995) *Ideology and the Image: Social Representation in the Cinema and Other Media*, Bloomington, Ind.: Indiana University Press.

O'Brien, P. (2006) *The Pacific Muse: Exotic Femininity and the Colonial Pacific*, Seattle, Wash.: University of Washington Press.

Pfaff, F. (1984) *The Cinema of Ousmane Sembène, a Pioneer of African Film*, Santa Barbara, Calif.: Greenwood Press.

——(2004) *Focus on African Films*, Bloomington, Ind.: Indiana University Press.

Ramsay, R. (2010) *Cultural Crossings: Negotiating Cultural Identity in Francophone and Anglophone Pacific Literatures*, Brussels: Peter Lang.

Robinson, D. and Robinson, K. (2005) "Pacific Ways of Talk: Hui and Talanoa," Social and Civic Policy Institute, Wellington, New Zealand and Council on Public Policy Education, Dayton, Ohio. Available online at www.scpi.org.nz/documents/Pacific_ Ways _of_Talk.pdf (accessed May 12, 2011).

Rony, F. T. (1996) *The Third Eye: Race, Cinema and Ethnographic Spectacle*, Durham, NC: Duke University Press.

Rouch, J. (1962) "The Awakening African Cinema," *UNECSO Courier*, 3 (March): 10–15.

Sharrad, P. (2007) "Strategic Hybridity: Some Pacific Takes on Postcolonial Theory," in J. Kuortti and J. Nyman (eds.), *Reconstructing Hybridity: Postcolonial Studies in Transition*, Amsterdam: Rodopi, pp. 99–120.

Shohat, E. and Stam, R. (1994) *Unthinking Eurocentrism: Multiculturalism and the Media*, London: Routledge.

Spivak, G. (1988) "Can the Subaltern Speak?," in C. Nelson and L. Grossberg (eds.), *Marxism and the Interpretation of Culture*, Urbana, Ill.: University of Illinois Press, pp. 271–313.

Taouma, L. (2004) "Gauguin Is Dead. . . There Is No Paradise," *Journal of Intercultural Studies*, 25 (1): 35–46.

Tomaselli, K. G. and Eke, M. (1995) "Perspectives on Orality in African Cinema," *Oral Tradition*, 10 (1): 111–128.

Tomaselli, K. G., Shepperson, A., and Eke, M. (1995) "Towards a Theory of Orality in African Cinema," *Research in African Literatures*, 26 (3): 18–35.

Ukadike, F. (1995) "New Developments in Black African Cinema," in M. Martin (ed.), *Cinemas of the Black Diaspora: Diversity, Dependence, and Oppositionality*, Detroit, Mich.: Wayne State University Press, pp. 204–240.

"Vilsoni Hereniko Interview" (2004), Native Networks, Smithsonian Institution. Available online at www.nativenetworks.si.edu/eng/rose/hereniko_v_interview.htm (accessed January 30, 2011).

Wayne, M. (2001) *Political Film: The Dialectics of Third Cinema*, London: Pluto Press.

Wendt, A. (1973) *Sons for the Return Home*, Auckland: Longman Paul.

Williams, M. (1986) "The Anxiety of Writing: Language and Belonging in New Zealand and Fiji," *SPAN: Journal of the South Pacific Association for Commonwealth Literature and Language Studies*, 22 (April): 93–104.

Wilson, R. (2000) *Reimagining the American Pacific: From South Pacific and Bamboo Ridge and Beyond*, Durham, NC: Duke University Press.

Winduo, S. (2000) "Unwriting Oceania: The Repositioning of the Pacific Writer Scholars Within a Folk Narrative Space," *New Literary History*, 31 (3): 599–613.

Young, R. (2004) *White Mythologies: Writing History and the West*, 2nd edn, London and New York: Routledge.

8 The intra-East cinema

The reframing of an "East Asian film sphere"

Kate E. Taylor-Jones

For many, Japan's defeat in the Pacific war was greeted with great jubilation, and for those who lived in Japanese occupied territories the defeat was especially important. The Pacific war was the end result of a series of Japanese colonial and imperial initiatives which started in the late nineteenth century.[1] Prior to defeat, the Japanese Empire had colonized Korea, Taiwan, and large areas of China including Manchuria and Inner Mongolia and had occupied Hong Kong, Singapore, the Philippines, Dutch East Indies (Indonesia), Burma, and Malaysia. Although the Japanese Empire may have ended over seventy years ago, its legacy lives on in many aspects of East Asian society, culture, politics, and government and as Kuan-Shing Chen (2010) notes, a continual examination of the colonial period is needed to fully comprehend modern politics and cultural trends in the region. This chapter is focused on one main form of cultural product, namely cinema. From as early as 1910 and particularly during the 1930s and 1940s, the Japanese Empire pioneered its vision of a "Greater East Asian Film Sphere" (GEAFS). This idea, clearly linked to the baggage of a harsh colonial rule, became consigned to history when Japan was defeated in 1945. However, as this chapter will explore, it can be seen as one of the first attempts to construct a cinema presenting a vision of a pan-Asian identity. The first part of this chapter will focus on the narratives told by the GEAFS, and the second part of this chapter will examine examples of modern cinema that re-engages with the legacy of the Empire and its vision of a pan-Asian cinema in new and unique ways. The chapter will focus on two key films *Perhaps Love* (Hong Kong and China, 2005) and *Cape No. 7* (Tawian, 2008) to extrapolate a vision of a new (since 1990) pan-Asian cinema.[2] The aims are to provide a discussion of an intra-East Asian cinema that creates and sustains its own narratives and mythologies.[3]

Throughout this chapter the terminology "pan" and "intra" are both used. "Pan-Asia" references the notion of an idealized "emotional signifier" used "to call for regional integration and solidarity" (Chen 2010: 213). In this way "Asia" as an entity becomes a tool of political and cultural negotiation (Ge 2000). Intra indicates the desire to look inward, to examine the tensions and narratives of Asia and not engage in a dialogue which has the West as a primary focus. There is a need to find and explore a new "frame of reference that take us beyond both the western frameworks that we are all a part of" (John 2010: 195) and "thus, the question of

Asia must not merely be pursued within the framework defined by the dichotomy of East versus West, but also should be considered as dealing with internal problems in the Asian region" (Ge 2000: 14). Thus, de-Westernization is a key part of this approach. There needs to be renewed focus on "agency on the part of Asia" and understanding and seeing "Asia" "not as an essentialist category, but rather as a contextualized position" (Wang 2007: 321). The central argument of this chapter is the fact that pan-Asian film is not a new development fuelled only by a desire to compete against Hollywood (returning once again to a binary of East and West), but an important part of *Asian* cinematic development. Seeing pan-Asian cinema in historical and culturally contextualized positions allows us to "propose and promote theoretical foundations whose concepts, comparisons. . . are rooted in, or derived from, the cumulative wisdom of diverse Asian cultural traditions" (Miiki 2007: 231). This is not an either/or (East/West) approach but rather a move toward a more flexible mode of understanding that traverses borders.

Pan–Asian colonial visions

The Japanese colonial empire is unique as one of the only non-Western empires of modern times (Myers and Peattie 1984: 6). The intricacies, politics, cultures, and economics of the Empire are vast and impossible to chart here but key is that from the beginning Japan engaged with cinema as an important aspect in the construction of its empire as a *transnational* unit (High 1995; Baskett 2008; Kushner 2007).[4] This trans-Asian empire's vision of an Asian identity was embedded in the imperial rhetoric of Japan. The Japanese colonial empire was marked by two key (and often conflicting) discourses (Saaler and Koschmann 2007). The first focused on the cultural and historical "sameness" of those residing in Asia and presented pan-Asian unity as a positive and necessary process to defend against Western imperialism. The "Greater East Asian Co-prosperity Sphere/*Dai-tō-a Kyōeiken*" as proposed by the Japanese would, in theory, unite all Asians (evoked through the notion of *hakko ichiu/*"Eight Corners of the World under One Roof") with Japan leading "less developed" Asian nations toward a bright and ultramodern future under Japanese rule (Shin and Robinson 2001). The GEAFS would aid this drive for Asian collectivity and would help educate and encourage the millions that resided in the Japanese Empire. This was a cinema that would reject a Western cinematic vision, as Japanese actor/director Kinugasa Teinosuke stated in a 1943 interview:

> In consideration of our current victories on the battlefield, we should quickly expel the movies produced by evil Britain and America from the "Greater East Asia Co-Prosperity Sphere," such as China, the Philippines, French Indochina, Thailand, Burma, Malaya and Netherlands India, and substitute them with enlightening and entertaining Japanese films.
>
> (Tadao 1943: 86)

However, this paternalistic vision of Japan leading East Asia to a bright future was in contrast to the strongly held imperial discourse offering a clear notion of

Japanese superiority and therefore difference from the rest of Asia. Consequently, despite the narratives of collectivity that were presented throughout the period, the GEAFS was part of a system that would just replace one binary hegemonic power structure with another. Conflict between the ideals of a pan-Asianism and the focus on Japan as different and superior resulted in continual tension between the colonizing government and the local population, which, especially in the case of Manchuria and Korea, was brutally repressed. Whilst the Empire's pan-Asian ideology was widely advertised via visual and literary propaganda (Kushner 2007; Baskett 2008) the everyday treatment of non-Japanese citizens in this Greater East Asian sphere was very different (Young 1998; Ienega 1979). This chapter is not in *any way* condoning or justifying the Japanese imperial project; however, the GEAFS was aiming to visualize an idealized narrative, *not* accurately represent reality. It is the *constructed* visualization of empire that this chapter is concerned with. This "vision of empire" that the Japanese wished to present (which again was not based on reality) was created not only for Japanese citizens but also for those residing in their colonies. Baskett's work on the Japanese Empire as a transnational cinema unit is particularly useful. In his charting of the Japanese film industry across its colonies he notes that "Japan envisioned that its Attractive Empire would unify the heterogeneous cultures of Asia together in support of a 'Greater East Asian Film Sphere' in which colonizer and colonized alike participated" (Baskett 2008: 3). This would also support the Japanese desire "To replace Hollywood as the main source of news, education and entertainment for the millions living under Japanese rule" (Baskett 2008: 25). Japan's articulation/visualization of pan-Asianism throughout this period is an important area of study for scholars from a variety of backgrounds since the discourses of this period have been key in the shaping of modern Asian narratives and dialogues of pan-Asian identity. Pan-Asian ideology in Japan was not a monolithic and unchanging narrative. It is true that by the late 1930s the intense militaristic focus of the Japanese Empire resulted in narratives of a united Asia been ignored in favor of harsh colonial control, but in the early stages of the empire there had been genuine excitement and commitment to the discussion and extrapolation of the ideals of pan-Asianism in a variety of formats.[5] In terms of film, the desire may have often been economically based, but many filmmakers, producers, and stars during this period understood the need to appeal and engage with local markets. In Shanghai, for instance, a popular and influential cinematic arena, Japanese production companies aimed to "exploit the established relationship between Shanghai cinema and Asian audiences (including overseas Chinese) so as to establish the basis of 'movies of the Greater Asia' and provide a springboard for Japanese films to enter the Asian world" (Yau 2009: 29).

In order to gain a clear understanding of the GEAFS the common themes of films in this period need to be examined. The GEAFS contained documentaries, dramas, romantic comedies, and musicals. Key in all of them was a frequent attempt to eradicate cultural, linguistical, and historical differences in order to construct an idealized (and "Japanified") pan-Asian subject.[6] An ideal personification of this was actress Ri Koran (real name Yoshiko Yamaguchi). Japanese by nationality, she was fluent in Chinese and during the 1930s and 1940s was a key player in the promotion of Sino-Japanese unity. Films like *China Nights* (China, 1940), *Soshū Nights* (China, 1941), and *A Vow in the Desert* (China, 1940) feature Ri Koran as a young headstrong Chinese woman who falls in love (despite her initial anti-Japanese feelings) with a Japanese man. Gradually she "learns" the error of her ways and is convinced of the validity of the Japanese ideas of a united Asia. As a "colonizer passing for colonized . . . Her border-crossing mobility and variable identity elicited a utopic Greater East Asia imaginary where national boundaries and the ethnic and linguistic markings were erased" (Stephenson 1999: 242). As the lead male (Sano Shjiū) in *Soshū Nights* states, "your resentment all comes from misunderstanding. We are here to help build a new Asia."

This "new Asia" would be an ultramodern place. Symbols of modernity such as trains and fast ships which allowed free travel across the Empire (in theory linking each nation to mainland Japan) are frequently presented in these films. *The Volunteer* (Korea, 1941), *Military Train* (Korea, 1938), and *Spring in the Korean Peninsula* (Korea, 1941), for example, all end with the train as a focal point (usually with a crowd waving Japanese flags as the train departs). Together with modern transport systems, the ideas of modern city life are frequent motifs presenting a vision of a united and developing East Asia with Japan as the dominant force driving the modernization process. These are seen in films such as *Sweet Dreams* (Korea, 1936) and *Fisherman's Fire* (Korea, 1939) as well as in the countless newsreels that preceded any film viewing in the empire. The mixture of cars, trains, and modern clothes placed the empire at the "apex of urban Modernization" (Kushner 2007: 44) and an ideal example of "Imperial Prestige" (Kushner 2007: 44). For example, in *Spring in the Korean Peninsula*, the modern meets the traditional as the film examines a cinematic production of the Korean folk legend "the story of Chungyhung." After the film is completed, the lead actress and the director depart for Tokyo to "learn all they can" from the modern center of the film industry. As the Pacific war developed, nations fighting together become the predominant overarching theme. National differences between the various nations would be eliminated in favor of a united Japanese empire and, since this was also the time where repression and abuse in the regions was the strongest, these films are the ones that raise the most discomfort in the modern viewer. *Suicide Squad on the Watchtower* (Japan, 1943), *You and I* (China, 1941), *Portrait of Youth* (Korea, 1943), and *Dear Soldier* (Korea, 1944) are just a few of the films offering a jingoistic focus on the military and evoking the need of the East Asian nations to unite behind Japan. As the father in *Dear Soldier* informs his son when he heads off for the Front, "what you have done is the best thing any son could have for his mother." His (dying) mother states "It takes hundreds of years for us to have this unique opportunity" (to fight/die for Japan). This cinematic imagining of pan-Asia was one the empire (mistakenly) hoped its citizens would help defend.

The defeat of Japan and the unearthing and vocalization of countless abuses and destruction the empire had inflicted on its colonies resulted in this cinema being marginalized and ignored for many years. But via the empire, pan-Asian cinema has been an intrinsic part, often very controversially, of East Asian cinema since its inception in the early twentieth century. As Yau astutely states, "movies of 'Greater East Asia,' conceptualized by Japanese filmmakers during Wartime, were one of the origins of the present East Asian Film networks" (2009).

A pan-Asian cinema of attractions: *Perhaps Love* and *Cape No. 7*

In 2005 the Hong-Kong/Chinese production *Perhaps Love* opened simultaneously in five major East Asian cities (Shanghai, Beijing, Kuala Lumpur, Hong Kong, and Taipei). Starring multilingual Ryukyuan/Taiwanese actor Takashi Kanishiro, Korean television star Ji Jin-hee, and Hong-Kongers Jackie Cheung and Zhou Xun, the film's cast was as pan-Asian as its funding, screening, and reception. Filmed in mainland China, funded by TVB (Hong Kong) and Astro Shaw (Malaysia), the film was distributed across East and South-East Asia by Hong Kong-based Celestial Pictures. *Perhaps Love* was just one of several films produced by Intra-Asian company Applause Pictures. Established by Peter Chan as a specifically pan-Asian production unit, features produced by Applause Pictures such as *Jan Dara* (Thailand, 2001), *The Eye* (Hong Kong and Singapore, 2002), *One Fine Spring Day* (Korea, 2001), and *Three* (South Korea, Thailand, and Hong Kong, 2002) have gone on to break box-office records across Asia (with *The Eye* also crossing into mainstream Europe and America). *Perhaps Love* focuses on the experience of a film director (Cheung) as he brings together two popular stars (Kaneshiro and Zhou) to make a film about the *ménage à trois* between a ringmaster, a showgirl, and a stagehand. Ji Jin-hee plays multiple roles as the narrator who functions in both the film world and the "real" world of the film production. Far from being the Chinese-language version of *Moulin Rouge* (USA, 2001), *Perhaps Love* centers on the notion of an intra-Asian co-production and narrative and can therefore be seen as "one form of a pan-Asian Cinema, claiming core Chinese-speaking markets and from there, venturing further a field into other Asian Territories" (Davis and Yeh 2008: 85). This form of pan-Asian cinema has been steadily growing since the 1990s as domestic markets began to contract which "necessitated investments schemes to amplify market potential and spread the risk" (Davis and Yeh 2008: 85).[7] For cinematic products to economically succeed there needed to be a much wider East Asian market for the film product. Just as the Japanese empire needed to create imperial subjects via their visions of the "Attractive Empire" (Baskett 2008), so too does contemporary pan-Asian cinema need to find an audience that moves beyond national or linguistic boundaries in order to compete with the Hollywood products which have proven so successful at border crossing (O'Regan 1992). So how does *Perhaps Love* aim itself at this market?

Perhaps Love uses one of the most powerful tools at its disposal, i.e. key Asian stars who cross both linguistic and cultural borders. Jackie Cheung (one of the four "Heavenly Kings of Cantopop") is a highly popular and well-known figure in Asian media, and his role as both the fictional ringmaster and the "real-life" director engages with several facets of his media persona. Zhou Xun is a known actress in Hong Kong and mainland China in both mainstream and art-house features. Ji Jin-hee is a well-known face from *K-Doramas* (Korean television dramas) such as *Love Letter* (2003) and *Spring Day* (2005), which have enjoyed popular success across Asia. All these media stars work as an "attraction" for multiple Asian audiences.[8] The casting of Ji and Kaneshiro who are clearly "traveling" star bodies engages in notions of agency between the respective involved regions and hence the pan-Asian viewing audience. Indeed, Takashi Kaneshiro's star status has been developed with this pan-Asian identity as its central selling point. Spokesperson for multiple international brands such as Biotherm, Mitsubishi, Volvic, Honda, and Sony, it is virtually impossible to visit any Asian city without seeing his face on a billboard. In her study on Kaneshiro, Eve Tsai (2005) notes that different facets of this star body engages with the various Asian nations in which it performs in different but linked ways. He is both a colonial symbol (Japanese via his Ryukyuan father) and a postcolonial one (due to his Taiwanese mother). For Japanese audiences, he operates as a sign of their continual accepted presence in pan-Asia despite the actions of the past. For Taiwanese audiences he is a successful symbol of their nation's ability to work and engage with the globalized pan-Asian markets. Just as Ri Koran (as discussed in the previous section) functioned as a symbol of Sino-Japanese engagement during the time of the GEAFS so too, via the body of Kaneshiro, the notion of a previous pan-Asian past continues into a new globalized world. However, Vivian. P. Lee criticizes the film for offering a "generalized ethnic identity" (2009: 203) and cites the film's inability to "measure up to the established benchmarks of the Western Musical" (2009: 202). Thus, for Lee, *Perhaps Love* becomes "a contemporary piece of filmmaking and a symbol of modernity that Asia now champions on the international screen" and for the West something "already achieved, if not surpassed" (2009: 202). What Lee is not acknowledging is that *Perhaps Love* is not *aimed* toward an international audience (rather an intra-Asian one) and that it is in fact referring back to a much earlier Asian film style. Musicals such as *My Nightingale* (China, 1943) and *Singing Lovebirds* (China, 1939) were shown in cinemas around the empire. *My Nightingale* was a star vehicle for Ri Koran and thus, in a similar fashion to *Perhaps Love*, utilized border-crossing stars to engage pan-Asian audience. A Japanese-Chinese co-production, *A Myriad of Colors* (1942) was a lavish musical staring Japanese and Chinese dancers and actors and was a popular hit (Fu 1997: 78). As Stephen Teo notes, the film also evokes "an indigenous practice of song-and-dance cabaret-style musical shows and films (as exemplified by the cycle of films starring Zhou Xuan or Ge Lan, made in Hong Kong in the 1950s and 1960s, or the Shaw Brothers musicals directed by the Japanese director Umetsugu Inoue in the latter 1960s)" (2008: 352). This is not to say that the films did not, and do not, engage with the Western musical form; rather the relationship is not simply a process of an Asian embodiment of Hollywood. This is not an indigenization of Hollywood; rather, it is an engagement with a variety of cinematic traditions both old and new. This is a shift "away from a Euro-American-centric knowledge production" (Ching 2010: 184) toward "new frames of references and new subjectivities" (2010: 185) that engage with forms and modes outside the Hollywood paradigm by offering an interplay between various older forms of

Asian film styles and the new pan-Asian modern musical. This is not aiming to establish a dichotomy of Eastern vs. Western musicals; rather, it is to focus the discourse on the contextualized processes that allow a film to be established in a specific Asian narrative of time and space.

Whilst *Perhaps Love* was conceived as a pan-Asian release, the second film to be examined is, in many ways, the polar opposite. *Cape No. 7* was a surprise hit since the modest budget, lack of famous stars, and first-time director made it at first glance unlikely to achieve massive popular success. In 2010 it became the highest grossing film of all time in Taiwan and went on to be released across Asia, performing extremely well at the box-office and in film festivals (BoxOfficeMojo 2008). The film is a romantic comedy set in the small Taiwanese seaside town of Hengchun, where Japanese pop-star Kousuke Atari (playing himself) is coming to perform. The mayor decides that the town needs a "homegrown" band to open the festival and engages visiting Japanese promoter (and Chinese speaker) Tomoko (Chie Tanaka) to organize the group. After a raucous town-wide audition the mayor's troubled stepson and failed musician, Aga, takes the lead and is joined by bitter traffic cop and ex-SDU (Special Forces) member Rauma, his father Olalan (both of Rukai tribe origin), teen church pianist Dada, mechanic Frog, an eighty-year-old Yueqin (Chinese lute) player Old Mao, and Malusan, a diligent alcohol salesman of Hakka origin. There is also a sub-plot dealing directly with the colonial period. In his job as a postman Aga illegally opens up a parcel from Japan. Inside he finds a collection of love letters from the 1940s from a Japanese teacher to his Taiwanese lover (also called Tomoko) whom he left behind when he was repatriated to Japan at the end of the war. Unlike *Perhaps Love,* the film was not "pan-Asian" in its production, cast (bar for Chie Tanaka) or funding. However, the narrative of *Cape No. 7,* despite being based in a small Taiwanese seaside town, is one that has engaged audiences across national and linguistic borders

Figure 8.1 Cape No. 7 (Te-Sheng Wei, 2008).

and deals directly with the legacy of the colonial period in a variety of ways. In joining the narrative of a lost colonial relationship to Aga and Tomoko's tumultuous path to romance, the film makes the link from past to present. More specifically, by focusing on the relationship between Japan and Taiwan, the film directly engages with the continuing legacy of the Japanese Empire.

Toward the end of the film Tomoko speaks with Dada's mother, Lin, a maid at the hotel where she is staying. Lin states "Japanese don't know how to feel," and it becomes apparent that she has had difficult relations with a Japanese man in the past. It turns out, however, that she is the granddaughter of the woman who was due to receive the missing letters, a narrative twist implying that, despite past problems, inter-Asian engagement and relations are impossible to ignore. This interplay between "colonizer and colonized" is further embodied in the casting of Chie Tanaka. Tanaka learnt Chinese as an adult and has become one of the most popular actresses in Taiwan. Similarities to Ri Koran then are clearly there. However the difference is that Tanaka is not offering the narrative of "becoming the colonizer" (as Ri Koran did) rather she is a sign of the new and productive interplay between the former colony and Japan. Ri Koran operated as a symbol of a pan-Asianism that was focused on subsuming Asian cultures and languages under one category (Japanese). However in *Cape No. 7*, although there are clearly still tensions, the relationship between Tanaka and the community develops into one that is based on mutual respect and friendship. Whilst Tanaka makes some cultural and linguistic mistakes (such as giving the band Rukai bead necklaces without fully understanding the meaning of them and frequently misunderstanding what is said to her in the local dialect) there is no sense of the film moving toward a "generalized ethnic identity" (Lee 2009: 203). This notion of an eradication of cultural individuality is something Lee sees as a potential problem for pan-Asian films aimed at a wider Asian audience. Rob Wilson notes there is the possibility that "Global production would send the transpacific local culture offshore and worldwide, resolving the tensions of imperial history and global imbalance into mongrel fantasy, soft spectacle and present-serving myths" (2006: 343). If this became the aim, then films that wish to engage a pan-Asian audience would need to ignore sites of clear cultural and historical tension such as the Japanese Empire to avoid the alienation of a particular element of the Asian market. However, the contrary seems to be taking place. Whilst there are no doubt many examples of recent pan-Asian films which fall under the category set up by Wilson, films that deal directly with the colonial past have actually become more common in the pan-Asian sphere in the past few decades. Examples can be found across the Asian spectrum from Japan (*TRY*, 2003; *Pride: The Fateful Moment*, 1998) and South Korea (*Once Upon a Time*, 2008; *2009 Lost Memories*, 2002) to Malaysia (*Leftenan Adnan*, 2000), Thailand (*Sunset at Chaophraya*, 1996), China and Taiwan (*Devils on the Doorstep*, 2000; *Seediq Bale*, 2011; *The Puppetmaster*, 1993; *City of Sadness*, 1989; *Lust, Caution*, 2007; and *Dou-san*, 1994). What many of these films have in common is a desire to interrogate and re-engage with the past as part of an ongoing debate on the current state of Asia rather than individual nations. A recentering (away from a continual focus on the West as the main point of reference) and a reassertion of the ideas of pan-Asia have taken place in several political and cultural forums (Chen 2010; Hu 2005). An example of this is the East Asian Film Festival circuit that has been an important element in the "re-centering" that has been seen across the Asian film industry (Iordanova 2010: 16–17). Film festivals as a site that provides "opportunities for exchange" are "important as a key transnational and infrastructural node that make new networks and alliances possible" (Iordanova 2010: 17). This new focus on border-crossing and exchange is giving life to the new pan-Asian cinematic movement. However, one thing that is clear is that filmic pan-Asian subjectivities are in a constant state of negotiation rather than a static entity. Knowledge systems are in constant flux, and the pan-Asian identity is something that is open to debate and interrogation in many of the modern mediascapes and ecologies taking place in global communication systems (Hu 2005; Iwabuchi 2004; Huat 2001). Taking as an example one of the films discussed here, *Cape No. 7* was initially banned in mainland China due to its perceived refusal to engage fully in the narrative of Japanese colonial brutality. The scene when Old Mao speaks fluent Japanese to Tomoko was edited out of the version issued in mainland China. His speaking Japanese was likely given that a Taiwanese citizen of his age, residing in Taiwan during the 1930s and 1940s would have received their formative education in Japanese not Taiwanese; however, this section was cut by Chinese censors who claimed that it may offend those who had suffered under Japanese colonial rule (Yunfei 2009). The piracy industry in mainland China meant that the uncut DVD was still widely available and internet chat forums and sites widely discuss the film and its various meanings, demonstrating that agency is something constantly being challenged and created (Pang 2006). In this way, the narrative of the "attractive empire" of pan-Asia can take place inside and outside dominant disciplinary and hegemonic structures (such as governments). The ways in which the narrative is taking place are myriad: from official government-funded joint agreements to international events such as film festivals all the way down to local internet forums. These are all formats that allow various processes of border-crossing to take place either physically a (film festivals, stars working in more than one national film industry, films being shown in cinemas around Asia at the same time) or in a less tangible way (internet discussions, popular film forums). This new pan-Asia is flexible and open to engagement at multiple levels.

Conclusion

This chapter has not, in any way, sought to present a vision of a united East Asia at ease with itself that can reject all forms of external influence. The memories of the colonial period and other traumas (civil war, mass civil unrest, military dictatorships, and economic crises, to name a few) that have shaped the face of East Asia since 1945 cannot be easily consigned to the past. Japan's continual refusal to accept and acknowledge its actions during the colonial period continues to present tension between that nation and many of the others that surround it. The continuing isolation of North Korea and the myriad of tensions inherent in the

People's Republic of China and other Chinese-language zones continue to this day and can often find their roots in the activities of 1895–1945. What is clear, however, is that the GEAFS, no matter how problematic, was a forerunner for the current focus on a pan-Asian working identity (Davis and Yeh 2008; Baskett 2010; Yau 2009). Recent narratives surrounding pan-Asian production have, whether by design or not, engaged with pre-existing narratives of pan-Asian identity. As stated in the introduction, de-Westernization is about the extrapolation of a framework(s) that allow for an Asia-centric focus. A closer analysis of the relationship between "Globalization and the Imperial and colonial past from which it emerged" (Chen 2010: 2) allows us to contextualize cinematic pan-Asian visions and constructs. It is this contextualization that allows us to see the interplay between the GEAFS and the new pan-Asian cinema, not caught up in questions of the West as a category of comparison but as debating a shared history, however contentious that shared history may be. In short, a de-Westernized inter-Asian cinema has forged and will continue to its own pathways and narratives both on and off the screen.

Notes

1 The intention here is emphatically not to conflate imperialism and colonialism. Japan was both a colonial power and an imperial power. For example, Korea and Taiwan were exercises in colonialism proper, while Japan's actions in China for the most part were more imperial than colonial, as illustrated by the puppet ruler of Manchuria. This is the reason why both terms are used in this instance.

2 Editors' note: given this chapter's focus on the history of pan-Asian film production, it has been decided to give the principal country of production as opposed to simply the name of the director, the first time each film is referenced. This is intended to help the reader understand how individual national cinemas have fitted into this process of transnational production within the East Asian film sphere and intra-East cinema.

3 The term "East Asian cinema" has come to reflect the film industries of primarily China, Hong Kong, Taiwan, Japan, and South Korea but can also engage with and directly reference the cinemas of other nations in the geographical area. This term itself is not unproblematic (Wang 2007: 319), and I am using it with acknowledgment that it is not a fixed or unchallengeable notion.

4 Seeing the Japanese cinema of this period as transnational in its conception is an alternative idea to the predominant construction of Japanese cinemas as a discreet and specifically national entity. See the work of Stringer (2011), Stringer and Phillips (2007), and Baskett (2008) for further reading on this.

5 Art, literature, philosophy, politics, economics, and cultural studies were all subjects where the ideas of a pan-Asian were discussed (Saaler and Koschmann 2007, Ge 2000, Shin and Robinson 2001). What pan-Asia would actually be was a much-debated point but it is important to note that this dialogue kept going well into the 1930s despite the government's renewed focus on the subjugation of the Japanese territories.

6 The increasing banning of the local Chinese, Taiwanese, and Korean languages in favor of Japanese in public (and cinematic) life would compound this.

7 Davis and Yeh (2008) note that this pan-Asian cinema has several manifestations, but due to space constraints this chapter focuses on films that Davis and Yeh have labeled "Intra-Asian" cinema: those "focused on East Asian audiences and indifferent to Western reception" (Davis and Yeh 2008: 91).

8 The question of how media stars are created and then function in the new globalized East Asia is an important topic that is beyond the scope of this chapter. For more information see Wang 2007, Shin 2009, Fung 2003, Siriyuvasak and Hyunjoon 2007.

References

Baskett, M. (2008) *The Attractive Empire: Transnational Film Culture in Imperial Japan*, Honolulu, HI: University of Hawai'i Press.

BoxOfficeMojo (2008) *Taiwan Yearly Box Office*. Available online at www.boxofficemojo.com/intl/taiwan/yearly/?yr=2008& p = .htm (accessed June 9, 2010).

Chen, K. (2010) *Asia as Method: Towards Deimperialization*, Durham, NC: Duke University Press.

Ching, L. (2010) "Inter-Asia Cultural Studies and the Decolonial-Turn," *Inter-Asia Cultural Studies*, 11 (2): 184–187.

Davis, D. W. and Yeh, Y. (2008) *East Asian Screen Industries*, London: BFI Publishing.

Fu, P. (1997) "The Ambiguity of Entertainment: Chinese Cinema in Japanese-Occupied Shanghai, 1941 to 1945," *Cinema Journal*, 37 (1): 66–84.

Fung, A. (2003) "Marketing Popular Culture in China: Andy Lau As a Pan-Chinese Icon," in Lee Chin-Chuan (ed.), *Chinese Media: Global Contexts*, London and New York: Routledge, pp. 257–269.

Ge, S. (2000) "How Does Asia Mean? Part I," *Inter-Asia Cultural Studies*, 1 (1): 13–47.

High, P. (1995) *The Imperial Screen: Japanese Film Culture in the Fifteen Years' War, 1931–1945*, Madison, Wisc.: University of Wisconsin Press.

Hu, K. (2005) "The Power of Circulation: Digital Technologies and the Online Chinese Fans of Japanese TV Drama," *Inter-Asia Cultural Studies*, 6(2): 171–186.

Huat, C. B. (2001) "Pop Culture China," *Singapore Journal of Tropical Geography*, 22 (2): 113–121.

Ienega, S. (1979) *The Pacific War, 1931–1945*, New York: Pantheon Press.

Iordanova, D. (2010) "East Asia and Film Festivals: Transnational Clusters for Creativity and Commerce," in *Film Festival Yearbook 3: Film Festivals and East Asia*, St Andrews: St Andrews University Press, pp. 1–37.

Iordanova, D. and Cheung, R. (2011) *Film Festival Yearbook 3: Film Festivals and East Asia*, St Andrews: St Andrews University Press.

Iwabuchi, K. (2004) *Feeling Asian Modernities: Transnational Consumption of Japanese TV Dramas*, Hong Kong: Hong Kong University Press.

John, M. (2010) "Locating Inter-Asian Dialogues," *Inter-Asia Cultural Studies*, 11 (2): 194-196.

Kushner, B. (2007) *The Thought War: Japanese Imperial Propaganda*, Honolulu, HI: University of Hawai'i Press.

Lee, V. P. (2009) *Hong Kong Cinema Since 1997*, Basingstoke: Palgrave Macmillan.

Miiki, Y. (2007) "An Asiacentric Reflection on Eurocentric Bias in Communication Theory," *Communication Monographs*, 74 (2): 272–278.

Myers, R. H. and Peattie, M. R. (1984) *The Japanese Colonial Empire, 1895–1945*, Princeton, NJ: Princeton University Press.

O'Regan, T. (1992) "Too Popular by Far: On Hollywood's International Popularity," *Continuum*, 5 (2): 302–351.

Pang, L. (2006) *Cultural Control and Globalisation in Asia: Copyright, Piracy, and Cinema*, London and New York: Routledge.

Saaler, S. and Koschmann, V. (2007) *Pan-Asianism in Modern Japanese History*, London and New York: Routledge.

Shin, G. and Robinson, M. (2001) *Colonial Modernity in Korea*, Cambridge, Mass.: Harvard University Press.

Shin, H. (2009) "Have You Ever Seen the Rain? and Who'll Stop the Rain? The Globalizing Project of Korean Pop (K-Pop)," *Inter-Asia Cultural Studies*, 10 (4): 507–523.

Siriyuvasak, U. and Hyunjoon, S. (2007) "Asianizing K-Pop: Production, Consumption and Identification Patterns Among Thai Youth," *Inter-Asia Cultural Studies*, 8 (1): 109–136.

Stephenson, S. (1999) "Her Traces Are Found Everywhere: Shanghai, Li Xianglan, and the Greater East Asia Film Sphere," in Yingjin Zhang (ed.), *Cinema and Urban Culture in Shanghai: 1922–1943*," Palo Alto, Calif.: Stanford University Press, pp. 200–222.

Stringer, J. (2011) "Japan 1951–1979: National Cinema as Cultural Currency," in D. Iordanova and R. Cheung (eds.), *Film Festivals and East Asia*, St Andrews: St Andrews University Press, pp. 62–80.

Stringer, J. and Phillips, A. (2007) *Japanese Cinema: Texts and Contexts*, London and New York: Routledge.

Tadao, Fukai (1943) "Shi'na tairiku eiga to Kyo?eiken eiga: Kinugasa Teinosuke Morita Nobuyoshi ryo? shi ni kiku" (Movies of Mainland China and Co-prosperity Sphere: Interview with Kinugasa Teinosuke and Morita Nobuyoshi), *Shin eiga (Film Spirit)*, January: 83–87.

Teo, S. (2008) "Promise and Perhaps Love: Pan-Asian Production and the Hong Kong-China Interrelationship," *Inter-Asia Cultural Studies*, 9 (3): 341–358.

Tsai, E. (2005), "Kaneshiro Takeshi: Transnational Stardom and the Media and Culture Industries in Asia's Global Postcolonial Age," *Modern Chinese Literature and Culture*, 17 (1): 100–132.

Wang, Y. (2007) "Screening Asia: Passing, Performative Translation, and Reconfiguration," *Positions: East Asia Cultures Critique*, 15 (2): 319–343.

Wilson, R. (2006) "Spectral Critiques: Tracking 'Uncanny' Filmic Paths Towards a Bio-Poetics of Trans-Pacific Globalization," in Meghan Morris, Siu Leung Li, and Stephen Chan (eds.), *Hong Kong Connections: Transnational Imagination in Action Cinema*, Durham, NC: Duke University Press, pp. 249–268.

Yau, K. S. (2009) *Japanese and Hong Kong Film Industries: Understanding the Origins of East Asian Film Networks*, London and New York: Routledge.

Young, L. (1998) *Japan's Total Empire: Manchuria and the Culture of Wartime Imperialism*, Berkeley, Calif.: University of California Press.

Yunfei, Y. (2009) "Cape No7 Controversy," Xinhua News Report, February 15. Available online at http://news.xinhuanet.com/ent/2009-02/15/content_10821637.htm (accessed May 15, 2011).

Part III

New (dis-)continuities from "within" the West

9 "A double set of glasses"

Stanley Kubrick and the *midrashic* mode of interpretation

Nathan Abrams

Although not immediately noticeable or obvious in his films, the Jewishness of Stanley Kubrick (1928–1999) was indelibly inscribed, forming the bedrock of his filmmaking, what George Steiner referred to as "the pride and the burden of the Jewish tradition" (1961: 4). As Paula Hyman observed, "Even secularized Jews were likely to retain a strong ethnic Jewish identification, generally internally and reinforced from without" (1995: 91). Geoffrey Cocks put it thus, "there in fact was – and is – always one Jew at the center of every Kubrick film. The one behind the camera: Stanley Kubrick" (2004: 32). Using Kubrick's adaptation of Stephen King's 1977 novel *The Shining* (1980), as the author's case study, in this chapter he will outline a *midrashic* approach to film studies that originated both before and beyond the Euro-American/Western/Eurocentric traditions in order to allow space for non-Western influences, experiences, and modes of thinking and theorizing Western film.

Midrash (Hebrew: lit. "to investigate" or "study") is the oldest form of Bible exegesis. An ancient tradition, it began within the Bible itself. Developed in the rabbinic and medieval periods and continuing in the present, it is the Jewish method of interpreting and retelling biblical stories that goes beyond simple distillation of religious, legal or moral teachings (Jacobson 1987: 1). It is a means of formal or informal elaboration on Jewish scripture, as a form of commentary, in order to elucidate or elaborate upon its deeper, hidden meanings. It fills in many gaps left in the biblical narrative regarding events and personalities that are only hinted at in the text. Midrash can therefore be highly imaginative and metaphorical, not intended to be taken literally, and is often "a springboard for creative readings of the text that are often at odds with – or even invert – its literal meaning" (Eisen 2003: 370). At the same time, it may simultaneously serve both as a means to make the text relevant to contemporary audiences and as a key to particularly esoteric discussions in order to make the material less accessible to the casual reader.

When it comes to exploring Jews and Jewishness, however, midrash operates at odds with the general trends in current Euro-American film studies which, in general, have almost completely ignored Judaism as religion, as both an analytic category of study and methodology, tending to focus primarily on the Holocaust and/or the image of the ethnically defined "Jew" who is implicitly assumed to be male (Michel 1994: 245; Valman 2007: 3). Furthermore, to date, it has taken as its primary task, "the locating, describing and analysing of films in which identifiably Jewish characters appear or those in which Jewish issues figure into the plot," restricting itself to "*explicit* content, assuming that Jews and their life, society and culture are being discussed or referred to *only* when they appear directly on screen" (Michel 1994: 248, 249; emphasis in original). In this way, film studies has taken on a very limited definition restricted to *visible* ethnicity.

In contrast, midrash allows us to penetrate deep into the film text, challenging the widespread approach to the Jewish/ethnic image on film as limited to explicit "content" analysis. In its focus on the subsurface, "implicit" (Rosenberg 1996: 18), symbolic or conceptual Jewishness and Judaism, that is where Jews, both ethnically and religiously defined, are "literally *conceived*, more than *represented*" (Brook 2003: 124), a midrashic approach uncovers what Ella Shohat has called "a hidden Jewish substratum" undergirding film. Furthermore, it reveals that, despite the absence of any such "ethnic" designation, Jewishness and Judaism are often "textually submerged"; they inhere in film, not only in those where such issues appear on the "epidermic" surface of the text (Shohat 1991: 220, 215).

Midrash allows us to see "Jewish moments" (Stratton 2000: 300) in which the viewer is given the possibility of "*reading Jewish*" (Bial 2005: 70), but not with certainty. Reading Jewish employs "a largely unconscious complex of codes that cross-check each other" (Bial 2005: 70), relying on the viewer locating identifiably Jewish characteristics, behaviors, beliefs or other tics, either explicitly, or by a range of undeniable signifiers. The "real-life" status of the actor/actress behind the depiction, in its conflation of cinematic role/persona with real life, provides a good place to start. But off-screen Jewish identities, although key, are by no means the only way of reading Jewish. Other important clues include historical and cultural references such as looks, intellect, behavior, profession, names, physiognomy, foods, verbal and body language, phenotype, aural, visual or emotional/genre signs, speech patterns and accents, hairstyles, anxieties, neuroses, conflicts between tradition and modernity. All of these require a prerequisite and prior knowledge "allowing individual viewers to identify these clues that represent things Jews and elements that can be read as possibly Jewish" (Krieger 2003: 388).

Furthermore, according to Henry Bial, a Jewish audience

> may glean Jewish specificity from performances that a general audience decodes as universal. Only Jews (or those who know the codes) will interpret these elements of performance as Jewish. While general audiences may recognize these performance practices as unusual, urban, or ethnic, they will not necessarily recognize them as indicators of Jewish cultural difference.
>
> (Bial 2005: 152)

Reading Jewish thus operates in a mode summed up by David Mamet's response when it was suggested that the majority of his audiences would not recognize the Jewish symbolism within his work. Paraphrasing the great Jewish scholar Maimonides (1135–1204), he replied, "Those that do, do; those that do not, do not" (quoted in Kane 1999: 362 n. 40). Leslie Kane suggested that Mamet's "response underscores the coded nature of the work, accessible on many levels" (1999: 362 n. 40). While Mamet's reply may be read as a sense of (defensive) insularity, suggesting a potential lack of desire for intercultural engagement, he is simply acknowledging that reading Jewish requires a frame of alterity to see beyond or beneath the explicit surface of a text. Daniel Bell described this as the individual who sees, "as if through a double set of glasses" (1980: 134) which, figuratively, creates a set of four additional eyes, consequently doubling Nöel Carroll's "two-tiered system of communication" (1998: 245) between Hollywood filmmakers and their audience. I would argue further that Mamet's approach is just as apt for midrash and reading Jewish in general.

Although, according to Frederic Raphael, Kubrick was "known to have said that he was not really a Jew, he just happened to have two Jewish parents" (1999: 105–106), using a midrashic mode of interpretation to read Jewish, the author will argue here that Kubrick's *The Shining* can not only be explored in a midrashic fashion, but also that Kubrick was offering up his own midrash and that his work itself is midrashic. Here, the author is influenced by the similarly midrashic models provided by Kane (1999) on Mamet, Rogovoy (2009) on Bob Dylan, and Diemling (2011) on Bruce Springsteen, all of whom considered their subjects in the manner which the author is proposing, that is to place Kubrick within Jewish cultural history in order to argue that a rewarding way to approach his work is to read it as the work of a mind immersed in Jewish (among other) texts and engaged in making midrash itself. Marc Michael Epstein (2011) cogently argues that not only does Jewish visual culture evince many examples of midrashic motifs but also that Jewish visual culture *itself* needs to be considered as a form of exegesis that mirrors, supplements, and occasionally subverts traditional midrash. Indeed, Kubrick was an enigmatic, elliptical, and frustratingly uncommunicative director. He refused to explain his films' purposes in part as a means to encourage, through exploration and experimentation, the possibilities of meaning and expression. "I think that for a movie or a play to say anything really truthful about life, it has to do so very obliquely, so as to avoid all pat conclusions and neatly tied-up ideas" (Kubrick 1960/1961: 14).

In his analysis of Kubrick's entire oeuvre, Thomas Allen Nelson observed,

> With the possible exception of *2001*, no previous Kubrick film contains as many important details or stimulates as many associative responses. *The Shining* requires several viewings before its secrets are released, and even though like a maze-puzzle it can be assembled into one or more interpretative designs, mysteries remain which intimate that there is still more.
>
> (Nelson 2000: 207–208)

For example, previous scholars have found some tantalizing but underexplored biblical echoes in *The Shining* (Žižek 2006; Hess 2010; Webster 2011). Most significantly, Paul Miers perceived this parallel: "the film ends with Nicholson bellowing in the maze like an Abraham just deprived of both the son and the ram" (1980: 1366).

Following Miers' suggestive analogy, and using a midrashic approach, the author will argue that the film can be read Jewishly, especially in its invocation of the binding of Isaac.

Certainly, in its central idea of a father seeking to murder or sacrifice his son at the bidding of a higher power, the narrative of *The Shining* resembles that of Genesis 22. Known as the *Akedah* (Hebrew: lit. "binding"), out of nowhere, God instructs Abraham: "Take now your son, your only son, whom you love, Isaac, and go to the land of Moriah, and offer him there as a burnt offering [*olah*] on one of the mountains of which I will tell you." Abraham and Isaac then journeyed for three days to a place called Mount Moriah where, at the crucial moment, an angel stays Abraham's hand and a ram caught in a thicket is substituted for Isaac and sacrificed. Abraham named that place "*Yehovah-yireh*" (Hebrew: "the Lord will see/look") because "he saw Him on the mount."[1]

Many of *The Shining*'s details parallel the *Akedah*. Just as God instructed Abraham, a mysterious force draws Jack Torrance (Jack Nicholson) to the Overlook Hotel, which sits high in the Colorado Mountains, an eternal place of mystery that transcends time according to Cocks (2004: 216). The name "Overlook" itself suggests a godlike higher power in its omniscience and omnipotence. One also cannot help noticing the coincidence of the words "Yehovah" and "Over" and that the word "*yireh*" can be translated as "looked." Danny (Danny Lloyd) is Jack's only son whom Jack tells, "I love you, Danny. I love you more than anything else in the whole world, and I'd never do anything to hurt you, never. . . You know that, don't you, huh?" Midrash also states that Abraham was silent during the three-day journey.[2] Likewise, as the family drives up the mountain to the hotel, Jack is irritable and bad-tempered, dismissive toward Danny's curiosity and distant from his wife.

Jewish tradition constantly stresses that it was never God's intention that Abraham kill Isaac. At no point in the biblical narrative does God explicitly instruct Abraham to sacrifice Isaac; rather that Isaac be brought up the mountain and be *prepared* as an offering. In an early form of what is today called intertextuality, the rabbis invoked other biblical sources to support this view, and no fewer than sixteen biblical passages prohibit child sacrifice as an abomination. Judah Goldin has written, "As everyone knows, nothing could be more repugnant to the God of Israel than human sacrifice" (1979: xiii). Yet in one midrash (*Bereishit Rabba* 56: 7), Abraham argues with God to let him carry on and complete the sacrifice. In this reading, Abraham is carried away, almost drunk with submission, obsessed by obeying God. In this respect, he compares to Jack who is literally drunk, as well as submissive to the higher power of the Hotel that orders the "correction" of his family. Since the declaration of Genesis 22 is clear – "Do not raise your hand against the boy, or do anything to him" – Jack is punished because he seeks to sacrifice his son against God's wishes. As Genesis 9:6 warns, "Whoever sheds man's blood, by man shall his blood be shed." Deuteronomy 28 outlines the consequences of disobedience to God's word – "Your carcasses will be food to all birds of the sky and to the beasts of the earth" – a fate that clearly applies to Jack (once his body thaws) whose frozen corpse inside the maze provides a lasting image at the end of the film.

The *Akedah* is central to Judaism. It is the focus of many legends, myths, and folklore. It forms a key part of the New Year's Day service when the complete narrative is read aloud. Many midrashim (plural) have grown up around the *Akedah*, and there is more than one interpretation of it, reflecting the deeply troubling nature of this story. It has since been deployed in Hebrew literature lamenting the loss of homeland and people. During the Middle Ages, in particular, the *Akedah* obtained a prominent place in Jewish liturgy. In the context of the murderous Crusades, it was held up as a test of the worthy, an example of devotion in faith, and its merit was invoked when appeals were made for God's mercy (Wellisch 1954: 57–58). In more recent literature and popular culture, Franz Kafka, Wilfred Owen, Dylan, Woody Allen, as well as *The Believer* (dir. Bean, 2001), have all addressed it.

Furthermore, Kubrick previously deployed the device of the *Akedah* in his *Spartacus* (1960). During the film's denouement, spurned by the wife of Spartacus (Kirk Douglas), Varinia (Jean Simmons), Crassus (Laurence Olivier) orders Spartacus and Antoninus (Tony Curtis) to fight a gladiatorial match to the death. Aware that the winner will endure an excruciating and prolonged death by crucifixion, each vows to defeat the other. Spartacus tells Antoninus that he loves him like a son and then stabs him to spare him further pain.

> In this closed system of destruction designed by the Romans, no divine hand stays Spartacus and no ram is caught in the thicket to substitute for Antoninus. Choosing to spare Antoninus the greater suffering, Spartacus accepts for himself the more prolonged, painful death. There is no hope of redemption.
> (Burton 2008: 13)

In *The Shining*, in contrast, in the closed system of destruction designed by Kubrick, the divine hand stays Jack and Danny is spared. Instead, Jack, trapped in the maze, becomes the proverbial ram caught in the thicket, the offering that The Overlook demands. Furthermore, the blood gushing forth from the elevator recalls the Chronicle of 1096 that recounts the martyrs of Magenza (Mainz). Remembering the *Akedah* and faced with the prospect of certain death or conversion to Christianity, the Jewish residents of the town resolved to sacrifice each other and to offer themselves in sacrifice in sanctification of the Holy Name "until there was one flood of blood" (Spiegel 1979: 19). In this respect, it is significant that the opening music of the film is an electronic rendering of *Dies Irae* ("Day of Wrath"), a thirteenth-century Latin hymn, possibly derived from the prayer "*Unetanneh Tokef*" (Hebrew: "let us tell"), recited as part of the Rosh Hashanah liturgy when the Torah passage recounting the *Akedah* is also read. Legend ascribes the prayer's authorship to the legendary Rabbi Amnon of Mainz (c. 4700–4800).

Just as Abraham is considered to be the father of the Jewish people, midrash invites those wearing a double set of glasses to read *The Shining*'s Abrahamic figure, Jack, as Jewish. *Contra* Cocks, who argues that the film's "abstraction of indirection avoids Jewish stereotyping" (2004: 220), using a midrashic approach to reading Jewish, although nowhere explicitly identified, Jack can be identified as a Jew through a series of stereotypical signifiers and other clues which, as a result, combine to give the viewer the possibility, if no certainty, at least conceptually or symbolically. As Nelson observed, "Jack appears to be a model of liberal politics and education – a writer and teacher, informally dressed in tweed jackets and sweaters, a man who apparently reads *The New York Review of Books*" (2000: 213). The novel certainly describes him as a "college fella" who talks "just like a book" (King 1977: 97). Thus, one of the first things that we learn is that Jack is defined by intellectual rather than physical activity, manifesting what is known as *Yiddische kopf* or "Jewish brains" (Gertel 2003: 132), tapping into a trend, dating almost as far back as to the invention of the medium itself, whereby Jews are defined by their minds rather than bodily traits. Jack is a city slicker, a wisecracking and humorous talker, all cinematic defining features of what Rogin has called "the Jew as brain" (1998: 49). In addition, Nelson's notion that Jack is a subscriber to one of the favored journals of the New York intellectuals is highly suggestive here, compounded by Patrick Webster's argument that Jack "may be losing his sanity and may soon be contemplating the murder of his family, but his liberal sensibilities were still shocked by the use of such politically incorrect and 'murderously' racist language" as "nigger" (2011: 111).

Furthermore, the use of yellow is prominent in *The Shining*. Jack drives a yellow Volkswagen during the entire three-minute opening sequence, as well as when he drives his family to the hotel. Nelson points out that as the film moves closer to Jack's madness, yellow becomes increasingly prominent (2000: 216). The Grady murder corridor is covered in faded yellow wallpaper; a lamp next to Jack's typewriter gives the paper a yellow texture; his face and eyes turn yellow like the yellow bourbon in his glass; the hallway in the Torrance apartment is decorated with yellow-flowered wallpaper; his face takes on a yellow hue while he stands

Figure 9.1 The Shining (Stanley Kubrick, 1980).

outside the bathroom with an axe; as he pursues Hallorann (Scatman Crothers), the interior lighting transforms the walls into evening yellow; and both the Gold Room and gold corridor suggest yellow. Further into the film, a waiter spills a tray of drinks over Jack. "I'm afraid it's Advocaat, sir. It tends to stain," he tells Jack. Advocaat is noted for its distinctive yellow color.

For centuries, yellow has historically connoted Jewishness. Jews were ordered to wear distinguishing yellow badges in the medieval period. A variety of sumptuary laws in fifteenth-century Italy established various markers as Jewish signs, including a circle cut out of yellow cloth for men and a yellow veil for women. A Jewish woman discovered in the street without her distinguishing yellow veil could be publicly stripped (incidentally, this was the sign used elsewhere to mark prostitutes who suffered the same punishment). Rebecca the Jewess in Walter Scott's *Ivanhoe* (1819), adapted into a 1952 film, wears a yellow turban, signifying her Jewish difference. These signs morphed into the yellow badge of the Nazi period, culminating in the yellow triangle for Jewish camp inmates. In this light, the Advocaat stain becomes emblematic of Jack's Jewish origins. It is a stain, a badge of shame, which points to his ethnic identification. The notion of "race" as stain was certainly a familiar one in the past. In 1920s England, for example, one anti-immigration Conservative MP argued that allowing any aliens to remain in Britain would be "a stain upon our British stock" (Schaffer 2008: 12). Later, George Orwell described the perception of Jewishness in the UK to "an initial disability comparable to a stammer or a birthmark" (1945: 167). Philip Roth also used it as the central motif in his 2000 novel *The Human Stain*. In a similar vein Daniel Boyarin wrote, "Jewishness is like a concentrated dye" (1997: 263). As Cocks puts it, "Grady spills the yellow liqueur Advocaat on Jack just as the Nazi 'law' marked Jews with the stain of prejudice, ostracism, and persecution" (2004: 246). Advocaat also sounds like the German, Dutch, French, and American English for lawyer (*advokat, advocaat, avocat,* and *advocate* respectively), a stereotypically Jewish profession. Finally, it links to Freud's essay on the uncanny, itself a source text for the film (Cocks 2004: 245).

Furthermore, Jack styles himself as "The Big Bad Wolf" of the Disney 1933 short *Three Little Pigs*. He utters the line, "Little pigs, little pigs, let me come in," as he chops down a door in his attempt to get at Danny and Wendy (Shelley Duvall). In the original Disney cartoon – and there are multiple references to these peppering the film – the wolf is disguised as a stereotypical Jewish peddler, complete with large crooked proboscis, eye glasses, black hat, thick Yiddish accent, and hand gestures. Although the wolf's disguise was later changed to that of a Fuller Brush salesman, the unaltered soundtrack remained until it too was re-edited (Cohen 1997: 25). Nevertheless, the anti-Semitic stain was not rubbed away.

Jack demonstrates other physical tics the West has historically ascribed to the Jew. In one sequence, he is framed inside the reflection of a bedroom mirror as he eats breakfast in bed, thus giving the illusion that he eats with his left hand. This draws upon age-old stereotypes of the Jew as "sinister." In medieval European Christian iconography, Synagoga and the Jews were typically represented as being on the left-hand side (in Latin, *sinistra* literally means "left") of Christ in depictions of the Crucifixion, the Devil's side (Lazar 1991: 54). Similarly, Wendy physically disables Jack during the course of the film, crippling his right leg, emphasizing the ability of the left, tapping into this same discourse.

Jack's disability is reinforced in a twelve-second uncut sideways tracking shot of Jack dragging his limp foot as he pursues Danny. This is not only "a visual marker of his difference" (Larsen 2002: 81) but also a subtle allusion to his Jewishness that historically has been coded in crudely stereotypical terms by a "clumsy, heavy-footed gait" (Muscat 1909; quoted in Gilman 1991: 228). As Sander Gilman has written, "The idea that the Jew's foot is unique has analogies with the hidden sign of difference attributed to the cloven-footed devil of the middle ages" (1991: 39). Certainly, Jack is represented as a satanic figure, and there are multiple comparisons between him and the Devil, alluding to classic Christian Judeophobia in which Jews were perceived as the Devil's mediators on earth and "given all the possible attributes and qualifications, all the images and symbols that pertain to the prince of the netherworld" (Lazar 1991: 40).

Ultimately becoming the sacrificial victim, Jack "fulfills the classical requirements of scapegoat: he is broken, crippled, outcast" (Kane 1999: 293). At the same time, Jack's limp alludes to his biblical namesake. After Jacob wrestles with the angel, and is renamed *Yisrael* (Israel), the damage caused to his thigh causes him to limp, possessing the gait of the slow and weak. In this respect, Jack's forename is significant. Roland Barthes considered the proper name to be "the prince of signifiers; whose connotations are rich, social and symbolic" (quoted in Webster 2011: 94), and the name Jack is replete with biblical allusion. Jack is short for Jacob (Hebrew: *Ya'acov*), the biblical patriarch, whose sons were the ancestors of the Twelve Tribes of Israel. Jacob was the son of Isaac, who cheated his brother Esau out of his birthright by fooling his blind father, but becomes nonetheless the father of *B'nei Yisrael* (Hebrew: Children of Israel), after his name is changed from *Ya'acov* (Jacob) to *Yisrael* (Israel) following his struggle with the angel. In *The Shining*, like Jacob, Jack awakes from a terrifying dream in which he murders his family and from which he awakens in a fright. The accompanying music is that of Krzysztof Penderecki's *The Awakening of Jacob* suggesting "Jacob's Dream" of Genesis 28:10–18 in which he dreamt of a heavenly stairway which angels were ascending and descending. "Jacob awoke from his sleep and said. . . 'How awesome is this place! This is none other than the abode of God and that is the gateway to heaven.'" And the inserted elevator is none other than a mechanical ladder or a gateway/stairway to heaven (Cocks 2004: 255).

Where Jacob rested is, in midrash, identified with Mount Moriah, the very same place where Abraham sacrificed Isaac. Further intertextual connections link Abraham with Jacob: both were "awakened to obligation by a Voice calling their name" (Kane 1999: 224); both received a new name in addition to their given names at birth (Abram/Abraham; Jacob/Israel); their descendants are both blessed by God who promises them both that they will multiply. Unlike Jacob in Genesis 28, however, when Jack wakes from his dream, he does not realize that, "Surely the LORD is in this place" but rather "I did not know it." His death/ punishment vindicates the presence of God, his frozen body and upturned eyes seemingly saying, "How awesome is this place! This is none other than the house of God, and this is the gate of heaven."

It has not been the author's intention here to reduce Kubrick to a single message or to suggest that he made "Jewish films" (whatever that may mean) with purely literal and exhaustive meaning. Indeed, Kubrick's work can be enjoyed without recourse to its Jewish aesthetic or vision. Yet, rather than diminish the interpretative possibilities of Kubrick's cinematic oeuvre, a midrashic approach allows us to read Jewish, that is to read it backward, to understand the impact and sweep of history that inform his canon, to illuminate the sources and scope of his work.

A midrashic approach helps us to understand how a text such as *The Shining* which, at first glance, appears to be firmly embedded in the codes, conventions, and discourses of Hollywood (even if it is directed by an auteur who was considered something of a maverick/outsider in the Hollywood system), encodes deeper, and not always Euro-American readings. In this way, a midrashic reading necessarily effects a specific "de-Westernizing" of the text by reclaiming and foregrounding Jewish references in an act that not only specifically challenges Western perceptions or stereotypes but also challenges, subverts, and confronts wider opinions, stereotypes of Jews and Jewishness that are not necessarily Western in origin per se. In this way, Kubrick, as part of the Jewish diaspora, can be seen as placing Jewishness as simultaneously within and outside of the "West." While such an approach may be particularly appropriate for Kubrick and Jewishness in film, it can be extended to any film or any non-visible minority. In this way, it moves us away from American and Eurocentric approaches to film studies to embrace non-Western ways of reading meaning into films, Western and otherwise, where it is not immediately apparent.

Acknowledgments

The author would like to thank Lindsey Taylor-Guthartz for her extremely useful comments on earlier drafts of this chapter.

Notes

1 *Yehovah* is a Hebraized version of the King James-type "Jehovah," a misapprehension based on combining the Hebrew consonants of YHVH with the vowels of "Adonai," but not actually a form that was ever used.
2 It is also suggestive that the opening sequence lasts three minutes.

References

Abrams, N. (2011) *The New Jew in Film: Exploring Jewishness and Judaism in Contemporary Cinema*, London: I. B. Tauris.

Bell, D. (1980) *Sociological Journeys: Essays, 1960–1980*, London: Heinemann.

Bial, H. (2005) *Acting Jewish: Negotiating Ethnicity on the American Stage and Screen*, Ann Arbor, Mich.: University of Michigan Press.

Boyarin, D. (1997) *Unheroic Conduct: The Rise of Heterosexuality and the Invention of the Jewish Man*, Berkeley, Calif.: University of California Press.

Brook, V. (2003) *Something Ain't Kosher Here: The Rise of the "Jewish" Sitcom*, New Brunswick, NJ: Rutgers University Press.

Burton, M. (2008) "Performances of Jewish Identity: *Spartacus*," *Shofar: An Interdisciplinary Journal of Jewish Studies*, 27 (1): 1–15.

Byers, M. (2009) "The Pariah Princess: Agency, Representation, and Neoliberal Jewish Girlhood," *Girlhood Studies*, 2 (2): 33–54.

Carroll, N. (1998) *Interpreting the Moving Image*, Cambridge: Cambridge University Press.

Cocks, G. (2004) *The Wolf at the Door: Stanley Kubrick, History, and the Holocaust*, New York: Peter Lang.

Cohen, K. F. (1997) *Forbidden Animation: Censored Cartoons and Blacklisted Animators in America*, Jefferson, NC: McFarland.

Diemling, M. (2011) "American Midrash: Biblical Motifs in the Work of Bruce Springsteen," in L. Dolezalová and T. Visi (eds.), *Retelling the Bible: Literary, Historical, and Social Contexts*, Frankfurt: Peter Lang, pp. 343–356.

Eisen, M. (2003) "Midrash in Emil Fackenheim's Holocaust Theology," *Harvard Theological Review*, 96 (3): 369–392.

Epstein, M. M. (2011) *The Medieval Haggadah: Art, Narrative, and Religious Imagination*, New Haven, Conn.: Yale University Press.

Gertel, E. B. (2003) *Over the Top Judaism: Precedents and Trends in the Depiction of Jewish Beliefs and Observances in Film and Television*, Lanham, Md.: University Press of America.

Gilman, S. L. (1991) *The Jew's Body*, London and New York: Routledge.

Goldin, J. (1979) "Introduction," in Shalom Spiegel, *The Last Trial*, trans. Judah Goldin, Philadelphia, Pa.: Jewish Publication Society, pp. i–xx.

Hess, N. (2010) "*The Shining*: All Work and No Play. . . ," *The International Journal of Psycho-Analysis*, 91 (2): 409–414.

Hyman, P. (1995) *Gender and Assimilation in Modern Jewish History: The Roles and Representation of Women*, Seattle, Wash.: University of Washington Press.

Jacobs, L. (1995) *The Jewish Religion: A Companion*, Oxford: Oxford University Press.

Jacobson, D. C. (1987) *Modern Midrash: The Retelling of Traditional Jewish Narratives by Twentieth Century Hebrew Writers*, Albany, NY: State University of New York Press.

Kane, L. (1999) *Weasels and Wisemen: Ethics and Ethnicity in the Work of David Mamet*, Basingstoke: Macmillan.

King, S. (1977) *The Shining*, London: New English Library.

Krieger, R. (2003) "'Does He Actually Say the Word Jewish?' Jewish Representations in *Seinfeld*," *Journal for Cultural Research*, 7 (4): 387–404.

Kubrick, S. (1960/1961) "Words and Movies," *Sight and Sound*, 30: 14.

Larsen, E. (2002) *The Usual Suspects*, London: BFI Publishing.

Lazar, M. (1991) "The Lamb and the Scapegoat: The Dehumanization of the Jews in Medieval Propaganda Imagery," in S. L. Gilman and S. T. Katz (eds.), *Anti-Semitism in Times of Crisis*, New York: New York University Press, pp. 38–83.

Michel, S. (1994) "Jews, Gender, American Cinema," in L. Davidman and S. Tenenbaum (eds.), *Feminist Perspectives on Jewish Studies*, New Haven, Conn.: Yale University Press, pp. 244–269.

Miers, P. (1980) "The Black Maria Rides Again: Being a Reflection on the Present State of American Film with Special Respect to Stanley Kubrick's *the Shining*," *Modern Language Notes*, 95 (5): 1360–1366.

Nelson, T. A. (2000) *Kubrick: Inside a Film Artist's Maze*, Bloomington, Ind.: Indiana University Press.

Orwell, G. (1945) "Anti-Semitism in Britain," *Contemporary Jewish Record*, 8 (2): 163–171.

Raphael, F. (1999) *Eyes Wide Open: A Memoir of Stanley Kubrick*, London: Ballantine.

Rogin, M. (1998) *Independence Day*, London: BFI.

Rogovoy, S. (2009) *Bob Dylan: Prophet, Mystic, Poet*, New York: Scribner.

Rosenberg, J. (1996) "Jewish Experience on Film: An American Overview," in D. Singer (ed.), *American Jewish Year Book, 1996*, New York: American Jewish Committee, pp. 3–50.

Roth, P. (2000) *The Human Stain*, New York: Houghton Mifflin.

Schaffer, G. (2008) *Racial Science and British Society, 1930–62*, Basingstoke: Palgrave Macmillan.

Scott, W. (2009) *Ivanhoe*, New York: Signet Classics. First published 1819.

Shohat, E. (1991) "Ethnicities-in-Relation: Toward a Multicultural Reading of American Cinema," in L. D. Friedman (ed.), *Unspeakable Images: Ethnicity and the American Cinema*, Urbana, Ill.: University of Illinois Press, pp. 215–250.

Spiegel, S. (1979) *The Last Trial*, trans. J. Goldin, Philadelphia, Pa.: Jewish Publication Society.

Steiner, G. (1961) *The Death of Tragedy*, New Haven, Conn.: Yale University Press.

Stratton, J. (2000) *Coming Out Jewish: Constructing Ambivalent Identities*, London: Routledge.

Valman, N. (2007) *The Jewess in Nineteenth-Century British Literary Culture*, Cambridge: Cambridge University Press.

Webster, P. (2011) *Love and Death in Kubrick: A Critical Study of the Films from* Lolita *through* Eyes Wide Shut, Jefferson, NC: McFarland.

Wellisch, E. (1954) *Isaac and Oedipus: A Study in Biblical Psychology in the Sacrifice of Isaac, the Akedah*, London: Routledge & Kegan Paul.

Žižek, S. (1989) *The Sublime Object of Ideology*, London: Verso.

——(2006) *How to Read Lacan*, London: Granta.

10 Situated bodies, cinematic orientations

Film and (queer) phenomenology

Katharina Lindner

This chapter suggests that one way of dislodging film (studies) from its "Western" hegemonic locations is to put "the body," and questions of embodiment, at the center of inquiry, in order to challenge the taken-for-granted orientations, perspectives, and (embodied) points of view of traditionally "Western" film (criticism). This includes the bodies *in* film, the bodies *of* film, as well as the bodies "behind," "in front," and "around" film that constitute the embodied contexts for its production, consumption, and theorization. The critique of the "Western" standpoint and orientation of much contemporary film theory and criticism presented here makes use of phenomenological debates around subjectivity as embodied and lived, as well as of queer critiques of traditional phenomenology, in order to begin to unpack the ways in which "Western," white, heterosexual, male subjectivity has been the structuring norm that film (theory) has been orientated "around" (Ahmed 2006: 115).

Rather than critiquing conventional and hegemonically "Western" standpoints and locations by proposing alternative centers, this chapter begins to challenge their taken-for-granted orientations. It is not only a matter of where we stand (when we engage in film criticism and, indeed, when we watch films). It is also a matter of which way we face, and what is, therefore, ahead of us, within sight and reach – and, conversely, what is behind us, out of sight and unreachable.[1]

The "West," for the purposes of this discussion, is therefore not a geographical location but a particular mode of being in, and seeing/perceiving, the world, a particular perceptive and expressive center from which the world unfolds – although this center is certainly grounded in some, often Western, geographical locations more than others. The non-Western approach to cinema proposed here can be considered "queer" in that it challenges "straightforward" accounts of our embodied (expressive and perceptive) relations to the world and to cinema. It accounts more specifically for non-normative embodiments and relations, and their affective, social, and political dimensions (although this does not, of course, mean that non-Western approaches are *necessarily* queer in this sense). Following, critics such as Richard Dyer (1997) and Sara Ahmed (2006) who highlight the centrality of heterosexuality to conceptualizations of race (and vice versa), the notion of "queer" employed here encompasses various non-normative embodiments of gender, sexuality, and race.

First and foremost, this chapter provides a conceptual critique and reorientation of various approaches to film and the cinematic experience. The argument presented is illustrated with particular reference to *Girlfight* (Kusama, 2000) and *The Gymnast* (Farr, 2006), two sports films produced within distinctly Western geographical locations (the USA), while featuring queer female characters in central roles. These films are considered to provide de-Westernizing potential "from within," so to speak, by "making strange" normative bodily relations and orientations from within the context of Western cinematic representation. A frustration, on the author's part, to come to terms with these and other sports films using established approaches is partially where the motivation for, and the orientation of, this endeavor unfold from. Vivian Sobchack expresses a similar sentiment in *The Address of the Eye*, where she writes that, although they have "grounded and circumscribed feminist film theory, both psychoanalytic and Marxist film theory in most of their current manifestations have obscured *the dynamic, synoptic and lived-body situation of both the spectator and the film*" (1991: xv, xvi; emphasis added).

Perhaps, this is not so much only a matter of "obscuring" lived experience, but of taking for granted a very *particular kind* of lived experience (Western, white, heterosexual, male) that becomes so normative and "habitual" (Ahmed 2006: 129–133) as to be unfelt. As such, Ahmed's (2006) account of queer orientations adds a phenomenological and corporeal dimension to Dyer's (1997) argument around the sociocultural construction of heteronormative whiteness as non-specific, as universal, and as "just human," as seemingly non-located and disembodied – rather than a *particular* manifestation and experience of race (and sexuality) – as well as to Dyer's calls to "make strange" whiteness and to highlight the *particularity* of the embodied experience of being white.[2]

Sports films such as *Girlfight* and *The Gymnast*, concerned, as they are, with the relationship between bodily movement/performance identity, subjectivity, and (narrative) agency, encourage us to think about different ways of reading bodies and bodily movement *in* and *of* film.[3] They also foreground the complex intertwining of gender, sexuality, and race via their representations of athletic bodies in action. Athletic female characters constitute, by definition, a queer presence within the male-centered and masculine (generic) context of sports (films). Female athleticism more generally carries queer connotations as it is associated with gender-inappropriate bodily forms and ways of moving through and taking up space (Young 1980), thus opening up possibilities for non-normative embodied spectatorial engagements.

Locations, encounters, orientations: cinema and (queer) phenomenology

The argument presented here is based upon a critical engagement with a range of contemporary and historical approaches to film from a queer perspective that attempts to dislodge the "straightforward" conceptual and theoretical assumptions underpinning these approaches. This is not an entirely new endeavor by any means. In part, its beginnings can be located in the critique of psychoanalysis and its place within film studies from a feminist perspective from the 1970s onwards (i.e. Mulvey 1975). The homogenizing and generalizing (white, middle-class, heterosexual, Western) tendencies of early feminist criticism were subsequently challenged by black, working-class, and lesbian feminists. The initial feminist arguments put forward did not "fit" with their specific understandings and *experiences* of oppression, and, importantly, with their frustrating, but also often pleasurable, encounters with cinema (i.e. Bobo 1995; Gaines 1986; hooks 1992). In a way, this was an initial move away from an abstract understanding of subjectivity, centered on (disembodied) vision, and toward what Adrienne Rich (1984) calls a "Politics of Location," which asks us to take into account the historical and sociocultural specificity of our locations and subject positions. What is not acknowledged, however, are the embodied and affective dimensions of differently located and orientated subjectivities. What is advocated here, then, is a move beyond a "Politics of Location" and toward what might be called a "Politics of Orientation," that accounts not only for "where we are (from)" but for "which way we face," and for our embodied and necessarily orientated existence in the world. Such an understanding allows for a critique, and a "making strange," of the normative directionality and orientation of a Western point of view, centered as it has traditionally been "around" the hegemonically white, heterosexual, middle-class male body and "toward" the non-Western, or other, Other that serves as a necessary point of identification against which the hegemonic center defines itself.

It is in relation to what Laura Marks calls "intercultural cinema" in *The Skin of the Film* (2000) that the embodied dimensions of cinematic spectatorship have been explored in some detail. With a particular focus on art-house, avant-garde and experimental films, produced by (diasporic) filmmakers working between cultures within a postcolonial global context, she identifies intercultural cinema as characterized by a representational aesthetic that provides access to "other" cultures through an articulation of, and appeal to, *embodied* memories and experiences. These films, suggests Marks, invite a sensuous engagement that resonates with specific socioculturally and historically situated knowledges and experiences that traditional (Western) forms of representation, and ways of *accounting for* those representations, might not be able to "grasp" (2000: xiii). For instance, Marks focuses on the significance of what she terms "haptic visuality" (2000: 162) and explores that ways in which certain kinds of images, in particular those that emphasize surface and texture, appeal to our sense of touch, thus evoking embodied knowledges and (sense) memories (2000: 71). As such, this type of cinema, located, as it is, both inside and outside the geographical West, can be seen as a non-Western (as per the definition introduced above) form of critique and, importantly, of theorizing; as a challenge to Western film and to Western film theory; and as an exploration of new aesthetic, theoretical, and political possibilities.

Jennifer Barker's phenomenological approach in *The Tactile Eye* (2009) focuses more specifically on mainstream, Western, filmmaking. Barker goes beyond Marks's notion of haptic visuality by going beneath the "skin" of the viewer and the film, and she considers "musculature" as one of the locales in which the cinematic encounter might take place. Barker suggests that the movies not only "touch" but "move us" – intellectually, emotionally, physically – as the cinematic encounter is experienced through modes of movement, comportment, and gesture. This mode of seeing is characterized by a *grasping* gaze that engages our muscles and tendons, allowing viewers to empathize with films *kinesthetically* because of the similarities in the ways in which both films and viewers relate to the world through particular ways of taking up, moving through and extending space. Like Marks, and following Walter Benjamin, Barker proposes a mimetic, rather than purely symbolic, relationship between the viewer and the film but acknowledges more specifically the materiality, corporality, and fleshiness of the body. This points to possibilities for *bodily* identification with the image and "with the sense and sensibility of materiality itself" (Sobchack 2004: 65); as opposed to/in addition to psychological identification with characters and/or narrative. Crucially, however, this focus on bodily materiality comes without an acknowledgment of embodied and "lived" differences. In this sense, Barker proposes a one-size-fits-all approach and the seemingly neutral, unmarked, and universal "human" body at the center of this work is, in fact, a very specifically, and hegemonically, orientated (white, heterosexual, male, Western) body.

If, as Sobchack argues, cinema uses "modes of embodied existence (seeing, hearing, physical and reflexive movement) as the vehicle, the 'stuff,' the substance of its language [and if] it also uses the structures of direct experience (centring, bodily situating of existence in relation to the world of objects and others) as the basis of the structures of its language" (1991: 5), then we should be able to account for the cinematic experience, viewing pleasures, and the political implications of film in relation to how films appeal to, touch, and move viewers based on their (individually and socially) embodied ways of "being in the world." Sobchack (1991, 2004) is, in fact, one of the critics who begins to do this. Drawing on Iris Young's (1980) work, she points to the ways in which gendered subjectivities are embodied and lived *differently*, with feminine bodily existence tending to be self-referred, lacking bodily unity, and experiencing lived space as enclosing and confining, as being positioned in space, rather than positing space – while Young (1980) also highlights the ways in which the athletic female body largely defies these gendered norms. Sobchack goes on to conceptualize a dialectical relationship between our ways of being in and perceiving the world, suggesting that our embodied perception of the world is based on the ways in which we inhabit our body in space and time. This opens up important ways of understanding the cinematic experience in terms of our "bodily existence," and based on an understanding of bodily difference that is *not* essentializing and *not* rooted in anatomy but based on the embodied histories, experiences, and memories that leave their "marks" on skins and bodies.

Generally, however, the significance of lived differences is under-explored in current debates about film and embodiment, as phenomenology itself remains a largely Western, white, heterosexual, and male-centered framework. This is a conceptual and analytical gap that is explored further here, by drawing on Ahmed's *Queer Phenomenology* (2006), which questions the orientation *of*, as well as the concept of orientation *in* (Edmund Husserl's and Maurice Merleau-Ponty's) phenomenology.[4] Husserl's phenomenology in particular "seems to involve an ease of movement" (Ahmed 2006: 138) that is characteristic of certain (white, male, heterosexual) bodies but not of others. Ahmed suggests that the mobile body, the body that "can do" things, can be read in terms of heterosexuality and in terms of white-ness. Its orientation is normative, non-particular, and seemingly universal and thus not even perceived as being specifically orientated.

The body, literally, provides us with a "point of view," and perception involves a "turning toward" certain objects and others. If we face the right way, and see straight, the objects and others that come into view, that are reachable, close, and familiar, are those that allow us to follow the straight line of genealogy and its specifically heterosexualized and racialized dimensions (see Ahmed 2006; Dyer 1997). Racialized bodies are queer in that they "make strange" the straightforward whiteness of phenomenal space. Ahmed argues that "the 'matter' of race is very much about embodied reality, [which] does affect what one 'can do,' or even where one can go, which can be redescribed in terms of *what is and is not within reach*. If we consider what is affective about the 'unreachable,' we might even begin the task of making 'race' a rather queer matter" (Ahmed 2006: 112 – original emphasis). A phenomenology of queer embodiments thus points to the ways in which sexualized and racialized bodies are shaped and directed by how they take up/extend space, and, conversely, to the ways in which spaces are shaped by the direction and orientations of the bodies within it.

Queer bodies might have a disorientating effect (on others) and they might also experience their own existence as disorientating because of the inability to "ground" oneself within normatively orientated (straight, white) phenomenal space. What Ahmed also suggests, however, is that bodies "take the shape" of what they "do" (repeatedly and over time) and thus, in turn, may shape the spaces they inhabit. This is precisely why the sports context, which involves the endless repetition of certain bodily movements in training, is of particular interest here. Such an understanding also points to the political and "empowering" sig-nificance of bodily activity – and this is, again, of particular interest in relation to the sports context and the significance of (disruptively and disorientatingly) queer female bodies within it. To be queer is to disturb the order of things and, to point to the origins of the word "queer" as a spatial term, to be "out of place," "oblique," "off the line," "twisted" (Ahmed 2006). The filmic articulation of a kind of twisted embodiment, an obliquely orientated subjectivity, is therefore one way of "making strange" the Western (white, male, heterosexual) orientation of main-stream cinema that is based on a very *particular* relation to, and perception of, space and other bodies and objects within it, while passing itself off as universal. This includes its often "straightforward" (Oedipal) narrative trajectories and aes-thetic conventions; it includes its "straightforward" articulations of identity, sub-jectivity, and desire, as well as time and space; and it includes the kinds of (visual) pleasures and viewing positions thus provided. This particular orientation and directionality of traditionally Western cinema is, in turn, echoed by the traditional theoretical frameworks employed to account for its characteristics.

Queer encounters: *The Gymnast* and *Girlfight*

What is suggested in the remainder of this chapter, is that certain instances of female athletic performance and interaction might be read, and felt, as queer moments – even, or perhaps particularly, within films that are otherwise characterized by straightforwardly Western representational conventions. *The Gymnast*, for instance, a film evolving around two female gymnasts who fall in love with each other, features two explicitly queer characters but follows a fairly conventional coming-out/lesbian romance narrative trajectory. In terms of its visual aesthetics, the film can equally be situated within a traditionally Western representational context. In fact, the clichéd story line of the uptight, (f)rigid, married, blonde, and white American protagonist, Jane (Dreya Weber), whose lesbian desires are awoken through her encounter with the exotic, dark-haired, tattooed Japanese-American Jew with a knife fetish, Serena (Addie Yungmee), who plays a slightly less central role, can be read as a reinforcement of rather problematic racial and sexual binaries. Racial difference can be seen to substitute for sexual difference, leaving normative and binary understandings of sexual difference and desire intact. However, the coherence of this largely conventional representational frame is variously disrupted, both through the "making strange" of the disembodied and distanced nature of the white, heterosexual, male (viewing) position, embodied by Jane's husband, David (David Simone), and by the foregrounding and privileging of the embodied existences of, and relationships between, the athletic female characters.

From the outset Jane and Serena's encounters are physical and tactile: they both engage in a kind of acrobatic activity, involving long sheets of fabric hanging from the ceiling of an empty theatre hall. This training/rehearsal space carries particular significance and is clearly distinguished, in narrative and aesthetic terms, from the otherwise white and straight world outside. It is a secluded space which only the athletes themselves have access to, with the occasional exception of their white female coach, the African-American male owner of the property, and Jane's white bisexual female friend. Notably, however, the white male characters who play relatively central roles in the film as a whole are excluded from this rather queer space in which the female characters feel comfortable and "at home" (Ahmed 2006).

This contrasts with their initial experiences of being "out of place" within the straight, white world outside the hall: Jane's excessive exercising (running and weight lifting) without any explicit narrative goal or purpose, can be read, and felt, as a bodily struggle against the sense of confinement within a space that does not "extend her shape" (Ahmed 2006). This is particularly the case in the opening part of the film, before her encounter with Serena, where Jane's frustrations with the dullness of her heterosexual marriage and a general feeling of a lack of purpose are explicitly emphasized. What Jane "faces," what is "in front" of her, is a path, or "line" (Ahmed 2006) that seems to foreclose action and desire. The de-Westernizing potential of these opening sequences in particular can thus be located in the film's "making strange" of the orientation and directionality of normatively Western, white, heterosexual space – and Jane's athletic activity can be read, and felt, as an attempt to reorientate and reshape both her body and the space surrounding it. The sense of female athleticism – by definition nonconforming, transgressive, and queer within a Western (representational) context – as an expression of frustration and rebellion, and linked to experiences of not fitting in and being out of place, is characteristic for a range of female sports films including *Million Dollar Baby* (Eastwood, 2004), *Stick It* (Bendinger, 2006), *Girlfight*, and *Blue Crush* (Stockwell, 2002). Variously, these films are characterized by the foregrounding of the physicality of the female body, via an audiovisual emphasis on muscles, sweat, heavy breathing, and physical exertion. Depictions of athletic activity thus serve as articulations of a bodily struggle, not necessarily against an opponent but against the sense of confinement and the closing down of possibilities for action and desire experienced by those non-normatively orientated bodies that are "out of place." Athletic activity literally shapes the body, and in the case of the female body this challenges conventionally gendered ways of moving through and taking up space (see Young 1980).

In *The Gymnast*, the rehearsal hall provides an unmarked, and not-yet-particularly-oriented space that is visually set apart from the outside world in a number of ways, including color: the sheets of fabric used by the athletes are a deep red, as are the inner walls of the building, which creates a warm and sensuous feel – a reading of the rehearsal space as somehow womb-like is certainly possible. Additionally, there is a visual emphasis on the malleability of the space surrounding the characters. At various points, we see the athletes covering their hands in chalk powder in order to improve their grip. There are a number of slow-motion close-ups of the athletes clapping their hands and rubbing their fingers together, followed by slow-motion shots of thousands of tiny specks of chalk seemingly floating through the air. The audiovisual emphasis on the contact between skin, chalk, and air adds a specifically haptic quality to the image (there are similar sequences in other gymnastics films such as *Stick It*). There are also a number of athletic sequences in which the sun rays that enter the hall through the windows become visible as they reflect off the dust and chalk filling the air, emphasizing, again, the particular consistency of space, countering hegemonic assumptions of space as universal, unmarked, and somehow always already given. This provides a sense of physical connection, and contact, with the bodies moving through this space, imbuing the image with a sensuous register that privileges a more fully embodied engagement, challenging conventionally Western perceptions of and relations to space.

The emphasis on *bodily* reciprocity and exchange that characterizes Jane's and Serena's interactions (within the training space) contrast heavily with the centrality of the one-directional white male gaze in depictions of Jane's relationship with David (outside this space). In fact, whenever white, heterosexual male characters do get visual access to the athletes in action, their exclusion from the women's physical bond is even more explicitly emphasized: they can *only* look on. The distanced, alienated, and disembodied nature of the white male gaze is made visible, and its orientation, directionality, and assumptions of (sexual) power and control are exposed and ridiculed. In these moments, the more general reappropriation of the athletic female body as an object of heterosexual male desire

Figure 10.1 The Gymnast (Ned Farr, 2006).

within popular culture is "made strange." This contrast in (bodily) relations is perhaps most powerfully asserted through the athletes' use of a technique called "porting." "Porting" refers to "a set of aerial moves that use a particular hand-grip, which is the only thing that keeps one of the aerialists from plummeting to the ground."[5] When using this technique, athletes are connected by a sense of mutual dependency. Their bodies are in physical and sensual contact with each other and/or the fabric, and it is through this emphasis on bodily contact and the sense of touch itself that the film articulates a "sense" of eroticism.

The use of long strips of fabric as sporting equipment is crucial to this. The performers not only engage in a kind of reciprocal and often sensual relation with each other but also with their equipment itself. In the first training scene, the instructor encourages both Jane and Serena: "Don't just hang there. Respond to the fabric," which both athletes do. They wrap themselves around the sheets as they wrap the sheets around their bodies. The material is smooth and strong and forms a kind of organic relation with the women's bodies.

The camera angles during athletic sequences also differ significantly from the "straightforward" depictions of the other spaces in the film. At times, the athletes seem to defy gravity. Their muscular and powerful bodies move freely and without inhibition in this space that accepts and welcomes the "shape" of their bodies and that is, in turn, shaped by their presence. It is a space that extends the shape of their bodies and thus opens up possibilities for action and agency (Ahmed 2006). The overhead shots and oblique, slanted, and twisted camera angles leave it unclear, at times, if the characters, and in fact, we as the viewers, are positioned upside down, right side up, sideways, forwards or backwards. Rather than creating a sense of confusion (as visual mastery and control of the space is denied), this can be read, and *felt*, as an opening up of possibilities and pleasure and as a foregrounding and "making strange" of the straightforward, restrictive, and conventionally orientated space depicted elsewhere in the film.

The significance of the fabric in inviting a more fully embodied engagement is asserted in a number of scenes in which the material denies the spectator direct visual access to the female body and its physicality. When Jane and Serena use the fabric as a hammock, it is only the outline of their bodies and their imprint on the fabric that is actually "visible." The movement of the bodies across the fabric articulates an eroticism that is not, importantly, based on looking. The link between the athletic physicality of the female body, the sense of touch, the fabric, and its texture and a specifically queer sensuality and desire is perhaps most explicit in a sequence when Jane is lying in the hammock on her own following a training session with Serena. Jane begins to move her hand across the fabric. The light from behind the material gives it a textured, see-through consistency. The play of light against/through the red fabric, through which we can "see" the outline of Jane's body and her moving hand, in addition to the slow and melodic score, create a sensual atmosphere and give the image an explicitly "haptic" quality (Figure 10.1).

The camera then cuts to a short scene of Jane back in her house, in the bathtub. A close-up of Jane's hand, her fingers tightening around the rim of the bathtub, suggests that she is masturbating. This is followed by a fantasy sequence in which images of Jane's hand caressing the fabric are superimposed over images of Serena during training. As Jane touches the fabric, she "touches" (the image of) Serena (Figure 10.2).

What is articulated here, then, is a sense of what it might "feel like" to touch, and be "in touch" with, this body. Serena's body is not necessarily desirable because of what it "looks like," but because of the kind of bodily existence and way of "being in the world" it embodies. The bodily relations depicted on screen in this sequence encourage a more fully embodied gaze – but they can also be

Figure 10.2 The Gymnast (Ned Farr, 2006).

read as an articulation of the kinds of queer embodied viewer engagements made possible by cinematic representations of female athleticism more generally. The sequence provides us with a "sense" of the physical connections between the materiality of the bodies represented on screen (Serena's body), the materiality of the film (through the superimposition that "incorporates" a range of contradictory temporal and spatial dimensions) and the materiality of the "viewer's" body (Jane's hand that "touches" the fabric/Serena's body/the image). This is an (embodied) articulation of desire that does not rely on conventionally Western binary differences and the subject–object distance underpinning such conceptions of subjectivity and desire. Generally, the film's articulation of queer subjectivity and desire *within and through* athletic performances can be seen to make "visible" the possibilities for more fully embodied, and queer, engagements that depictions of athletic performance provide – outside of and/or in addition to the more conventionally straightforward viewing pleasures on offer. In particular, the film highlights possibilities for perceptive and affective relations to cinema that are very much centered around ways of "being in the world" that challenge the normatively Western emphasis on the supremacy of vision (especially notions of a gaze that penetrates, conquers, and controls the three-dimensional space constructed on screen). It also challenges our taken-for-granted assumption about what is "in front" of us, and therefore reachable and knowable, through its "twisted" articulation of subjectivity and desire.

In *Girlfight*, a boxing film featuring a Latina protagonist, Diana (Michelle Rodriguez), the queerness of the female athlete is not linked to an explicit representation of queer sexuality (as in *The Gymnast*) but articulated exclusively via representations of bodily performance and embodiment. This is the case with regard to most filmic representations of female athleticism, as the openly lesbian female athlete, and particularly the non-white lesbian female athlete, continues to represent something of a taboo. In fact, Diana's relationship with her Latino boyfriend, Adrian (Santiago Douglas), who is also a boxer, challenges us to think through the troubling implications of the *heterosexual* queer female body as well as through common conflations of (bodily) gender performance and sexuality. Diana embodies a queer subjectivity in that she fails to conform to the bodily norms of gender and race: her body is extremely muscular and powerful, hard rather than soft, and clearly "out of place" – both in the homosocial space of the boxing gym and in the social-cultural space of the film as a whole, which is situated within a working-class Latino community in New York.

In the opening part of the film, Diana seems uncomfortable "in her own skin" and has an alienated relationship to her body that does not "fit," in a social and in a bodily/embodied sense. She fails to inhabit social spaces (school, home) comfortably and gets into physical fights with her classmates and with her father. The opening sequences in particular, in which the camera focuses on Diana leaning against the wall in her high school's hallway, with students cutting across her body and the frame in a constant flow of (straightforward) movement, can be read, and felt, as an articulation of Diana's queer orientation: she faces the wrong way and we are asked to share her disorientation.

Taking up boxing, against the wishes of her father, her brother, and the majority of boxers and trainers in the gym, is depicted as a response to a sense of embodied discomfort, or, rather, of disembodiment. Initially, Diana is "out of place" within the gym and has a disorientating effect within this male-centered space. However, the boxing space has appeal for her because it allows for the literal reshaping of the body: what bodies "do do" over time affects what they "can do" (Ahmed 2006). The initial training sequences foreground Diana's raw and unpolished physicality, and there is a sense in which she does not know how to use her body. Ahmed (2006) suggests that the impossibility of action arises from a lack of "fit," that is from incompatible orientations, between spaces, bodies, and objects/tools. Diana's embodied experiences of a lack of fit, and therefore a lack of possibilities for action and agency, mean that she is not (yet) "in tune" with her own body and its capabilities.

Girlfight, like most other female sports films, can certainly be read as an instantiation of the tomboy narrative (see Creed 1995), in which the development of a mature heterosexual femininity is put into crisis through engagement in sport, only for it to be finally recuperated by the climactic formation and celebration of the heterosexual couple (i.e. *Wimbledon* [Loncraine, 2004], *Love and Basketball* [Prince-Bythewood, 2004], *Bend It Like Beckham* [Chadha, 2002]). The alternative is punishment and/ or death (i.e. *Million Dollar Baby*). However, *Girlfight* can also be seen, and *felt*, to follow a sensuous trajectory from alienation, disembodiment, disorientation, and being "out of place" to embodiment, reorientation, and feeling "at home," that "makes strange" conventionally Western narrative trajectories and visual pleasures and that might resonate with the embodied experiences and memories of queer viewers in particular.

The incoherent movements and lack of boxing action in the initial training sequences are foregrounded by the lack of aestheticizing music and the sounds emanating from the body and its contact with the environment. At one point we see Diana looking at herself in a broken mirror in the boxing gym. What is reflected back is a disjointed and cut-up image, underlining the sense of disorientation and the lack of bodily unity inscribed on her character. The static framing of these early boxing sequences, the lengthy, distanced shots and lack of editorial action parallel the lack of action and agency in the gym. They serve as embodied articulations of the sense of frustration felt by those bodies that reside in spaces that do not extend their shape. The static framing (particularly within the generic context of the boxing film in which editing tends to aid, rather than undermine, the action) invites an embodied spectatorial response, a sense of embodied frustration about a lack of bodily agency that might be characteristic of and/ or familiar to (some) queer viewers.

Throughout the film, and as the result of intensive training, Diana's movements become increasingly smooth and confident. This is paralleled by a change in editing, which becomes more dynamic, and by the introduction of aestheticizing music. Diana begins to experience her body as pleasurable, as a source of agency, and as a body that "can do" things. Viewers are invited to empathize, *kinesthetically*, with the increasingly assertive and confident movements of a queer body that is not so much out of place anymore. The film articulates an almost utopian sense of being "in place" in a training sequence that shows Diana moving from side to side with breathtaking power and agility, shadow boxing, throwing punches, ducking, and taking pleasure in her body's capabilities. The extreme slow-motion framing allows us to trace Diana's movements across the surface of the screen. The movements of individual muscle strands under the skin and the glistening droplets of sweat moving along its surface highlight texture and foreground the corporeal dimension of the action, inviting the spectator to adopt a haptic, grasping gaze. The slow-motion framing highlights the dynamics of bodily movement by allowing the viewer's gaze to linger on, be in awe of, and "grasp" the complexity and smoothness of the interactions between different muscle groups and body parts. Diana's, the film's, and the viewer's movements are aligned, encouraging us to sway along and inviting empathetic engagements in kinesthetic, bodily terms (Barker 2009).

In another notable sequence of haptic and sensuous quality, the camera lingers on Diana's head and shoulders from behind as she trains on the speed bag. The smooth contours of her powerful and muscular body are outlined by the soft lighting from above, emphasizing the surface and texture of Diana's skin that bears the (muscular) contours and marks of the "painstaking labour" that, according to Ahmed, is involved "for bodies to arrive in spaces where they are not already at home [and] to inhabit spaces that do not extend their shape" (2006: 62). It articulates a perhaps utopian "sense" of proximity, intimacy, and contact with a body that is capable of action and that has come to be "in place" and "at home."

In this sense, *Girlfight* can be seen to follow a rather conventional narrative trajectory that leads to the climactic formation of the heterosexual couple, as Diana and Adrian are reunited toward the end of the film. However, it can also be *felt* to follow a sensuous trajectory, providing possibilities for (embodied) engagements and pleasure outside of/in addition to the kinds of straightforward viewing pleasures centered around a conventionally Western "point of view." As such, the film's (embodied) articulation of a queer subjectivity encourages a particular "somatic mode of attention" (Csordas 2002: 241), and might "touch" and "move" spectators in ways that resonate with various kinds of oblique and twisted ways of "being in," relating to, and perceiving the world.

Conclusion

As this discussion of *The Gymnast* and *Girlfight* indicates, the phenomenological approaches to film by Marks, Sobchack, Barker, and others, as well as Ahmed's "twisting" of phenomenology and phenomenological account of (racially and sexually) "twisted" bodies, provide a useful tool for an exploration of bodies in, of, and around film that not only puts the perceptive and expressive body at the center, but also accounts for the specificities of embodied existence in a way that challenges the universality of the white, Western, male, heterosexual norm. It does so by highlighting that this norm constitutes not only a particular point of view, from which we can see and know the world, but a way of facing the world by being orientated in certain directions and thus making certain bodies and objects, but not others, reachable. It accounts for the differences in our embodied and affective ways of being in and perceiving the world. As such, "De-Westernizing Film Studies" does not necessarily mean changing one's *point* of view, but it does, perhaps, imply turning around, facing familiar objects and others from a different angle, and, more importantly, facing new, unfamiliar objects and others – those, that might have been in the background or behind us. It also means acknowledging one's specifically situated and orientated existence, without taking certain centers and orientations for granted. This approach allows us to acknowledge the embodied dimensions of, for instance, race and gender, without, importantly, essentializing those differences. As such, the argument presented here opens up possibilities to reconceptualize questions of identification and desire in ways that account for the corporeal and "lived" dimensions of subjectivity.

Notes

1 Thomas Csordas describes "facing" as a "somatic mode of attention" (2002: 241–246) that allows us to be "touched" and "moved" by the proximity of others.
2 In *Performing Whiteness* (2003), Foster, for instance, begins to do this, by locating and identifying the particularities of the ways in which whiteness has been performed and re-performed throughout the history of cinema, to the extent that it has come to be seen as natural, universal, and non-particular.
3 In *The Address of the Eye*, Sobchack draws on existential phenomenology to provide a conceptualization of film as a "body." This is, importantly, not to suggest an anthropomorphic similarity between the human body and the body of the film; instead, it points to similar modes of *embodiment*. Jennifer Barker's argument in *The Tactile Eye* (2009) is based on similar assumptions.
4 See in particular Husserl's *Ideas: General Introduction to Pure Phenomenology* (1969) and *Ideas Pertaining to a Pure Phenomenology and to a Phenomenological Philosophy* (1989), as well as Merleau-Ponty's *The Visible and the Invisible* (1968) and *Phenomenology of Perception* (2002).
5 Available online at www.thegymnastfilm.com/thegymnast_flash.html (accessed September 1, 2011).

References

Ahmed, S. (2006) *Queer Phenomenology: Orientations, Objects, Others*, Durham, NC: Duke University Press.
Barker, J. (2009) *The Tactile Eye: Touch and the Cinematic Experience*, Berkeley, Calif.: University of California Press.
Bobo, J. (1995) *Black Women as Cultural Readers*, New York: Columbia University Press.
Creed, B. (1995) "Lesbian Bodies: Tribades, Tomboys and Tarts," in E. Grosz and E. Probyn (eds.), *Sexy Bodies: the Strange Carnalities of Feminism*, London and New York: Routledge, pp. 86–103.
Csordas, T. (2002) *Body/Meaning/Healing*, Basingstoke: Palgrave Macmillan.
Dyer, R. (1997) *White*. London and New York: Routledge.
Fanon, F. (1967) *Black Skin, White Masks*, London: Pluto Press.
Foster, G. A. (2003) *Performing Whiteness: Postmodern Re/Constructions in the Cinema*, Albany, NY: SUNY Press.

Gaines, J. (1986) "White Privilege and Looking Relations: Race and Gender in Feminist Film Theory," *Cultural Critique,* 29: 59–79.

hooks, b. (1992) *Black Looks: Race and Representation,* Cambridge, Mass.: South End Press.

Husserl, E. (1969) *Ideas: General Introduction to Pure Phenomenology,* London: George Allen & Unwin.

——(1989) *Ideas Pertaining to a Pure Phenomenology and to a Phenomenological Philosophy,* Dordrecht: Kluwer Academic Publishers.

Marks, L. U. (2000) *The Skin of the Film: Intercultural Cinema, Embodiment and the Senses,* Durham, NC: Duke University Press.

Merleau-Ponty, M. (1968) *The Visible and the Invisible,* Evanston, Ill.: Northwestern University Press.

——(2002) *Phenomenology of Perception,* London and New York: Routledge.

Mulvey, L. (1975) "Visual Pleasure and Narrative Cinema," *Screen,* 16 (3): 6–18.

Rich, A. (2003) "Notes Towards a Politics of Location," in R. Lewis and S. Mills (eds.), *Feminist Postcolonial Theory: A Reader,* Edinburgh: Edinburgh University Press, pp. 29–42. First published 1984.

Said, E. (1978) *Orientalism,* New York: Random House.

Sobchack, V. (1991) *The Address of the Eye,* Princeton, NJ: Princeton University Press.

——(2004) *Carnal Thoughts: Embodiment and Moving Image Culture,* Berkeley, Calif.: University of California Press.

Young, I. (1980) "Throwing Like a Girl: a Phenomenology of Feminine Body Comportment, Motility and Spatiality," *Human Studies,* 3 (1): 137–156.

11 Has film ever been Western?

Continuity and the question of building a "common" cinema

William Brown

This chapter considers the comprehension of narrative film from a cognitive perspective in order to propose that a key aspect of cinema, namely movement, or what this chapter will call continuity, is universally comprehensible and that all humans, regardless of culture, can understand it. The chapter will use this as the basis for proposing that cinema exists in what Michael Hardt and Antonio Negri (2009) might term the realm of the "common." If cinema is understood as "common," then this raises questions as to whether cinema is "Western" such that it needs to be de-Westernized, or indeed as to whether it has ever been Western at all.

Is cinema universally comprehensible?

Many are the anecdotes to suggest that people do not understand films when first they see them – with many confirming, whether consciously or not, a racist Western ideology concerning attitudes toward supposedly "primitive" audiences who do not "understand" advanced Western technology. Marshall McLuhan, for example, reports – without providing detail or evidence – that African audiences could not understand *The Tramp* (Chaplin, 1915) "because they cannot make the literate assumption that space is continuous and uniform. Non-literate people simply don't get perspective or distancing effects of light and shade that we assume are innate human equipment" (McLuhan 2001: 313).

Furthermore, Joan Rosengren Forsdale and Louis Forsdale endeavour to reinforce this Eurocentric (and racist) perception of film comprehension by stating that "some primitive peoples have shown repeatedly their inability to identify the content of pictures (both still and moving pictures) when they first encounter them" (Forsdale and Forsdale 1966: 9). Unlike McLuhan, the Forsdales do at least provide some "evidence" for their claims, although it is neither direct nor empirical but based, rather, upon anecdotal testimonies of supposedly "primitive" encounters with cinema. Not only is this evidence unreliable; it is also at times plain contradictory. For example, the authors twice cite Richard Griffith, who reports on Robert Flaherty's experiences of screening *Nanook of the North* (1922) to Eskimos, claiming first that the Eskimos did not even recognize Nanook, before then arguing that the Eskimos were so drawn in by the film that they mistook it for reality (Forsdale and Forsdale 1966: 11–12). The question of how the audience could not recognize Nanook and yet also mistake his image for a real person is not explored by the Forsdales.

Although McLuhan's and the Forsdales' argument in part tallies with the apocryphal myth regarding audiences fleeing the oncoming train during the first Lumière screenings in Paris in 1895, a myth perpetuated by Kim Newman (2002: 221–222) but debunked by Tom Gunning (1989), the problematic and potentially racist conclusions drawn by their assumptions toward primitive (read non-Western) audiences point to the ongoing role of cinema "as a potent organ of colonialism" (Ukadike 1994: 31). That is, McLuhan's and the Forsdales' tenuous arguments can be understood as the justification of the imperialist project in that Westerners "must" educate, in these examples, Africans and Eskimos in film literacy.

However, although "exposing" the racist ideologies that seem to underpin McLuhan's and the Forsdales' work has merit, there are more empirical reasons to dismiss their arguments – thanks to scientific work done on film cognition using "naive" spectators ranging from young children without much experience of film and television to adults who have never seen a film or television.

Smith et al. (1985), for example, have found that pre-school children (three to five years of age) not only recognize that they are viewing images and can not only discern objects and actions within those images, but they can also follow the thread of an action across different images, i.e. in a film that involves montage. Furthermore, in a second experiment by the same team, 62 percent of four-year-olds and 88 percent of seven-year-olds were found to comprehend montage. That is, children get better with time at perceiving whether there has been a change of location, an ellipsis of time, whether alternating images are supposed to be depictions of actions taking place simultaneously, and/or whether images are supposed to be the point of view of characters within the diegesis of the film that they see. Bearing in mind this improvement in film comprehension over time, it seems that even from an early age children can more often than not recognize many of the narrative (i.e. editing) strategies involved in filmmaking and what they mean.

Naturally, the children that took part in Smith's experiments might, even from the age of three, be used to film and television such that they can follow relatively or very sophisticated shows. This leads to the conclusion that narrative film comprehension is not necessarily universal but something learned, even if quickly and from a young age. In fact, the improvement with age that Smith et al.'s results show would indeed suggest that narrative film comprehension is learned, because otherwise one might contend that it should come to us "whole" and not improve over time.

However, further evidence suggests that adults with little or no familiarity with film and television can comprehend films, too. That is, if it is a common argument that cinema "has the advantage of speaking directly to the senses of [its] audience, without the coding and decoding inevitable with written language" (MacDougall 1976: 147), then this argument has more recently found support from cognitive research. Hobbs et al. (1988) have found, for example, that tribal villagers in Kenya who had rarely seen films in any medium could comprehend a filmed narrative, even when various "point of view" techniques were in operation. Meanwhile, Schwan and Ildirar (2010) obtained similar results when showing films to inexperienced adult viewers from southern Turkey. This chapter will now explore the second of these two experiments in some detail.

Schwan and Ildirar showed various clips to twenty adults who had never seen a film or television before, even though all knew about television and all had photographs in their household. They also showed the same clips to seventeen adults who had owned a television for between one and three years but who did not frequently watch it (not daily, and mostly for the news), as well as to nineteen adults who had owned a television for more than ten years and who watched it daily. The clips featured various techniques, including abrupt changes of viewing position (shot-reverse shot), POV shots, pans, and temporal ellipses. Schwan and Ildirar

> found no instances in which an inexperienced viewer was unable to understand a film clip as a pictorial representation of a real-world scene. We also found no instances of a viewer mistaking a film clip for reality. Inexperienced viewers tended to interpret the films as referential depictions of existing places, persons, and events.
>
> (Schwan and Ildirar 2010: 973–974)

Like Smith et al., Schwan and Ildirar did discover that experienced viewers could more easily comprehend certain techniques than inexperienced viewers, suggesting that "perceptual and cognitive capabilities acquired in natural settings are not sufficient" (2010: 975), but that the differences between the experienced and inexperienced viewers were not particularly pronounced – at least for the comprehension of certain techniques. Though the inexperienced adults could describe accurately the contents of images, they did not necessarily infer that a shot of an exterior of a house, followed by a shot of a woman sitting in a room, meant that the woman was sat in that house. Nor did POV shots register as such; "the inexperienced viewers seemingly had no idea of the camera as a substitute for an active looker" (Schwan and Ildirar 2010: 975). Pans and shot-reverse shots, however, were predominantly understood by the inexperienced viewers, while ellipses (jump cuts) and cross-cutting (simultaneous events) were also more easily comprehended than not. For Schwan and Ildirar, this latter finding in particular suggests that "a familiar line of action is essential for the interpretation processes of inexperienced viewers; a line of action helps them overcome unfamiliar perceptual discontinuities" (2010: 975).

The results of Schwan and Ildirar seem indirectly to be corroborated by Germeys and d'Ydewalle (2007), who found that (European) film viewers follow a filmed conversation in spite of the violation of the so-called rules of continuity editing. In other words, it would appear that narrative comprehension is dependent not so much on editing as on continuity. Continuity, here, does not necessarily mean that the action must be continuous and unbroken, since even the inexperienced viewers in Schwan and Ildirar's experiment could follow action across jump cuts and cross-cutting more often than not, but it does mean that recognisable lines of action, or continuity, or movement, must be visible across the shots such that we can infer how one leads to the next.

Continuity editing: a contingent universal?

If the comprehension of a "line of action," or of what in this chapter we will term "continuity," comes naturally to viewers, then perhaps the comprehension of editing does not, insomuch as some, if not all, editing techniques must, as above, be learned and incorporated into film comprehension. Given this distinction between continuity and editing, what are we to say about continuity editing – a technique often associated with classical and contemporary Hollywood? To address this question, we shall turn to David Bordwell's work on "contingent universals."

Bordwell proposes that continuity editing is a "contingent universal," in that the techniques of continuity editing, such as the shot-reverse shot, are "arbitrary devices" that are also "widely present in human societies" (Bordwell 2008: 60–61), with Bordwell providing examples from films as diverse as *Yaaba* (Ouedraogo, 1989), *Suvorov* (Doller and Pudovkin, 1941), *Al-ard/The Land* (Chahine, 1969), *Dip huet seung hung/The Killer* (John Woo, 1989), *Toni* (Renoir, 1934), and *School Daze* (Spike Lee, 1988). Bordwell says that it is not important whether the comprehension of contingent universals is "biologically prewired or culturally acquired." Rather, it is important to think of "conventions as norm-governed patterns of behaviour, and [of] artistic goals [. . .] as effects" (Bordwell 2008: 62–63). That is, a film and the techniques that it employs may have a certain "meaning" when considered from the perspective of cultural conventions and codes, but that meaning is only one of the effects of the film. Films produce many sorts of effects, some of which are universal – not in the sense of being genetically hard-wired (there is no gene for film comprehension), but in the sense of relying on contingent universals.

Motion is, for Bordwell, a prime example of a contingent universal: "We did not evolve in order to be able to watch movies, but the inventors of cinema were able to exploit a feature of the design of the human optical system to create a pictorial display that is immediately accessible to all sighted humans" (2008: 63–64). That is, all (sighted) humans visually detect motion (a "universal" attribute), even if the movies were only invented through a specific set of ("contingent") historical circumstances. Moreover, Bordwell extends his argument beyond motion to entrances and exits from the frame and to shot-reverse shot cutting, not least because "face-to-face personal interaction is a solid candidate for a cross-cultural universal" (2008: 64).

Bordwell argues that we can identify variations of the shot-reverse shot structure in all of the films listed above, and more. Again, it is not that certain or all of these films do not require culturally specific knowledge, for example in identifying allegorical figures, but even these "higher" elements have as their basis the "contingently universal cues" that Bordwell describes (2008: 66–73). In this way, "some features of the films we study, for whatever reason, are manifested across cultures and may thereby create convergent effects," or effects that have "cross-cultural power[s]" (2008: 74).

The above discussion raises several issues, some of which will be important in bringing this chapter toward the notion of the common. Schwan and Ildirar argue that continuity is universally comprehensible, while Bordwell seems to take this a step further by saying that the conventions of continuity editing are universally, if contingently, comprehensible. And yet, there seems clear evidence that the "meaning" of some editing techniques needs to be learned – otherwise we would understand all editing techniques "automatically." Bordwell here tries to pass under the term "contingent" the fact that anyone can, and many people do, learn the conventions of continuity editing, such that they become universal. In some senses, there is evidence to suggest that continuity editing *is* universally comprehensible; it *is* the system of filmmaking that many, if not most, audiences in the world have in common, as Bordwell himself maintains (2008: 77). That is, continuity editing is, metaphorically speaking, the *lingua franca* of cinema across the world, even if we must recognize the existence of many diverse styles of filmmaking from all over the planet. And yet, if editing must, unlike continuity or movement, be learned, then Bordwell's position is open to critique.

After Bordwell, continuity editing might be "easy" to learn (2008: 64), and it may well be a form of filmmaking that has global reach. But Bordwell's claim to legitimacy via the claim to universality could also be construed as an apology for the imposition of a certain type of filmmaking on people who perhaps would (and do) find greater levels of self-expression using other techniques. In other words, claims to universality might, in contrast to this collection's title, constitute precisely the Westernization of film. Furthermore, if we all (easily come to) "understand" continuity editing, this might make of us all "experts" on films the "higher meanings" of which we do not in fact understand. That is, anyone can lay claim to understanding a film even if they have no knowledge of the culture from which it springs.

With regard to this second conjecture, Bordwell's argument that a meaning is only one of a film's possible "effects" perhaps merits reiteration. This is not to say that we should not strive to understand a film within the context of the culture(s) from which it springs, but it also is not to reify a specific meaning as a given *telos* for a film. It may well be that we cannot understand each other; it may well also be that humans walk around with different and contradictory understandings of the same films, even if some are "more informed" than others. But the impossibility of perfect communication, interpretation and understanding is not a reason to reject outright communication via audiovisual means. In fact, the impossibility of perfect communication demands effort ever more to improve understandings, not least by basing higher understanding on the "cross-cultural universals" that Bordwell describes.

But is this all just the "Westernization" of cinema? For, Bordwell's theory of continuity editing as a contingent universal runs the risk of using the word universal to legitimize what historically is contingent, rather than using the word contingent to qualify the word universal. It is historically contingent that it was "in" Hollywood that continuity editing was most powerfully developed. It is contingent because this happened for a variety of reasons that were very much of their time and place (and for an overview of these reasons, see, *inter alia*, Bordwell, Staiger, and Thompson 1988). To "universalize" the contingent might be to legitimate Hollywood, therefore, as the universal system and style (however heterogeneous it is).

Redefining continuity editing

Given the possible problems with Bordwell's position outlined above, it is important to make clear what this chapter is proposing here. This chapter is not proposing that continuity editing is a style that is or even should be universally adopted. Alternatives to continuity editing are more than evident in an enormous range of films, from 1920s Soviet montage to Bollywood musicals from many eras. In addition, Teshome H. Gabriel has, among others, written about how there are alternative aesthetics to "Western-style" continuity, such as films that focus not on action but on the environment in which that action unfolds (Gabriel 1989: 57). Such a switch in emphasis might be achieved, Gabriel proposes, by filming in long shot and with a static camera rather than focusing on the individual in close-up and medium shots. Gabriel attributes such aesthetics to Third Cinema, though the fact that we see filmmaking of this kind in movies as diverse as *Zire darakhatan zeyton/Through the Olive Trees* (Kiarostami, 1994), *Sud pralad/Tropical Malady* (Apichatpong Weerasethakul, 2004), and *Meek's Cutoff* (Reichardt, 2010) suggests that these techniques have, or have acquired, a global reach in the same way that Bordwell proposes that continuity editing does. Put differently, these techniques are neither exclusively "Western," nor "non-Western." As the inclusion of an American Western (*Meek's Cutoff*) in the above list should make clear, these, and perhaps all sets of, techniques are (in theory) available to filmmakers from all over the world. As such, all cinematic techniques exist not as the exclusive property of one industry or one nation or (as we might understand Third Cinema to be) from a shared ideological perspective, but in the realm of the "common" – a term that shall be considered in detail across the remainder of this chapter.

Now, techniques might be "common" (as in "shared" or "widespread") but, as proposed above, the common basis of cinema is, arguably, continuity itself. Continuity here is not (exclusively) the sense of continuity that is produced through the techniques of continuity editing. Continuity here is more simply *movement,* or change over time – be that change within *or* between shots. Gabriel's proposed film (about a hunt) that consists of a long shot that lasts for several minutes and which is taken with a static camera (1989: 57), might seem to involve little "change" when compared to an edited sequence that involves numerous shots, each in close up or medium shot, and with a camera that is moving sideways, forwards, and upwards all at the same time. However, while both of these sequences involve different *rates of* movement (or speeds of change), both nonetheless involve change over time, or movement. This is the definition of continuity that this chapter wishes to propose: change over time, or movement. *All films* involve change over time, as is irrefutably made clear by the fact that all films have a running time, even if that running time is variable (for example, projecting a film at twenty-four or sixteen frames per second), and even if within that running time we see only still images. *All films* therefore involve continuity, and continuity is, as this chapter will show, the basis of a "cinematic commons" – the reason being that continuity as defined here does not obliterate difference. It does not demand that all films be made in the same way, because this chapter also proposes, as we shall see, that editing, or the techniques that filmmakers choose to use, are the root of difference (and that no two films are the same, even if they have continuity, or movement, in common).

However, in order for this argument to be made, the chapter must naturally engage with the term "continuity editing" as it has traditionally been understood. That is, the chapter must wrest new meaning from the phrase "continuity editing" such that it is not a term associated with a particular style generally thought to be Western or from Hollywood (even if that style has a pan-global presence, as outlined above). Instead, "continuity editing" becomes the editing (which implies diversity, as we shall see) of continuity (or movement, which is the underlying "universal" of cinema, and which is also, as this chapter has tried to demonstrate, universally comprehensible). In this way, the chapter can propose a "cinematic commons" that will allow us to ask whether cinema has ever been Western.

As per the Greek word for movement, κινημα, the continuity of movement is "cinema," and this continuity, or movement, is the universal element of cinema that all (sighted) humans can understand. It is the constraints placed upon movement via editing that are harder to understand, and which, as the above cognitive approaches suggest, require learning – even if that learning is, after Bordwell, "easy" (Bordwell 2008: 64).

If continuity is defined as movement, then editing itself is the editing of continuity, or the editing of movement, of κινημα. It is not quite, then, that continuity is truly cinema, and editing is something that takes us "away from" cinema; rather, the two in conjunction are important constituent elements of cinema. From this perspective, there is not one (the Hollywood) mode of continuity editing; instead all films "edit continuity," or movement, in a different way, depending on the ideas, emotions, culture, and story that the filmmakers wish to express, and/or the audience to which they wish to appeal – to name only a few factors that might affect a film's look and feel. The appeal here to "universal" comprehension is not, then, a case of legitimizing Hollywood continuity editing over other systems. Instead, it is a/ the key part of the process of filmmaking itself. If all films are edited differently, then there are as many editings of continuity/movement as there are films in the world; but what unites them, what they have in common, is the *process* of editing continuity, or movement, or change over time – as opposed to the reified "style" that is traditionally understood as Hollywood (or classical) continuity editing. To appropriate Bordwell's language, editing styles are contingent, while movement/ continuity is universal – such that all films "edit continuity."

Cinema: property or common?

Tom O'Regan has argued that "the procedures, the norms and practices of Hollywood [. . .] are transferable rather than intrinsically the property of Hollywood" (O'Regan 1990). If the procedures, norms, and practices of Hollywood, which are understood here as continuity editing, are not the property of Hollywood, then Hollywood is instead the "property of the rest of the world" (O'Regan 1990). O'Regan raises compelling questions regarding the "ownership" of Hollywood, questions that might seem to provide a solid foundation for de-Westernizing film. However, this chapter wishes to take a different stance, not by challenging what is whose "property" within the world of cinema but by challenging the notion of property itself. Discussions of property always already suggest participation in the practices of capitalism, or Empire, as Hardt and Negri (2009: 9–15) make clear. In place of property, Hardt and Negri propose the concept of the common. In order to make clear how cinema is or might be common, we must define what "common" might mean.

The past twenty years have seen a growth in work that addresses the issue of collective endeavour in the economic context of increasing levels of privatization. Two examples include Jean-Luc Nancy's (2000) concepts of "withness" and being singular plural, and Hardt and Negri's (2004, 2009) concepts of the multitude and the common, which have all arisen in the face of the increasing hegemony of Empire (Hardt and Negri 2000). Empire itself is not necessarily the same as "old school" imperialism, as Hardt and Negri explain:

> the coming Empire is not American and the United States is not its centre. The fundamental principle of Empire [. . .] is that its power has no actual and localisable terrain or centre. Imperial power is distributed in networks, through mobile and articulated mechanisms of control"
>
> (Hardt and Negri 2000: 384)

What this means for Hardt and Negri is that power itself has been decentered and that meaningful "opposition" to it is similarly not the privileged struggle of the few in various "central" locations distributed across the globe. Instead, as Empire has spread to cover the whole terrain, it has also brought into being the potential for collective endeavour, or the work of the multitude, because the drive toward globalization inevitably puts into contact groups that can self-organize into resistance against the hegemony of Empire.

"Empire" in the above sense will seem abstract and perhaps contradictory. It will seem abstract because it talks of Empire as having no center (Empire is in this sense "invisible"), and it will seem contradictory because there are visibly persistent examples of "old school imperialism" in the world. However, this abstraction is "essential to both the functioning of capital and the critique of it" (Hardt and Negri 2009: 159). Hardt and Negri argue, after Marx, that it is the abstraction of labour that allows for commodities to have exchange value. While we live in a world that reifies labour through its products, such that some forms of labour acquire greater value than others, it is the abstract view – of seeing not types of labour but the shared element of labour – that enables a common to come into being (workers from different trades can unite). And it is only through the production of the common that capital can be challenged. In this sense, abstraction becomes a necessary condition both for Empire and for resistance to old school imperialism and Empire itself. It is for this reason that Empire sows the seeds of its own destruction, because while mechanisms of control persist, the potential for overthrowing them also increases as the world becomes "globalized."

It is in view of the necessity of abstraction for resistance that Hardt and Negri argue that:

> [t]he most important change [. . .] takes place inside humanity, since with the end of modernity also ends the hope of finding something that can identify the self outside the community, outside cooperation, and outside the critical and contradictory relationships that each person finds in a non-place, that is, in the world and the multitude.
>
> (Hardt and Negri 2000: 384–385)

In other words, Hardt and Negri argue not for the production of specific tools for resistance but for an abstract change "inside humanity," whereby thought extends beyond the immediate and visible world/the self, and which recognizes in the widest sense that there is no outside of the community. That is, all human beings are interlinked and interdependent, and we *all* form the community that Empire has brought into contact with itself.

In a similar vein, Jean-Luc Nancy argues that we are only ever with each other in the world. For him:

> Both the theory and praxis of critique demonstrate that, from now on, critique absolutely needs to rest on some principle other than that of the ontology of the Other and the Same: it needs an ontology of being-with-one-another, and this ontology must support both the sphere of "nature" and the sphere of "history," as well as both the "human" and the "nonhuman"; it must be an ontology for the world, for everyone – and if I can be so bold, it has to be an ontology for each and every one and for the world "as a totality," and nothing short of the whole world, since this is all there is.
>
> (Nancy 2000: 53–54)

To say that there is only the world, in which irrevocably we take part, might seem like a totalizing discourse, but core to both Hardt and Negri's concept of multitude as well as to Nancy's "being singular plural" is that this holistic thinking ("nothing short of the whole world") must be plural *as well as* singular. That is, our differences must be recognized (plural), but so must our interdependent nature (singular).

Transferring Hardt and Negri and Nancy's ideas to cinema is not a matter of seeing that cinema and capital are perfect mirrors of each other, for this is not quite so. It is, however, to adopt a mode of looking at cinema, whereby we do not privilege American (read Hollywood) cinema as the "center" – even if it "occupies a privileged position in the global segmentations and hierarchies of Empire" (Hardt and Negri 2000: 384). But nor is it to exclude Hollywood cinema. It is to look at *all cinema,* and in the same way that "[l]anguages mix and interact to form not a single unified language but rather a common power of communication and cooperation among a multitude of singularities" (Hardt and Negri 2004: 138), so, too, might we see not a single unified system of filmmaking (continuity editing in the traditional sense of the term), but a common power of cinematic communication and cooperation among a multitude of singularities (continuity editing as put forward here). The new definition of continuity editing proposed here means that cinema is not a single, unified style, even if Hollywood-style continuity editing seems to predominate (but only ever by varying degrees – never totally, because continuity editing never existed in a unified or reified form). Instead, there are only singularities, or single films (perhaps even single moments in films), that share the common power of communication and that cooperate in the world.

Hardt and Negri propose that:

> the common [. . .] is both the final product and also the preliminary condition of production. The common is both natural and artificial; it is our first, second, third, and *n*th nature. There is no singularity, then, that is not itself established in the common; there is no communication that does not have a common connection that sustains and puts it into action; and there is no production that is not cooperation based on commonality.
>
> (Hardt and Negri 2000: 348–349)

While the model of "production" here might well apply literally to film productions, which are, on the whole, precisely the endeavour of collective groups of people, this quotation also demands a more abstract interpretation. That is, conceptions of "Western," Third, or any other cinema, are in Hardt and Negri's terms "singularities" that are underwritten by the common. The "de-Westernizing" of film, then, does not necessarily entail proposing alternatives to Western/Hollywood cinema. Rather, it is to conceive of cinema "as a whole," and to see it as a "common." It is not that *Yaaba* is any more or less cinematic than, say, *Captain America: The First Avenger* (Johnston, 2011). Both are cinema, and to "de-Westernize" film is not to challenge the West by pointing out the importance of work from the East, the South, or from anywhere else. It is to challenge the politics of West/Other thinking as a whole, such that we can ask whether film has ever truly been "Western" at all.

Conclusion: the power of love

The issue of power remains: Hollywood has a "preeminent market position" across the globe (O'Regan 1990) and it dominates the thinking of many people regarding what cinema is. In the same way that Hardt and Negri call upon their readers to rethink property, so, too, do they argue that "[t]he primary form of power that really confronts us today [. . .] is not so dramatic or demonic but rather earthly and mundane. We need to stop confusing politics with theology" (Hardt and Negri 2009: 5). To "de-Westernize" film, then, should not be to perpetuate the same system of property, power, and, therefore, domination that has existed up until now, and which might be the case if the intended *telos* of "de-Westernizing" film were to relocate, or redistribute "filmic power" from Hollywood to another location (simply to recognize other cinemas, be they mainstream, art house, political, amateur, whatever). Power and property are mutually reaffirming concepts that legitimize the same system. In the realm of the common, however, there is always only ever a democratic, or non-proprietorial, distribution of power. This (recognition of the) distribution of power is based upon love, a concept that this chapter will introduce only tentatively as a result of limitations of space – but in earnest nonetheless.

The "de-Westernization" of film via the concept of the common belies the possibility that film has, in reality, never been Western at all. A common world is one based on mutual influence, and in which power relations are not exclusively defined by subjugation and domination; rather, they are actively promoted by equality through diversity. After Hardt and Negri, and after Nancy, there is only being-with-others, there is only communication.

To think and to act in this way is to adopt a politics of *love*. In other words, "love is an essential [if overlooked and often rejected] concept for philosophy and politics" (Hardt and Negri 2009: 179), and by extension, this chapter argues, for film and film theory. This is not race love or nation love, or patriotism, which "are examples of the pressure to love most those most like you and hence less those who are different" (Hardt and Negri 2009: 182). This is love as "the constitution of the common and the composition of singularities [. . .] a love based on the encounter of alterity" (Hardt and Negri 2009: 184–187). Such an encounter, it could be argued, aims to displace an encounter with the other – for example, that of European colonialism with the non-Western world – that is overwhelmingly based on fear, arrogance, and ignorance, and that engenders hate and oppression, rather than "love." In cinematic terms, this means not to love certain films over others but to love all films. Not cinephilia as the preserve of privileged films or viewers, but cinephilia as the love of cinema as a whole. This is not a philosophical project in the sense of loving wisdom; instead it is a sophophilic project that recognizes the wisdom of loving.

Continuity as defined here might be the line of action, or movement, that is universally comprehensible. Although continuity is in this sense akin to κινημα/ movement, cinema itself is the process of editing continuity/movement. Every film "edits continuity" in a different way. To love cinema, then, is to recognize cinema as endlessly diverse (there are only ever different "editions" of movement/continuity) and to recognize the equal, interlinked, and interdependent nature of films (plural) in the world of cinema (singular). In doing so, not only is cinema de-Westernized, but we are also compelled to ask whether cinema has, indeed, ever been Western at all.

References

Bordwell, D. (1996) "Convention, Construction, and Cinematic Vision," in D. Bordwell and N. Carroll (eds.), *Post-Theory: Reconstructing Film Studies*, Madison, Wisc.: University of Wisconsin Press, pp. 87–108.

——— (2008) *Poetics of Cinema*, London and New York: Routledge.

Bordwell, D., Staiger, J., and Thompson, K. (1988) *The Classical Hollywood Cinema: Film Style and Mode of Production to 1960*, London: Routledge.

Forsdale, J. R. and Forsdale, L. (1966) "Film Literacy," *Journal of the University Film Producers Association*, 18 (3): 9–15 and 26–27.

Gabriel, T. H. (1989) "Third Cinema as Guardian of Popular Memory: Towards a Third Aesthetics," in J. Pines and P. Willemen (eds.), *Questions of Third Cinema*, London: BFI Publishing, pp. 53–64.

Germeys, F. and d'Ydewalle, G. (2007) "The Psychology of Film: Perceiving Beyond the Cut," *Psychological Research*, 71 (4): 458–466.

Gunning, T. (1989) "An Aesthetic of Astonishment: Early Film and the (In)credulous Spectator," *Art and Text*, 34: 31–45.

Hardt, M. and Negri, A. (2000) *Empire*, Cambridge, Mass.: Harvard University Press.

—— (2004) *Multitude: War and Democracy in the Age of Empire*, London: Penguin.

—— (2009) *Commonwealth*, Cambridge, Mass.: Belknap Press of the Harvard University Press.

Hobbs, R., Frost, R., Davis, A., and Stauffer, J. (1988) "How First-Time Viewers Comprehend Editing Conventions," *Journal of Communication*, 38 (4): 50–60.

MacDougall, D. (1976) "Prospects of the Ethnographic Film," in B. Nichols (ed.), *Movies and Methods: An Anthology*, Berkeley, Calif.: University of California Press, pp. 136–150.

McLuhan, M. (2001) *Understanding Media: The Extensions of Man*, London: Routledge. First published in 1964.

Nancy, J.-L. (2000) *Being Singular Plural*, trans. by R. D. Richardson and A. E. O'Byrne, Palo Alto, Calif.: Stanford University Press.

Newman, K. (2002) "Panic in the Cinema," in L. J. Schmidt and B. Warner (eds.), *Panic: Origins, Insight, and Treatment*, Berkeley, Calif.: North Atlantic Books, pp. 221–252.

O'Regan, T. (1990), "Too Popular by Far: On Hollywood's International Popularity," *The Australian Journal of Media and Culture*, 5 (2). Available online at www.mcc.murdoch. edu.au/ReadingRoom/5.2/O'Regan.html. (accessed May 3, 2011).

Schwan, S. and Ildirar, S. (2010) "Watching Film for the First Time: How Adult Viewers Interpret Perceptual Discontinuities in Film," *Psychological Science*, 21 (7): 970–976.

Smith, R., Anderson, D. R., and Fischer, C. (1985) "Young Children's Comprehension of Montage," *Child Development*, 56 (4): 962–971.

Ukadike, N. F. (1994), *Black African Cinema*, Berkeley, Calif.: University of California Press.

Part IV

Interviews

Editors' note on interviews

The following chapters are edited transcripts of interviews conducted by the editors of *De-Westernizing Film Studies* (Saër Maty Bâ and Will Higbee) with a range of artists, filmmakers, producers, composers, writers, critics, editors, and academics that took place between May and September 2011. Due to the logistical difficulties of ensuring the participation of this wide range of interviewees, the interviews were completed using a variety of methods: via email and VoIP as well as face to face.

Interviewees were asked to respond as they saw fit to six questions (circulated in advance) that it was felt encompassed the aims and issues addressed by the *De-Westernizing Film Studies* project. The interviews are therefore intended to offer a different perspective from the previous chapters and, at the same time, engage with them. Thus the interviews form an integral part of this book and further the editors' firm belief in the insights that are to be gained when scholars and filmmakers enter into dialogue with one another. We are grateful to all those interviewed for generously giving their time and insights to this book.

12 "There is no entirely non-Western place left"

De-Westernizing the moving image, an interview with Coco Fusco

Do you perceive film as, predominantly, a universal art form or medium?

I wanted first to clarify one thing. All of the questions you sent me in advance refer specifically to "film" and none of my production work is in what I consider "film." I have exclusively made videos art. I studied film semiotics a long time ago, and there was a time in the 1980s and early 1990s when I had a limited involvement with writing about postcolonial film and curating. However, since that time I have left that world for a number of reasons. Firstly, because the independent film circuit that existed in New York began to disappear becoming absorbed in a kind of international commercially oriented kind of distribution network and so there wasn't really a context in which to work. I also felt that the creative energies I was interested in and the kind of experimentation with the moving image and with narrative was going on in video art.

I feel in a way very distant from questions such as "is film a universal medium?" because it's been almost twenty years now since I even thought about myself in terms of a relationship with film. So if it's OK with you, I will respond in a more general sense to your questions in relation to the moving image, particularly because of current patterns of reception now which mean that cinemas arc disappearing by the day here and the vast majority of screen time is spent in front of digital screens and looking at video. Is that OK?

That's absolutely fine; one of the reasons we wanted you involved in this project is because we feel you have a different take on these questions than other people we are interviewing because of your work as a multimedia artist and video artist

I think the thing to say is that, for artists, "film" has become a material that one chooses to use to achieve a particular look, but not because one is interested in participating in a formally enclosed discourse on film. People appropriate already-made films, people shoot in film sometimes and then transfer to video to have a particular look, or they shoot in video to make them look like film, but now there is considerably more fluidity and a lot of it has to do with cost and viability of

Figure 12.1 A Room of One's Own: Women and Power in the New America (Coco Fusco, 2005).

film; it's just not a viable format if you're working as an artist and it's not been a viable format for many filmmakers for some time now.

What you're saying already opens up something very interesting and important which is, if we're talking about this whole idea of "de-Westernizing" film, what do we actually mean by film? Do we mean the material object that is 35mm? Are we talking about a particular look; are we talking about a particular approach? Is it a shorthand for cinema more generally and the actual processes of exhibition and distribution and audiences? So we're happy for you to interpret and respond to these questions in relation to the moving image or visual culture rather than "film" specifically

In that case, in response to the first question, I would say that if the question was "Do I see film as a universal medium?" I don't, and for a number of reasons. I think that, historically, it emerged in certain parts of the world first and then spread very quickly. But I don't think that, as a model of image production, that it has ever been universal because films have not been produced everywhere in the world. They may have been *seen* everywhere in the world but I don't think there's ever been a time in history where film production was going on everywhere in the world. That said, "Do I think the *moving image* is a universal medium and art form?": yes. Because I think that one of the things that has happened, particularly with the more recent developments in digital imaging technologies and video technology, is that it is now financially possible for the vast majority of people in the world to engage in some kind of image production – whether it's with a cellphone camera or with a small consumer camera, or with a still image camera that has a video component. I feel much more comfortable that I'm based in reality when I say that the majority of the world's population has access to some kind of image production now [in 2011], than I would have if you'd asked me this question twenty or thirty years ago. And there are also mechanisms of distribution – however uneven they are – that allow more image production from more parts of the world to be seen. Finally, there is definitely media literacy that, in my opinion, if it is not universal is quite close to being universal. I have been to some pretty remote places in the world, whether it's the Amazon jungle or parts of Africa that are pretty underdeveloped, or islands in the South Pacific. There might not be running water, but, if there's an electrical line, I know I'm going to see a screen and I have seen them just about everywhere. I've seen people using cellphones in remote areas and developing solar power for running their media far out in the desert in Australia and things like that. So, yes, I definitely see it as a universal form.

One further question around the idea of the film as a universal form: do you think that there is a universal "language" of the image? You were talking about the way in which technology, the means of production and the networks of distribution are more readily available than ever before, does this necessarily entail that there is a common or universal way of reading or understanding these images?

Well I think that there are a number of factors that contribute to a certain degree of homogeneity. One important factor is the dominance of Hollywood-style media production and reception. The further away you get from cosmopolitan centers, the more likely it will be that the range of the kind of images available is much narrower but what transmits the furthest is the most commercial. So really derivative action flicks will play all over the developing world and so on and so forth. Also there is a way that multinationals and their promotional media extend all over the world; so you see Nike commercials or McDonald's commercials just about anywhere on the planet and they pretty much follow the same format, even if the language has changed, or if the actors, or the physiognomy of the actors changes from one place to another. So I think that certain commercial forms do dominate and have an influence. I also have witnessed how music video is consumed all over the world – townships in South Africa, for example – and the way that popular-culture consumption socializes the majority of viewers to think about image production in a particular way. Now, that said, of course you're going to find variations from place to place; there are certain images that are taboo, there are certain storylines that are probably unacceptable in one place or another, there might be the dominance of an indigenous form in a particular place. For example, India has its own particular paradigms for musicals and for different kinds of narratives that are part of their cultural traditions and the very rich film tradition that exists there. So you might see some different modes of production and reception in a context like that. Or China, which has a very strong film industry as well as controlling its own television production. But I don't think that those indigenous forms in different parts of the world completely disrupt or transform the dominant pattern [i.e. Hollywood-style media production and reception].

The second question is about thinking of the West as a category that's always shifting, unstable and in motion. And whether or not you think that the West or Western is defined by strictly geographical frameworks

No, because I think that it's more of a symbolic category and not an actual geographic category. This is something that many postcolonial theorists such as Trinh T. Minh-ha have talked about: that there's a West in every non-West and that there's a non-West in every West. There was a time when the West was distinguished from the rest of the world due to the fact that it was the site of imperial power and colonial power. Dominant ideas, dominant languages, dominant political forms and dominant cultural forms thus emanated from this West out to the rest of the world. However, we're no longer in that kind of world. It is true that English, Chinese, and Spanish are the most spoken languages in the world – and two out of three are Western languages. But I don't think that this has so much to do with place any more than it has to do with capital and information flows and practicality (the need to be able to have communication systems that cross borders, so there's more and more kind of consolidation around fewer and fewer languages in order to facilitate transnational communication). And while this certainly is rooted in a kind of colonial past, I think even if you could argue that, in an economic sense, there are still superpowers, culturally speaking we have to think in a different way about what constitutes superpower status at this point in time. I also think that in the theorizing of cinema, yes, there was a more Marxist-driven analysis of film history that looked at the West as dominant industries; that imposed their product on the rest of the world and, in doing so, socialized the rest of the world to want to consume those products over their own productions, but also to see themselves through the symbolic paradigms of Hollywood cinema. But I think that what we're talking about now is Hollywood styles versus non-Hollywood styles and about senses of time, space and pacing and the use of language in film. There was a period when there was a lot of grandstanding around experimentation with different kinds of cultural consciousness, different ways of seeing and being in the world – I know that Teshome H. Gabriel was talking about senses of time and space and Jorge Sanjinés in the 1970s was talking about collective practices and indigenous languages and indigenous ways of being. Maybe I'm wrong, but the way I look at it at this moment in time is that those are more the concerns of anthropology and documentary filmmaking than they are of the kind of cultural product that is consumed as entertainment by the majority world population. Today, whatever we understood to be Western cinema has been to an extent infiltrated, transformed and disseminated by the inclusion of many different kinds of narratives from many different parts of the world. In much the same way, rock music, once a specifically British and American phenomenon, has now taken on a completely different life in Mexico or Argentina or different parts of Asia. Indeed, in some ways, the infusion from other cultural points in the globe has rein-vigorated forms that are already exhausted in our Western context. In the filmic world, look at Iran at this point as an example, or some of the production coming out of different Asian countries at the current time. There's a way in which these cinemas have extended – reinvigorated, even – the idea of an intelligent, auteur-ist, narrative film, the kind found in the 1970s, which was driven by storytelling, acting and visual metaphors rather than by special effects and action. So you can see that these forms that once had been thought of as "Western" move into dif-ferent parts of the world and that's where there is the greatest energy; *not* in the USA. I don't think that we are very good any more in this country [the USA] at producing those sorts of auteurist narratives. As a matter of fact, I think that if there are any auteurs left [in the USA] they are probably moving into television because it's very difficult to get support or even distribution for that kind of film production in this country at this point. So, in this respect, the issue of whether it's in the Western or non-Western mode of thinking is less relevant today. Those kinds of oppositions are much less viable now because of the way in which a certain kind of cinema is essentially disappearing from the West and other forms of image production have become sites of far greater creativity and experimentation. It is also because whatever is left of that old tradition has already been taken up in what we would understand to be non-Western spaces.

What you're saying here also brings to mind recent work by the French journalist and sociologist Frédéric Martel and his idea of "multiple mainstreams"; thinking not just in terms of Hollywood as the only dominant center, but also as one mainstream or one center of audiovisual production amongst many others; citing Indian cinema, Nollywood and the *telenovela* in South America as other examples. Our third question leads on from the idea of thinking about the West in conceptual terms. What do you understand by "non-Western" modes of thinking theorizing and making film? And does that kind of understanding have any effect on your work?

Because of the expansion of access to consumption of media and information that has taken place all over the world, I feel that it is very hard now to find places where you have so-called "non-Western" forms of thinking that remain intact and are able to be disassociated from what we understand to be the West. This is precisely one of the ways that Hollywood and the American music industry have tried to stay afloat; by making sure that they're consumed everywhere. So I'm less inclined to accept this notion that there are "non-Western" ways of thinking, although they probably are contexts in which certain aspects of the experience of visuality is different because of the pace of consumption, the diversity of screen experiences and the existence of other cultural forms. For example, I was just in Cuba at the beginning of June. Now Cuba was never an entirely non-Western country; it's a place that was one of the first testing points for Hollywood cinema at the beginning of the twentieth century. Filmgoing is an important part of the leisure experience of the middle class. At the beginning of the Cuban revolution they made a big deal about taking cinema out into the countryside but, well before the revolution, most audiences were (and continue to be) made up of middle-class people for whom watching film and television is very normal. So Cubans don't necessarily see Hollywood as foreign. And as the state has shrunk and its capacity to control media has diminished, more and more Cubans, through both legal and illegal means, are accessing more and more media from different parts of the world. They are also increasingly able to produce media from different parts of the world, now that it's legal to have a cellphone in Cuba. That said, the average number of hours that people spend watching is much less than in the USA. No one has 24/7 internet access; no one can stream easily; no one can stream from home. They may be able to stream from a government ministry if there's a really good satellite connection but, in general, the internet connections are slow, and, just like with every other kind of technology, access to media is still relatively limited. So when I went there recently, I spent a week basically without 24/7 email access, without being able to stream, without being able to watch movies on a computer, with a limited number of hours of television a day, with a limited repertoire of films – and it was actually very relaxing. So I see not only that the pace of consumption is much slower there, the range of consumption is also more limited. Which is not to say that there aren't people walking around with knapsacks full of pirated movies and video games and that there aren't expert technicians who can hack into Playstations and all kinds of machines to make them work, so that Cubans can play their pirated games or pirated movies on them. So there are ways in which they are improvising the means to be able to consume but it's nowhere near the level of over-saturation of information that I would experience living here [in the USA]. So that, to me, is the kind of difference we are talking about: it is a quantitative difference, which can, at a certain point, become a quali-tative one because Cubans don't experience the kind of "image fatigue" that I experience. At the same time, because Cubans have lived for so long in a place with state-controlled media, Cubans have a lot lower tolerance for official streams of information. Whereas I would maybe sit through a CNN news report, they will shut off an official news report very quickly or not even turn it on and not pay attention. And yet, this is not about a strictly "non-Western" mode of consumption.

What you're talking about is different levels of consumption and exposure, essentially

And different attitudes toward the image; Cubans have learnt to be much more skeptical about what passes as information than I think most people are in the USA.

So are you suggesting that it's also a question of how they adapt those existing Western codes to their own viewing and creative practices – the application of continuity editing from Hollywood, for example? It's not a question of there being some kind of non-Western mode of thinking or practice that is completely divorced or isolated from those Western influences?

No. You know people went through that. Film theorists in Cuba, directors during the high point of New Latin American cinema – people like Tomás Gutiérrez Alea and Julio Garcia Espinosa – who wanted to talk about "imperfect cinema" and about dialogical exchange with spectators, developing modes of production that would allow viewers to think critically. But they're not there anymore. That's not where the conversation is. And that was based on a very oppositional binary model of there being Hollywood, on the one hand, as a capitalist, ideologically dominant and controlling entity and then, on the other hand, the revolutionaries of the rest of the world who were trying to subvert that entity. People just don't talk in that way any more and, if they do, they don't get the same kind of attention paid to them as they once did because I don't think that most people – in or outside of the film industry – really believe it.

So the next question is based round a quote from Robert B. Ray, where he asks, "What could be a more exact definition of the cinema than the crossroads of magic and positivism or a more succinct definition of film theory's traditional project than to break the spell?" Do you see your own work as in any way located at a form of crossroads? Does your work break spells, be they theoretical or practical?

Once upon a time, when I was in college, we were taught – and this was in the late 1970s early 1980s – that we had to subvert dominant cinematic discourses and never try to make classic realist narrative and that, if we were women, we had to be Feminists, and classical realist narrative was masculinist, and that we couldn't offer opportunities for all kinds of eroticized looking at the female body or the male body, and that we should not allow our spectators to be sutured into an imaginary space. I learned all of that. And many of the people who mentored me during that time still adhere to a certain kind of skepticism about the practices that take a less critical stance vis-à-vis those paradigms. However, I don't adhere to that kind of insistence on deviating from popular forms; in part because I'm more interested in parodying those forms, working with them, playing with them, or even enticing audiences to look at things that they might not otherwise look at by presenting them in a format that makes them more familiar and palatable. It is also because I think that there's less and less of an audience for that kind of high, theoretical, super-intellectual image practice. Audiences generally don't appreciate being clobbered over the head with a voice-over that scolds them about what they should be or shouldn't be feeling.

Do you think it also links back to what you were saying a moment ago about moving away from that absolute division in the Third Cinema paradigm between Hollywood on the one hand and a politically engaged, experimental or non-mainstream, avant-garde cinema, on the other? The sense that these apparently absolute binaries or positions are either not there any more, or they are no longer relevant

I don't think that they're relevant because I don't think they're rooted in the social reality that we experience in the present. I also think that media literacy has changed radically since I was a child. I grew up in the 1960s, there were five television channels and a local movie theatre and 90 percent of what was on TV was pretty straight narrative. The rest conformed to a magazine format that was an adaptation of vaudeville, variety shows along the lines of the Ed Sullivan Show. Movies on TV were mostly movies from the 1930s, 1940s, and 1950s that were transferred to television to fill the hours that weren't filled by the production of sitcom and news. We didn't have 100 channels and we didn't have music video, which has completely changed the way that young people experience media. We didn't have the possibility of putting our own images into circulation. Nor did we have a cinema that reflected all those other kinds of media production, unlike today. Now you turn on the TV and half the commercials are made to look like they were shot by amateurs. Even television series, popular television series, are shot to look like reality TV or to look like they were made by an amateur, or to look like a *cinéma vérité* documentary – like a lot of the popular cop shows. So there's a way in which the mainstream has become polluted with all these vernacular or amateur forms, and vice versa. And there is a way in which all these people, who are not professionals, try to mimic these styles that they see on television and film in their own production. That kind of mirroring was not a part of the image world that I was raised in. So this idea that there's a need to step outside and look critically at something that is a self-contained dominant form doesn't make sense to me any more because there isn't a self-contained dominant form. Gaming is probably more of a space where you have a commercial hegemony. But, even here, smart kids, by the time they are teenagers, have hacked into those games and begun to transform them. So it's not that I don't recognize that there are really pronounced economic differences, and technologies that are only accessible when you have millions and millions of dollars. Rather, I don't think that patterns of production and reception are such that it makes sense to talk about the need to find a space 'outside' from which to critique a paradigm. I think that critique can be made manifest through a variety of means and that the very intellectualized mode of 1970s and 1980s independent film is not necessarily the most effective way of communicating one's distance from dominant forms today.

What do you think is the most effective way then, to pick up on that final thought?

I think there are different kinds of experiments that are interesting for different reasons and at different moments. For example, there was a moment in the late 1990s and early 2000s when people who were working in new digital media were playing with ways to take control of the web, to leverage the presence of a dispersed but massive audience in order to transform or to disrupt the hegemony of certain systems and modes of communication. In other words, politicized hacking had a moment, and this was a really important moment. There's also the example of the Iranian filmmaker Jafar Panahi, who is under house-arrest. His most recent film [*This is not a film*, (2011)], which was partly filmed on a cellphone, was sumuggled out of Iran to be screened at Cannes. Who would have thought that Cannes would show images from a cellphone within the context of the festival? Look at what has happened with social media and its use in relation to political movements in the Middle East or elsewhere. There are ways that bloggers have taken up a role in the production of images and cultural information that would have been unthinkable even ten years ago. Now this may have to do with my own aesthetic sensibilities or with my political sensibilities, but I'm more interested in how people with less access subvert the system with a little than I am with what happens in Hollywood in terms of innovations in gaming or 3D. Because I feel like what's happened in the commercial end of media production is that everything is organized around trying to extract more capital from consumers and also about trying to find the latest technological innovation able to get people into a cinema. So what's left of cinema at this point is just special effects, films that you have to see with special glasses, that you have to see on a big screen. But that doesn't speak to me in a way as a kind of innovation that I would even take that seriously, as anything other than a machine for extracting money – not much else.

This brings us back to the question of developments in digital technologies and new media and the opportunities they bring to a whole group of people to take control of the means of audiovisual production. Would you say that, rather than gaining access to the same production materials and distribution networks as Hollywood, it's actually about using new media to challenge the mainstream and find a completely different audience?

Not a different audience, it just finds an audience. I mean the thing that Hollywood had to its advantage was it had a kind of hegemonic control at the level of distribution. And that's what was killing independent film – there was no way to compete with Hollywood's control of film houses, control of advertising, control of commercial promotion time. So you could make a great movie but the chances of it being seen are minimal. I was at a conference in April [2011] where director Todd Haynes was speaking. He's just made a big production for television of *Mildred Pierce* (HBO, 2011), his first foray into television, and he was talking about two things: one, the evaporation of money for the kind of independent film that he has made up to now, and second that more people will see *Mildred Pierce*, one production, than the sum total of viewers for all of his films prior to that time. So what Hollywood – and here I mean Hollywood in a more generalized sense of studio film production – digital media and the Internet has done is to open up the possibility of lateral distribution that doesn't go through those circuits that are controlled by the system. And that is its strength, that you can get your work out there to a sizeable audience. And it's more and more the case that there are filtering systems that make it possible for people to get to the audiences that they need to communicate with. So Facebook helps in Iran and Egypt and elsewhere to organize people and there are similar things going on in China and Cuba and other places where, up until the present, regular citizens had very limited access to information other than what the state provides and, in the case of the United States, other than what Hollywood and mainstream television would provide. Obviously the numbers are not the same but they're enough to cause a ripple in the system.

Our next question, I think actually we've touched on already: do you think that de-Westernizing is principally an economic, political, institutional or artistic process and does it extend from earlier cinematic movements such as Third Cinema? And what's it doing differently?

I think that when these kinds of propositions and arguments were originally conceived, they were conceived of as all of them: economic, political, institutional, and artistic. I mean, if you go back to what Latin Americans were thinking about in the 1950s and 1960s it was about getting around the hegemony of Hollywood, it was about developing economic systems of production, state film industries in Mexico, Brazil, Argentina, Cuba, and elsewhere that could circumvent Hollywood control and that could create bases. It was political; the idea was that these would be centers for the production of national cultures and regional cultures and that it was institutional. There was a lot of effort put into building those national film industries and pumping money through them to engender national cinemas in parts of the world that hadn't had them. It was artistic in the sense that there were directors and theorists who were talking about Imperfect Cinema and Third Cinema – in other words different forms of practice that would be more faithful to cultural realities in other parts of the world and that would form a counterpoint to the Hollywood model. Did those issues come up earlier? Well, there was film production in different parts of the world. In Africa, under colonial rule, virtually all the productions were of foreigners coming in and doing ethnographic film or films for the colonial governments but in Latin America and in Asia there were productions before the kind of "postcolonial moment" – not a lot, but some – and also in India, I would imagine. As far as I know, the work was not necessarily driven by an anti-Hollywood stance. I think that that kind of political awakening

I associate with the postcolonial period of the 1950s and afterwards. So was there a political agenda involved? As far as I know I would say "no" that there wasn't a political agenda at that point of what we might call "de-Westernization." Maybe it was actually going in the other direction, it was more to prove how Western we are.

But what is it doing differently? The thing is, I don't even know what de-Westernizing film is anymore! But what I can tell you is this: I teach; I've been teaching for seventeen years. A lot of the stories in the films and videos that I show to my students from time to time are stories that I'm very familiar with. But I'm a kind of anomaly in this country in that I travel a lot, I go to developing countries, I have a reference point for understanding what the world looks like outside the USA and outside New York. Most of my students, especially the ones from the USA and Europe, don't have this frame of reference. And they're still shocked when I show a video that depicts poverty in the Third World. They're still unaccustomed to film that is based on a folk tale from West Africa. Or a story showing how people in a repressive authoritarian state respond at a very personal level to that repression with all kinds of escapist ways of thinking and being. Or how artists use extended allegories in those contexts in order to convey critiques that they can't state explicitly. So all of these things – both the kind of rootedness of storytelling in popular traditions that come from other places and the social realities of other places – are still a surprise to my students. And so, to me, I take that as a sign that, for all my talk about how "de-Westernized" we are, there still is a very narrow view of the world that the majority [in the West] hold and that there are still stories, points of view, social realities and political histories that are not part of a universally recognisable canon. That's not a product of a kind of colonial obsession with negating other cultures. I think it's a product of the narrowness and provincialism of majority audience viewing. It's more and more the case that more and more stories from different parts of the world enter our system [in the USA or the West] but that doesn't necessarily mean that everybody can see them or even wants to see them. I still get e-mails ten years after the fact from people who were in classes of mine a long time ago, saying: "I remember this weird video you showed me about 'X' and I was wondering if I could find a copy of that." So, that to me is a signal that, in a way, at the level of a collective culture imagery, there still is something that is "de-Westernizing" about certain kinds of media texts. More, I would say, than certain forms of communication.

One final question: Does de-Westernizing film studies mean rejecting entirely dominant Western modes of thinking, production, criticism, and practice? Is this even possible?

No I don't think it's possible. In the same way that I would argue at this point that there is no entirely non-Western place left, I don't think you can get rid of ways of thinking, ways of seeing, ways of speaking, and ways of understanding that have defined and shaped your experiences for most of your life. You're always going to have it. I mean, I'll always have that in me and I am a person who was trained in a Western tradition. I was educated in Western educational institutions, I learned and read predominantly Western canonical traditional texts as part of my intellectual formation, I speak Western languages. I am not going to be able to erase my hard drive, so to speak. I don't think any of us can, really. And then there is the question of what does that really mean at this point in time? To me, issues of cultural difference at this point have more to do with social experiences and their relationship to information consumption than they have to do with cultural particularities and specificity.

13 De-Westernizing film through experimental practice

An interview with Patti Gaal-Holmes

Do you see film as a universal medium/art form?

It depends entirely on what type of film is being referred to here, and so we are already getting into specifics and not universality. Some films are more "universal" as they are purely about reading the images (and music) as opposed to having to follow dialogue and a narrative text: Godfrey Reggio's trilogy (*Koyaanisqatsi: Life out of Balance* [1982]; *Powaqqatsi: Life in Transformation* [1988]; and *Naqoyqatsi: Life as War* [2002]) comes to mind. For example, the viewer can be led by the hypnotic narrative flow offered by Philip Glass's music and the diverse images of humanity or nature depicting aspects of beauty, deprivation or global destruction. A deeper understanding of the trilogy is, however, enhanced by having knowledge of the films' focus on the complex relationship between man and nature.

The ubiquity of Hollywood (dominant, narrative) cinema, across the globe, can perhaps misleadingly identify film *as* a universal medium. This is, however, not the case, since certain visual metaphors or motifs are culturally specific and are not easily translatable.

If I think of a specific case of attempts at film's universality, it is in the approach of African director Ousmane Sembène, who considered the power of film – as opposed to printed literature – as a valuable tool "to represent and to communicate with the masses" (Murphy and Williams 2007: 51). In this way, film could be used to impart important sociopolitical information, to inform and educate literate as well as illiterate viewers. For Sembène this was particularly important as he understood the need to present an accessible Africa for Africans: "I had read all that was written about Africa by both Europeans and Africans; and nowhere did I find my Africa: the Africa of the workers, the farmers, the women; the Africa that suffers but also struggles" (Gadjigo 2004: 37). In other words, through accessible narratives and recognizable contexts African viewers could identify with their situation, hopefully eliciting some form of change and opening up debates on issues important to them. This is the case with Sembène's final film, *Moolaadé* (2004), which focuses on female circumcision. Sembène's films, are, however, perhaps less accessible to Western viewers who cannot identify with the language, landscapes, and way of life that might be unfamiliar to them. I would therefore suggest that while film is a universal *tool* which can be used in diverse ways, I would not say that the film text is universally accessible.

Do you consider the West as a category that is always shifting, in motion, and therefore unstable? Should this "West" or the "Western" be perceived solely as, or through, geographical frameworks?

The boundaries of the West are forced to shift and change from time to time as they accommodate themselves to economic and sociopolitical changes, but stringent attempts are made to maintain its dominance by upholding Western ideologies. The idea of the West has a certain stability as long as enough people believe in it, but this too changes and, as a result, the West has to find new ways to reinvent its validity.

From a personal viewpoint I have never had the certainty of the West as a separate construct to the non-Western, as I was born to German and Hungarian immigrants in South Africa and grew up with multiple cultures, languages, and geographies (that I have lived in/with and can claim as part of my genealogy). This has resulted in my understanding of these terms (West and non-Western) as a fusion without a fixed sense or internal orthodoxy; and in my mode of operation either one or the other is utilized.

I do not believe the concept of the West or "the Western" can or should be perceived solely through geographical frameworks because the West has infiltrated the whole globe. This is explicitly evident in the Western brands and consumer goods prevalent in non-Western countries but also in the prevalence of non-Western products in Western countries. This fusion is also evident in the cross-cultural and multi-racial world which we inhabit. The conception of the West may, however, be useful to form generalizations of certain geographical areas where Western dominance is prevalent, but this should be used with an air of caution and not as definitive. This fusion of West/non-Western is explicitly evident in films such as Alejandro González Iñárritu's *Babel* (2006) where West and non-Western are not clearly separated by geographical frameworks. Western infiltration can be seen in examples such as the tourist bus, full of predominantly Caucasian Western sightseers (initially looking out from the enclosed "protection" of their bus), traveling in a remote part of Morocco; or the Western dress adopted by the Japanese business men and young students in Japan. Alternately, the infiltration of non-Western cultures is evident in the reliance of the American couple on a Mexican servant/house-help who is central to the "successful" functioning of their family.

What do you understand by non-Western modes of thinking, theorizing and making film?

One problem with attempting to conceptualize non-Western modes of thinking is that it problematically essentializes the discourses as being separate to Western modes of thinking; of being envisaged as a binary opposition (even if this is not the intention). Instead, conceiving of modes of thinking as constantly shifting and changing and seen within a hybrid space – i.e. a toing and froing *between* different cultural modes of articulation – may be a more apposite perspective. Homi Bhabha identified this as operating more through a level of negotiation, "a space of translation" (Bhabha 1998: 37). I would say that it is important to understand thinking, theorizing, art/filmmaking as coming out of this hybrid mix unconfined by fixed parameters of West/non-West and, crucially, as a fusion/mixing between spaces. This fusion is evident in the "Drawings for Projection" of South African artist, William Kentridge, who so eloquently combines European and African influences in his short films focused on apartheid and post-apartheid South Africa.

Perhaps elucidation of the original question can be found by asking the following, further questions: Where did modes of structured thinking originate? Where/when did the written word as discourse begin? How are these forms of pinning thinking down (through the written form) taken into an oral tradition; and worked from oral into written form and then into the film text? How is the text infused by what is lived? What then are non-Western modes of thinking and theorizing? Are these more intuitive approaches that are not insistent on explicit rationalization? Are they less confined by fixed boundaries, an openness of approach unbounded by structured systems? How can one even begin to make these divisions in thinking, when there has invariably been more of an infusion between West/non-West, rather than their existence being seen as fixed entities confined within set parameters? And what of non-Western filmmaking born out of oral traditions of storytelling, rather than of a literary or theatrical format? Are these impulses still prevalent when thinking, theorizing and filmmaking have passed through Western modes of operation?

Judy Purdom identified that the word "hybrid" can be "deceiving in inferring a balanced coming together of two identities" when instead "[t]he experience of hybridity is far more complex and more likely to be a clash of cultures than a comfortable union" (Purdom 1995: 22). This clash then may be essential for an ongoing process for probing and asking further questions about modes of thinking or theorizing that may at times appear intransigent, but carry no weight when taken across, or into, other cultural/theoretical/critical spaces of negotiation. There is perhaps the hope that some median form can be reached for an understanding of a particular type of whole, but in the end it is the fragmentary that prevails, offering only field notes for articulation to work from.

How does such an understanding affect your work?

I don't really think about this (West/non-Western) when I make work. I make work that I feel needs to be made. The camera is a tool, just like a pencil or my body, which is necessary for expressing what needs to be said (and this is often not fully understood or determined at the outset). I am currently preoccupied with the meaning of "home" and in thinking about the distinction between my African and European roots and how this may determine ways of thinking, theorizing, approaching my work. And in even knowing whether I am African (non-Western?) or European (Western?): there is so much of both within my mode of operation. As a case in point, about two years ago, someone visited my studio (in

Figure 13.1 provisionally free (Gaal-Holmes, 2010).

Portsmouth, England) and said that it had a real European sense to it; and more recently another visitor said he could see Africa in it. These are sentiments which cannot be separated from my approach to thinking, theorizing and making films. But what is certain, in general, is that there is not one orthodoxy, not one way that is "the way." Inherent in all my approaches is an awareness that there are other possibilities (other languages, other landscapes, other gestures). I think this lends an openness to thinking and a lack of confinement or rigidity in my approaches to the work.

In her essay on Walter Benjamin's Arcades Project, Margaret Cohen discussed his approach to historiography as being one which gave equal measure to dreams, illusion and the sundry scraps and findings of evidence necessary to compose history. She identified that Benjamin's "notion of 'rescuing critique' exemplified his favourite practice of disjunctive conceptual montage" (Cohen 2004: 210). I am very drawn to this idea of "disjunctive conceptual montage" as it makes the greatest deal of sense for foregrounding the notion that one uses whatever it is that one finds, whatever is necessary, whatever works or speaks best. This means that there are no tightly fixed parameters within which to work, but rather the fluidity of intuition, observation and recognition.

I believe that there is an emotive value present in different forms of cultural or linguistic expression that elicits a kind of response of being on familiar ground. These deeply held sentiments are difficult to express: it may simply be the case that a connection is sparked through the way that a word is uttered, the gesture someone makes, or the way an object looks. This emotive value may also come through the manner in which thought processes are articulated: i.e. like a language within a language.

Again, I am not really sure about the division "Western/non-Western" with regard to myself and my practice. I just approach the work in the way that seems necessary. Since birth there has never been only one language, culture, geography that has been the defining one in my world. My father was Hungarian, my mother is German, and their common tongue was French. I was born in Africa with my mother looking often to her northern skies with longing and my father mute on his escape from Hungary in 1948. My mother tongue is German, although I was educated in English (and Afrikaans as a second language). I am a Belgian national, although I feel no affinity at all to Belgium as a defining factor in my identity, except that one of my sons was born there and my father – after being stateless for some years – was given Belgian nationality. Furthermore I have no idea how I should be culturally defined if this ever becomes necessary: as a British-based South African/German/Hungarian artist? So when the artist Anselm Kiefer says "My biography is the biography of Germany" (Lauterwein 2007: 29) I ask: which biography then is mine? When Madan Sarup asks: "Who am I? Shall I look at my passport to find some clues about my identity?" (Sarup 1996: xiv). I take out my passports: South African, German and Belgian (current or expired) but they only give clues, which are very diffuse. Rather than something definite, I think of identity construction as being in a continual state of fragmentary transmutation. There are moments of cohesion, but essentially the fragmentary prevails, so there is a continuous state of negotiation and renegotiation. This then translates into my modes of thinking, theorizing and approaching practice.

Robert B. Ray, an academic with particular interest in critical practice, once asked, "What could be a more exact definition of the cinema than 'the crossroads of magic and positivism'? Or a more succinct definition of film theory's traditional project than 'to break the spell'?" Do you see your work as located at some form of crossroads? Does your work break any spell(s), theoretical and/or practical?

I am not sure if my work breaks any spells or sits at some form of crossroads, but the relationship between theory and practice has been (and continues to be) of particular interest to me. This became particularly evident to me whilst undertaking research and writing toward a historical (as opposed to practice-based) Ph.D. on 1970s British experimental filmmaking; and in questioning the processes of production inherent in writing and art-making. The approaches taken as an artist in the studio differ considerably from the type of academic rigor required for the writing of a historical thesis. Although creative practice has its own internal rigor or/and constraints, usually defined on the artist's terms, there is not the same need to justify every claim through evidence; and a more intuitive way of working can guide the artist: for both the inception and the completion of a work.

I worked on a project intermittently alongside my Ph.D., where I thought closely about the relationship between theory and practice. This was initiated by my reading of Keith Jenkins' *Re-thinking History* (which I found to be a particularly influential text); and I had earmarked so many pages to take notes from. In one specific citation Jenkins, discussing the positioned nature of the historian, references the Russian Futurist poet, Velimir Khlebnikov as follows:

> The past that we "know" is always contingent upon our own views, our own
> "present." Just as we are ourselves products of the past so the known past
> (history) is an artefact of ours. Nobody, however immersed in the past, can
> divest himself/herself of his/her knowledge and assumptions. There are,
> then, few limits to the shaping power of interpretive, imagining words.
> "Look" says the poet Khlebnikov in his *Decrees to the Planets,* "the sun obeys
> my syntax." "Look," says the historian, "the past obeys my interpretation."
>
> (Jenkins 2003: 15)

I loved the idea that sun *obeyed* his syntax. This was a kind of an expectant grandeur
on Khlebnikov's part – calling the cosmos to attention – as if this were possible!
Therefore instead of taking notes conventionally from Jenkins' book – in a notebook
or on a computer for example – I "drew" the contents of selected pages onto
A3 pieces of handmade Khadi paper. Some notes and quotations from Jenkins'
book were taken down and random mark-making also took the form of abstract
images. These "drawings" were then sewn into an artist's book – perhaps an
attempt at cohering my arbitrary responses. In order to take the process of distilling
the written form into more minimal abstract and drawn images further, each
A3 page was refined into a simpler and smaller A6 form. These became a series
of small artist's book called *distilling history,* with each page having either a word or
a few words or abstract images on it. What was made apparent through this
process was that in taking another avenue to imbibe a text, new referral points in
another "language" were divulged. In this respect the intention was that a dialogue between the processes of working as an artist and the analyses of texts for
research would open up the possibility for further chance encounters to occur. It
was hoped that some form of osmosis would take place: that through an open
form of drawing the text could be inscribed into my brain.

I also found the way of the studio useful for theoretical/critical research
and experimented with making quick drawings of shots/scenes from a film, as an
aide-mémoire and as another way of gaining entry into a film text.

Robert B. Ray used the example given by anthropologist, Michael Taussig
when discussing the need for a "graphicness" in approaching film criticism,
having the ability to maintain a sense of film's influential and widespread appeal
(Taussig discussed commercial Hollywood cinema here), yet also offering a
critique. Taussig suggested that what was required was a need to "penetrate
the veil while retaining its hallucinatory quality" which would involve the dual
interpretive purposes of "reduction *and* revelation" (Ray 1995: 10). I therefore
asked myself, was there inherently some way of entering the text (in the case with
Jenkins a history book, though it could just as easily be a film too) by taking an
oblique angle to gain entry to the text, and once inside, offer up new ways of
reading? Ray suggested that the "reduction and revelation" could be found in
alternative approaches informed by avant-garde practices of experimentation, as
well as in cross-disciplinary approaches to research and practice: "This process of
invention-by-extrapolation involves translation between disciplines: as John Cage
once explained, 'One way to write music: study Duchamp'" (Ray 1995: 47).

Do you think that de-Westernizing film is principally an economic, political, institutional, or artistic process? For example, does it extend from earlier cinematic movements, such as Third Cinema?

I am not entirely sure what the intentions of the processes of de-Westernizing film are, but perhaps they are attempting to rupture some of the more conventional institutional approaches to film studies and film production? If so, I'd say yes, perhaps it does extend from earlier cinematic movements, as Third Cinema activists/directors Fernando Solanas and Octavio Getino would say, "with the camera in one hand and a rock in the other" (Solanas and Getino 1997: 49). What is de-Westernizing film doing differently? Perhaps attempting to open up new spaces for discourses to occur.

Does de-Westernizing film studies mean rejecting entirely dominant Western modes of thinking, production, criticism, and film practice? Is this even possible?

No, definitely not rejecting wholesale; I don't believe this to be possible or useful. One cannot invent a new language entirely and why would one want to when there are many aspects of any language that are useful? One should work with the existing ones, shifting, changing, adding and contesting where necessary.

References

Bhabha, H. K. (1998) *The Location of Culture*, London and New York: Routledge.

Cohen, M. (2004) "Benjamin's Phantasmagoria: The Arcades Project," in D. S. Ferris (ed.), *The Cambridge Companion to Walter Benjamin*, Cambridge: Cambridge University Press, pp. 199–220.

Gadjigo, S. (2004) "Ousmane Sembene and History on the Screen: A Look Back to the Future," in F. Pfaff (ed.), *Focus on African Films*, Bloomington, Ind.: Indiana University Press, pp. 33–47.

Jenkins, K. (2003) *Re-thinking History*, London and New York: Routledge.

Lauterwein, A. (2007) *Anselm Kiefer, Paul Celan: Myth Mourning and Memory*, London and New York: Thames & Hudson.

Madun, S. (2007) *Identity, Culture and the Postmodern World*, Edinburgh: Edinburgh University Press.

Murphy, D. and Williams, P. (2007) *Postcolonial African Cinema: Ten Directors*, Manchester: Manchester University Press.

Purdom, J. (1995) "Mapping Difference," *Third Text*, 32 (autumn): 19–32.

Ray, R. B. (1995) *The Avant-Garde Finds Andy Hardy*, Boston, Mass.: Harvard University Press.

Sarup, M. (1996) *Identity, Culture and the Postmodern World*, Edinburgh: Edinburgh University Press.

Solanas, F. and Getino, O. (1997) "Towards a Third Cinema: Notes and Experiences for the Development of a Cinema of Liberation in the Third World," in M. T. Martin (ed.), *New Latin American Cinema*, Vol. I: *Theory, Practices, and Transcontinental Articulations*, Detroit, Mich.: Wayne State University Press, pp. 33–58.

14 "With our own pen and paper"
An interview with Teddy E. Mattera

Do you see film as a universal medium/art form?

Yes, I do see it as a universal medium and art form.

Do you consider the West as a category that is always shifting, in motion, and therefore unstable? Should this "West," or "the Western," be perceived solely as, or through, geographical frameworks?

It is indeed difficult to decide and define the notion of the "West" or "Western"; so I would agree (though with reservation) that it is, as a category, always shifting, in motion, and therefore unstable. On the one hand, the notion of the "West" is my reality as an urban and international citizen as much as it is that of someone from Europe, the many Americas, Australia, Japan or China, amongst other places. On the other hand, the same notion is generally defined through and by geographical frameworks (i.e. West/East; Global North and Global South). In such frameworks it is the West or Global North, which seems to enjoy the surplus of everything and therefore appear to be controlling "everything."

What do you understand by non-Western modes of thinking, theorizing and making film? How does such an understanding affect your work?

What I understand by "non-Western modes" is that I attempt to "deconstruct" these Western modes and, in so doing, introduce what and who we, as Africans, are; what we think, feel and hear as Africans.

Robert B. Ray, an academic with particular interest in critical practice, once asked, "What could be a more exact definition of the cinema than 'the crossroads of magic and positivism'? Or a more succinct definition of film theory's traditional project than 'to break the spell'?" Do you see your work as located at some form of crossroads? Does your work break any spell(s), theoretical and/or practical?

I believe that filmmaking is about "making and breaking the spell." Cinema is an ancient tradition in African societies. The first peoples of the world – the San and

Khoi of Southern Africa – have often had to tell the visual and aural story of the land around them in the burning embers of a desert fire. In a similar way, the men tell of the hunt – which animals set foot in the desert, whether it was male or female, injured or fit – purely by reading the tracks or imprints on the sand and infusing them with meaning.

Cinema is about infusing meaning into images and sounds. The picture had to be seen first in the mind's eye of the storyteller and then transmitted evocatively to that of the listener. Therefore I see cinema as an aural and visual ritual much like our ancestors did. Like the Sha-man and Sha-woman who perform their rituals when they visualize, listen and heal, whether it comes by divine inspiration or is curated by our ancestors. (African) cinema, whether rural or urban, is a ritual performed at the crossroads where spells are broken and new ones made, sometimes seamlessly and other times in more direct and obvious ways (e.g. through the use of montage).

Do you think that de-Westernizing film is principally an economic, political, institutional, or artistic process? For example, does it extend from earlier cinematic movements, such as Third Cinema? What is it doing differently?

Third Cinema is, simultaneously, a derivative and partner of revolutionary processes and outcomes. It resembles liberation theology, which had to redesign God to suit the times; for who would worship a God that did not support the struggle?

De-Westernizing film may be a new idea, conceptually speaking, but it is not a new concept. As a case in point, many (African) filmmakers, from Haile Gerima to Med Hondo, Ousmane Sembène and Djibril Diop Mambéty, have "de-Westernized" film or cinema by including their very own experiences in Europe and elsewhere

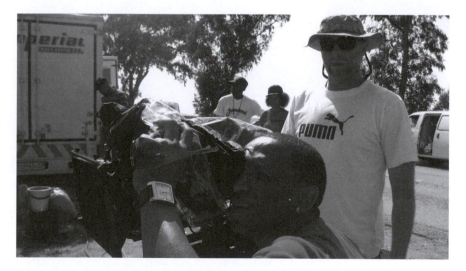

Figure 14.1 One Way (Teddy E. Mattera, 2006–2007).

into their films. Africans who have spent time in Europe have made a variety of films about Africa, ranging from nostalgia to political agitation and styles of storytelling that suit the oral traditions from long ago. This is what de-Westernizing is and has been doing (differently) from the kind of current copycat behaviour that we see from a contemporary globalized generation of African filmmakers. The latter, predictably, ask the problematic question: When will film and cinema be "globalized" rather than "Westernized" or "de-Westernized"?

Does de-Westernizing film studies mean rejecting entirely dominant Western modes of thinking, production, criticism and film practice? Is this even possible?

The lines of demarcation are not as easily visible as we would like them to be. It is almost like asking a child of mixed blood or mixed parentage whether s/he is black or white. The truth is that s/he is both. What matters is how the child can take the best, and then learn about the worst, from both parents so that s/he can make informed decisions and be able to take responsibility for those decisions. It is in fact the essence of filmmaking: making decisions during writing, shooting, acting, lighting, editing, financing etc., then living with and learning from those decisions rather than hiding away from them. For now, it seems that the history of cinema and film and their making is/will mainly be told by the victors (the West). Unless we make, show and distribute African cinema we will only help to fill a pen we do not own with ink as it writes cinema's story. We must own our own pen and our own paper to write and distribute our own stories: African solutions to African problems.

15 "To colonize a subject matter is to learn nothing from it"
An interview with Jonnie Clementi-Smith

Do you see film as a universal medium/art form?

Yes, film is most definitely a universal medium and art form. Storytelling through music and images has always been a universal medium and art form for as long as there have been humans. A major difference between film and other forms of expression, such as theatre, exists within film's automatic movement, it apes/imitates reality.

As an art form film tries to unveil the human spirit, to reveal in life a reality unnoticed. As the philosopher and metaphysicist Henri Bergson, writing in the early twentieth century, suggested, art does not create, it unveils aspects of reality that have been previously unnoticed; it should add to an understanding of the human condition.

As a commodity industry, film has many functions. It usually revolves around some form of control and escapist fantasy, or complex issues trivialized and packaged for bite-sized consumption – the end result being to block truth and the human spirit, deaden minds and create robotic behavior.

Finally, like the human brain, film deals in images; words are just signs for the images created in the brain; hence film is a more universal medium than language.

Do you consider the West as a category that is always shifting, in motion, and therefore unstable? Should this "West," or "the Western," be perceived solely as, or through, geographical frameworks?

Assuming that you mean the West in film, you could argue that commercial film everywhere is Westernized, that industrial film is a capitalist commodity (this is especially true in Hong Kong where I am currently based) and that, as a commercial medium, film shifts with fashion and style, though not in ideology.

Hong Kong is where I have the film cooperative, DogStar, made up of Asian and Western filmmakers dedicated to creating works that push the boundaries of the medium; films that do not shy away from potentially difficult issues. Part of the Collective's call to arms is to try and reinvent Hong Kong film as an industry that takes risks, as with the Collective's first film, *The Surroundings* (Yang Zheng Fan, 2011), commissioned by the Freshwave Film Festival (Hong Kong) where it won best cinematography, or *The Offerings* (Clementi-Smith, Henderson, 2012), selected as one of the Finalists for the 2012 International Documentary Challenge at the Hot Docs Toronto Festival. In recent years the Hong Kong film industry has lost itsway being eclipsed by Mainland Chinese film – unsure of where its national identity lies.

I see differences more in terms of commercial industry vs. art practice. Most commercial Chinese films are shot in a Western way, using continuity editing, and narrative-led action – classic Hollywood techniques – though, arguably, small budget, independent art films using long takes, fluid stories, decentered actions, possibly depth of field (instead of classic montage, and non-professional actors) could be classified as Western too.

I think that technique should not be classified as either Eastern, or Western, though of course all films tell stories that can very much be linked to culture and national identity.

However, a fundamental difference between Western and Eastern cultures does exist within communication and how it is used to either create harmony, consensus and balance, or rhetoric (i.e. to state an issue and argue a point of view). Another way to describe this would be conflict leading to resolution vs. balance or harmony. This highlights a major difference between Western and Eastern modes of thinking, which can be reflected within film. It could be argued therefore that Hollywood narrative film, like the ethics of Roman culture 2,000 years ago, has set a benchmark to be either copied or broken.

What do you understand by non-Western modes of thinking, theorizing and making film? How does such an understanding affect your work?

With my work I certainly never think, "Well today I am going to make a Western – or Eastern – centric film"; I do not see film as either conflict resolution or simply the creation of balance or harmony. I am more likely to dive into the abyss, divine a way through the chaos, and hopefully bring back an illumination, an unveiled truth.

I never think in terms like "non-Western" modes theorizing and making film – only film academics do. Film is neither Western nor Eastern but, as stated previously, a universal language. Film breaks into the categories of industry, and artistry, a point that leads to the issue of money, and who is paying for it, which also affects the film's distribution and hence the film's exposure. The Internet has, to some degree, helped to balance this situation.

Indeed Western modes of thinking could be described as rather abstract and clinical but, personally, I prefer a more embodied approach. In the case of my restaging of Maya Deren's *Divine Horsemen* (2005), it was about being true to the spirit of Deren, and the cosmology of voodoo, something the Cherel and Teiji Ito cut of the film released in 1985 never did. I looked for similarities between Deren's film artistry and voodoo cosmology to help release the inherent similarities between the magical form and the image within both. As a remix then, my restaging took a certain mimetic approach which highlighted the difference in similarity, a translation to create a new form yet hold onto the inherent quality or spirit of the original.

With my documentary installation, *People Inbetween* (2007), again all subjects are treated the same, with no agenda; therein, the trance possessions of the Urvedic

demon exorcisms and the working-class Sri Lankan spaces are as valid as the traditional Dutch burgher spaces; no prior conceptions, or agenda. It is about releasing
durations of time in the intervals of spaces, and the people's stories within – "the
value of zero, the rhythms of life caught in time between actions" as Deren would
say [Deren, cited by Jackson 2002: 159]. To force an ideology, or a film style onto
a subject that does not flow or resonate with it is to colonize or colonially exploit it:
maybe this is Western. The way that a film is shot should not ethically, or conceptually, clash with the content or images of the film: this is true of documentary.

This happened in Sri Lanka after the devastation of the 2007 tsunami. Western
film crews actively encouraged the children to be more traumatized, to play victims
for their own ends. I heard this from Timothy Barco, a Sri Lankan filmmaker and
child psychologist, who witnessed it at first hand.

To colonize a subject matter is to learn nothing from it but merely prop up
one's ego, one's own agenda. Within my documentary work I try to release the
image and hence unveil the soul of the work, something that, in turn, allows the
stories, places, spaces, and people, time and hence meaning, to shine in the film.
All this explains the absence of techniques designed to lead a viewer, such as,
voiceover, the use of long takes, directly involving the subjects in the making
of the work, and few preconceptions: this is neither Eastern nor Western,
neither resolution through conflict or balance, but truthful, however chaotic that
may be. Like the true nature of life, film is chaos with the illusion of a veneer
of order.

The Surroundings, the film I have shot in mainland China as Director of
Photography, uses long static takes, an extreme depth of field, non-professional
actors and very little lighting (if any). We kept the non-professional actors in
character off-frame to allow natural sounds to mix with the sounds of the acted
situation; hence the off-frame sounds flow around the image, creating a more
truthful atmosphere. This could be described as Eastern, Taiwanese filmmaking,
or the ideals of André Bazin, Eric Rohmer, and the French New Wave (or even a
combination of the two). Mary Steven, Eric Rohmer's editor has mentored this
project, which is more a matter of the techniques of truthfulness against the
techniques of manipulation, to allow the story to evolve within the mise-en-scène
of the frame instead of being manipulated by the montage.

**Robert B. Ray, an academic with particular interest in
critical practice, once asked, "What could be a more exact
definition of the cinema than 'the crossroads of magic and
positivism'? Or a more succinct definition of film theory's
traditional project than 'to break the spell'?" Do you see
your work as located at some form of crossroads? Does your
work break any spell(s), theoretical and/or practical?**

I think all film is magic with the illusion of positivism.

Film is the manipulation of time; on one level, it is time travel. All thought in
film, including Third Cinema, New Wave, Montage, Long Focus, the Cinema of

Hunger, or Garbage Cinema can be present at all times, in the here and now, like memories in a brain.

I never go into a film thinking: "this is what it will be." Filmmaking can be a magical process; the best films release, uncover, and unveil something – moments of *photogénie,* as Jean Epstein would say – meaning film's power to reveal, within the most mundane image, magic beyond the capacity of words to define. I never try to go looking for these moments, if they happen, they happen. In my own work, they are usually revealed in post-production.

I try to keep to small intimate crews, personal visions. This can be dangerous as it opens up the possibility of either film magic, or failure. Nevertheless, to make good films means taking risks, jumping off the precipice into the void, or as Deren would say delving into the abyss to reveal truthful experience (Deren 1946: 21).

I look for the intervals, the rhythms of life. All my works deal with time (the rhythms of nature) and humanity (a human touch is very important). Through this, I try to achieve a form of distant intimacy. This could be described as a major element of magic. Lately I have tried to explore the power of nothing, and the notion of difference in repetition, a form of creative mimesis that is also used in trance possession and shamanic magic to objectify fears of the unknown, of the Other. This is highlighted in works such as *Les Maîtres fous* (Jean Rouch, 1954), where the *Hauka* act out the oppressive forces in their lives in order to control them.

Filmmaking is about revealing time, which is caught in light, emotions, and reality; in essence the face of things, their nature. Indeed, on a technical level, to over-light a scene in a film is to wipe away the emotional face of what is real. A light touch shows the essence of things. The cinematographer reveals with light, the actors reveal with their bodies, the director reveals the souls of things. This could be thought of as magic but I think this is more about reality and life; film is reality.

With each new film, I try to be open and let the nature of the space in and the story to shine through in time, to be supple and strong, like a reed in the wind.

Do you think that de-Westernizing film is principally an economic, political, intuitional, or artistic process? For example, does it extend from earlier cinematic movements, such as Third Cinema? What is it doing differently?

I think that institutions need to de-Westernize their thinking; this is partly a political process as the hegemony of thought has been a political process in institutions and education. I would like to see a little more of the paradoxical nature of film within film theory, a more baroque approach which acknowledges a more chaotic structure and less the ideals of conformity and consensus. Indeed an issue I have is that unless film theory is written in English it is predominantly ignored.

Industrial film will always lean toward the Hollywood system, and, due to a lack of resources and money, film as an artistic medium will always lean toward methods exemplified by Third Cinema and the Cinema of Hunger – small crews, and personal visions.

Does de-Westernizing film studies mean rejecting entirely dominant Western modes of thinking, production, criticism and film practice? Is this even possible?

For me de-Westernizing film studies is about de-Westernizing academic thought. I see the problem as an academic one, not in the mode of production, or thinking, but in the way that thought in film is interpreted by film academics. There will always be two modes of filmmaking, which are either the dominant commercial industrial process, or the artistic personal expressive process. These may be categorized as Eastern and Western but this does not mean that this division is strictly or solely geographical. Most film production, and this is true of Hong Kong, is commercial and Westernized.

Film as an art form – i.e. films that talk directly to the soul and try to unveil realities that have not been expressed before – will always be marginalized. This is partly due to the tension between artistic and industrial processes but also the way that film is taught. This is the only medium with this tension. In other creative forms, such as writing, painting, theatre, etc., there is not the same differentiation between commercial and artistic processes. In many ways, this highlights the importance of film as a universal medium and a communication tool for unveiling reality, or propaganda manipulation.

As Gilles Deleuze says in *Cinema 2: the Time Image* [1989: 164], "Cinema is dying, then, from its own quantitative mediocrity, has degenerated into state propaganda and manipulation, into a kind of fascism which brought together Hitler and Hollywood, Hollywood and Hitler." To quote Deleuze again, "the brain is the screen." I don't believe that linguistics and psychoanalysis offer a great deal to cinema. On the contrary, the biology of the brain – molecular biology – does. Thought is molecular." Film has tended to be hijacked by linguists for their own ends. Interestingly, innovative research within neuroscience, such as that conducted by V. S. Ramachandran in the USA, backs up this premise.[1]

Film deals in concepts, in feelings, thoughts, and images that cannot always be put into words. Epstein, with the notion of *Photogénie* that he developed in the 1920s understood this.[2] It has a power to communicate directly to the brain. To analyze and explain what cannot be analyzed and explained (as, in my opinion, some film academics do) is to risk misrepresenting an entire medium. This leads to a further problem: where to place film studies as a subject within academic thought, and institutions. In any case, limiting film studies to an over-analytical narrow style of thought and writing limits the subject not the films. Filmmakers, in contrast, tend to operate within a fluid and close-knit community in which many styles of work can be made from multiple perspectives and for a variety of audiences.

References

Deleuze, G. (1989) *Cinema 2: The Time Image*, London: Athlone Press.

Deren, M. (1946) *An Anagram of Ideas on Art, Form and Film*, Yonkers, NY: Alicat Bookshop Press.

Jackson, R. (2002) *The Modernist Poetics and Experimental Film Practice of Maya Deren, (1917–1961)*, Lampeter and New York: Edwin Mellen Press.

Willemen, P. (1994) *Looks and Frictions: Essays in Cultural Studies and Film Theory*, Bloomington, Ind. and London: Indiana University Press and BFI Publishing.

16 "Isn't it strange that 'world' means everything outside the West?"

An interview with Rod Stoneman

Before we get to the series of questions that form the basis of this interview, you wanted to say something about your background in relation to this project [*De-Westernizing Film Studies*]?

Yes. Very briefly my political background is formed in part by coming from this part of the world [south-west England/Northern Hemisphere], but I went to university in the early 1970s when the bow-wave of 1968 had its effect and politicized culture. By the time I began to study English literature at the University of Kent and a postgraduate diploma in film at the Slade School of Art (University College, London), there was already a sense that a new agenda had been created, emanating from the punctual moment of 1968 and that a key component of that agenda was the realization – even if I hadn't any direct experience of it – that there was a rather large part of the world which was not properly mapped onto or connected with the northern part, the West, where we were; and, worse than that, that there were the continuing legacies of imperialism (of which Vietnam was the obvious example at that time). After graduating from the Slade, I became involved on the board of [the British film studies journal] *Screen,* wrote articles for that magazine and others like *Afterimage* and *Undercut.* Then there was a short time on the dole, freelancing, and then running a cinema within an arts center in Bristol called the Arnolfini. All of those things were quite speedy and short-term, so after doing the Slade's postgraduate course I had two or three years back in the south-west of England and began some independent filmmaking and, indeed, a part-time assignment as a consultant for Channel 4.

So that is the background to going to work full-time for Channel 4 [in the early 1980s], which was a very different experience because obviously there was the formidable structure – the intimidating institution of fortress television – but Channel 4 itself was trying to do television differently with its legislated remit to innovate in both the content and form of television and reach niche audiences with new forms of broadcasting. That translated into bringing people into television who were not already internal to it – in the sense of not being professionally involved and set on a career path within British television. Television has been rather more enclosed and exclusive both before and since this experiment.

"Outsiders" would have included Liz Forgan from the women's page of *The Guardian*, or Naomi McIntosh, who had been a professor at the Open University, and this was certainly true of someone like me right out on the edge from *Screen*, the London Filmmakers Co-operative, SEFT [Society for Education in Film and Television] and the IFA [Independent Filmmakers' Association]. But, it was compatible because the whole notion of the Channel 4 was to open a space for new voices that would reach new audiences. There were a whole range of areas that our department supported and programmed to increase diversity and push the boundaries of television: they included experimental cinema, low-budget fiction, political documentary, and personal documentary. But obviously in the context of your exploration of de-Westernizing film studies, the one area I should focus on within the work of our department, Independent Film and Video, was the concerted attempt to show films and programmes from Africa, Asia, and Latin America on British television. We moved from the term "Third World" to "the South" (labels are very important in television). And so "South" seemed a better brand. Personally, I've always disliked the phrase, "Developing World" because, actually, I think it should be matched by the phrase "the *Over*developed World," which is where I think the West is at the moment! So underdeveloped has to be thought through in relation to parts of the planet that are overdeveloped and our need to retract from the economy of perpetual growth.

And so we began in 1983, at the beginning of Channel 4, in a relatively fragmentary and piecemeal way, by assembling seasons from different continents and countries: New Cinema of Latin America, Africa on Africa, *Caméra arabe*, and Vietnam Cinema.

Our starting point was clear: Channel 4 sailed under the flag of radical pluralism, and our approach was, in a number of different areas, to privilege "direct speech." An example would be the *People to People* series of programmes, which was enabling communities of interest – whether they be miners' wives or young people in Northern Ireland or Italians in London or transsexuals – working with professional filmmakers to be able to talk directly, or have something approximating direct speech. Of course there is always a degree of mediation, but we were trying to reduce that mediation hugely. In a certain way our frame of reference from Africa or Asia would also have been direct speech. There is a way that a clear political documentary is always interesting but that it does not extend to the lived texture of everyday life seen from another part of the planet, which is available in a fiction film. I have to just say in parenthesis that I think it is particularly tragic that at a point when people are flying civilian aircraft into buildings there has never been a more important moment in the life of a planet to hear, see, and feel how other places live and work – their cultures – and yet actually that's at a time when the Western media have never been more enclosed, cut off, or insular.

Anyway, after that initial phase of anthology seasons for Channel 4, a mixture of mostly fiction and some documentaries grouped around one country or film culture – Latin American, African or Vietnamese cinema – of which there were about half a dozen of these seasons, often with a supportive context, a documentary or educational booklet, there was a breakthrough resulting from the success of the seasons: we got a slot. That can't be underestimated. Then we expanded to a regular weekly slot called *Cinema from Three Continents*. I stole the title from the festival in Nantes, and told the Jalladeau brothers [Philippe and Alain], "You should take this as a compliment, we're nicking your title!" So *Cinema from Three Continents* ran for about thirty weeks, it was scheduled for 10 o'clock on a Sunday night, which is not a bad time, and mixed films from different parts of the [global] South. So that was really a breakthrough, and I think one index of its success was that BBC2 also started programming films from these parts of the world. As we know, imitation is the most sincere form of flattery. I realized when I went to FESPACO [the pan-African film festival in Ouagadougou] suddenly there was a BBC2 man outbidding me for the rights to the best African films. But I thought that this form of competition was entirely excellent; to get one part of television competing with another in a progressive aim, that was great. So we moved from the seasons to a long-running Sunday cinema slot and we added a mid-week, mid-evening magazine programme (*South*), which had three runs. The programme schedule is divided into quarters of the calendar year in television, so it would be a series of about twelve programmes, and *South* had short elements, it was a magazine programme but, crucially, like the bigger project of *Cinema from Three Continents*, all the individual pieces were made by "Southern" filmmakers.

I remember going to Tunis once, at the Carthage Film Festival, and calling filmmakers together – of course you've only got to say you've got a bit of money for production and filmmakers gather round – and the late, great Youssef Chahine was there, along with various others, and I said, "Look we're trying to set up this magazine programme so if you have any ideas send them through and we'll pay you proper money to make some of them." And, perhaps understandably, there was a lot of suspicion: "What are you trying to do? What are you taking from us now?" And Chahine just cut through the crap and he said, "Look. You fuck Rod, Rod fucks you. You all have a good time and it works in both directions." A rather vulgar metaphor, but the crucial thing was we were paying properly for films to be made (£15,000–25,000 for short commissioned pieces) and Channel 4 was gaining by showing those films.

I remember equivalent meetings in Cape Town and Johannesburg, as I came into the room, a theatre group from the Markets sat around, and they began by asking, "What are you going to do for us?" I replied, "I refuse those terms – precisely on the basis that this should be an exchange. You are not mendicants. What can you do for me? What can you produce that is fantastic and will work on British television?" which is perhaps a rather heavy-handed way of putting it, but it's certainly more dignified than saying, "Oh God, you poor beggars, we've got to give you some money and feel a bit less guilty." Horrible stuff. But those are the kind of distorting relations that you have to find a way through.

And the other thing alongside *Cinema from Three Continents* and *South* was that as we continued going to film festivals, like FESPACO, like Havana, buying the best recent films, but we also began to move to putting production money

into new films that were to be made – called "pre-purchase" in television trans-
actions. It's actually ironic because it contradicts the market: if you see a great
feature film that is finished and you buy it – in those days anyway – it would have
cost between £12,000 and £15,000, conceivably up to £20,000 for three trans-
missions over a five-year period. The difference between these figures, by the way,
the price depends on how long the film is, how well the distributor negotiates, has
it won prizes, or if the BBC's going for it as well, then it gets competitive. Putting
money into a film before it's been made – even though it's much riskier and
you're not sure how it will turn out – is much more expensive. So you'd be putting £25,000, £35,000, £50,000, occasionally £75,000 into a feature film, and
because of the economy of production in Africa – I was particularly focused on
Africa – that makes a big difference, you know; that pre-purchase £50,000 was
hard currency, it was commitment, it was confidence in the project, which helped.
Obviously there were other funders in the francophone areas (the French state
contributed money in various forms), WDR and ZDF in Germany were other
European television stations occasionally doing this. So that seemed to me to be a
move towards a much more productive and more useful and proactive relationship with filmmakers in those parts of the world, and basically this added up to a
concerted attempt to put, in fictional and documentary formats, non-Western
forms of image-making, sound-making in front of a British television audience.
And although there are, of course, limitations to watching cinema on television, it
soon had a real and tangible effect and supported these films in theatrical distribution as well.

Anyway, that's a sketch of my experience in a television context, before and
outside the academy, before we talk more about film studies and the academic
domain.

Let's move on to the questions. Do you see film as a universal medium/art form?

Well the intellectual framework in which I was trained at university was structural
theory, new French theory, and that of course means that the moment I hear the
word "universal" I reach for my revolver because universal is, exactly, a natur-
alizing ideological delusion. While I do, of course, accept that film is relatively
accessible across cultures, nothing is "universal" or "natural." It brings to mind
something I read in *Scientific American* once when I was a younger. There were
some anthropologists in New Guinea and they were talking to a group of New
Guinea islanders who had never had access to Western media in any form. So the
anthropologists used a Polaroid instant camera to take a photograph of the tribal
chieftain – his head and shoulders – then they passed him the photograph and
asked, "What do you think of that?" The chief replied, "I don't know; it looks like
a coloured leaf to me." One of the anthropologist said, "Actually, it's an image of
you. It's a picture of you that I've just taken on this machine." And explains,
"Look, there it is, it's taken from the side: that's your nose, your ear, your chin."
But the tribal chieftain insists, "That's not me. I've got two eyes, there is only one

eye on that thing you've done. It isn't a picture of me." And that story for me was a kind of crucial epiphany enabling us to imagine ourselves outside of a frame that has been entirely naturalized and universalized by the (Western) media.

And trying to think about cultural specificity – which, as I said, is also part of the baggage of the *Screen* theory that I carried into work in television – all these years later, I'm sitting down in Paris at the rough cut of *Tinpis Run* (Pengau Nengo, 1991) which is the first feature film coming out of New Guinea. Seeing this rough cut – and in all these things, whether it be Papuans or Brits or Americans, whoever, you'd always be trying to feed stuff into the understanding of how the film's going to work, as a premonition for the audience, without playing Miramax and wearing jackboots and saying, "We want the opening re-cut or the ending changed." There's this sequence where, as I recall, some people from the village are outside and they're arguing and fighting – it was a mess. And then I said, "I have completely lost the narrative here, I can't see what's happening." And they said, "Well you know the first argument takes place in his village, and then they go to the other person's village and that's where they have the fight." And I said, "Well how am I going to know that? It just looks like the same village." And they said, "Well of course anyone can see they are two different villages because the huts in that village, which are near the sea, are all two feet off the ground on breeze blocks, and the huts in that village, which are up on the mountain, are sitting on the ground because they're not near the sea." And I said, "Well, thank you for pointing this out to me, but, frankly, that detail is not visible to a Western audience and we need this film to work for British television. However, I don't want you to introduce completely extraneous distortions to your filmmaking just for us," and they said they would think about it and they came back with a brilliant solution. They just added two shots of the two guys in a pickup truck going from one village into the hills to the other village! You see, they knew that it doesn't destroy the rhythm of the film, it doesn't harm the language of the film, and mere Brits, who are not used to the huts on stilts or whatever, understand the important narrative points. So that's a small but typical example of how, when we were involved in the making of the film, and not just buying a finished film, we would have some effect on it but with a care and (I hope) respect to ensure that we weren't saying, "Oh, we want an action scene here or a sexy ending there," or some such. So that, for me, is an example of film working as a universal medium.

A second set of questions. Do you consider the West as a category that is always shifting, in motion and therefore unstable? Should this West or even the Western be perceived solely as or through geographical frameworks?

I don't really have clear answers to these questions. I think that, as we know from Heraclitus, a long and pre-Socratic time ago, everything is shifting and in motion; nothing stops, it is all changing. The same is true of interactions between the global North and the global South. Any illusion that it is stable and fixed is dubious and should be examined. In terms of geographical frameworks, it's based on geography because most of Africa, Asia, and Latin America is in the South and most of the North is in the North! But obviously we are now living within a globalized monoculture, which interpolates around the world and exceeds its geographical provenance.

But it's complex: you've got music from Africa, which through slavery goes to America and then makes blues, and then it's incorporated into white American music and then white Brits start imitating the blues in the 1960s – John Mayall and many others are playing the blues here – that supports the black people who were already making this music in America. So that's an example from the 1960s of a zig-zagging motion: music that came from Africa goes to America, crosses back over to Britain, goes back to America stronger and then the West discovers Ali Farka Touré (from Mali) and a version of this music happens in Africa as though it has never really left that continent! And then he works well with Ry Cooder in LA. It's great, isn't it?

I think one of the things we are getting at is that the West or the Western, beyond being a sort of geographical location, may evoke a certain kind of cultural or ideological way of thinking and perceiving film. We were talking about labels in television earlier – does that have a kind of resonance for you?

I think it does. Antonioni made a film called *The Passenger* (1975), and there's a scene where the journalist, played by Jack Nicholson, says to a guerrilla leader in the Sahel something like "Can I do an interview with you?" And the guerrilla leader says, "Mr Locke there are satisfactory answers to all your questions, but I don't think you understand how little you can learn from them. Your questions are much more revealing about yourself than my answers will be about me." So that's the difficult thing: how we understand that even our questions are predicated on habits, perspectives, ways of thinking.

One other little recent example which is fresh in my memory happened by a sort of accident when Larry Sider, who organizes the School of Sound every two years in the South Bank in London, asked me to be the interlocutor for [Burkinabé filmmaker] Gaston Kaboré and to do a session talking specifically about his use of sound and the deployment of music in his films. So because I have known Gaston for a long time – we put some Channel 4 money into some of his films in the 1980s and 1990s – I was happy to do this. And Gaston was very articulate and clear in the session, and I thought it seemed to have gone down well. I didn't realize until I got an email afterwards from Larry that unconsciously it had had exactly the de-Westernizing effect we are talking about. Apparently over the years there's an interesting mixture of people who go to the School of Sound: it's a productive combination of filmmakers, composers, technicians, academics, students, musicians. But this whole particular mixture of people have, in the end, tended toward the "Walter Murch" approach to sound design in a certain way.

And so therefore, without much forethought or anticipation, without any careful planning, bringing Gaston to the School offered a radically different perspective. West African filmmaking has a very divergent starting point in terms of culture, politics, financing as well as its use of sound and music. Gaston said things like, "Well, I tend to make films every four to five years because finances are so difficult that every film has to count; it has to be something that I mean, it has to come from a particularly close and interactive relationship with the culture and history that I grew up in. And even if you think it's kind of outside of historical time you know actually for us it's functioning in our epoch and referring to the time it came from. Although I'm not a musician this is what I'm trying to do when I use music and this is how it relates to our musical tradition and how it works." And all of that stuff is, of course, so different from what most School of Sound attendees expect because they come from a culture where people say, "What's your next project?," "Well, you tell me!," where someone will pay you to make a commercial project. Gaston couldn't think of being *given* a project to make. He is not a filmmaker looking for a career or money when he's making a film. His approach is, frankly, a much more simple and integral recording of direct sound, and – I'm not saying he only uses two soundtracks – but he's not playing at a kind of level of accumulated naturalized codes that someone like Murch works with – who is a brilliant editor, for sure. By contrast, unwittingly, all these differences that decenter and displace Western modes came into focus at the School of Sound by talking to Gaston.

Authenticity and identity – that is what Gaston brought to the debate. Authenticity – which I know is a tricky term because we should say the "rhetoric of authenticity" – is, in relative terms, something very important for a filmmaker from West Africa like Gaston, who has always and inevitably been very involved in a broader picture, cultural politics; something that isn't necessarily true of many Western filmmakers. I think it's only healthy because, apart from suggesting that there are other ways to make films, it also says, "Take a simple camera, take a simple means of recording sound and see how these sounds and images can go together." It's not about some kind of techno fetish of expensive and sophisticated equipment. Actually, an imaginative image with an intelligent sound is much more effective than a kind of Red Cam and then digital effects, CGI etc., etc. . . .

I think that anecdote leads us quite well into our next question, which is what do you understand by non-Western modes of thinking, theorizing and making film?

It is good that you mention modes (in the plural) because it is clear to me – taking African cinema alone – that there's considerable diversity and difference in the domain. There was a lot more coming out of West Africa and Francophone Africa than the Anglophone or Lusophone spheres of influence. Obviously South Africa was in a sort of isolation in that epoch – it hadn't quite returned to civilization – and the Maghreb, I mean there's unevenness even with that. Tunisian cinema was in a very productive phase then, maybe now Morocco has come forward.

These things come and go in constellations, which are always changing as your question suggests. There's also some curiosity about the layers of determinations – maybe it's to do with some interaction in the colonial epoch? Why is there not more coming from, Anglophone Africa in relative terms? I mean obviously Nigeria and Nollywood is now an example of autonomous indigenous cinema, although a lot of it is rough stuff in terms of quality.

I would say actually that there is a sort of possessiveness in Western attitudes and much Western support for African cinema that is totally self-serving. A few years ago, in 2005, I went to a conference, plus exhibition, plus season in San Salvador in Brazil, which was about the relationship of Brazilian and African cinemas. And when I went into the room to present my paper, there were the French cultural attaché and his assistant giving out photocopies of articles written in French to the people coming in through the door. They had been somehow offended that the Brazilians had asked an *Anglophone* to talk about African cinema.

In fact, the French had said to the Brazilians, "We will build a bridge between Brazil and Africa," and the Brazilians apparently replied, "We don't need you to build bridge, we'll do it ourselves!"

Let's move on now to the fourth question. It starts with a quote from Robert B. Ray where he asks "What could be a more exact definition of the cinema than the crossroads of magic and positivism or a more succinct definition of film theory's traditional project than to break the spell?" Do you see your work as located at some form of crossroads? Do you think your work breaks any spells, be they theoretical or practical?

I've got problems with this question. This may be my limitation, but for cultural reasons the word magic signifies something very problematic for me. It's often used in dubious ways in our society – you know, most people who talk about magic can't form a sentence without the word "energy" in it. I support film theory's traditional analytical project of breaking the spell. I think it was Coleridge who said, "Do we pull the petals off to count them and see how a flower works, or do we stand back and just appreciate it?" I'm very much of the former mindset that says let's see how it works; let's de-naturalize the invisible systems we live within, if we can. Finding new forms of analysis and creativity to break up the specious and mystificatory. Of course positivism is preposterous but magic is just as difficult for me to relate to.

Why is that? Why is it difficult to relate to?

Well because magic is an unstable term that's been so misused by reactionaries and mystics, in our culture anyway. Positivism is problematic for other reasons. Like empiricism in film studies, it seems to me to be often, if not exclusively, a uniform of displacement and resistance to theory. As Adorno once wrote, "They offer the shamelessly modest assertion that they do not understand – this eliminates even opposition, their last negative relationship with truth," which is a way of blocking progressive analysis, not trying to come to terms with it. I'm just saying that, from where I'm coming from, magic can be a dubious domain.

That's fair enough. Let's take the idea of the crossroads. What is there? It's a space. But what is *within* the crossroads? What is to be negotiated at the crossroads? What is to be found there? Does it function as an entity? Or as a framework? Would you relate to *a* crossroads?

As you know, I live in Ireland where there has been dancing at the crossroads for many a century. I suppose this goes back to one of the first things I was saying, that we are in a situation where the one-way transmission of one form of industrialized culture from the USA is pervasive. So the small area that I have focused on, whether it was for the wider public in Channel 4 or in courses taught in the Huston School of Film and Digital Media, has really been about trying to provide a critique that points toward some degree of reciprocal exchange: films, television, music, even games should celebrate the diversity of the world. Although, frankly, the hegemony of the bottom left-hand corner of the USA, coming almost entirely out of Los Angeles, is very difficult to shift in a situation

Figure 16.1 Wild Field (Nguyen Hong Sen, 1979).

where the global audience is 100 times more likely to view a Hollywood product than any other form of film.

Like my strange example of African-American and British music, it's more complex and messy as soon as you look closely at the specific interrelations. But there has to be a better form of exchange that can relativize and undermine dominant industrialized culture – and that's where I put my efforts. I think when our students see *Wild Field* (Nguyen Hong Sen, 1979), where two Vietcong guerrillas hide from American helicopters by taking their baby under the water in the air bubble of a plastic bag in the Mekong Delta, that's already a shock to the system. And very different to the exhilarating aggression of helicopters going down on the village in Coppola's *Apocalypse Now* (1979) with Wagner blaring. It gives people something to think about – it's a commutation test because it's such a different spatial and political perspective. Then maybe at some point they travel to Asia, maybe encounter Vietnamese culture directly and it all begins to get more interesting. I mean, my eldest son just spent eighteen months teaching English in Oaxaca in Mexico. I don't even have to hear it from him, I know it will have changed him completely, changed his perspective for the rest of his life. And if that's what you mean by crossroads, then great.

Do you think of de-Westernizing film as primarily a political or ideological artistic process? For example, does it extend from early cinema movements such as Third Cinema and, if so, what is it doing differently?

I think that Third Cinema was a particularly sharp-edged instance of a challenge to Western film and my first encounter with that would have been seeing *Hour of the Furnaces* [Solanas and Getino, 1970] when I was at the Slade. It is an extraordinary film though slightly distorted because it's some sort of strange version of left-Peronism, if I remember rightly. We need a much more complex and broad model because, as your question suggests, it is actually a complex interaction of economic, political, institutional and ideological processes and that is what keeps academics in work – trying to see the interrelationship between these various determinations! And all these dimensions are in movement.

What is it doing differently? I would say it is, precisely that de-centering or re-centering of seeing from another place, which means that what it has to say and how it has to say it is bound to be different, inevitably. And that difference relativizes something, which gains its power through saying: "This is the thing. This is how it is for us. This is how *we* do things." So as soon as Gaston [Kaboré] says, in a modest way, "I do things like this" (and, because that's different at some level) it reminds me of how I've always felt about the avant-garde, for example. Makers of experimental forms of film don't see themselves as making a political incision but, at some level, they are also questioning the way that dominant forms of film work on us.

Here's one last Gaston Kaboré example – there is a moment in *ZanBoko* (Kaboré, 1988) where two women sit down outside their huts in a village and one woman has a baby and she hands the baby to an elder daughter to look after and

Figure 16.2 ZanBoko (Kaboré, 1988)

they chat. "How's the baby?," "How are things going with your husband?" As they talk there is a lilting, I can't even describe it, each of them makes a gentle background hum under the other's words, when one is talking, the other is going "mmmm. . . aahh." For me it's a perfect instance of an everyday tenderness that is possible between people. I mean what they're doing is perfectly recognizable "universally," to use that dangerous term. Everywhere around the world women talk about how the homes are going, how their babies are doing, and how their domestic space interfaces with other domestic spaces. Whether it's in Manhattan or Mali, forms of those exchanges and conversations go on. But the actual texture of it in Moré outside in the countryside somewhere near Bobo-Dioulasso, is completely specific and different. The result is a double movement of something that can be recognized in other cultures but is also, clearly, a different form and version of it. It's the same, but different. Actually a very gentle and affectionate version of it – that's probably *not* quite how it sounds in busy New York or Paris or any other speedy metropolis – for me that double movement is exemplary and that's the effort; to try and open questioning and curiosity in different places. But it's uphill work because I think all these years later, the [global] South is basically still a source of commodities and a repository for tourism, and, as we all know, tourists never talk to anyone – they get shown round the Mosque on the way to the beach, but that's about it.

Interesting. So we come to de-Westernizing film studies – does it mean rejecting entirely dominant Western modes of thinking, production, criticism and film practice, and is this even possible?

Well we've certainly got to try, after all there's no alternative. I wouldn't want to sneer or be cynical about that, I think that early encounter with theory always made me say: "What is this discourse for? Who does it serve? How does it function?" I read something from Žižek about black rape after the New Orleans flood where he argues that, even if it's factually true, raising it is racist, because picking up on that fact has a different affect in the world: firing a black rape and a white rape into discourse is no longer equal because they are feeding on very severe inequalities and very severe imbalances of power.[1]

Coming back to film studies and film theory: it's great that as it proliferates it is finally beginning to think about films from other parts of the planet. But there is always the danger that it just becomes an enclosed and self-sufficient academic exercise rather than having any effect. "The point is to change it" as someone once said in a famous manifesto. I mean someone described academic life to me recently as "playing air guitar" [*laughs*] and that points precisely to the weakness of the academy: Where's the public? Where's the interaction? How enclosed and institutional are our discourses, our ways of thinking?

Another thing we have to think about is our use of language and terminology as well as our institutional agendas: we have to try and find new ways of thinking and new ways of living as Nietzsche suggested. In order to do that we need to relativize and show what's at stake. I think it's interesting that in, say, the history of art and, say, musicology, you have the (relatively new) terms "world art" and "world music" introduced. And I'm still wrestling with this because, clearly, it seems to me that looking at, say, visual or musical culture in China or in Mozambique should of course already be part of any substantial exploration of these cultural genres. But is there a problem because you are importing a frame of reference or an angle of approach which is a Western thing, how we look at Western art? And so I'm not sure: is it *still* a problem to just widen the frame and now suddenly call it world art? Isn't it strange that the term "world" actually means everything *outside* the West? As if we are looking at it through Western eyes, or try to find Western meanings in it, we're trying to see how it fits.

So do the same binaries stay in place?

Yes. One of the best challenges to the binary thinking we all live within is to be found in Roland Barthes's last lectures, which were called "The Neutral," where he was trying to find a way out of the structural limits of binary thinking.

And there's a space, a liminal space between these binary positions?

Absolutely. In the dialect of south Devon the word "dimpsey" means dusk, or crepuscule in French. I heard my parents using this word as a child growing up in Torquay, but now it is in danger of being lost as regional patois is swept away.

To come back to the original question, does de-Westernizing film studies mean a disengagement with Western modes of theorizing and representation? And if so is that even possible? Given what you have said in relation to your example of blues music?

I think in a way you're probably right because one can try to introduce a more reflexive mode into one's forms of thought by thinking about thinking – and if anything keeps Marx's and Freud's agendas still going it's because the spaces that they opened continue to be reflexive. This reflexivity is a kind of feedback loop, which at least keeps us from falling naively into the unconscious assumptions that keep the world the way it is. But having said that, there's nowhere else to go, there's no dry land on which to stand. As Wittgenstein said about the philosophy of language, it is like rebuilding a ship at sea. There's no dry dock to take the boat into to examine it, so we just need to develop better forms of exchange, of sensitivity and respect to be able to understand the world with adequate complexity.

The possibility to have ideas in the public space is long overdue to return. Phil Wickham down in the museum [the Bill Douglas Centre, University of Exeter] organized this event at the NFT [National Film Theatre in London] on the twenty-fifth anniversary of Channel 4, and I gave a talk and showed eight or ten extracts from the range of material our department was supporting, including *South* and *Cinema from Three Continents*, and the *Screen* article by Hannah Andrews reviewing this conference described what I'd said as "nostalgia." And, I have to say, that irritated me – not because it is any problem to have someone criticizing my position, but because, clearly, I'd not managed to convince listeners that our experience of Channel 4 has to be fired forward into the media we have at the moment rather than putting it in some museum case for a twenty-fifth anniversary conference. I mean, I think our work should have been surpassed by new generations doing more and doing better. At the time, it wasn't like, "Hey, we've achieved it all." Quite the opposite: our feeling was great frustration that we couldn't do more. But, you know, there are occasional moments of optimism that fragments from the past can help change the future.

Note

1 See 'Some Politically Incorrect Reflections on Violence in France and Related Matters. 4. The Subject Supposed to Loot and Rape Revisted', available online at www.lacan. com/zizfrance3.htm (accessed February 16, 2012).

17 Beyond stereotypes and preconceptions

An interview with Farida Benlyazid[1]

Do you see film as a universal medium/art form?

I think it is; the language of the image is in a way more universal than writing or even the spoken word per se. In Morocco, as in all Arab countries, the language spoken is different from the written one, which remains static with reference to the Koran and the [linguistic/cultural] unity of Arab nations. For example, an uneducated person may not be able to understand political speeches, given in literary Arabic but grasps the images that could accompany them.

Turning to the question of film as art, I would say that the approach to it is a personal matter that does not embody a condition of original specificity though, of course, one must show a degree of sensitivity toward, and interest in, art. Moreover, one must, to a certain extent, open up to the diversity of other human cultures, irrespective of the fact that one is from the Orient or the West, educated or uneducated. As a case in point, during a debate following an open screening of *Une brèche dans le mur* (Ferhati, 1977), the first film I produced, someone told me it was a pity that illiterate people could not understand it. However, as soon as that person finished, a woman stood up in the audience and said that this was not necessarily true: "I have never been to school and yet I have understood it very well."

Do you consider the West as a category that is always shifting, in motion, and therefore unstable? Should this "West" or "the Western" be perceived solely as, or through, geographical frameworks?

All societies are in a state of continual mutation, unless their members are considered from outside these societies. Let me explain: it has been noted that persons who have emigrated and been immersed into another culture safeguard their culture of origin as the supreme point of reference, whereas societies they have left evolve to such an extent that these emigrants find themselves somewhat disorientated when they return home.

One cannot tackle this question from a geographical perspective. For example, geographically speaking, the Arabic "Almaghrib," or "Morocco," means "Occident/West"; Morocco is within the Greenwich Mean Time zone. Conversely, one can talk of Oriental and Western cultures. In other words, these are two different ways of relating: one to the notion of time, and the other to the world. In the latter, the Western model is very aggressive and the Oriental one constantly on the defensive. However, an interaction between the two is inevitable, especially in the current phase of globalization and in the use of new [digital] technologies.

What do you understand by non-Western modes of thinking, theorizing, and making film? How does such an understanding affect your work?

For me a Western film is one that promotes Western values as the best and indisputable. This is not always the case though, as John Boorman's *The Emerald Forest* (1985) illustrates. I would class this film as a non-Western film of Western origin; it is the only Western film I am aware of which ends with the non-prevalence of Western morality.

The perspective through which I make films reveals another form of thought that is neither better nor worse but one that makes us ponder another possible becoming for the human being – outside stereotypes and preconceived ideas.

Robert B. Ray, an academic with particular interest in critical practice, once asked, "What could be a more exact definition of the cinema than 'the crossroads of magic and positivism'? Or a more succinct definition of film theory's traditional project than, 'to break the spell'?" Do you see your work as located at some form of crossroads? Does your work break any spell(s), theoretical and/or practical?

It is a good definition, I think. I say "yes" to magic as long as it is art, and "no" when it becomes formulaic mode of representation. I once took part in a colloquium, alongside some Hollywood filmmakers, on the laws of the market in relation to the cinema. The Hollywood filmmakers complained about the directives imposed upon their creative freedom for the sake of abiding by market norms. For my part, I said that for us [African and Arab filmmakers from the Global South] things were different: given that we have no market, our productions remain modest but we also have a precious freedom that is so necessary to creation.

As for film criticism, it is not my profession. I still watch films as a good spectator and become a critic only later on, i.e. once the magic is over. Moreover, when I am working, film theory is not my major concern; it is present for sure, but only implicitly. It is as if I'm afraid somehow of losing track of my inspiration if I uncover its mechanisms in a scientific or theoretical way. Instead, I must trust my intuition; I want to continue to believe in the magical aspect of things: Soviet director [Sergei] Paradjanov used to say that he dreamt of sequences first and then shot them the following day.

Do you think that de-Westernizing film is principally an economic, political, institutional, or artistic process? For example, does it extend from earlier cinematic movements, such as Third Cinema?

I do not really know enough about the movements and ideas that you are talking about but I can tell you that, for me, Western cinema production is fundamentally ideological. This cinema certainly inspires aspects of my work but, at the same time, it is not my only source of inspiration. In effect, since childhood I have been lucky enough to have seen Indian, Egyptian, and, later on, Japanese films. [Yajushiro] Ozu remains, for me, one of the greatest filmmakers in the history of the cinema.

Does de-Westernizing film studies mean rejecting entirely dominant Western modes of thinking, production, criticism, and film practice? Is this even possible?

I believe that everything is conceivable. Things take time to materialize but, from the moment that the question presents itself to you, to me and to others, this course of reflection is under way.

Note

1 Interview translated from the French by Saër M. Bâ and Will Higbee.

18 "About structure, not about individual instances"

An interview with Daniel Lindvall

Do you see film as a universal medium/art form?

To answer this question we need to look at, initially, what we mean by "universal." Do we mean (a) "universally comprehensible" or (b) "universally accessible"? In the former case my answer would be a qualified yes, in the latter a strong no.

First, the idea of film as "universally comprehensible." Ultimately the human brain is preprogrammed for making use of communication systems following a common human logic that, theoretically, enables any two human beings to enter into reasonably successful communication. The spoken (and sometimes written) language of a film poses obvious problems of understanding and more or less subtle shifts in meaning through translations. Filmmakers' social and cultural frames of reference may differ from those of an audience and thus affect interpretation. But its use of images, not least that of the human body with its more universal direct language – body language and facial expressions – renders film more immediately universal than art forms based entirely on written and/or spoken languages.

Second, the idea of film as universally accessible. There has been a lot of talk, much of it in very utopian terms, and over the past twenty years, of the democratizing implications of new, cheap technology. Nollywood is perhaps the most successful story of a national film industry being facilitated by home-video technology. But whilst cheap(ish) digital cameras, computers with software for filmmaking, and the Internet as a means of distribution certainly continue to change the playing field, it should be clear that no global, utopian change has (or looks likely to) come about. Access to even "cheap" equipment remains very unequally distributed (along national/regional, class, gender and ethnic lines), as does access to the kind of knowledge and training needed for successful filmmaking. Also, budgets do matter. Stars and/or the latest, most high-end technology, for instance, are by no means guarantees for success, though they help. Genuine access to film as an art form also means access to an audience, to visibility. Here we should note for example that the Internet, rather than becoming an alternative distribution channel and a utopian-democratic disseminator of information in general, is increasingly coming under corporate control. Looking at the first couple of decades of the "Internet revolution," Foster and McChesney sum up the evidence so far:

> though there are an infinite number of Web sites, human beings are only capable of meaningfully visiting a small number of them on a regular basis. The Google search mechanism strongly encourages implicit censorship, in that sites that do not end up on the first or second page of a search effectively do not exist.
>
> (Foster and McChesney 2011: 20)

They continue by citing statistics showing that the top ten websites in the USA accounted for 75 percent of all page views in 2010, up from 31 percent in 2001 (Foster and McChesney 2011: 20). By this I do not mean that those of us who wish to see more equal (universal) access to film art and moving images in every respect cannot or should not make the best use we can of the opportunities that new technology offers, but only that our assessments of the current state of affairs and the immediate possibilities need to be realistic.

Do you consider the West as a category that is always shifting, in motion, and therefore unstable? Should this "West," or "the Western," be perceived solely as, or through, geographical frameworks?

It is a very unstable and difficult category. For one thing, what is its opposite? Today it is certainly not "the East," though up until the end of Stalinism in Eastern Europe it might have been, in which case "East" versus "West" meant the ideological opposition between "liberal democracy" and so-called "communism." Talking about "the East" or "Eastern" today, which is hardly ever done, invokes Orientalist and racialist ideas. Rather, today we either hear the very vague term "non-Western" or, automatically think along the lines of the "Global South," thus treating "West" and "North" as synonyms.

It is very unhelpful to think of the "West" solely in geographical terms. For one thing, this would make all culture, all forms of thinking and politics within this region by definition "Western." This would logically lead to an impossibly vague, complex, contradictory term. In reality, this "geographical" thinking tends to give way instead to simplified, homogeneous definitions that reinforce an opposition, along implicitly racialized lines, between what is "Western" and what is "Other." This is not only historically misleading (think only of the great influence of classic Arab civilization on post-Renaissance "Western" civilization), but also serves to ideologically isolate subordinate classes in "Western" and "non-Western" nations from each other. European and North American representatives of the ruling class (the political and economic elite) are certainly well aware of this when they smugly use the term in this way, referring to the "Western values" of democracy, tolerance, free speech, women's rights, etc.[1] The mirror image of this usage of the term is when conservative voices in the "South" refer to greed, moral decay, imperialist warfare, lack of respect for nature, etc., as "Western." Whatever remains outside of such a binarism then becomes either invisible or perceived as "foreign." The result becomes a false choice of allegiance between "Western" and "non-Western" that obscures the complex history of human development as well as real conflicts of interest within nations/regions (notably class conflicts) as well as real common interests between groups (such as classes) across the "Western"–"non-Western" divide.

I believe that "Western" could today best be thought of as an ideological framework of ideas shared by Triad (European Union, North America, Japan) ruling classes. The aim of this ideological framework is to serve primarily these ruling classes themselves and secondarily other ruling classes globally, but only in so far as this does not conflict with Triad goals. In other words, the goal is for the major transnational corporations to create and uphold, at whatever cost, as beneficial conditions as possible for the exploitation of the earth and its peoples. Popular classes in the geographically Western and non-Western nations are all at the receiving end. This framework currently consists of neo-liberal economics (the "Washington Consensus") and "humanitarian imperialism," that is, instrumentalized human-rights discourse (strictly minus socioeconomic rights!). The naïve idea that the economic crisis would automatically weaken the resolve of the ruling class to push through neo-liberal policies has been completely discredited by now, not least by the fact that policies identical to the infamous Structural Adjustment Programs are now being imposed even on European Union member states, notably Greece and Portugal. This ideological framework can slide toward more openly authoritarian positions, even as far as fascism and outspoken "honest" imperialism, as the global crises (economic and environmental) develop. The signs are already there. And they can be read in films as well. For instance, equally condescending and authoritarian attitudes toward the geographically Western working class and the general population in geographically non-Western nations can be found in many films generally considered to be, in Anglo-American parlance, "liberal." These include the recent Danish Oscar-winner, *In a Better World* (Bier, 2010), a textbook example of how racism abroad becomes classism at home,[2] and another celebrated Oscar-winner, *The Hurt Locker* (Bigelow, 2008), which airbrushes away Iraqi victims in a cinematic statement almost the equivalent of Donald Rumsfeld's chilling remark that "We don't do body counts on *other* people" (emphasis added).[3]

Finally, however, I must say that I am rather sceptical of the use of these terms ("West," "North," "South") as political and cultural distinctions. It may be hard to avoid using them entirely but we should be very careful not to let them blind us to the differences and very real contradictions within these geographical areas and the urgent need to build international political and cultural cooperation based on democratic opposition to global corporate rule. In the field of film and culture production, as in many other areas, the battle to preserve and strengthen commons against the constant threats of enclosure is central to the development of any democratic alternatives. Representatives of "Western," i.e. neo-liberal, economic policies have long been busy pushing for the creation and strict enforcement of enclosures within all fields of culture and knowledge, for instance strongly promoting "intellectual property rights." Such policies, of course, have strong supporters among the upper classes in the geographical South as well. Against this ever-increasing commodification of culture we need to establish and defend structures that recognize that culture is a natural commons – an ongoing complexly collective process fundamental to society – and that grants a more egalitarian access to this process than does "the market." A healthy culture needs to be fertilized by the thoughts of many minds, not just those of an elite minority.

Throughout film history there has been a multitude of attempts by progressive movements to make use of filmmaking. Today, more than ever, we need to strengthen all such projects involving popular organizations (unions, community organizations, grassroots NGOs, etc.) and strive to create global grassroots networks for the embedding of a democratic filmmaking (and film studying) culture that is up to the task of challenging "Western" ideology globally. Simultaneously we must defend public, state or local, cultural institutions and programs and do all we can to make them serve the common good, not (directly or indirectly) "the market." In today's economically, politically, and militarily interconnected world there should be no shortage of stories of equal relevance to, say, a Swedish and a South African audience.

What do you understand by non-Western modes of thinking, theorizing and making film? How does such an understanding affect your work?

By "non-Western" modes of discourse and filmmaking practice I would, personally, refer to modes that challenge the above ideological framework. However, the term is by its nature so inclusive, being simply of a negating character ("non"), that it is in practice almost useless and possibly dangerously misleading. It lends itself far too easily to the kind of ideological smear tactics of guilt by association that are such a staple of dominant ("Western," as defined above) ideology.

Robert B. Ray, an academic with particular interest in critical practice, once asked, "What could be a more exact definition of the cinema than 'the crossroads of magic and positivism'? Or a more succinct definition of film theory's traditional project than 'to break the spell'?" Do you see your work as located at some form of crossroads? Does your work break any spell(s), theoretical and/or practical?

My modest work as editor of *Film International* and freelance writer could be seen as being located at the crossroads suggested by Marx's eleventh thesis on Feuerbach: "The philosophers have only interpreted the world in various ways; the point is to change it."[4] Thus my work is located at the crossroads of interpretation and promotion of positive change: it includes breaking the spell of dominant liberal ideology as well as promoting films, filmmakers, and film cultural organizations that, in some way, help us understand the world better and/or represent democratic alternatives.

Do you think that de-Westernizing film is principally an economic, political, institutional, or artistic process? For example, does it extend from earlier cinematic movements, such as Third Cinema? What is it doing differently?

It is essentially a political process, though not simply one of narrow "cultural politics." It is political in the sense of being about structure, not about individual instances. There is a need to think about the totality of the social structure within which every instance of cultural practice takes place and, through dialectical interaction with which, it gains its ultimate meaning (its ideological effect). Attention to totality – i.e. realistically appraising the social playing field, fully understanding what we are up against – is not only a prerequisite for effective action, but, as Antonio Gramsci might have put it, by tempering the expectations with which we invest individual instances of cultural practice, it also functions as a form of intellectual pessimism that preserves the optimism of the will from rapid disillusionment following upon intellectual over-optimism.

It is a truism to say that history is all we've got to learn from. The mistakes and successes of earlier movements provide invaluable lessons for us. Despite often difficult circumstances, there has been, historically, such a wealth of varied movements and attempts to challenge dominant film culture that there is no easy way to sum up in a few lines or paragraphs what should be done differently today. However, I will make a few tentative points based on my own impressions from studying radical film history on and off for twenty years.

1 We should avoid "aestheticism." Specific styles or genres are not progressive or reactionary per se. They can generally be adapted to a variety of political uses, the best and the worst. Filmmakers' personal cultural backgrounds and inclinations, intended audiences, aims of a film, available budget, etc., are all things that do and should influence aesthetic choices. We need to make use of many genres and many styles in many films to challenge the dominant, "Western," worldview.

2 We should avoid "big man" thinking. However much we might deservedly admire individual filmmakers (an Eisenstein, a Sembène or a Loach), culture is always a collective human project, and any attempt at democratizing culture must be openly conscious of this and continuously challenge the distinction between a minority of producers and a majority of consumers, a distinction that reinforces the general social distinction between those who do and those who don't have voices (that count). Participation, rather than a handful of "masterpieces," is key to lasting progressive change. Perhaps no other aspect of progressive culture received worse press after the demise of the latest period of cultural and political radicalism in the 1960s and 1970s. Then, with the advent of the Internet, it became almost taken for granted that a new

participative, non-hierarchical ("flat") culture would automatically manifest itself. As we now know (see above) this will not happen of itself.

3   We should not accept simplified dichotomies of Hollywood versus rest of the world, entertainment versus great art, or, for that matter, the geographically defined "Western" versus the geographically defined "non-Western." Historically, far too often attempts at challenging dominant "Western" commercial culture ("Hollywood") have resulted in versions of its distorted mirror image reproducing similarly hierarchical film cultures, whether as local/national commercial film industries or as elitist "art cinemas" or, generally, as combinations of both, functioning to preserve "natural," anti-democratic social distinctions between producers and consumers of culture. Systems of support invariably reinforce this false choice as it is "accepted" to argue against the *direct* (but not *indirect*) interests of capital in the name of preserving "great art" as defined in some pseudo-objectivist, aestheticist fashion by an intellectual elite. It is far more difficult to argue in favour of greater democracy and the right to self-representation not only in a national/geographical sense but for subordinate groups and classes. The former type of "art cinema" serves as a mark of cultural "distinction" for educated classes and as a PR tool for nations and regions (for instance in attracting tourism).

At the same time, instances of resistance exist within every form of film production. Everywhere films that are, in some way, worthwhile exceptions to the logic of dominant, "Western" ideology are being made, even in Hollywood.

Does de-Westernizing film studies mean rejecting entirely dominant Western modes of thinking, production, criticism and film practice? Is this even possible?

Allowing the narrow definition of "Western" mentioned above, it may be possible to answer "yes." However, according to the broader definition certainly intended by the question here, this kind of absolute rejection is obviously neither possible nor desirable, as should be clear from the above. Such rejection seems to me to be the opposite of critical thinking, pointing toward some kind of "racialized" essentialism that can never serve the oppressed anywhere but only, possibly, alternative elites.

Notes

1 Almost invariably such "Western values" are also, implicitly or explicitly, presented as wedded to "free market" capitalism, i.e. neo-liberalism.

2 See D. Lindvall, "In a Better World: 'The White Man's Burden'," *Film International*, February 28, 2011. Available online at http://filmint.nu/?p=891 (accessed July 3, 2011).

3 Fox News, "Transcript: Donald Rumsfeld on 'Fox News Sunday'," November 2, 2003. Available online at www.foxnews.com/story/0,2933,101956,00.html (accessed July 3, 2011).

4 Editors' note: Karl Marx originally wrote the Theses in 1845. The first English translation appeared in 1938 in *The German Ideology*. See "Theses on Feuerbach," available online at www.marxists.org/archive/marx/works/1845/theses/original.htm (accessed December 2, 2011).

References

Foster, J. B. and McChesney, R. W. (2011) "The Internet's Unholy Marriage to Capitalism," *Monthly Review*, 62 (10): 1–30.

Fox News, "Transcript: Donald Rumsfeld on 'Fox News Sunday'," November 2, 2003. Available online at www.foxnews.com/story/0,2933,101956,00.html (accessed July 3, 2011).

Lindvall, D. (2011) "In a Better World: 'The White Man's Burden'," *Film International*, February 28. Available online at http://filmint.nu/?p=891 (accessed July 3, 2011).

Marx, K. "Theses on Feuerbach." Available online at www.marxists.org/archive/marx/works/1845/theses/original.htm (accessed December 2, 2011).

19 "Still waiting for a reciprocal de-Westernization"

An interview with Mohammed Bakrim[1]

Do you see film as a universal medium/art form?

Cinema is a universal art form in so much as it is a language that gives rise to a plurality of expressions made from sound and image. As narrative, film also draws from intellectual schematics common to humanity, that are themselves born with/in the narrative form – hence the universal success of American cinema. But cinema is also underpinned by cultural codes that assure a certain grounding in a specific environment. In short, we are faced with a universal language that expresses itself through localized [cultural] codes, which can also be seen as a means of translating a specific relationship to time and space. The "plan américain" (a medium-long shot, used to film a group of characters) was so specific to the character of the American West that it became classic. Film language is thus transformed by cultural codes. The same is true for the use of the close-up in Egyptian cinema or the wide shot in Sub-Saharan African cinema. The arrival of sound cinema further reinforced this evolution toward a greater "cultural specificity" from an apparatus that had originally been seen as technically neutral. Dialogue in sound cinema offered further "local" opportunity to cultures that were supposedly sustained by orality.

Do you consider the West as a category that is always shifting, in motion and therefore unstable? Should this West or even the Western be perceived solely as or through geographical frameworks?

The West is far from limited to solely its geographical dimension: it's a political and ecomomic category as well as being (above all) a form of representation that haunts the collective imaginary of people from the Global South, where it is perceived as a lifestyle and a particular relationship to time and space. This dichotomy – a split between the "here" of Morocco and the "there" of the West, where the latter is perceived as an Eldorado – runs through the characters who typically appear in films by Moroccan directors. Abdelwahed, the lead character in the docu-fiction *Alyam Alyam/Oh the Days!* (1978) by Ahmed Manouni could be seen as an emblematic figure of this looking toward the horizon of the

West as a space of liberation or escape. His arrival in Casablanca at the end of the film shows that, ultimately, everyone must be content with the kind of "West" that they can attain through new behaviour patterns.

What do you understand by non-Western modes of thinking, theorizing, and making film? How does such an understanding affect your work?

As a critic, I don't resort to an idea of the Western versus the non-Western or not in my initial reading of a film at least. First of all, I try to analyze a film from the point of view of cinema as a "universal" medium. I then try and deal with the film's own particular imaginary in relation to a number of aspects: the representation of women, its relation to time and space, the rhythm of the narrative. . .

Robert B. Ray, an academic with particular interest in critical practice, once asked, "What could be a more exact definition of the cinema than 'the crossroads of magic and positivism'? Or a more succinct definition of film theory's traditional project than 'to break the spell'?" Do you see your work as located at some form of crossroads? Does your work break any spell(s), theoretical and/or practical?

I would rather say that theory prolongs the pleasure of viewing a film, that a critic is someone who has transformed their love [of film] into a theoretical object. If there is any interruption at all, it is provisional, momentary, lasting no more than the time we need to decrypt what precisely fascinates us in order to, in the end, return to acknowledging the strength and magic that film possesses. Theorizing film is an enlightening process aimed at bringing a different audience to different fascinations and magical moments, which at times presumes an informed rather than passive way of thinking about cinema.

Do you think that de-Westernizing film is principally an economic, political, institutional, or artistic process? For example, does it extend from earlier cinematic movements, such as Third Cinema? What is it doing differently?

The economic level is where this issue is acutely present, in the form of an economic interdependency that determines the type of scripts and proposals that non-Western filmmakers put forward for funding. This competition to obtain funding from different [Western] sources is, in fact, detrimental to authentic expression. Once, during a colloquium on the subject, I put forward the idea of a "Fonds Sud aesthetics" to designate those characteristics common to several films – Moroccan, Lebanese, Mauritanian, or Chadian – funded by Fonds Sud.[2]

I joked that "the colour of money influences the type of framing" in order to underline the demands made on cineastes from the Global South to rewrite their scripts. Of course, such script revisions end up standardizing the artistic choices that these cineastes are able to make, such as: to favour shots of disadvantaged city outskirts, romantic interior scenes invoking Orientalism and marriage, scenes of circumcision or of the Islamist lurking nearby. As a result, dare I say, we are still awaiting a reciprocal de-Westernization.

Does de-Westernizing film studies mean rejecting entirely dominant Western modes of thinking, production, criticism, and film practice? Is this even possible?

Within the West there are films, critiques, and theories that privilege an alternative approach [to dominant Western modes], acknowledging diversity and plurality. I am thinking of [Jean-Luc] Godard's *Film Socialisme* [2010], a radical illustration of this approach, or the highly empathic writing of Charles Tesson [editor at *Cahiers du Cinéma*], who was recently appointed head of the *semaine de la critique/* critic's week at [the] Cannes [Film Festival]. Therefore, this is a global dialectical movement: the point is not to refuse Western modes but to build an alternative that is underpinned by an understanding of otherness and a critical way of thinking.

Notes

1 Interview translated from the French by Saër M. Bâ and Will Higbee.
2 Fonds Sud was created by the French in 1984 to assist in the part-funding of production, post-production, and rewriting of films from all countries in Africa, Latin America, and selected countries from the Near and Middle East and Asia and Central Europe. Funding is provided by the French Ministry of Culture and Communication (via the Centre National de la Cinématographie) and the French Ministry of Foreign Affairs.

20 "Moving away from a sense of cultures as pure spaces"

An interview with Deborah Shaw

Do you see film as a universal medium/art form?

"Universal" is always a loaded term as it inevitably fails to consider the experience of many people, which it dispenses with if they provide an exception. Yes, vast numbers of people throughout the world have access to film, and film watching forms a regular part of their leisure time/education. However, a large number of people living in poverty and/or in remote areas do not have access to film, or to the technology required to watch film. Many cannot afford to buy cinema tickets, or cable film channels, so may watch pirated copies of films on DVD, with piracy rife in many countries. Having said this, film along with television programmes are the most widely consumed art forms.

Do you consider the West as a category that is always shifting, in motion, and therefore unstable? Should this "West," or "the Western," be perceived solely as, or through, geographical frameworks?

In some respects, we have a clear idea of the West. It is associated with Western European and North American developed countries, and represented in power blocks such as NATO (the North Atlantic Treaty Association), which has twenty-eight members.[1] Nevertheless, a look at this list of nations opens up the complexity when we start to consider the concept of the "West." There are other countries seen as "Western" which are not part of this military alliance for historical reasons, such as Austria, Ireland, Sweden, and Switzerland. What about Australia and New Zealand which are considered part of the West, yet are geographically distant from Europe? Is Russia part of the West? What about Israel? Is it a Western country located in the Middle East? It may be made up of many European immigrants, but many Jews in Israel originated from Arab countries and speak fluent Arabic as well as Hebrew. This is even without mentioning the Palestinians who make up a large proportion of the population and for whom Palestine is an Arab country.

Even the seemingly clear-cut case of the USA, for many the center of the "West," is not so clear-cut. It has many immigrants from Africa, China, Japan,

Vietnam, many of whom are American citizens, and have brought with them their food, religions, languages, and belief systems, and so on. The concept of the West is, then, far more complex than many acknowledge, and there is no simple list which can tell us who is part of the West, where this is located, and who belongs in the "West." Is it a place, a set of values and cultural practices, a political power block? Does it rest on ethnicity, religion, colonial legacies, and/or migratory practices? There are no simple answers to these questions.

The site of the "West" often depends on who is doing the defining. Mexico can be seen as another illustration of this. It is a former Spanish colony (New Spain) which achieved independence in 1810, and while the majority of the population are *mestizo* (of Spanish and indigenous descent and heritage), some are indigenous and much of the elite ruling classes are very clearly of Spanish descent. Syncretism can be found in religion (Christianity and Aztec and Mayan practices and beliefs) and philosophical systems with beliefs coming from indigenous Aztec and Mayan traditions as well as the Enlightenment, and Marxism, to give a few examples. Most Mexicans would consider themselves part of the West, yet many in Europe and the USA would exclude them from this category. Similar points could be made of most other Latin American countries: where, for instance, would we place Argentina and Brazil in the West versus the rest carve-up of the world, with Argentines and Brazilians largely seeing themselves as Western, and many in Europe and the USA excluding them from this category. In popular thought, the West is for many the USA and Europe, but this is about the power of the media and lazy thinking.[2]

What do you understand by non-Western modes of thinking, theorizing, and making film? How does such an understanding affect your work?

This answer clearly follows on from the previous one. If we cannot be entirely clear what constitutes the "West," we can also not be entirely clear what is non-Western. I always like the anecdote told to me by my colleague [at Portsmouth University], Ann Matear. She tells of a trip to Peru where Quechua-speaking women put on their traditional costume for the benefit of tourists, and as soon as the photographs were taken and the tourists departed, they took these off to reveal "Western" clothing underneath. Traditional song and dance would be produced for the benefit of those on the tour buses. What this anecdote reveals is that culture is rarely, if ever, "pure," and that there is no neat distinction between "Western" and non-Western: transnational movements of peoples and ideas must be considered when we study culture and cultural artefacts.

None of us can know "the world," but consumers are given a sense that we can do so through the market: thus, we have "world" cinema, "world" music, the BBC's "World" Service. My understanding of non-Western modes of thinking means that I try to situate myself and acknowledge that however much "world" music, "world" cinema or "World" Service (of which I am a fan) I listen to, I cannot know the world. I live in England, and the view of the world and "non-Western" culture is filtered through the marketplace and the media, and what I have access to and time and inclination to seek out. My understanding of films outside of my areas of knowledge will be limited, even with access to these. Subtitles will not magically allow me to understand all the cultural, social, and political meanings within texts that are made in nations of whose culture I am unfamiliar with. In short, academics and critics' work needs to show an understanding of our limitations and not pretend we know "the world." Many of us are students of cultures that are not our own, and an acknowledgment of our ignorance is an excellent starting point to begin asking the right questions.

My work always seeks to understand and problematize terms that have been used sometimes lazily. Thus, in one forthcoming chapter I take apart the term "transnational" and its usage in film studies, and in another article (2011) I reconsider how the notion of "world cinema" has been applied, and I know I am not alone in this endeavour.[3] At *Transnational Cinemas*, we always welcome articles that are prepared to take on accepted thinking of these terms and bring something new to debates. To give one very simple example of critical thinking that needs to happen: Why is the term "foreign film" used so uncritically in popular and academic discourses. "Foreign" to whom? Why are Hollywood films in the global market not seen as foreign, when a film from Spain would be seen as foreign in non-Spanish-speaking countries? We often forget that "foreign" is an entirely relative and value-laden term linked to power.

Robert B. Ray, an academic with particular interest in critical practice, once asked, "What could be a more exact definition of the cinema than 'the crossroads of magic and positivism'? Or a more succinct definition of film theory's traditional project than 'to break the spell'?" Do you see your work as located at some form of crossroads? Does your work break any spell(s), theoretical and/or practical?

Others would have to be the judge of whether my work breaks any spells; however, I do always attempt to consider the political, social, and ethical implications of films. There are always (at least) two levels of watching a film: one rooted in pleasure and the other in critical readings. The first viewing of a film may be entirely pleasurable, but then it is important to "break the spell" that the text has imparted. In my work I have also paid particular attention to forms of representation: How are women and men represented? How are gays and lesbians represented? Is a tourist gaze directing the camera? And so forth. Am I, as a viewer, complicit in the othering processes in play? How can I step outside of the pleasure points which are so central to film and reveal the power structures at play, a process which produces another form of pleasure for me and hopefully for readers?

I also cannot say whether my work is at some form of crossroads, but I try to be as comprehensive as possible in my readings of films and let the texts reveal the most appropriate approaches. Film is such a rich area in that the most productive readings require the critic to engage with such a broad intellectual field.

Do you think that de-Westernizing film is principally an economic, political, institutional, or artistic process? For example, does it extend from earlier cinematic movements, such as Third Cinema? What is it doing differently?

This is a broad question, and the answer depends on where one focuses: with the filmmakers, and production companies, or the academics involved with such a process, and cinema journal editors, and publishers. As I am an academic and journal editor, I will limit myself to this focus. Lecturers have a social and ethical responsibility when deciding what to teach our students, and journal editors and researchers should ensure that film means more than US productions and European art cinema. We cannot know the whole world of film, as I have already discussed, but we can try to ensure that lesser-known films and film scholarship from around the world are represented in our activities. For instance, in the case of the journal *Transnational Cinemas*, we aim to publish articles on films and film industries from all over the world, when, that is, authors engage with questions relevant to the theoretical field.

In relation to the question on Third Cinema, Third Cinema has a specific political agenda, and approach to filmmaking. In very simple terms, for theorists and filmmakers such as Fernando Solanas and Octavio Getino, films were a vehicle to promote revolution and the magic of cinema was abandoned for a goal to awaken the political consciousness of the spectator. A project to de-Westernize film has to consider film in a much broader sense and cannot stipulate any single approach to politics or aesthetics. We are also in an age of digital filmmaking, which has brought the tools of filmmaking to many more and has allowed many so-called non-"Western" people to become filmmakers, although the means of exhibition and distribution are as elusive as ever to those without money.

Does de-Westernizing film studies mean rejecting entirely dominant Western modes of thinking, production, criticism and film practice? Is this even possible?

We need to move away from a sense of cultures as pure spaces. We should question the centrality of US cultural production and the disproportionate amount of screen time and air time it receives, along with hegemonic ways of seeing and conceiving art. However, cultures interact on so many levels that we cannot, nor should we, turn into an anti-Western thought police, rather we should, wherever possible, provide spaces for voices across the globe to be heard.

Notes

1 These are Albania, Belgium, Bulgaria, Canada, Croatia, Czech Republic, Denmark, Estonia, France, Germany, Greece, Hungary, Iceland, Italy, Latvia, Lithuania, Luxembourg, Netherlands, Norway, Poland, Portugal, Romania, Slovakia, Slovenia, Spain, Turkey, the United Kingdom, and the United States.
2 I am grateful to Stephanie Dennison (University of Leeds), with whom I discussed these ideas in relation to Brazil.
3 My analysis of the concept of transnational cinema can be found at "Deconstructing and Reconstructing 'Transnational Cinema'," in S. Dennison (ed.), *Transnational Film Financing in the Hispanic World*, Woodbridge: Tamesis Books: forthcoming, and the analysis of "world" cinema is in "*Babel* and the Global Hollywood Gaze," in *Situations: Project of the Radical Imagination* 4(1), 11–31 (2011).

21 Nu Third Queer Cinema

An interview with Campbell X

Do you see film as a universal medium/art form?

Film is a visual medium, but also a storytelling medium. All cultures tell stories and draw. There are also soundscapes in film that immerse us more in the experience of the film. In fact, sound is very important for creating mood: the tone of voice, the atmospheric sound, the Foley effects; all add to the immersive experience. I feel that going to see a movie or looking at a DVD is like sitting round a campfire and hearing a story that comes alive. In that way it is universal. However, in the characters, protagonists, and contexts of dominant Western films, this is not the case, not least because movies represent the imagination constructed by Eurocentric, hetero-patriarchal imaginings.

Do you consider the West as a category that is always shifting, in motion, and therefore unstable? Should this "West," or "the Western," be perceived solely as, or through, geographical frameworks?

The "West" is a frame of mind. The frame of mind that says: films with an all "PoC" ("People of Color") cast will not be "commercial"; that believes that PoC = straight African descent urban dysfunctional violent young male = "commercial"; that women need not even bother to try telling any stories as the latter are "special interest" or derisively referred to as "chick flicks"; that no matter how good you are as a filmmaker, if you are not validating "white" hegemonic hetero-patriarchal capitalistic ideals through your choice of images and story you will not have access to substantial funding and will be pushed to the margins.

What do you understand by non-Western modes of thinking, theorizing and making film? How does such an understanding affect your work?

In order for me to have non-Western modes of thinking, I first have to empty my brain of "white noise" – the pervasive commercial way of thinking that dictates that stories are not allowed to be funded/filmed unless they start from a Eurocentric perspective. It is then important for me to read books, listen to seminars, and very importantly look at films/pop promos that de-marginalize people of African descent. The films and artists that were important for me in terms of inspiration, as a newbie (i.e. fledgling) filmmaker, were *Looking for Langston* (Julien, 1989), *Daughters of the Dust* (Dash, 1991), *Sankofa* (Gerima, 1993), *Pressure* (Ové, 1976), *Burning an Illusion* (Shabazz, 1981), *Tongues Untied* (Riggs, 1989), and singers and rappers Erykah Badu, Arrested Development, Janet Jackson, Soprano, Dead Prez, Nas, and Mos Def.

To speak across the African diaspora is important to me. By this I mean developing relationships with "QPoC" (Queer People of Color) in non-Western contexts; listening to stories from our foremothers and forefathers in the African diaspora such as Frantz Fanon, Aimé Césaire, Haile Gerima, Marcus Garvey and Malcolm X, Huey P. Newton, and Angela Davis, Zora Neale Hurston, and Langston Hughes.[1]

Working toward a non-Western practice in a very Western medium is a work in progress for me. In all my films, I try to create a QPoC aesthetic and storytelling. It is a challenge to do this with limited resources and outlets for showing this kind of work. In addition, as my work is about memory/shame and loss, I do not believe in the binary notion of "positive/negative" characterizations or storylines. Instead, I like to explore the dark corners of "minority" cultures: i.e. the areas we are taught to be ashamed of, the amnesia we create to support new narratives to "better" ourselves. And I want to create images for those of us whose histories are unwritten or erased and show how we deal with the shadows of our ancestral stories.

Robert B. Ray, an academic with particular interest in critical practice, once asked, "What could be a more exact definition of the cinema than 'the crossroads of magic and positivism'? Or a more succinct definition of film theory's traditional project than 'to break the spell'?" Do you see your work as located at some form of crossroads? Does your work break any spell(s), theoretical and/or practical?

My films attempt to break the spell of dominant Western hetero-patriarchal Eurocentric narratives/images. These pervasive images are all around us in the cinema/TV/magazines/billboards; they put us (the cinematic minorities) in a dreamlike state and zombify us in order to create identities using the very tropes set out to annihilate us as beings. My stories tend to put African descent, usually dark-skinned women, in the center of the frame. And yet I also aim to be inclusive in all my work in terms of ethnic, age, gender identity, sexual orientation in front of the camera as well as behind it.

As cases in point, in my film *Legacy* (2006) I explore the legacy of the transatlantic slave trade and how it has affected generations of people of African descent. In *Fem* (2007), a butch (lesbian/bisexual masculine woman) homage to queer

Figure 21.1 Legacy (Campbell, 2006).

femininity (femmes), I examine femmes in queer culture and explore a butch lesbian gaze through both desire and appropriation of dominant mythology. I am currently in post-production with *Stud Life*, a feature film which is a LGBTQ (Lesbian, Gay, Bisexual, Transgender, Queer) love story set in a black urban cultural framework and featuring a stud (masculine lesbian). In *Paradise Lost* (2003) I examine an LGB (Lesbian, Gay, Bisexual) Caribbean identity in a non-sensationalist way. It is an intimate, autobiographical film about growing up lesbian in the Caribbean and includes interviews with my parents and LGB people in Trinidad. In this film my mother reveals reading [Radclyffe Hall's novel] *The Well of Loneliness* (1928) as a teenager.[2] All of these films give a diversity of images one would never see in dominant cinema and television.

Do you think that de-Westernizing film is principally an economic, political, institutional, or artistic process? For example, does it extend from earlier cinematic movements, such as Third Cinema? What is it doing differently?

The concept of Third Cinema certainly influences and continues to have an impact on my work. However, I depart from it in that it never addressed issues of sexuality in relation to orientation or gender identities/fluidity. It remains hetero-patriarchal and so is excluding ideology/theory. In addition, New Queer Cinema, which looked as if it was going to be subversive in questioning the canons of hetero-patriarchy and an assimilationist view of LGBTQ people, ended up being another vehicle for "white" lesbian and gay filmmakers. Theorizing and making films using a "Nu Third Queer Cinema" perspective could be truly inclusive. This Nu Third Cinema would acknowledge that the experiences of white-skinned privileged LGBTQ people are specific. This cinema would amount to a new theorizing around film; it would not make the Eurocentric queer gaze appear to represent the "universal gay." It would eliminate the tyranny of the Eurocentric view of queer culture as being the "authentic/real" voice of all LGBTQ people. In addition Nu Third Cinema would deal with the specificity of "white" representation so "white" can no longer remain invisible and unnamed yet dominant.

Does de-Westernizing film studies mean rejecting entirely dominant Western modes of thinking, production, criticism, and film practice? Is this even possible?

We need to borrow from critiques and practices which question and subvert the straight "white" male gaze but we also need to be mindful of what we use as guidance. When Laura Mulvey wrote that iconic essay "Visual Pleasure and Narrative Cinema" (1975), it was revolutionary in re-examining Western cinema, although her assumption was that all men are the same. She never mentioned race or culture. There was no concept of a queering of that gaze either, as Jackie Stacey would later explore in "Desperately Seeking Difference: Desire Between Women in Narrative Cinema" [*Screen* 28 (1), 1987].

Western media construction of so-called minority communities is so pervasive; the MTVization/Hollywoodization of global culture seems so powerful now and unconquerable. However, there are still chinks for guerrilla filmmaking and for those with a "Third Eye" (those filmmakers who bring a different perspective to the body of films). Likewise, within academic postcolonial critical theory, important and exciting work is being done by Shamira Meghani, Sandeep Bakshi, Serena Dankwa, Sarah Lamble, Sara Ahmed, and Lynne Fanthome.

PoC in general, and QPoC in particular, do not have the luxury to allow our stories/histories to be told by others or even to give up trying to get stories out there to audiences. We have to resist and make trouble in spite of being seen as the "killjoy" described by Sara Ahmed in *The Promise of Happiness* [Durham, NC: Duke University Press, 2010].

Notes

1 Editors' note: Fanon (1925–1961), psychiatrist, writer, philosopher, and revolutionary from Martinique; Césaire (1913–1928), poet, politician, and author from Martinique; Gerima (b. 1946), Ethiopian filmmaker; Garvey (1887–1940), Jamaican Black Nationalist journalist and political activist and founder of the United Negro Improvement Association; Malcolm X (1925–1965), American religious, political, human-rights activist, founder of the Organisation for Afro-American Unity; Newton (1942–1989), American political and human-rights activist, co-founder of the Black Panther Party; Davis (b. 1944), American author and political activist; Hurston (1891–1960), American author; and Hughes (1902–1967), American activist and author.

2 This was the first British novel that dealt with lesbianism and was banned for forty years in case young girls were corrupted by its content.

22 "To start with a blank slate of free choices"

An interview with Kuljit Bhamra

Do you see film as a universal medium/art form?

The answer to that is yes, I think it would be difficult not to consider it as a universal medium or art form, because it is so all pervasive. We could talk more about it but I think the answers will unfold in the following questions.

We can keep that in mind. The second question was how do you consider the West to be in terms of a category: is it always shifting, is it always in motion and therefore unstable? Should this West, or even the Western, be perceived solely as or through geographical frameworks?

Yes. I think that the West is probably *unstoppable* rather than unstable! I don't really relate to it as a geographic area; definitely the West has certain values that seem to permeate the rest of the world. If you go to India, Bombay (Mumbai), or other countries there is a certain Western ideal that people aspire to. The whole thing about Good and Evil and the character of the hero and the villain, for example, are very simple components that represent the West in terms of – I don't know if it's really American or Western – but there seems to be a need for humans to somehow witness, in action, the Good versus Evil. My concern is that it's usually the West that comes out on top! It is this particular dynamic that I refer to when speaking of "the West."

Following on from that, how do you then see the example in the case of Indian cinema or Bollywood that there is an adaptation of that, or an influence of that, in relation to that kind of Western theme of the Hero, or of Good versus Evil or a kind of alternative?

Even before the Indian film industry evolved into what we now call Bollywood, there were still very strong Western influences. All films (except the very few art-house productions) are musicals, with dance sequences and camera angles inspired by the likes of Baz Luhrman and Busby Berkeley – all combined with simple plots lifted from popular Hollywood productions and Spaghetti westerns. Recent Bollywood productions all have choreography in the style of Michael Jackson's "Thriller" – strangely now with groups of Russian dancing girls! I don't really like Bollywood now, and it's a difficult subject for me. Bollywood nowadays has almost nothing to do with the rich Indian culture we all expect from an Indian production. If you examine the music – even with productions like, dare I say it, *Slumdog Millionaire* (Boyle, 2008) – you'll find that "subtracting" vocals from the songs would leave you with a mediocre pop backing track, which I think is a shame. Occasionally, some Indian sounds and twangs are thrown in to satisfy or somehow distinguish the original country source of the production. I've recently come to describe Bollywood as "the worst of both worlds" (!) because in the old days before technology got a grip of music recording production and film and sound recording, there was a richness in content and artistic context. However, in recent years if you listen to and watch a Bollywood movie or a Bollywood song sequence there's nothing Indian in it at all apart from costumes and a skin colour. And that's something I think that still reflects a very strong colonial mentality in India, where people aspire to be Western or something. My friends and colleagues in Mumbai have developed a "conveyor-belt" mentality in the industry. Films are produced to make a short-lived impact (but maximum financial gain) rather than an ever-lasting impression. These attitudes, I feel, have been imposed by current Western culture and ideals.

It's strange because I sometimes feel that the diasporas, the people that left India, have retained Indian culture more: we're sort of frozen in time, you know. My parents came to England in the mid-1950s and somehow British Indians have retained parts of a culture that no longer exist in India. I was in Bombay last year during *Diwali* – you know, the Festival of Light – and I was looking forward to enjoying the celebrations being bigger and more glorious than here, but they said "Oh, no, we don't do *that* here anymore!"; I expected to see fireworks going off all night – just like they do in Southall, "Oh, no, we don't do that anymore." "Really?".

The Westernization thing has somehow got hold of India in an unfavourable way for me, and it's a shame because some of the beauty of what I have known India to be musically and also cinematically seems to have got lost.

What do you understand by Western modes of thinking, theorizing, and making film? How does such an understanding affect your work as a composer, as a music composer?

I think I'm a bit of a rebel, actually. I don't wake up every morning and say, "I'm going to be a rebel today" but because I'm a self-taught musician and I never belonged to any guru system or learning system. I'm a self-taught musician and producer – I have been my whole life; I have a recording studio downstairs in my house, a record label – and all of that has come out of me jumping into the deep end. I've never formally studied business or music, you know, I was a very good Indian boy and studied civil engineering (!) and then left it to go into music. Sometimes I think that my parents still feel they're not sure exactly what I do. But in answer to your question, a non-Western mode of thinking would be something that doesn't conform to what people expect because the Western model is so all-pervasive that people expect that. If you take the Bhangra phenomenon in the UK, for example – and I always say that Bhangra is a British invention – you had acid-Bhangra, house-Bhangra, Bhangra R&B, so it's always followed a Western trend, and there seems to be a need to want to be approved or endorsed by the Western world. When I was churning out Bhangra records in the 1980s we were selling 100,000 units, 200,000 units – we could have easily got to number one in the charts in the UK, but none of the Indian shops were Gallup-registered.[1] How success is measured amongst Indian musicians even today relates to how success-ful they have been in the West. Whether you're selling 200,000 units in Mister Patel's corner shop somehow is not the measure of success but if you're in America, you are in the charts, you've got management, and you're on tour then somehow that's successful! So I suppose being non-Western you have to be slightly nonconformist, and personally I've always looked at breaking rules and pushing the envelope somewhat. In all the albums that I've done, without any exception, if there were ten songs on the album, I would have done eight for the masses and then thrown a couple in for the artists and people who understand my musical journey. So in recent years I spent a lot of time working on breaking the mould and stepping outside the box because I don't want to do what other people have already done. It's a trap as well because, say I produce a song and it becomes a hit, then for the next year I would have people knocking on my door saying, "We want to make a record; we want it to sound like that one that you did." But I did that two years ago: why would I want to step back in time? But there are lots of dynamics at play – I think it's not just about the art, it's con-nected to fashion, it's connected to being accepted by your peers. All of these – I would call them "simple" pleasures or "shallow pleasures" – seem somehow to drive that whole scene, which is quite sad, frankly. So in recent years, especially since I got my MBE[2] and I've been acknowledged for the work I've done, it's given me an extra boost in terms of feeling that what I'm doing is acknowledged and somewhat worthy in its cause. Consequently, I've now become a bit more extreme in terms of my artistic directions. Having said that, if you're a fish, you can't avoid water can you? That's probably a terrible analogy but we are working in this Western mould and it is all pervasive and unstoppable and I think some-how I try to reach a balance by stepping outside and breaking certain laws in terms of the way I play my tabla drums and the experimental ways I'm com-posing and recording – but not so radically that it leaves the mass audiences behind because, at the end of the day, I'd like as many people as possible to hear what I'm doing.

You seem to be saying that non-Western is a kind of mentality, a position or even an attitude that is nonconformist and that seeks to challenge or subvert rather than something that is located in a particular geographical location?

That's correct. I think that when we say Western it probably *is* located (geographically speaking) in the Western world. But I don't actually know *where* the Western world is.

Well it depends where you're standing, I suppose.

I thought I was standing in the Northern World! It's probably America and England and this model of the Bruce Willis character in films that saves the world; "there's a problem, so let's fix it," you know, "we've got twenty minutes to save the world." So many films are saying that?! There seems to be that predictable and boring model. Similarly, if you took Bollywood (and most Indians would tell you this), all the films have the same story – or at least a familiar, particular plot. I find the fact that people want the comfort of that form of entertainment quite strange. Maybe it's part of being human: somehow I feel that I have to balance where people are with where I'm going to take them. I don't think you can transform the way people think unless you really get that where they are is a perfectly valid place for them. The current trend in Bollywood filmmaking works for most people – it's just not the place for me – it doesn't make a difference! I know I'm talking like it's all bad and wrong. I don't actually mean it that way. I just mean to say that stepping back a little, we can see that it's perfectly valid – this whole Western model of values and ways of thinking – but at the moment it's not for me. Of course there's a place on this planet for everything, but I think that I must accept that something is valid before I can assume to be in a position to somehow transform it. I think if I came at it from a position of trying to fix it, I wouldn't succeed in that way. So I suppose what I'm saying is that there needs to be a balance creatively in my work as a composer and musician and in order to create that balance, I need to be aware of where people are and where I'm going to take them. And to be aware that neither one of them is actually better than the other. I mean, globally speaking, we're all going to do what we do and then we're going to die, so everyone's life is perfectly valid and what everyone does is what everyone does. But it would be a shame, I think, if people lived their lives without being aware of the choices that they had to make. And part of the problem – if I can call it that – with the all-pervasive Western style of thinking and production is that very few people realize that there is other stuff out there. Why isn't there an Indian singer in the charts right now? I mean there's got to be a mission to stop that happening. We've got a black president of America recently, why wasn't there one before? How long is it going to be before we get an Indian Prime Minister in England? There's got to be some underlying mission against that, I say. And so I think you have to somehow accept those things and then slowly wean people into where you are as an artist.

Robert B. Ray, an academic with particular interest in critical practice, once asked: "what could be a more exact definition of the cinema than 'the crossroads of magic and positivism'? Or a more succinct definition of film theory's traditional project than 'to break the spell'?" Do you see your work as located at some form of crossroads?
Does your work break any spell(s), theoretical and/or practical?

I make a point of all my work being, if not collaborative, then from collaborative sources. The crossroads suggests to me that you have a choice of where to go. I think it's similar to what I said in my previous answer in terms of either standing at the crossroads or being very clear about which direction to take. And if you are clear about the direction to take, does that mean you are not aware that there can also be a crossroads?!

Because I've done so much in my career, it is quite easy for me to get bored with myself and my style of creativity, so I make an effort now to work with other creative people collaboratively. In order to do that, I have to be ready to completely readdress my values and my previous directions.

In terms of breaking spells practically, I think that my attitude toward playing and de-mystifying the tablas is very unusual, I like the "artisan" side of things; I'm quite practical and have enormous admiration for musicians – especially those who make their own instruments. I find the whole process from creating an instrument from wood, metal, hide and clay and then learning to play it magical! The last recording I produced was an album called "Heartfelt" with young London-based singer called Shahid Khan. Shahid won a talent competition at the age of sixteen. I was a judge on the panel and was blown away by his singing talent. In an attempt to revive the old Hindi film sound, I decided to record the album with a live string section and produce the recording using vintage analogue equipment. Nowadays, recordings are usually done digitally, using computers. This method allows one to correct and "perfect" the recordings by using computer applications. I have felt for a few years now that the resulting music – although technically flawless – sounds empty, hollow and soulless. Using analogue equipment meant that the musicians had to practice and play together until the songs sounded as good as a performance, rather than as separate computer files that could be compiled later. While I don't think I broke any spells doing that, people in the industry remark "Oh my God, really?" when I explain the process to them. I see the use of the computer as a Western way of working. Although the use of computers in producing music and films has been revolutionary, I feel that the computer is not a replacement for a creative mind, instrument or camera. Many people think that "they are their tools." Just because you have the latest model computer doesn't make you a talented musician, artist or filmmaker. Many people now have access to software Final Cut Pro, Garage Band, Photoshop, etc., However, I am concerned that many of them feel that owning the software could make them a successful artist. If you own a really good mobile phone, does it enable you to make really good phone calls?

Could you say a little bit more about that context or idea of the crossroads – you talked about how collaboration is possibly breaking traditions and breaking spells – could you say a little bit about your experience and place as a musician and composer working within cinema, within the film industry?

Well, here, again, I've never formally studied writing music for film, but I'm someone who throws himself into the deep end and figures out how to do it. Then, I study what's been done before and whether I like it and its process. I explore if things could have been done differently or more efficiently.

I recently wrote the soundtrack for a film entitled *The Winter of Love* (2011) produced and directed in Southall by Shakila Taranam Maan.[3] I collaborated with both Indian and Western orchestral musicians. The main character theme is played on a *berimbao* which is a single-stringed Brazilian instrument. The whole soundtrack was recorded on my old analogue two-inch tape-recorder. It sounded great! More recently, I played tabla on Tim Burton's *Charlie and The Chocolate Factory* (2005). I was thrilled to discover that the Oompa Loompa theme had a Bhangra beat to it! Coming back to the current state of Bollywood, with the mandatory Michael Jackson dance routines, I would definitely *not* put that in if I was directing a new film. I would want my film to stand out by being different. Unfortunately, the trend amongst other creators is to play safe and use existing formulaic models, most of which have been tried and tested by the Western film industries. So they want to do what they think has worked before at a low risk cost. I'm more of the thinking that the higher the risk the higher the reward – or the higher the failure! As an artist, I would say that I am more driven by commercial success. This doesn't mean that I sell out on my own artistic integrity, but I like questioning things, and I like breaking styles of working – and I really believe that magic comes out of that and I'm always looking for that; whether it be in writing music for films or whether it be in writing songs for an artist, or playing live. [Put differently,] I think there is a big difference between being commercially driven (that is following formulaic templates that guarantee a certain monetary success) and being driven by a desire to make a difference to a wider audience. I am passionate about what I do and would like my work to reach as many people as possible. Some artists are happy even if only one person has been provoked into thinking. Personally, I feel that creations should be made available to as many people as possible (unless the project is otherwise such). I believe there is a way of balancing the two worlds to benefit both audience and artist.

We've got two more questions. The first of those is whether your understanding of the de-Westernizing film is principally economic, political, institutional, or whether you think it's an artistic process? Do you think it's doing anything different from earlier cinematic movements such as Third Cinema, for example, and if it is doing something different or things are happening differently at the moment, what is it that is different?

Well with the first part, I don't think you can just separate the artistic from the political or the social. I think they're all entwined but we need to give them categories so we can talk about them – but you can't talk about anything in isolation because it's all part of life. So I don't think it's just about considering these things artistically; I mean, we can, that's why we categorize them but generally they're all connected. I think also that if we take the example of the art house movie (and I'm talking about Indian cinema now) you can put on the TV channel or stick on a DVD, and you know it's an art-house movie – you can tell just by looking at it. So there must be a drive to keep it art house, otherwise it would become mainstream. I think that artists have always had the same struggles even if the mediums may be different, technology may be different. Imagine that you're someone who has never experienced classical music before and then someone gently persuades you to a concert at the South Bank and you end up loving the experience or a piece of music you heard there. It's not fair to assume that you will return soon with a few of your friends to see another concert. The invisible boundaries that classical music performance of being slightly elitist and snobbish will still be there. It's almost like there's a club mentality, an invisible wall around it, and I think that something similar can be found in art-house movies and movies that are trying to not conform to Western ideals: it will always be a small portion – I think it needs to be small just by virtue of what it is.

I think there is something like a sense of value in it – I don't want to use the word "elitist" – but there's a sense that this smaller group of people who understand and appreciate the kind of risks that certain artists take and the fact that they're not going to compromise to just attract a mainstream audience or for similar reasons; so [this smaller group] can sense a feeling I suppose that you are working in a minority but a minority who value the art they're producing.

Does de-Westernizing film studies mean rejecting entirely dominant Western modes of thinking, production, criticism and even practice? If we think about de-Westernizing film studies in this instance as a kind of conceptual term, does it mean that you have to reject all those kind of Western influences, modes of thinking, ways of working and so forth? Is that even possible? Can you start from zero and reject those terms entirely?

I might have answered that before: you can't reject something unless it's there. The phrase "de-Westernizing" as a general context has the word "Westernizing" in it. It's a sort of vicious circle, isn't it? I think that, as I mentioned before, you have to be aware – if you're somebody who is inspired by de-Westernizing, I'm talking about film here – but if you're someone who is inspired by that, then I think you really have to honour and validate what is there already. You have to respect the choices made by others. There are valid and credible sets of approaches and methods of working within cinema, Hollywood or Bollywood, even if they might not be for me. It's not simply about just rejecting modes of thinking as a reaction. It's about glancing at the other side of the coin. One side needs the other! You yourself couldn't even conduct this research if the word *Westernizing* didn't exist! So, therefore it is unfair to purely reject ideals and principles based on our dislike of a mainstream cultural superpower. One needs to start with a blank slate of free choices.

Also, bound up in this idea of de-Westernizing, is the question of whether we are just replacing one binary position with another – if, for example, de-Westernizing means rejecting dominant Western modes of thinking production and criticism are you just replacing one hegemony or mainstream cultural superpower with another. Does that get you anywhere? Is that realistic anyway?

I think it's important to identify the purpose of one's mission. If one's work is fuelled purely by a rejection or dislike of Western systems and modes, then I don't think it will make a difference. In my own work, I hope that I don't set out to be a rebel or antagonist just for the sake of it. I feel that I can make a difference with my work. As creators in the film and music industry, we are constantly evolving and toying with various ways of thinking, operating and creating. However, it dismays me to see many creators employ what they perceive as "success templates" from the West.

Notes

1 Editors' note: Bhamra is referring to the polling, or statistical research branch of the Gallup Organization. Gallup was the pollster company that used to compile the pop-music charts in the UK, based on sales from Gallup registered/affiliated stores. "You only really need to about 20,000 units to be in the top 10. We were selling bucket-loads five-times, ten times more than that. But why isn't there one [in the top 10]?"

2 "Member of the British Empire," UK recognition for outstanding achievement/service to an area of public interest granted to a selected number of British citizen by the Queen on her birthday.

3 "The film was originally released under the title *A Quiet Desperation* (2001). A surge in interest 10 years later caused [Maan] to re-release it with a new edit and titled *A Winter of Love*. In the process, she managed to make some further edits that she had always wanted to" (Kuljit Bhamra, email correspondence with the editors, November 29, 2011).

23 "The crazy dream of living without the Other"

An interview with Olivier Barlet[1]

Do you see film as a universal medium/art form?

Édouard Glissant wrote: "I believe that we should abandon the idea of the universal. The universal is an illusion, a deceptive dream. We ought to conceive of the world as wholeness, that's to say as a known quantity and not a value sublimated from particular values" (1996: 136). The notion of the universal is thus problematic as it denies both differences and singularities: under the pretext of universality, the West speaks in the place of the Other. Controversies that cut across the political sphere in France are still typical of this denial of history, and there are numerous examples: in 2005, the preposterous debate on the benefits of colonization and the remarks made by politicians during the riots in the *banlieues* [deprived urban peripheries of many large French cities];[2] in July 2007, the speech by President Sarkozy in Dakar [Senegal];[3] and in 2009–2010, the debate on French national identity.[4]

Therefore a film is not universal in the sense that it cannot speak for everyone. However, it does address the universal since, as a communication tool employing universal codes, film can be understood by those who are willing to see and hear it.

Do you consider the West as a category that is always shifting, in motion, and therefore unstable? Should this "West," or "the Western," be perceived solely as, or through, geographical frameworks?

The West is constantly evolving. At the same time, it does possess historical constants concerned precisely with imposing its "universality" on those who take issue with it. This imposition has been achieved through a power struggle that has passed through the slave trade, slavery, colonization, and their continuing negative legacies. Its humanism has fed upon these historical contradictions, made law by the "Code Noir"[5] and then in colonial law books, where the Other is simultaneously viewed as a commodity to be sold and a soul to be won; a savage to be kept at a safe distance and a potential citizen.

The aforementioned power struggle conveys a sense of geography but, since it is also inscribed in the Other's collective psyche via an internalizing of racial hierarchy and of inequality, that same geography also dissolves into the realms of thought. Which alienated person has not, at least partly, integrated their alienation into an understanding of themselves and of the world? In this way, the inequality decreed by the Western "universal" remains all-pervasive.

What do you understand by non-Western modes of thinking, theorizing and making film? How does such an understanding affect your work?

In a similar way to my response to the previous question, the concept of "non-Western" cinema is, in itself, problematic, since it would seem to reinforce a mythical duality. In the economic domain, this can be seen in the funding mechanisms that are offered to the cinemas of the [global] South and in international co-productions. There is no autonomy in the world of cinema, only negotiations and compromise that are as much economic as they are cultural.

On the other hand, films draw from a diverse range of cultural codes, which must be taken into account in any critical analysis. Must one systematically make clear, through a combination of in-depth research and scholarly exposition, the codes of this "world of reference," the foundation of "possible worlds," elaborated by the reader or the viewer, and alluded to by Umberto Eco in *Lector in fabula* [1985]? Or, on the contrary, must one consider these symbols as self-explanatory and therefore just formulate one's own perception of them? The risk is that exoticism and Orientalism triumph but, as local symbols and inscriptions are not unequivocal, subjectivity, and it follows that, subjectivity, and therefore the codes of reference used by the individual who writes, will always predominate. So it is not "difference" but the relationship *to* the work of art that matters.

Robert B. Ray, an academic with particular interest in critical practice, once asked, "What could be a more exact definition of the cinema than 'the crossroads of magic and positivism'? Or a more succinct definition of film theory's traditional project than 'to break the spell'?" Do you see your work as located at some form of crossroads? Does your work break any spell(s), either theoretical and/or practical?

Certainly not. Isn't that the difference between film criticism and academic approaches to the cinema? A critique of relation is possibly lyrical and embraces or rejects the film rather than analyzing it.

Of course, the critic's keen and sharpened gaze is different: its attention to framing, mise-en-scène, and the actors' performance, to sound and narrative structure, or even its attentive listening to moments of discoveries, inferences, and to influences and ruptures, superimposes itself on the pleasure as spectator. But this distance does not "break the spell." And yet, sometimes I find myself leaving a film screening without having taken in all the intricacies of the story because my attention had been captivated elsewhere within the film.

Do you think that de-Westernizing film is principally an economic, political, institutional, or artistic process? For example, does it extend from earlier cinematic movements, such as Third Cinema? What is it doing differently?

On the pretext of opposing globalization and freeing ourselves from its grasp, we draw from metaphysics of de-Westernization whose utopian ideal is apparently to cut Africa off from the world by reconnecting with the crazy dream of living without the Other. The indiscriminately used term "African cinema" only serves a perpetual return to that isolationist and reductive mode of thinking. Its globalization does not take any account whatsoever of the pronounced diversity of cultures, the hybridity many African directors' cinematic works, and their biological *métissage*, of the virtual absence of any definable national cinematographies, and, even less so, of continental ones, as well as the quasi-general lack of cultural policy and cinema industry, the latter being the only criterion which could possibly warrant the use of such a denomination. "African cinema" is a myth maintained in order to reinforce the fact that it is confined to a position of difference, akin to a generic category per se ("like the Western" says [Congolese filmmaker] Balufu Bakupa-Kanyinda) the codes of which will then be defined in a supposedly learned fashion.

"Third Cinema" theory came to break away from Hollywood and auteur cinemas in order to develop a radical consciousness. Thus, "Third Cinema" stuck to a form of political commentary that struggles to account for the type of ruptures at work in cinema today. This type of ideological analysis is synonymous with telling "African cinema" what it should be by also trying to define what an African film language "from an African perspective" might be.

These expressions make up part of what [academic] Abdoulaye Imorou calls "the untouchables": reassuring expressions, fortifications against the deep-seated fear of a return to the colonial and which one cannot deconstruct without immediately being accused of playing into the hands of a (neo)colonial ideology and wanting to return Africa to the "heart of darkness." If, on the other hand, a critic shares with the culture from which a work of art emerges a sensibility that is grounded in the critic's own lived experience and a knowledge of the [cultural, cinematic, geographical] terrain, this can serve to enrich the critic's analysis, to clarify specificities, to reveal hybridities. All of this brings an undeniable quality and additional "flavor" to our understanding of the artwork. That doesn't mean, however, that the critic holds some truth, simply an understanding that is possibly subject to caution, just like all knowledge called upon by another voice. The critic's involved vision is crucial for shedding light on an artwork, but it should not be dogmatic. Critics should not position themselves as experts, for they would risk removing themselves from the sphere of criticism itself. It is rather the poetry that they are able to extract from their cultural proximity to the artist that constitutes the strength of the critics' conviction.

Does de-Westernizing film studies mean rejecting entirely dominant Western modes of thinking, production, criticism and film practice? Is this even possible?

A danger looms on the horizon and concerns us all: overplaying the notion of alterity. For this would be to endorse the dominant discourse (be it Western or African) on Africa of the West as the norm and Africa as difference/otherness/ outsider. In order to make itself understood, this discourse must unambiguously emphasize difference [between Africa and the West], to make Africa appear like an alien world and Africans as alien to the West? Basically, it is about reducing or masking the similarities that would place Africans on a level footing with the rest of the world, even though it is clear that African societies are governed by the same rules as societies elsewhere. To challenge/discuss this dominant discourse means that clichés and illusions are never far away, but these are widespread precisely because otherwise one is not listened to. The danger is therefore that one drifts toward an affective discourse where the commonly held position is that one "loves Africa" and must serve it. What is at stake, as Abdoulaye Imorou (again) suggests, is not to grant the artwork the status of an affective object but rather of an object of study in its own right.

On the other hand, it is essential to also think through the implications of the Other as occupying an irreducible position. For to not know the Other and not to recognize oneself in the Other is to cease searching for similarities in order to leave the Other to exist independently of oneself. We must aim to miss the Other, otherwise, in hitting the target, we kill them, elaborates Eduardo Viveiros de Catro in *Métaphysiques cannibales* (2009). To miss the Other is to lack some-thing of the Other, to be able to love still and, therefore, to be capable of searching for the Other in the Other. It is essential to occupy this position of the anti-Narcissus in order to not think about the world in universalizing, general categories that lead us to try and comprehend how, in others, such categories manifest themselves. It is, on the contrary, to accept a multiplicity of perspectives, and therefore the opacity and irreducibility of things.

In my opinion, this double move forms the basis of solidarity.

Notes

1 Interview translated from the French by Saër M. Bâ and Will Higbee.
2 On the so-called riots, see Jim Wolfreys' evaluation, one year on. Available online at www. socialistreview.org.uk/article.php?articlenumber=9872 (accessed December 4, 2011).
3 Editors' note: the Dakar speech has generally been considered as colonial or "unacceptable." Available online at www.zeleza.com/blogging/african-affairs/nicholas-sarkozy-s-unacceptable-speech-boubacar-boris-diop-trans-french-wan (accessed December 4, 2011).

4 Editors' note: this debate emerged from Immigration Minister Eric Besson's desire to launch "a major discussion on 'national values and identity.'" Available online at www.france-today.com/2009/10/french-national-identity-grand-debate.html (accessed December 4, 2011).

5 A decree passed by King Louis XIV of France in 1685 that defined the conditions of slavery in the French colonial empire.

References

Anon. (2009) "French National Identity: The Grand Debate." Available online at www.france-today.com/2009/10/french-national-identity-grand-debate.html (accessed December 4, 2011).

de Catro, E. V. (2009) *Métaphysiques cannibales*, Paris: Presses Universitaires de France.

Diop, B. B., "Nicolas Sarkozy's Unacceptable Speech." Available online at www.zeleza. com/blogging/african-affairs/nicholas-sarkozy-s-unacceptable-speech-boubacar-boris-diop-trans-french-wan (accessed December 4, 2011).

Eco, U. (1985) *Lector in fabula*, Paris: Grasset.

Glissant, É. (1996) *Introduction à une poétique du divers/Introduction to a Poetics of Diversity*, Paris: Gallimard.

Wolfreys, J. (2006) "France: One Year After the Riots." Available online at www.socialist review.org.uk/article.php?articlenumber=9872 (accessed December 4, 2011).

24 "De-Westernizing as double move"
An interview with John Akomfrah

Let's kick off with the first question. Do you see film as a universal medium or art form?

I think this is a little bit like the debate on socialism: there is what one might want and what actually exists. Or let's start with film as a kind of technology. One would like to think that it functions as a universal art form; one would like to think that it functions that way, or at least one would desire that to be the case, but I don't think that that is what actually happens.

The differences that actually exist in cinema, whether it's about how the technology impacts on different parts of the world, for example how it is accessed, or the phenomenological experiences of cinema, these elements are so different, so marked by difference, should I say, that it's difficult to hold that idea of difference and universality in the same sentence. So, for instance, it's clear that large parts of the world, especially those where cinema died as a kind of functioning entertainment unit in the 1960s, early 1970s, and 1980s, most audience experiences of the moving image are not actually by the cinema; it's via small screens, it's about images which have been manufactured by the digital camera or manipulated digitally, edited digitally, shown on small screens, largely domestic settings, and so on and so forth. Now, if you believe all the arguments around identification and suturing, all the screen theory baggage, if you believe that, if you still think that those theories have a purchase, then that must mean if people are not having those ontological experiences of the cinema, then cinema is not a universal medium. It just can't be. If you believe the positions screen theory put forward about how spectatorship is constructed, the psychic processes involved and how much that's really a sort of an existential relation between subject and screen – and by screen I think they mean normally quite large things – well, most people don't have that experience of cinema anymore. For large parts of the world that experience stopped at a certain moment, historically; it returned, the image returned, but never in quite the same way. So it's in those terms that I would qualify one side of our debate about universality.

The other is that, clearly, at the level of narrative storytelling, for instance, it's clear that, while there may be recurring motifs and archetypal figures, themes and so on, the whole Joseph Campbell theses about the way in which folk functions in the everyday life, how they impact on storytelling and narrative is very different – very marked by difference across the planet – so that what might require translating, deconstructing, explaining in *Uncle Boonmee Who Can Recall His Past Lives* [Apichatpong Weerasthakul, 2010] for instance in Accra, may not take so much explaining in Berlin or Thailand.[1] And so the idea that there's a kind of unmediated access to narrative, which is open to all across the planet regardless of gender positions, class positions, and so on – regardless of nationality and ethnicity – is just a little bit too difficult to pull off.

And I have to say that's necessarily the case because otherwise the whole point of cultural studies, the whole point of film studies loses its value. If the thing is already apparent and universal and natural and everybody gets it, then what the fuck is *the* point of studying it? [*Laughs.*] If questions of location and questions of scholarship make no difference to our experiences of cinema, if everybody from Ljubljana [Slovenia] to Kigali [Rwanda] can "get" *Film Socialisme* (Jean Luc Godard, 2010) or *The Colour of Pomegranates* (Sergei Paradjanov, 1968) or *Battleship Potemkin* (Sergei Eisenstein, 1925) then the game is over for people like me and you because our job is done. I mean, there's no necessary need for intellectual interventions in the space between subject and screen that says: "Look, actually, there is something to talk about, this isn't just what it appears; there might be things to unpack, things to deconstruct" and so on. And so for all those reasons it feels to me that the question of universality needs to be there because clearly now everybody across the planet knows what an image is – the cinema is not a club or cult anywhere on the planet. At the same time, what they feel about, what they think of it, how it is used and functions are all very, very marked by difference.

Could we just follow up very briefly on this point? You talked before about technology – and you've spoken elsewhere about the possibilities of digital technology in terms of the universality of the art form. On the one hand, you're talking about the universality of understanding immediately the meaning in the images that we see, but isn't there also a sense in which the possibilities of digital technologies potentially open up a new kind of universality for audiences, the possibility of greater interconnectivity?

Absolutely. And I think the operative word from me is "potential." There seems to me to be potentialities, to use a kind of a [Giorgio] Agamben phrase, that are inherent in digital technology that now make it possible for a renewed universalist discourse around cinema to take place. And it is already happening because what the promise of the digital allows is a certain kind of circumventing of the political economy of cinema. Before the intervention of the digital, the political economy of cinema required that essentially productions outside of the metropolis functioned in a relation of dependency to the metropolis. Pretty much along the same lines as the traffic in crops, currency – so, in other words, the center was where it's at, it dictated what you did. If you shot a film you had to first buy the stock here. And of course, once it was exposed, send it back here to be processed, and so on and so forth. Very, very few countries in the South had laboratories beyond the black and white. Even at highpoint of cinema in these countries – and by highpoint I'm talking the moment of postcolonial euphoria when people really did take seriously the idea of political and cultural freedom, i.e. that we were going to make our own image and so on. In Ghana, even in those moments, it was only really possible to process black and white. So the flow of traffic of images, the flow of traffic of cinema pretty much mimicked the flow and traffic of all other resources in the world. Pretty much up to the promise of the digital in the past fifteen to twenty years, I'd say. And the transformation is quite remarkable because it does mean not simply that people in different parts of the world have access to the same thing but it's also this promise that they can do the same thing with access: and that's quite remarkable. In other words, the fact that you could get your hands on a Panavision camera in Ghana in 1971 did not mean that you could shoot *McCabe and Mrs. Miller* [Robert Altman, 1971], you know, because if you were able to shoot *McCabe and Mrs. Miller* you wouldn't be able to process it in the same way, with all the tricks of the trade. For instance, in Accra in 1971, in order to pull off the "desaturated" look by pre-flashing, pre-exposing some of the stock to a certain color, would have been a nightmare if you had to send the material back and forth. Not impossible, but just a nightmare. Now all of that immediately gets taken out of the equation because the package of the digital is exactly that: it's a package and it has no way of differentiating between how it arrives in Lagos and how it arrives in London. You could buy a Final Cut Pro package from Apple for use in Conakry and it will come with everything that I would get when I order it in London. So the promise of delivery is absolutely complete: when it arrives, it is exactly what is says on the tin; so that makes a profound difference to, and changes I think, to the question of access. And so it seems to me that there are two ways of seeing the cinema that are now rendered slightly problematic. The first, a slightly older and lingering, albeit radical, one, said that people who are not at the center of power don't have access to the technologies of cinema because of imperialism, [because] of political economy's dominance and subordination, and all the rest it; they don't have access *ergo* the cinema is unfair; I am talking here basically about the classical anti-imperialist critique of the cinema. That language seems to me now to be rendered slightly obsolete by what's going on. The second, slightly problematic, way of seeing cinema is a certain neo-liberal universalist language which says that because this stuff is available it must mean that the need for struggle over ownership of resources is also over. I don't believe that. In other words, the translating of the kind of Francis Fukuyama End of History thesis[2] into image making – which is pretty much what you're getting in quite a lot of magazines now, such as *Wired*: "it's a global village; everything is fine now we're all able to gain access." I don't think that's the case. I think there is a certain amount of truth to it; that's simply how our planet functions today, the opening up of markets which have in the past been developed or closed is now a reality. There is a global traffic of everything including images but that traffic does not necessarily get rid of all the questions of political economy. For instance, you can make your film in Nigeria but trying to get it beyond a certain confine, ethnic, or geographic, you still need the same old boys to intervene. So, there are still lingering questions of political economy and subordination, of domination by one part of the world over the other, which have not gone away: it's difficult to make a *Harry Potter* in Lagos. That's still, as far as I can tell, not on the cards! And the reasons are very obvious ones! They're the same ones that they were twenty years ago – in other words there are certain mechanisms by which images are disseminated across the globe which haven't really been touched that much. They may be shaken slightly, they might have the confidence knocked about how much they can control the market but they're still intact, there are people who can still make billions out of images and people who can't.

If we move onto the second question, then, which is whether you consider the West as a category that is always shifting, in motion and, therefore, unstable. The second part to that question is whether we need to think beyond the idea of a geographical framework for what the West might actually mean.

My answer would be "yes, yes, yes," to all of those, starting with the last. I mean, clearly you have to think beyond geography when it comes to trying to evaluate quite how a notion of the West could help you to understand certain national cultures or identities on the planet. Geography just doesn't help. What do I mean by that? Well, for instance, the whole question of diaspora – especially the African diaspora – seems to me to problematize the idea that one can locate the concept of the West purely in Europe or within European borders. It seems to me that what we know of the African diaspora as it is, let's say for instance in the New World, took shape from the sixteenth century onwards, as an entity that is marked by a series of hybrid traces and clearly a key one of those traces is the European trace – the "Western trace." Without that trace clearly that entity would not exist and I don't mean that just in the negative sense: every major intellectual from the New World – from Frederick Douglass to C. L. R. James, from Édouard Glissant to Patrick Chamoiseau have made that point quite forcefully when you push them.[3] I'm just watching a television documentary series on the Caribbean made in the 1980s and presented by the great Stuart Hall. And in the episode on Martinique, Aimé Césaire makes that point very clearly and emphatically: "I am a product of French culture," he says. "That does not mean that I am not also of African descent, but I am quintessentially a product of French culture." So, it seems to me that for a man who sits in the Caribbean, which, if my geography serves me right, is really very far off the radar of the West (geographically), if somebody of that stature in that region can say that, then it seems to me that the question of geography is of very little value in evaluating what one means by "Western." The conundrum of geography, let's call it that, just doesn't fully account for the persistence of the term, otherwise North

American culture in general would not be part of this – it is just not, geographically, in the same space. At the same time, like all rhetorical devices, tropes, and so on, clearly, at the heart of it [the category "West"], there's also a lingering sense that geography is important. You know, a guy has just taken to shooting and killing about 100+ people in Norway and, when you look at the website that he's put out, what is frightening is still the sense – for people like that – that there is a geographical entity called Europe, a space marked and imbued with "Western values." For people like that, those values are the ones that are threatened by outsiders who are coming into that geographic space. So in that kind of discourse, which is not confined to just nutcases who wield guns, there are still lingering sentiments – romantic or otherwise – that somehow the European domain is the repository of something called "Western values." And when you listen to the recent pronouncement of our British Prime Minister, David Cameron, on multiculturalism, you know that this insidious combination of geography and fantasy, this White Mythology, is not going anywhere anytime soon. I don't think we should forget that; there's a sense in which people who play deconstructionist games always think the only game in town is theirs: "I say Western doesn't exist *ergo* everybody else believes that" – well, that's clearly not the case in this instance.

We were talking earlier of the idea of race as a construct and of nation as a construct – academics can sit around and say "we're in a post-national moment, the nation that doesn't exist" that doesn't mean that nation doesn't still have an incredibly strong hold and mean something and can be used for political, artistic or ideological means.

Yes, exactly. Rather than it being seen as something we've arrived at by a series of protracted set of negotiations between different corners of our globe, the "Western" is still seen by many a set of values that owe their origin to a singular geographic space. And therefore the sense of that repository being under threat is still a very powerful political tool. It is an exclusionary rhetoric that underpins quite a lot of cultural strategies increasingly in Europe. And is also a lived reality for quite a lot of contemporary Europeans. And I don't mean in a sort of old-Marxist "false consciousness" sense; I think there are, let us say, productivities to that idea which are still in motion and still working: some good; or at least acceptable. And some not good at all. But it seems to me that the problem is not really to do with whether one could say that the notion of the West is a repository of one specific place. The problem for me is the idea that because it "originated" in that space, it can now only be protected by, contained by and embodied by that space – that's what I don't buy because clearly the ongoing histories of various forms of diaspora seem to me to throw that into question. There were many connections, many elective affinities between the French and Haitian Revolutions between the likes of Robespierre, and Toussaint L'Ouverture.[4] And this symbolic exchange was not confined to the leadership: your average Haitian revolutionary soldier believed too that there was a connection between what they were trying to do and what had happened in the Métropole. Basically, that symbolic evoking of a post-geographic sense of what constitutes the Western has shaped the history of the modern in ways that one cannot account for by simply linking the Western to the European in any simple, causal way. Take the anti-colonial struggles, for instance. Because there you see some of the complexity of the traffic I am alluding to. Many of its leaders were consciously attempting to throw off something "European," be it a history of political rule or economic incarceration. But many of the figures who were involved in the African liberation movement – and I don't know one who isn't formed in this way – either studied here (I mean, in Europe or North America) or were very aware of this idea that they were taking something from "here" over "there": whether it's Marxist theory, Keynesian economics or Eisenteinian cinema; people very consciously felt that their intervention in a space, which they saw as much as kind of a geographic space but also a space of mentalities, was about taking certain things and taking them elsewhere. [Ousmane] Sembène, when you spoke to him about how he decided [to get into filmmaking], said "I wanted to talk to more people, I realised the novel wasn't, so I went to VGIK in the Soviet Union to study cinema, to take it back." And he had no qualms about saying: "Look, for me, my practice, the way in which I was initiated into this thing just says that the notion of the West is a kind of unstable epistemic category because I'm already infected by those values, I've taken a course, I've taken them back and I'm going to put it to use. Now, I'm not going to reproduce it in some crude mimetic way but my cinema will still be marked by the trace of the location which I took this from." And he meant that across the board: technique, approach, understanding of function and so on. So when we talk about African cinema and stress its aversion to interiority, for instance, well, that's not just because of an unblemished, African griot cultural translation of cinema; it is also because of a Sembènian understanding of Soviet cinema. So, for me, celebrating the difference of African cinema, for instance, involves highlighting the qualities that are not unique to it. To not do that is to repress and deny the persistence of "Western values" in the emergence of different cinemas. But to do that also by implication involves problematizing, complicating, and "disassembling" what passes for conventional understandings of the geography of those values.

You can't have one without the other: if the notion of the Western is now inherently unstable, then so are its "pure opposites." They are no less "unsullied" and "uncontaminated" by this instability.

We can build up on that reference with the next question. What it is that you understand by non-Western modes of thinking, theorizing, and making film? How does such an understanding affect your work?

In my mind, it's very direct my understanding of that difference, very direct. I mean, I grew up with a passion for cinema; by the time I was twenty I had seen

I think every variety of it on the planet from Bollywood with my young Asian friends in west London in the early 1970s to French cinema on television, to Russian cinema – Tarkovsky being a particular favorite. A repertory cinema – the Paris Pullman – was around the corner from where I lived off the Fulham Road in London and so, in my teens I watched everything from the classic Italian neorealist films to the new American independent cinema. So I was never fooled by the idea that there is one cinema. My experience has said there are different forms and some slightly more mystifying to me as a child than others. When you first see Tarkovsky's *Mirror* [1975] and you're seventeen it takes some . . . you know, when you see Passolini's *Salò* [1975] that mystification turns to a sense of shock. And the shock really has to do with the protean forms the cinema could take, the many guises it arrives in. And at some point you think: "Shit! These differences *need* to be understood – I mean, I need to get my head around what it means," and that moment was going really to review films for *Framework* in Pesaro [1984] in Italy when they had this massive retrospective on Indian cinema. And they showed everything: the early years, the classic Bollywood films from the 1940s and 1950s, the art cinema revolt of Satayajit Ray and Ritwik Ghatak, the power of political cinema and the avant-garde cinema of the 1970s, and what struck me looking at the avant-garde stuff in particular – the films of Mani Kaul and Kumar Shahani, for instance, or even some of the later Ghatak – was that here was a difference marked by a willful desire to *be* different. You know this isn't just an accidental difference, it's not like watching Tarkovsky's *Mirror* where you're like "Okay, if I understood what he was saying, if I knew something about the history I could get it because this guy is trying to say something to somebody like me in his setting." When I saw these films, I thought "Wow, these are people who are really genuinely trying to say something different here. You really do need to change the way which you think about the medium to understand that they are coming from a very, very different place to most of the film's you've seen." Everybody has the film that does that for them but once that's happened, then you realize actually that's been all along. So I would say that the 1980s was the moment for me when I thought, "Okay let's just understand what this genie is because it is clearly out of the bottle for you, John Akomfrah, now." And now I don't think it's being romantic or kitsch or trendy or whatever the phrase is to say that. I think what I know now of cinema is that there may well be a set of rules that inform and, by implication, form the dominant forms of it – be it Bollywood, middlebrow Russian cinema or Hollywood, there may be kind of a set of rules working with those for what we could call the "Western values" but for all of that there's always people from a very different space. The first film that really made me think, "Now let's just think about this" was Mani Kaul's *Dhrupad* (1982). *Dhrupad* is probably the slowest film I've ever seen, I mean this film makes a virtue of being slow. You can't recoup the slowness as something quaint; it's not like watching [Romanian filmmaker] Miklós Jancsó's films where the ten-minute roll is a series of movements. No, this is just a static shot of a group of people sitting on a rooftop playing a piece of music. And it goes on for a whole ten-minute roll without moving – it's just there. And slowly, you think, "Shit, so let me get this straight, there's this musical form called *dhrupad* which has a slow build, the tempora comes in and then, slowly, the voice starts to mimic how the tempora is working; and it's working with very few notes – if one could call them notes – because they're not really notes; nothing is being hit. There is no stable referent, except the frame, but the frame is doing exactly what the voice and instruments are doing. They're all slowly, just evolving." And I thought "Wow!" – it was a moment of epiphany for me. That was 1981–1982 when I saw *Dhrupad*, and I thought it was just a one-off film. It's only when I went to Pesaro in 1984 and saw [the above-mentioned Indian films] that I realized there is a whole load of this stuff – not just one. And it changed me.

So there was a realization that it wasn't just one exception or exceptional film? More specifically, it was to do with a non-Western approach to the image?

Yes. It wasn't just some structural anomaly – this really was a default for a certain way of coming at cinema, which has positioned and set its difference up as completely against all the rules by which the cinemas that I kn[e]w that, for want of a better word, one can only call "Western" worked. It was just radically different, and the difference was not about an aesthetics of hunger, it's not *cinema nôvo*, it's not Third Cinema. In other words, it did not seem as if it was infused by a political rhetoric; it was a formal rhetoric which happens to be and had positioned itself as difference, as alterity in the most marked way that you can see alterity in existence. I mean I was just, "Wow! This is really taking-no-prisoners cinema. And not loud." It's not the opening of *Memories of Underdevelopment* [Tomás Gutiérrez Alea, 1968], or the *The Hour of the Furnaces* [Octavo Getino and Fernando E. Solanas, 1970] which has these beating frenetic drums saying "I'm different, I want to come and take over your life and your wife." It's not that. This is a kind of refusenik manifesto, a secessionist manifesto which is not playing by any of the standard rules of trespass. It had set up its camp on the margins and was very happy to be there. It had its own forms of address, forms of legitimation and was working with those – absolutely. Now, when I subsequently spoke to these filmmakers, they of course mentioned all these other figures from the so-called Western canon who were as much an influence as the Indian epic forms that fascinated them. So, Mani [Kaul] was absolutely fascinated and obsessed with Matisse, Kumar was absolutely fascinated and obsessed with Brecht (as indeed was their mentor and teacher, Ritwik Ghatak), and so these are not hermetically sealed places of worship or encampment: they are clearly porous enough to be influenced by, inflected by an understanding of the outside. But the outside was not so menacing as to banish alterity. And that's a complicated thing to pull off, to say, "Yes, I'm a universal figure but I speak the language of the local," which is also as painstakingly constructed as the universal. That is the important thing: that both are constructions. None of these filmmakers were saying "Oh, there is a Western form which is a-historical and fixed and then there is me who is non-Western and a-historical and fixed." I've never come across that, I've never come across. . . I mean all the cinemas that one could call non-Western, whether their "non-Western" approach is to question spectatorship or storytelling or production, all of them, always, have their differences marked by and via an understanding of the West and the Western. I mean, at the very least, some of the ways in which the technology is deployed alone is.

Do you think they're also always working counter to the dominant trends or forms within their own culture? You were talking about how the kind of films that really stopped you in your tracks were clearly "setting up their own camp," which was not in the center or the mainstream and actually doing something very different. So in a sense they're producing that kind of creativity and uniqueness from a marginal position, even within their own culture?

Even within their own culture, it seems to me. And that's either in terms of where the audience is at, or where the cinema in their country is positioned in the world-cinema firmament. So in the case of Ousmane Sembène, he was making films in a country [Senegal] where people were watching him and Charlie Chaplin at the same time. He never had the majority audience; the majority audience was always for Charlie Chaplin or Bollywood cinema. He always functioned, and I'm talking here just about spectatorship and audiences, as a minoritarian figure in Senegal. But there are other examples, the national cinema doesn't rely on the foreign import to sustain itself as a film culture – India, for instance – where the filmmakers I'm talking about definitely place themselves in some form of complicated opposition to the national cinema – and that could be Satayajit Ray and Ritwik Ghatak in India, Edward Yang and the great South Asian film-makers, such as Hou-Hsiao-hsien – they are not where the dominant cinema is at, at any one time. In fact, if you were to take most of those figures out of the equation you would pretty much think that cinema is a universal form in which people make love, have romances, die, and so on. The stock formats, formulas, genres you will find all over the world; the comedies, the *policiers,* the thrillers, especially now; every country that I go to will have its stars who are crossovers from the music industry, whether it's in Korea, Japan, or Nigeria. And the films really are pretty much vehicles; it doesn't matter what the genre is – comedy or drama – they are the vehicles by which the cinema gets to the outside world, gets to their audiences in that world. And at the same time as you're getting that, you will also find within those cultures, coexisting with those dominant cinemas, maverick ones formed by the same idea that somehow they are going to do something different. And this is not because they don't know the other stuff. In other words there is no Adamic myth behind what marks non-Western cinema as different anymore – even if there ever was, and I'm not sure there was, it certainly isn't there anymore. Most people who are making films that are quite difficult "non-dominant," non-traditional, are aware that they are functioning in a space in which they are definitely *not* (1) the only cinema; (2) the dominant cinema; (3) the one with the audience on its side *en masse* – and this cinema functions with those three recognitions.

Could we just follow up on that in relation to your own work? You talked about the epiphany of seeing those Indian films. Do you think that informed your work in terms of allowing you to realize [the existence of] a multitude of approaches, be they artistic, political, etc., or was it more specific in that there was also something within [these films] that spoke to your work, in terms of a manifesto that you could follow, or artistic influences that made you feel that this was a different way to approach my own practice as a filmmaker?

I took the new Indian cinema seriously enough to realize that to try and reproduce it in any simple way would be a fallacy. And that was the real lesson actually that I took from them. Here was a cinema questing for uniqueness but its specificity was built on trying to find a way in which it could harness its understanding of how cinema had functioned to date across the world with what it felt had to be said anew about its culture and its location. That seemed to me to be the main lesson that I took from those films. Sometimes it raised formal questions that I thought, "Okay, I can take this and reformulate it for our setting. And sometimes the lesson was simply a confirmation and legitimation of a certain approach that you are taking vis-à-vis your location. I mean, you know when you watch the radical cinemas of the 1960s and 1970s, e.g., Solanas and Getino's *The Hour of the Furnaces* – which has one of the most extraordinary openings I've ever seen – there's a particular use of black space given to the unseen that's important, which is formally, politically, and culturally important. And so in a sense what I am saying is that sometimes the cinemas merely confirmed where you were at and why you needed to be in that space. Sometimes they genuinely gave you an approach that you thought you could take forward with you in that space. I don't think in that sense I'm that different from how non-Western forms have worked in Western spectatorship. If you go back for instance to that famous year, 1959 – and people talk about the (French) new wave revolution and so on – but really between 1952 and 1959 most of the major revolutions were not from Europe at all. From *Rashomon* (Kurosawa, 1950) and to *The Apu Trilogy* [Ray] the whole world suddenly thought "Fuck me, these non-Westerners have a trick or two up their sleeve." Kurosawa's impact from *Rashomon* onwards on the new Hollywood of the 1970s is still to be documented. I mean the guy was massive. And between 1952 and 1959 you couldn't get any more non-Western than *Rashomon*. These are films marked by a sense of alterity, visually they just looked so different. Actors were different: they looked different, they spoke differently, they ate differently, they *sat* differently. And yet this was a cinema that clearly seemed to understand something about what we need here (and by here I mean in the Western enclave).

Figure 24.1 Rashomon (Kurosawa, 1950).

And people took from them with "extreme prejudice," as they say. And a lot still continue to take and learn from them. And so I'm not sure that my relationship with these cinemas is that different actually from what's been the standard traffic, if you want, between the two poles – the so-called Western and non-Western. I would say that there has been a kind of crossing of thresholds and borders, which seems to me to mark, and always has, that dichotomy for individuals and film-makers – and it's worth bearing that in mind I think.

Our next question is based around a quote from Robert B. Ray where he asks, "What could be a more exact definition of the cinema than 'the crossroads of magic and positivism'? Or a more succinct definition of film theory's traditional project than 'to break the spell'?" Do you see your work as located at some form of crossroads? Do you think your work breaks any spells, be they theoretical or practical?

I love the idea of the crossroads. It does wonders and sometimes has literally been the subject of films that I've worked on, for instance *The Last Angel of History* [Akomfrah, 1996]. The whole of the [Black Audio Film Collective's, BAFC] oeuvre is about that theme. For example, [filmmaker] Sergei Paradjanov and indeed [composer and conductor Krzysztof] Penderecki are figures that have meant a lot to me over the years: one because of a certain understanding of chromatism in its broadest sense, the sonic chromatism of Penderecki, and the other in terms of just how one of the most discarded and reviled of cinematic techniques – the tableau – can be commandeered for other uses. You know, most filmmakers say, "We make cinema because it's not theatre," and there's a sense in which *theatre* in cinema is a real pejorative term, a term of abuse. But the tableau is a theatrical device par excellence and it seems to me that in the work of Paradjanov one could see ways in which one crossroad, the one between cinema and theatre could be breached, so that became very useful for us; one, for economic reasons and two, for political and cultural reasons as well. So I think there's a sense in which the notion of a crossroad, of liminal spaces between different worlds, contact zones if you want, has been important to what I do. It was clear from the very beginning that since there were no traditions of Afro diasporic cinema except in the most recent sense, what we made will be formed out of residues, elements of the old, i.e. non-Afro diasporic sensibilities and approaches. And that was important not simply because that was how all new forms came into being. But this is also how diasporas are formed. They are crossroads formations. That was very clear to us from the very beginning: the absence of the ruin meant that you had to construct some, even if all you were constructing were half finished monuments – you had to build something.

Derrida would be very happy!

Another important figure for me. On a related tangent though, I think the notion of magic – and I'm taking that in its broadest sense, the alchemical sense – was also important because in alchemy there is this notion of the *negredo* or the moment of blackening, when something turns from base material to something valuable – it's a moment of transmutation and transfiguration, and that's where magic has value in alchemy, it's about that process of transformation, not transformation but transmutation, and both categories are absolutely central in what we've been trying to do. They've certainly been important in what I'm trying to do because a lot of it is to do with acquiring material that has "non-cinematic" use – be they artifacts, photographs, writings, accounts that are not the traditional forms of cinema or that the cinema is supposed to use. It's about taking things that have inherently "non-cinematic" value and forcing them into that space in which they begin to acquire the resonance of the cinematic, for example, forcing a line-up of photographs to say "We are part of the procession of the real; we too are partaking in this creating of narrative in which subjectivities can be understood. We too can take part, it is not just actors, not just scripts – we too are legitimate to cinema." So, if I understood correctly what you've offered here, which is really three keywords: "positivism," "magic," and "crossroads" – I can certainly say something about magic and crossroads. The "positivist," yes, I have a kind of slightly knee-jerk aversion to the phrase but I know what it means. Positivist epistemologies have always just meant having some faith in what you see, giving some legitimacy to things as they are available to us, and it's just a wonderful way of getting cinema right to put those two phrases together, because, in a way, the magic undercuts the positivism because it says that there is value to things unseen, which are valuable in understanding what you're looking [at] and that's pretty much in a nutshell how I would approach the cinema.

Do you think that de-Westernizing film is principally an economic, political, institutional, or artistic process? Does it extend from the cinematic movements such as Third Cinema, most obviously, and finally if it does what is it doing differently? One more thing to say about this notion of de-Westernizing is that we're not setting it up as a given, or a clearly defined concept. The whole point of this project is to extrapolate a series of thoughts and ideas as to what de-Westernizing might actually be. So it would be great if you could offer your thoughts as to what you understand the term to actually mean. There are no guarantees or certainties. We want to problematize it by putting it out there.

I think the notion of de-Westernizing was always implicit in some ways in pretty much all of the avant-gardes in cinema – especially the ones from non-Western spaces. Now, how interesting and convenient and strange is that!? But what it seems to me happens is that, depending on where people see themselves, they privilege either a cultural move, an aesthetic one, a political one or an economic one. But there's always implicit in the non-Western, avant-garde gesture what I would call a double move of alterity. There's always a double move at work. And a double move more or less always takes this form: it says "I recognize the potency – adversarial or otherwise – of a presence, that presence I am going to call the Dominant, Mainstream, Western logos. And I'm going to impute these values to it – political or economic or cultural dominance. And then I'm going to say: 'I'm not going to be that.'" So there's always this diagnostic and prescriptive move, this double move at work in order to have a de-Westernized discourse, that double move has to be there. In other words, however right or wrong the protagonists in that drama are in making that move, however successful or futile the gesture, they definitely always start by saying: "This is something and that is what it isn't. And those two, very distinctive, things are me." I'm saying this and I'm doing that at the same time. Now the rhetoric is not necessarily always an explicit one – i.e. it isn't necessarily a moving-image piece accompanied by a manifesto all the time. Sometimes the work itself is both a manifesto as well as the rhetoric. But, quite a lot of the time, there is definitely also a kind of ontological separation between a manifesto, which is a set of diktats and positions papers, which say: "We are about the aesthetics of imperfection, about the aesthetics of *creolité* or whatever and because we believe those things we're going to make this." There the double move is absolutely clear. Where it's much more difficult is where there's the collapse of those ontologies, where the rhetorical gesture seems to be absent and only really found in a kind of muted way in the piece of work. But you look closely enough and you could see the argument, you could see the traffic of that double movement in the work itself. Take the Indian Mani Kaul's work, for instance; it's clear that this isn't a cinema functioning with the rhetorics of imperfection, either deliberately or unconsciously. By any description, this is incredibly well shot, in a way that could only be possible with a certain attachment to classical cinematography; it deploys color in a way that is also clearly out of a certain attachment to Matisse. So he is saying: "I like that sense of color and angularity that can only come by knowing someone like Matisse." But then he goes to say, "What I want to do is to tell you what that enchantment with Matisse means in this setting. I like the flattening that's going on with the great Frenchman, but, hey, rather than his red and green and blue all the time, how about some ochre?" And you could just see it in the very framing of the image, a new sense of the frame – a *re*newed sense of the frame is being offered to you (i.e. the manifesto), which then becomes the basis for the re-enactment of a difference – and that is the gesture. You can see both at the same time but you have to know both in order to see it. So there, the "de-Westernizing" impulse moves from the actor to the subject, to the viewer. There you are asked to do the work. So it seems to me that's really what the difference might be: in the absence of a manifesto – explicitly stated and available – the viewer is then being asked to somehow gather the remnants of that manifesto by what they're seeing, either there and then or in the interviews with the filmmaker afterwards. And that double move seems to me almost to be a default of various forms of cinema across the world today. Watching Abbas Kiarostami's *Five* [*Dedicated to Ozu*, 2003], for example, that film seems to be saying: "if you didn't get it in the first six films. . . I'm gonna tell it to you, like, as straight as I can. I ain't one of you. I never was." You know what I mean? So then you are forced to think, "Hmmm, well that guy may well be saying something about de-Westernizing and the need to move beyond." The "beyond" seems to me a very valuable term here. The "beyond" here is not a kind of cut; in other words, people are not severing those links completely, absolutely with the something. Sometimes it's a strategic cut. It's a bit like the difference between a digital cut and a photochemical one. The digital cut takes an epiphenomenal form; it's a rhetorical cut, it's the promise of a cut because people want to keep doors open, sometimes. So Kiarostami might make the most "impenetrable gibberish" one minute and then he's back with Juliette Binoche the next minute doing a French road movie. That's how I would characterize the de-Westernizing gesture – always characterized by that "double move," which is a move for elevating a space of difference informed almost by [W. E. B.] Duboisian double consciousness. Otherwise it's just a primitivist gesture. And that seems to me different. A guy who comes out of the ghetto in Accra clutching a DVD of a television melodrama ('cause that's really what most Nollywood is) who says: "I don't know your cinema. I am formed by watching nothing you've ever made and this is my film." That's not a de-Westernizing gesture. That's something different.

The idea of de-Westernizing cinema then evidently presupposes a kind of connection, immersion or association with the West?

It has to. And here I am reminded forcefully of Marx's critique of the theory of value. The de-Westernizing move can only be fully grasped as a relational aesthetic, born out of engagement. There has to be some elective affinity for the gesture to be meaningful. Otherwise there is really no value, no resonance, it seems to me.

Which leads very well to the final question: does the de-Westernizing of film studies mean rejecting entirely the dominant Western modes of thinking, production, criticism and film practice, and is it even possible? So it's a continuation of that conversation isn't it?

There's a way in which de-Westernizing could simply be one of those rhetorical flourishes that you get in all radical discourses. It could simply be a way of saying: "the tree of liberty needs occasionally to be refreshed by the blood of patriotism." Equally, it could mean that, while there is something valuable in a kind of film studies orthodoxy, by introducing the term "de-Westernizing" one is simply saying, "Well, we need a 'beyond' this." We need to move again to the next level, even if the next level is one that has no promise of finality, no promise of perfection, no promise of success. Because the very act of saying that then gives notice to the currently existing orthodoxy in film studies that there is dissatisfaction with the way in which it's functioning. And there is, to that extent, it seems to me, no problem – I have no problem at all – with people saying to me, "Let's just chuck the whole shit over the edge." You might not be able to make it but the trying seems to me to be an important gesture. To say film studies, cultural criticism has settled into a kind of comfortable way of seeing the world, where there are books and books and books about the same people over and over and over and over again with maybe one other chucked in: ten books on Orson Welles, fifteen books on Truffaut, blah blah blah. In any of these film publication magazines, it is the same thing over and over again. Basta! Enough! So, I get the point. Will it succeed? Who cares?! It doesn't matter. Who cares whether it succeeds? It's just that punk gesture alone that's important. That refusenik manifesto that says, "We're tired of this shit," you know what I mean? "We're tired of this shit because *it* is tired!" It may well have been radical to have Raymond Bellour talking about difference and suture in 1974 but when that is the dominant way in which every film has to be put through the mince of identification theory then it's time to look elsewhere. And it is time to look elsewhere, it seems to me. Not sufficient attention has been paid to the huge legacies of work and what they really mean, what the implications of that work are. Hou Hsiao-hsien. . . it's thirty years now that this guy has been at this; in the thirty years that people have been banging on about Truffaut and Godard: I get it. But I still don't get Hou Hsiao-hsien. I still don't get it. In other words, what he has of value, the implications of what he's doing and has been doing with a whole range of collaborators is absolutely amazing. Will you find a book on that? Probably not. And even if there are now a few books on him, the number of them is certainly not commensurate with his significance. Or likely to significantly reorientate the hierarchies of that orthodoxy.

Talking of Hou Hsiao-hsien – are there any other filmmakers or film cultures that you think are currently espousing this idea, pushing it and finding something different and exciting and potentially "de-Westernizing"? Apart from at Smoking Dogs Films, of course!

One of the things that happens when you go to festivals now, especially if you look in the experimental, "New Horizons" sections is that you see something really interesting going on. And that is why I am keen for the de-Westernizing act to not have a geographical fix. It seems to have spread all over the shop – from Andalusian kids making films about anarchists in the border regions of France and Spain to young Chinese filmmakers who are just pushing the notion of a frame – literally – over the edge. And so that's one thing. And if you come out of the festival circuit and you just look around – I happen to live in London, so I'm exposed to the cheek-by-jowl existence of many ethnicities, communities in this region – it's clear that how people are consuming images is quite different. So I have an independent cinema that I can go to one day to watch *Four Seasons* [Jiwarangsan, 2010], and I cross the road and I can find stacks of Nigerian popular films [Nollywood], literally, like, feet apart. And that seems to me to be saying something very, very new about how the de-Westernizing gesture functions and should function or should work. One of the ways in which it could work is simply by us recognizing the change in circumstances in which people consume images.

What do you think about the film festival as a privileged site for an encounter with some of these images? What is its "de-Westernizing potential" if we can put it that way. Is it bridging a gap? Does it need to? Does it remain a privileged site or is there some way, with technology and through the Internet, that is doing something different?

The festival traditionally has liked to think of itself as that, and there is a way in which it functions like that. It was a place where all difference collided and met and sat at the table of cinema. I think that what is now even more clear is that it is finding it difficult to hold all the strings of this thing together, partly because it has its own questions of taste that now don't quite include Nollywood cinema or Congolese cinema – they just don't function in the same way as the older, modernist cinemas because some of these gestures are not modernist gestures; they occupy vanguardist positions vis-à-vis the current mainstream, by default, and that seems to me to be the other thing that's kind of unique and different about at a de-Westernizing impulse and gesture: it arrives, sometimes against its will, in this position of the double move because of the way in which the center is now constructed. It just arrives there. It's a discursive gesture, not because it wants to be. So Congolese cinema sold as a DVD opposite the Rio Cinema doesn't want to have a relationship – necessarily – with *Meet the Fokkers* [Roach, 2004], it just does. That's just the fucking way in which the planet currently operates! But sometimes absolutely remarkable symmetries also happen when, for instance, you go to the Rio and it's showing *The Tree of Life* [Malik, 2011], and you walk across the road and you can buy Kunle Afolayan's *The Figurine* (2010). And there, for just a moment, what constitutes both the center and the margin are occupied by de-Westernizing gestures, which is what's unique about this moment, and I don't know any other moment like this. I don't know it, I have to be honest, because when *The 400 Blows* [Truffaut, 1959] or *Le Mépris* [Godard, 1963] were in the space that Kunle Afolayan's *Figurine* was/is in, it was very clear that *The Thomas Crown Affair* [Jewison, 1968] was in the Rio. . . I'm not sure it's necessarily a permanent condition or whether it will go on forever but it's clear when you watch *The Tree of Life* that this is someone who is very consciously trying to live the "beyond" as a mainstream possibility – as mainstream as Fox Searchlight can get. It's obviously not the entire juggernaut of Hollywood behind it but it's certainly a very big truck from that camp that is pushing that film and the power of Cannes in those instances works because, clearly, there are ways in which, without it being from that space, and going to Cannes, that journey would be slightly more complicated. For one, it wouldn't be made!

If an interesting filmmaker such as Didi Cheeka was to come from Lagos and say to investors here, "Well, guys, I'm a filmmaker, I want to work with you, make something, and I don't have any money." I don't think that film would be idolized in the same way as *The Tree of Life*. So, some of the old certainties are still necessary even for these de-Westernizing gestures. Some of the old certainties around questions of taste and propriety and entitlement and the representative fragment that are in effect vestiges of the old art cinema firmament will be called upon to adjudicate and license and make available these new gestures. Will they triumph? I don't know, but it seems to me that as a way of recognizing things which are happening, as a wish for the academic curriculum to change, as a kind of history of cinema with a difference, as a means by which one accesses new insights, you can't do it without at least privileging a term that might get close to that, if it's not that. And without that, all those things remain either hidden or out of place. Without that gesture then what you're saying is more Orson Welles books, further marginality for Hou Hsiao-hsien, no recognition of the new political economies of cinema, and so on. And it just seems to me that some term needs to intervene to shake the whole thing up a little bit for people to begin to look at different things. And the ones you respect, the journalists and the critics you respect, are doing it: I read an article by Mark Cousins from the Sheffield Documentary Festival on one of Mani Kaul's films – he just died a month ago of cancer – a film that I never in a million years thought I would ever see anybody of that caliber going in search of; it's a film called *Siddeshwari* [1990], a remarkable film celebrating the life of an Indian singer – and Mark wrote a pretty brilliant piece on it! When that happens, you know something has changed. Because that film is not just on the margins, it's on the margins of the margins. It's Alpha-fucking Centauri. It's so far away from most people, and yet there's something about it, and you think, "Oh yeah, of course they should see it. . . why not? Because it is fucking brilliant, Yeah." [*Laughs.*] I'm done guys.

Notes

1 Editors' note: Campbell (1904–1987) was a scholar of myth; some of his key theories about the functions of myth can be found in *Occidental Myths* (1964). Available online at www.folkstory.com/campbell/scholars_life.html (accessed December 4, 2011).

2 Editors' note: Fukuyama is an American author, economic, and political scientist. Reference is being made here to his book The End of History (1992), an excerpt of which can be found online at www.marxists.org/reference/subject/philosophy/works/us/fukuyama.htm (accessed December 4, 2011).

3 Editors' note: James (1901–1989) was a historian, journalist, and activist from Trinidad. For details, please consult "The C. L. R. James archive." Available online at www.marxists.org/archive/james-clr/index.htm (accessed December 4, 2011).

4 Editors' note: Robespierre (1758–1794) was a French politician and lawyer and an important figure in the French Revolution. L'Ouverture (c. 1743–1803) was a Haitian revolutionary, statesman, and abolitionist; his army defeated both the French and British forces during what turned out to be a twelve-year slave revolt; that insurrection transformed the island of San Domingo into the free independent republic of Haiti. One of the key reference history books on the San Domingo revolution remains C. L. James's *The Black Jacobins: Toussaint L'Ouverture and the San Domingo Revolution*, first published in 1938.

References

Center for Story and Symbol, "Joseph Campbell: A Scholar's Life." Available online at www.folkstory.com/campbell/scholars_life.html (accessed December 4, 2011).

C. L. R. James Archive. Available online at www.marxists.org/archive/james-clr/index.htm (accessed December 4, 2011).

Fukuyama, F. (1992) The End of History and the Last Man, New York: Penguin. Available online at www.marxists.org/reference/subject/philosophy/works/us/fukuyama.htm (accessed December 4, 2011).

Index